THE COMPLETE
ERIC CANTONA

EVERY GOAL EVERY GAME

BY DARREN PHILLIPS

EMPIRE
PUBLICATIONS

First published in 2009

EMPIRE PUBLICATIONS
1 Newton Street, Manchester M1 1HW
© Darren Phillips 2009

ISBN: 1 901 746 58 5 - 9781901746587

Cover design and layout: Ashley Shaw

Printed in Great Britain by: Digital Book Print Ltd, Milton Keynes, UK.

CONTENTS

INTRODUCTION

The career of Eric Cantona was remarkable, transforming English football at a time when the game was growing in popularity following a decade when it was the 'problem child' of British sport.

During the previous decade, hooliganism had seen clubs banned from European competition, while the English national team attracted an assortment of nutters and lunatics that repelled anyone with a brain. Domestically football saw a series of disasters that culminated in the Hillsborough Tragedy bringing matters to a head. The aftermath of the disaster proved a turning point. Within a few years most terracing had made way for bucket seats and with seating women and children began attending games in larger numbers. When Sky Sports signed a £304 million TV deal in 1992, football hit the big time. 'A brand new ball game' pronounced Sky's advertising and it was hard to disagree as chairmen, managers and player saw pay rises unimaginable just a few years before.

Yet the end product differed little from what had gone before. The 1980s had seen most of the best English talent go abroad, the players left behind were coached to play 'direct' football as per the theories of Charles Hughes, the FA's Director of Coaching. The result was a game based on scientific probablity rather than creativity, a game that prized the set-piece above the precise through-ball or ornate dribble.

In 1989 and 1991 Arsenal won the league playing this disciplined type of football under manager George Graham, eclipsing a pass and move Liverpool team that seemed like a throwback to happier times. The football aesthete looked abroad for thrills - in Italy in particular the game played was unrecognisable from the kick and rush style beginning to infect all levels of the English game.

This was the state of the national game Eric Cantona discovered as he sought to re-invigorate a career that had hit the buffers. The Frenchman had undoubted talent but seemed too easily distracted by petty greivances and clashes with authority. Having fallen out with referees, managers, fellow professionals and club owners, Cantona had finally burnt his bridges in France by retiring from lowly Nimes.

With nowhere left to turn, he made a last attempt at footballing salvation in England. It turned out to be an inspired decision, although things initially didn't go all that smoothly. Having been offered a trial by reluctant Sheffield Wednesday manager Trevor Francis, Cantona ended up at Leeds. However Howard Wilkinson, a Hughes convert, seemed at a loss as to how to effectively utlise him. Cantona was tall but too creative to merely play at centre-forward, his tendency to 'drop-off' not only confused the opposition but eventually team-mates used to a rigid 4-4-2 formation purpose built for the First Division of the early 1990s.

Having helped secure Leeds the Division One title in 1992, contributing to a run-in which saw them overhaul a stuttering Manchester United team that should have had the title wrapped up long before Easter, Cantona began the following season by netting a hat-trick in a 4-3 Charity Shield win over Liverpool. Yet Leeds' form dipped alarmingly over the coming months, the champions falling to mid-table and knocked out of the European Cup by Glasgow Rangers.

Defeat at Ibrox proved the turning point for Cantona's relationship with Wilkinson. When he was substituted, in the middle of a performance best described as peripheral, the Frenchman stormed down the tunnel. A lengthy absence from the team followed during which Eric returned to France. The end appeared to be nigh for his English sojourn.

It took a speculative enquiry from Manchester United chairman Martin Edwards to alter the course of recent football history. United were struggling for goals and, having missed out on the 1992 title, lacked the confidence needed to sustain a title-challenge through 10 gruelling months. United manager Alex Ferguson had seen numerous bids for strikers re-buffed until Leeds enquired about re-signing Denis Irwin. Following a polite refusal, Edwards cheekily asked about Cantona. When a flat refusal wasn't forthcoming the door to the most influential signing in the last 20 years was pushed ajar.

Cantona's impact at Old Trafford was immediate. Frequently, managers and supporters discuss 'the missing link', the signing that transforms a good team into a great one - it is mentioned so often that it has become a footballing cliché. Yet Cantona was the missing link personified. Within weeks supporters went from fearing the worst to believing anything was possible. Never before has the stroke of a pen so trasformed the atmosphere of a club and its supporters. What followed was a five year Old Trafford career that defied belief.

There was nothing indifferent about Cantona, when he was good he was brilliant, when he was bad, the whole world turned on him, the club and the supporters. That Cantona's achievements still mean so much to Manchester United fans and cast a considerable shadow on the game is undeniable. It wasn't just that he played the starring role in United's first title triumph for 26 years, or that he set the ball rolling in Ferguson's long-term quest to knock rivals Liverpool 'off their f★★king perch' nor that his brand of instant justice at Selhurst Park in 1995 attracted more attention and column inches than any incident at a football match that anyone could remember, nor that when he returned the following season he became the first man to win the FA Cup and League Double single-handedly (or that's how it seemed).

No, it was the manner in which he did all these things that set the heart racing. Cantona was a footballer with immense ability who wasn't afraid to show it, who helped shatter the prevailing tenets of Charles Hughes and scientific football once and for all and paved the way for the foreign players and managers that dominate today's Premiership and turned it into the most watched sports league in the world.

Some may argue that Cantona didn't 'do it' in Europe, others nit-pick that the opposition he faced week after week wasn't world class and that his international career amounted to very little. What cannot be denied is that he introduced a brand of football into this country which hitherto had been regarded as foreign, untrustworthy and (the greatest barb of all) unsuccessful.

> *"It's a panic buy. In my opinion he's a flashy foreigner, he'll score goals for United....only when they're two up"*
> EMLYN HUGHES, NOVEMBER 1992.

With the benefit of hindsight the reaction to Cantona's move to United was hilarious and looking back many famous figures failed to see that Cantona was 'the whole new ball game' made flesh. Someone prepared to try something that wasn't in the manual, craft a chance when nothing was on or shoot for goal when logic dictated he should have squared it.

This book is a tribute to the great man's career. It features in-depth reports of every game he played in England and summaries of a nomadic French club career and an on-off international one.

FAMILY LIFE

Pedro Ruarich of the left leaning often anarchist and fiercely autonomous Catalonia was a Republican fighter in the Spanish Civil War. After being wounded in battle, he was unable to retreat behind his own lines as so few safe enclaves existed. The prospect of trying to blend in and live under the victorious General Franco lacked appeal and with no guarantee that he would survive if he were to give up his arms, Pedro had only one option.

With his young girlfriend by his side he crossed the Pyrenees to live in exile. It was not Catalonia but was as near as he could get to a home from home. Like many refugees from the conflict the couple shifted from camp to camp before moving on to Marseilles where the influx of expatriate Spaniards had gathered. After some years his life settled down. He married and had a daughter Eleonore. When France was invaded by Hitler's troops Pedro was labelled an undesirable and placed in a concentration camp, returning to Marseilles after the war. He lived in the city for the rest of his life.

The island of Sardinia had joined a unified Italy in 1861. Reliant on an arable economy, Sardinians were used to frequent depressions and shortages, and during these inhabitants tended to flee to Marseilles rather than the Italian mainland. France offered opportunities and a plentiful supply of work where Italy was often riven by petty regional conflicts and, later, under Mussolini, a Fascist dictatorship.

Joseph Cantona was one of those to join the large Italian community in the city. He settled down, married Lucienne and had a son Albert. First generation migrants Albert Cantona and Eleonore Ruarich met, married and had three boys. Born in 1963 Jean-Marie was the eldest, Joel the youngest came into the world 17 months after what turned out to be the middle son Eric. Each carried the same independence and dignity which bordered on rebelliousness through their parents.

It is often said that Liverpool, Glasgow and New York only

notionally stand in the countries they are recognised to be part of. The same is undoubtedly true for Marseilles. The very nature of port cities: that they are gateways for trade as well as people thus creating their own civic and cultural activities, makes for places which have a distinctive soul – a melting pot of races, colours, accents and attitudes that produce a culture seperate from the rest of the country. This 'difference' is reflected in a certain state of mind. All four cities are anomalies certain to sway against the national consensus. All four have been branded as militant, it's the price paid for not being submissive and accepting one's lot.

Despite his Mediterranean roots, Eric was born in Paris during a spell in which his parents resided in the capital before returning to the Cantona family home which was shared by three generations. Eric Cantona was no son of the capital city. He was a son of Marseilles.

His new home was unusual. It had started out as a cave measuring just nine square metres located in Caillols on the boundaries of the 11th and 12th arrondissements of Marseille overlooking the hills of Gardaban and Cassis. It had been used by the Germans as a look out point during the occupation but had been built from scratch and lovingly developed by Eric's paternal grandfather Joseph, a mason, after his grandmother had discovered it in 1955. In the beginning it was little more than a single room separated from the elements by a strip of curtain. 11 years later, when Eric was born, much building had taken place and there now stood a number of rooms. The family preferred rural life. Alongside a number of family values it shaped young Eric and ultimately his football.

Marseille is a city of extremes. Though the country's largest commercial port and a bustling city only second to Paris in size, to the east it boasts mountain ranges which rise almost 4,000 feet from lush forests. To the west lies Provence with its range of fishing villages and to the north slightly smaller mountain ranges are dwarfed by the Montagne Sainte-Victoire.

The weather is just as disparate. Summers range from mild to hot and dry. In those conditions city based Marseillais would travel out to Caillols to enjoy the view and the weather. Winters could be humid when they started but by January and February the icy cold Mistral winds ripped through from the Alps. Nearby Provence, now a mecca for bon viveurs, has long attracted artists from all over the continent.

Already proud of its distinctiveness, Marseilles made the most of its culture. Intellectuals and artists had flocked there under the reign of King René of Anjou and the number of museums, libraries, restaurants and galleries reflect this cosmopolitan population. By the end of the 18th century statistics demonstrated that somewhere in the region of half the population were not indigenous, a couple of hundred years later political and economic migration swelled the numbers further. There was virtually no point of Europe or Sub-Saharan Africa which had not been woven in to the fabric of Marseille. Part of that cloth included a heady mix of Mediterraneans which eventually formed the Cantona family.

True to their lineage the Cantonas injected Mediterranean sensibilities such as the value of a strong and happy family. Reflecting on his childhood Eric Cantona has said, "I am a son of rich people but in our house riches have never meant money, luxury or spending. Frankly, I wish that all those children who ask for my autograph could have, at the start of their lives, the same values which were passed on to me by my family in the hills of Marseilles."

The gentle ambience of the countryside appealed to the Cantonas, each of whom enjoyed typically rural pursuits such as walking and hunting. Other passions included the arts and football. Just like his family home, Eric Cantona's football career had humble origins. Like many children he played most of his football in the streets with anything that could be kicked making do as a ball – one was rarely available – cobbles were pitches and garage doors served as impromptu goals. However, there was no substitute for a football.

Olympique Marseille became a feature in his life as a toddler and in 1972 came a taste of the Stade Vélodrome atmosphere at its most raucous for a clash with Ajax in the second round of the European Cup. The Dutch side swept to a 6-2 aggregate victory and impressed Eric much more than his own team. OM's line-up included Josip Skoblar who at that stage held the Golden Boot with 44 goals from the previous Ligue 1 season and winger Roger Magnusson who laid on many of those strikes.

By 1974 he was a disciple of The Netherlands team and their pioneering, fluent style of play known as total football. Rinus Michels had a host of talented players at his disposal and devised a system where any player who was forced out of position had it filled by a colleague. Whether the ball was in defence, midfield or attack, the whole XI could go forward or back as opportunities arose. Compared to the often dogmatic systems employed previously, Michel's theory was revolutionary.

On the field Eric, like many of his contemporaries, looked to shine as an individual, a failing Eric's father made clear to the youngster after one particular defeat as a junior. Eric had tried to be the star in one game and this had been to the detriment of his team. Without enraged shouting or finger pointing Albert delivered a tactical insight, "there is nothing more stupid than a footballer who pretends to be more indispensable than the ball. Rather than run with the ball, make the ball do the work, give it and look quickly. Look around quickly and you will be the best. Look before you receive the ball and then give it and always remember that the ball goes quicker than you can carry it."

An eager learner, Eric took his dad's advice onboard and quickly jumped through the age ranges, eventually playing in teams with boys that were often five years older. At the same time the young Eric railed against certain decisions and frequently fell out with officialdom. Junior football provided a first experience of injustice during the summer of 1978.

His Caillols side had just won the Cup of Provence after a 3-0 victory over Vitrolles in the final. It was the first leg of a possible league and cup double. The following weekend his team needed a draw against Vivaux-Marronniers but with five minutes remaining Eric's side trailed 1-0. All of a sudden the youngster broke out of defence and started beating opponents. His weaving, apparently aimless run suddenly headed towards goal as Eric realised there was a possibility he could score. By now half a dozen Vivaux players lay in his wake as he shot just a few yards away from goal but as he did so the referee's whistle sounded because the official had noticed that Eric's bootlaces had come undone and the rules stated that they should be tied. The chance had gone and for nothing more than a minor detail, the league was lost. It was a bitter lesson.

At the Grand Bastide secondary school in Mazargue Eric met another man who would help form his attitude to the game and ultimately shape his career. Célestin Oliver, an Algerian by birth, had been brought over from his local club in Mostaganem and became a French Cup winner with Sedan and a member of the national side which finished third in the 1958 World Cup. Soon after his return he was bought by Olympique Marseille and managed an array of professional teams after hanging up his boots in the mid-sixties.

Eric put his thirst for success down to Oliver who also convinced him that glory could come with honour and be achieved without compromising the game's true principles. His guidance, along with others, put Cantona on the road to becoming a professional. Yet, although many clubs recognised the youngsters potential, most were reticent about bringing the teenager into their fold. Even at this early stage Eric's reputation went before him.

Nice seemed to be favourites to land Cantona. Many of those who had guided his career as a junior certainly recommended it as the next step. The club lay not far from Marseilles but Eric rejected the offer after a visit to Auxerre, a town 400 miles north of his home town. Situated between Paris and Dijon, Auxerre lacked the romanticism of the Côte d'Azur. A manufacturing and industrial hub, the local area was also renowned for producing some of the country's most distinctive wines.

Eric had initially been excited about linking up with Nice, a club which had nurtured the talents of Josip Katalinski and Roger Jouve - both of whom Cantona held as idols - but after visiting the club he left disappointed with the feel of things. Family was important for Cantona and he felt none of the warmth he was used to. At Auxerre there was a very different atmopshere. He came back from his visit there laden with souvenirs after meeting Guy Roux and Serge Dubord. It helped make up his mind, even if it would be a wrench to leave his close knit family. However success was the driving force and Eric harboured the conviction that he could one day return to taste glory with Marseille.

FRENCH CAREER

AUXERRE

GUY ROUX HAD been in charge of team affairs at Auxerre since combining playing and management duties in 1961 at the age of 22. He had been associated with the club for almost nine years at that stage but played with only minor distinction. The club had little merit either. They were a mediocre outfit who played in the Burgundy regional league, attracting crowds of no more than a couple of hundred. When they advertised for a successor to manager Christian Di Orio there were few replies. Roux, who had spent a month with Crystal Palace watching training and studying the set up, was one of the few to bother and he was also the youngest candidate.

His tone seemed desperate. In a formal letter he promised he would "do whatever is needed for the club, even chop the wood" but in other words and deeds he did enough to impress the chairman Jean-Claude Hamel, gambling on the importance of enthusiasm rather than experience. Roux's initial salary was 600 francs per month, much less than most coaches would accept. However Roux had impressed the chairman with his tactical acumen and willingness to work within a tight budget. Regardless of the level he operated at, his housekeeping style was unique. He cajoled farmers into donating dung from their goats to fertilise the pitch and training fields; fans and players' wives were asked to produce and sew the team's training kit. Although there is no reliable record that he chopped wood, he did double up on other roles taking a number of duties in the evening as he was the only person still knocking around the Stade de l'Abbé-Deschamps.

The ground was developed in line with the club's unprecedented rise. The local authority helped out and in time a centre of excellence was established. The club's full name 'Association de la Jeunesse Auxerroise' translated into English roughly meant Auxerre Youth

Association and the title was apt under Roux who made developing young talent his guiding principle. The fruits of this labour brought success.

Roux's system has been compared with the blueprint which existed at Manchester United in the post war years. The status, history and means of the Old Trafford club and AJA as it was known were poles apart but it in terms of nurturing footballers they were very similar. When, as inevitably happened, a player left for a bigger club, there would be a handsome sum received in exchange which could be ploughed back into the system which quickly became self-funding.

However, there was more to this man than a willingness to muck in or encourage frugality. No matter what he expected high standards from his employees. Throughout the country, he had a network of people who would report on his players' every move. The stories of Roux dragging errant players out of local bars and clubs were numerous. And, with Paris just an hour away via toll roads, he received regular reports from those taking money in booths, he noted the mileage of cars and was even known to feel the bonnets of vehicles outside his players' homes to determine whether they had been partying in the capital that night.

By the time Eric arrived in Auxerre they had risen, under Roux's guidance, from a lowly place on the amateur ladder to Ligue 2 and professionalism within four years. In 1979 the club surpassed all expectations by reaching the French Cup final only losing to the highly fancied FC Nantes in extra-time. Within a year Auxerre were promoted to the top flight as champions of the second division.

Everything felt right to Eric who, after rejecting initial reservations from his family, decided he would join AJA. Auxerre had stayed in Ligue 1 with a fair degree of comfort thanks, in no small part, to the presence of Polish forward Andrzej Szarmach who had contributed so richly to the "golden age" his national side enjoyed from the early 1970s onwards. His elegant, flamboyant play fitted into French football well and he became an instant role model to Cantona who joined the club just after his 15th birthday, a year after Szarmach had arrived from Polish side Stal Mielec.

It didn't take long for Roux to realise that in Cantona he had the "most brilliant of his trainees". A youngster to be named as one of the best half dozen or so schoolboys in the country. As befitted his manager's billing he was also permitted from time to time to train with the first team. Pitting some of his most promising juniors and those outside the first team picture against senior players was something Roux tended to do towards the end of a season to lift his apprentices and keep his senior men grounded. In one such match in the spring of 1982 the matches were played in this format and Cantona, who had graduated from fourth team to become one of the youngest third team players, was a substitute given his chance in the second half.

He was matching boys three to four years his senior for skill and strength on a weekly basis and though it was not his intention he forced one particular member of the first team to struggle. Never a person lacking in confidence, Eric frustrated the experienced defender Lucien Denis so much that he felt there was no option but to commit a foul every time the youngster had the ball.

His development continued apace. That summer he won a place in the French youth team and with that a chance to mix with some of the stars of the national side as games were mostly timed to take place just 24 hours before the 'first' team played. That was the case for his debut against Switzerland which acted as a curtain raiser to a full international - a World Cup warm up with Bulgaria in Lyon. Cantona grabbed the last goal in a 3-2 win. The main feature played before 45,000 fans ended in a goalless draw.

A year on and Eric was in the Auxerre reserves. The 1983-84 season ended with him playing a huge part in winning the French Third Division. With 20 goals he was second top scorer behind his friend Bernard Ferrer who had graduated from the highly successful L'Institut National du Football in Clairefontaine. 700 youngsters made applications each year but only two dozen gained a place which emphasised Ferrer's promise and the attraction of Auxerre as a first professional calling.

There were tales of equipment being broken when Eric was on the losing side - not just at football but any sport the trainees turned their hands to - and while playing for the second string there emerged a first showing of the temperament he would later become known for on the field of play. Indeed after one bad tempered game Cantona was met in Auxerre's car park by, as legend has it, seven irate opponents who wished to finish the business started on the pitch. Four spent part of the evening in hospital for their trouble.

His chance finally arrived on the biggest stage with a Ligue 1 debut on 22 October 1983 against Nancy. Patrice Garande, who had been unable to find the net with any regularity in recent months, was placed on the bench, the 17 year-old Eric filling a vacancy alongside Szarmach. It proved a good pairing and while the Pole did all he could to lay on a goal for his teenage partner during a routine 4-1 win, it wasn't to be. Though there proved to be plenty of confidence on display when a move started in defence found its way to Cantona inside his own area, a Nancy attacker bore down on him but was beaten with an impudent nutmeg. Another chance came against Lens but like all young men Eric had to complete National Service now he had reached 18.

Yet as Roux knew, there would be no question of square bashing or other matters associated with military induction. Sportsmen became members of the Joinville battalion in Fontainebleau just outside Paris. There would be high living rather than crack training though still a need to remain fit as games would have to be played for Auxerre at the weekend and there was no question of regaining a berth in the first team. That required the same training and fitness schedule as the others were able to undertake. At Guy Roux's suggestion Eric, along with Ferrer, took his year as quickly as possible.

Alongside his club commitments, Eric turned out for the Army team which played games throughout the world including many French colonies. From Cantona's point of view the most prominent was Gabon in West Africa. Roux knew the extent to which the high life was lived during National Service but he told his trainees to enjoy themselves although he still wanted to see a certain standard of play and commitment when they had those weekend passes.

L'ENFANT SAUVAGE

THE 1984–85 CAMPAIGN was a huge turning point in Cantona's fledging days as a footballer. He came into the reckoning again towards the end of the season and managed his first goal in the highest division at home to Rouen in mid-May. 26 minutes from time he galloped to meet the ball 35 yards out and despite a sodden pitch zipped the ball across the floor and in.

Near the end of that same month came a pivotal game against Strasbourg. There was a chance of UEFA Cup qualification but with half an hour remaining Auxerre trailed 1-0. Then Eric received the ball in his own area, moved upfield before shooting from 25 yards, the ball flying into the top right hand corner to earn Auxerre a European place – the coach assured Eric he would be a fixture in his plans from then on.

Auxerre's new hero and Ferrer had maintained the hedonistic atmosphere of their service at Fontainebleau. Both had been out until 4am on the morning of the game. Roux either never found out or turned a blind eye. He may even have had an alternative plan to concentrate the youngster's mind having taken soundings about the seriousness of the relationship with Ferrer's sister Isabelle.

However, at the beginning of the next season there was a setback. A bout of flu ruled Cantona out for a game at Nice with Roger Boli coming in as a replacement and scoring in an impressive win. Guy Roux decided not to change the team for the first leg of the opening round of the UEFA Cup meeting with AC Milan a few days later and a 3-1 win against one of the continent's powerhouses and former European champions proved encouraging. Sticking to the maxim 'never change a winning team', Roux saw no reason to omit Boli even now Eric was fully fit. When Milan, inspired by Franco Baresi, scored a convincing 3-0 win in the return leg, Eric was only introduced during the second half but could not help reverse the situation ending Auxerre's UEFA Cup adventure.

What happened next came as something of a surprise: Roux accepted a season long loan offer for Cantona from Martigues, who were then bottom of the second division. At first it was something of a shock but the player soon realised there was more to this than helping out another side. Eric's girlfriend was a student at the University of Aix-en-Provence and used to visit Auxerre when on vacation. It was clear this was no passing liaison and a lengthy period could be spent to ensure the relationship was given every chance to succeed and that, rather than pine for his love, Eric's life and career might flourish. A Peugeot 104 packed beyond its capacity left for the South within a week, Eric moved in to Isabelle's small flat and when the season ended she had finished her degree and returned to Burgundy.

Regular football honed Eric's skills and increased his ability to cope with the demands of the higher standards that would be required to maintain week in, week out in Ligue 1. But football became not so much a secondary thought but something to consider alongside the development of his relationship. 15 games produced four goals – a respectable ratio – but more important was his contribution to the side which, as may be expected, Guy Roux kept a close eye on. Watching his charge when he could and receiving regular reports.

Eric began with a bang, scoring on his debut against Montceau and in December, with his appearances yet to reach double figures, he was dismissed against RC Grasse. Another member of the Cantona family, Eric's brother Jean-Marie, was present and in the aftermath reacted badly to a comment made in the crowd after the red card was shown. An attempt to reach the person he regarded as the offender ended in his hand being cut as he leapt a dividing fence for a 'discussion'. Eric, noticing the commotion involving his brother, came over but was led away before he got anywhere near the incident which was quickly resolved.

A further dismissal came against Cannes but there was little mind paid to anything outside the actual football played. Aggression was a necessary evil which needed to be channelled in the right way as a player developed. Rough edges had been knocked off youngsters before and Roux, who put what he euphemistically termed as "bad moments" down to "a temperament from the south", had seen more than enough to convince him that a full professional contract would be offered in the summer of 1986 and with that the promise of a place in the side. The deal was put to Cantona after the final game of the season.

Marriage to Isabelle, which many were only told about after it happened, and a home in Yonne, a town just 12 miles away from Auxerre, meant life could not have been better for Eric. Yonne was a quiet place which allowed him to switch off when not training or playing. There was also an opportunity to undertake those favoured countryside pursuits in the nearby hills and forests.

There remains the possibility that if Cantona had not gone to Martigues his career could have been jeopardised by his relationship. Certainly his time at AJA may have been a short one and Roux, who had seen lovesick teens go off the boil before, was clever enough to recognise that a life in football could only be happy and complete when he was able to give his professional career undivided attention.

His experiences on Joinville, as hedonistic as they may have been, possibly helped too. Many of the pleasures adolescents seek were out of his system. The French media are very different but lurid the tabloid headlines some young professionals in the UK endure never hit Eric. He came back to Burgundy balanced. Not only as an individual without angst but also as a footballer with those rough edges knocked off.

Auxerre finished fourth in 1986-87, an improvement of three places and half a dozen points and qualified for the UEFA Cup for the second time in three seasons - some achievement given the financial means and relative inexperience of the squad.

Eric, who sat out just two league games, was the club's top scorer with 13 and tied as seventh best marksman in Ligue 1 behind home grown talents such as the experienced Bernard Zénier and Philippe Fargeon of champions Bordeaux along with imports such as Uruguayan Enzo Francescoli and Argentina's Alberto Márcico. It was something which caught the interest of the French Football Federation and further international recognition with the under-21s coached by Marc Bourrier.

Cantona was in at the beginning of a bid to win the European Championship at that level. It was a lengthy programme with a group stage before a knock-out competition that would culminate in the 1988 final. The campaign got underway with a game against a strong USSR side in Le Havre. A couple of Cantona goals shaded the contest 2-1 - a commanding

header and a drive from the edge of the area helping Les Bleuets to victory. After six games East Germany, who had inflicted France's only defeat, were edged out by a point as France finished top of their four team section advancing to a two legged quarter-final clash with Italy.

France had been eliminated in the last eight of the three previous tournaments but came through this one 4-3 on aggregate against the beaten finalists from two years before. A 2-1 win in the home match proved crucial when the teams shared four goals in Italy. In the semi-final with England, the French won the home leg 4-2 with Eric the star attraction. Cantona was able to create the first and score a sublime second before the visitors had conjured up anything approaching a threat. The latter saw Eric receive the ball just inside the England half with six would be tacklers beaten by a number of feints and dribbles. Eric tore into the inside-left channel then worked his way into the area. He banged the ball a few inches inside the near upright and into the top corner. For good measure he laid on France's last goal with a confident back-heel which Stephane Paille read perfectly. England fought hard and drew the home leg 2-2 but France cruised through to the final with Greece.

The Greeks had never progressed beyond the group stage prior to this event and despite overcoming Czechoslovakia and most impressively Holland in the last four they were underdogs. 80,000 Greeks provided an unforgettable atmosphere for the first leg and again Cantona impressed, coming closest to scoring. After a home attack was broken down the ball was cleared for Eric to chase. He latched on to the ball and went clear of the defence. As the keeper had no protection he raced out, slamming Cantona to the floor with a tackle which would not have been out of place in a rugby match. As the challenge was outside the area the keeper, as was normal at the time, receiving only a yellow card. The resulting free-kick came to nothing. Greece were swept aside 3-0 in the second leg but by then Eric had been banned from the national team following a comment he had made about national coach Henri Michel.

Eric's debut at full international level had come against West Germany and he had marked it with a goal. It may have been no more than a late consolation to a couple of Rudi Völler strikes in a 2-1 defeat but it showed his predatory instinct. Cantona got himself onto the end of a cross-field ball played into the area and slid between two defenders before poking it in from half a dozen yards. Despite that, Michel seemed no fan of Cantona preferring many of his peers from the under-21s and only affording him four more opportunities. Two of those had come with the senior side experiencing problems qualifying for the 1988 European Championships. Michel may have felt his policy was justified. With Cantona in the forward line they only mustered a 1-1 home draw with Norway in October 1987 while East Germany secured a 1-0 win which finally ended French qualification hopes. The other outings came in friendly internationals.

For all his accomplishments, it became clear towards the end of the 1987-88 season that Eric needed to leave Auxerre. The UEFA Cup run was ended after just two games - Panathinaikos going through 4-3 on aggregate despite the French team shading the second encounter by the odd goal in five. The Greek side accounted for Juventus at the next stage so it was no disgrace, but better had been hoped for. Eric arrived at his decision just two days before the 2nd leg of the semi-final of the under-21s European Championship following a bitter defeat in the quarter-finals of the French Cup to Lille. Now 22 he had almost 80 appearances under his belt and had represented France at every level.

Auxerre had finished a very disappointing ninth in the league, far lower than expected and, despite Roux's claims that youth was the reason, there was no talking Eric around and with such an impressive CV he had no shortage of offers. The papers splashed stories about the transfer request and its timing ahead of the under-21 game. Many writers debated a common criticism that Cantona struggled to raise himself for more run of the mill games. An outstanding header in that game (which was also televised nationally) saw him leap late to cushion the ball into the net. Many suspected his manager was quite happy with the situation as, for all the admiration Cantona received, Roux may have been worried that the situation would deteriorate over time and stretch their working relationship to breaking point in any case.

There had been other disciplinary issues, including a sending off for a leaping, bone crunching challenge on Nantes' Michel Der Zakarian which earned Eric a dismissal and a three match ban. During the 1986-87 season there had been another episode which possibly mapped out what was to come. He was fined for giving the club's goalkeeper, Bruno Martini, a black eye during a disagreement as they cleared snow from the pitch prior to a match.

So much interest was generated by his potential move from Auxerre that Cantona decided to employ an agent, Alain Migliaccio, to do the negotiations. All aspects of the clubs were looked at but it boiled down to financial and sporting issues. With those criteria to the fore there were two clubs to consider in the final analysis - Matra-Racing and his boyhood favourites Marseille. There was a three week window to mull things over.

The suitors were a contrast in many ways. Marseille were the team Eric had supported as a child and a club on the up thanks to the riches of Bernard Tapie. Matra, owned by the company of the same name, were similarly ambitious and had acquired the club formerly known as Racing Club de France. Both had agreed a fee of 22 million francs (£2.3 million). The fee was not only reflective of Eric's talents but Roux's talent spotting and fostering of young players. It further increased Cantona's profile and would improve the finances of Auxerre.

Marseille's owner, politician and businessman Bernard Tapie, had one of his coaches Gerard Banide, visit the player to discuss his role at OM. Banide impressed upon him his plans to use as him as a playmaker on a visit to Burgundy. Tapie had bought the club in

1986 not long after Olympique Marseille rejoined the top flight. A determined businessman, Tapie applied simple business logic to OM, employing the best talent available. Eric's home town club certainly seemed to be on the up.

Despite a late bid by Jean-Luc Lagardere, president of Matra, Eric soon made the inevitable choice, pronouncing "The Vélodrome was waiting for Cantona". It seemed that childhood memories along with the lure of home had proved too hard to resist yet even as the pen was literally in his hand ready to apply a signature on the contracts drawn up there was one last twist.

A message came through to Eric's agent via a phone at the Stade Velodrome. AC Milan were said to be making a late bid and Silvio Berlusconi was doing all he could to get a message through before any deal was signed. Marseille's representatives expressed their worry and respectfully asked if Eric needed some time to think. He may have dithered for a split second but no more than that. By the time the question had been posed the pen was hovering just above the paper, nevertheless Eric signed - the deal was done.

MARSEILLES

17TH AUGUST 1988 was a momentous day for Cantona who in his sixth game scored a first goal in Olympique Marseille colours against Matra-Racing of all clubs. His career there had begun with some frustration as from the first game to the fifth the lack of goals seemed something of a burden. Regardless of the goals he created, and there had been a sufficient number of them for Jean-Pierre Papin and Philippe Vercruysse, the relief was evident in Eric's celebration and the reaction of the home crowd.

PLAYING FOR ONE of the best sides in France, Eric expected to add more caps to the five he had already earned. When he was omitted from Henri Michel's squad of 16 for a game against Czechoslovakia Michel explained, "Eric is not on his best form". 48 hours after the squad announcement Cantona grabbed a brace in a 3-2 win over Strasbourg, creating the other for Papin. On that kind of evidence Cantona simply could not agree and made no secret of his annoyance in a post-match interview stating: "I will never play for France again as long as Henri Michel is manager. Don't speak any more about him.

It's a choice between Michel and me," before adding "I would like it to be known that I think he is one of the most incompetent managers in world football. I was reading an article by Mickey Rourke, who's a guy I really like, that the people who award the Oscars are a bunch of shitbags. I think Henri Michel is not far from being included in that."

Despite an apology and claims he made the comment in the febrile atmosphere of an interview conducted in a dressing room he effectively tendered his resignation from the national side. A ban of 12 months was quickly imposed which meant he would miss the second leg of the Under-21 final against Greece. Following a 3-0 French victory, Eric's colleagues were eager to remind a national television audience of his importance while fans held up a banner stating: "One person is missing – Cantona". As tended to be the case where Eric was involved the reason for the fallout had been coming for sometime.

The senior side had continued to struggle and when a number of the high flying youngsters were given opportunities – albeit in friendlies – for full caps many felt that Michel was trying to alleviate pressure being brought to bear by his employers, fans and the press rather than actively promote the youngsters. It wasn't just his own treatment which irked Cantona, it was also the lack of tactical nous and spine shown. For the player it seemed his fortunes 'swirled in the wind'. Over a two year period 50 different players were used and most, as far as Cantona was concerned, were only plumped for when the press called for them regardless of the team's requirements. As a consequence Michel's achievements – guiding the nation to a World Cup semi-final in 1986, third place after being controversially beaten by West Germany in 1982 and of course winning the 1984 European Championships as hosts – was tainted by failure.

In the event, Michel was soon dismissed after the senior side could only manage a 1-1 draw against Cyprus in Nicosia during late October just a month after the ban came into force. Michel Platini came in as a replacement and Eric was welcomed back soon after, appearing in a friendly with Sweden in Malmo at the beginning of the 1989-90 season, he gave the Scandinavians a torrid time, the 4-2 win ending a long unbeaten run for the hosts.

MATTERS MAY HAVE been redressed in that arena but at club level, despite Marseille winning the French league and cup double, there was unhappiness. Eric had only scored twice in 22 games, over half of which he had missed due to disciplinary problems. His problems culminated during a friendly against Torpedo Moscow. The match, broadcast live on television aimed to raise funds for those affected by the Armenian earthquake, was hosted by Sedan who were close enough to Marseille for the fans not to be put out by the travel but who had a much smaller stadium - one more appropriate to the crowd expected to turn up. A justifiable substitution was made as jeers rained down from the stands. When Eric threw the hallowed white shirt in the referee's direction as he left the field the outrage increased and a two-match ban was imposed by the club which effectively became indefinite after a hastily arranged loan was agreed with struggling Bordeaux.

Bernard Tapie was quick to condemn Cantona's actions saying: "A player who throws his shirt on the ground, even if he has scored three goals in the match, must be sanctioned because that's not what we expect from sport. This doesn't correspond to the idea which I have of football in general and of football at Olympique Marseille in particular."

He went on to suggest psychiatric help may be necessary and a quick thinking TV company did just that – even if Eric was not directly involved in the analysis. His findings surprised everyone... bar Cantona. He summarised that in a game that he was not only intelligent but honest while the player's statement claiming that he was, "happy to be crazy. The world in which we live is boring. Anyone who is different from the ordinary is considered crazy. I express myself without thinking. I say what I feel" - was given an express vindication.

Eric admitted his guilt and the erroneousness nature of his action saying: "By throwing away my shirt I was wrong... but only in terms of the image it created of me and in terms of my career."

Before making his exit from the Stade Vélodrome he expressed no regret about not satisfying either his or the fans' expectations as he would be back to do just that. Any hope of redressing opinions would have to wait of course and signs on the field were good. Waiting at Bordeaux with new manager Aimé Jacquet was Jean Tigana who, though born in the African state of Mali, had grown up in Marseille and played for the same Caillols junior club as Eric. He not only welcomed Cantona at the ground but provided an instant hand of friendship and understanding.

BORDEAUX & MONTPELLIER

AT BORDEAUX CANTONA played 11 games and scored six goals but continued to court controversy after missing training. The player contested claims this was a regular event by the club's president and claimed he skipped just one session on the day his dog died claiming he had awoken to find his pet collapsed on the floor. He reported to the ground in the afternoon a short time after his dog was put down. Whatever the truth of that matter, there was no extension of his time with the Girondins.

With no route back to Marseille, a further temporary home had to be found and Eric moved to Montpellier, 80 miles along the coast. Already at the club was Stephane Paille, a long standing friend who had joined just a few weeks earlier following seven seasons at Sochaux where he had come through the international ranks playing as a junior in many of the same teams as Cantona, including that all conquering under-21 side having made his senior bow for Les Bleus in 1986. In Montbéliard he had helped the club gain promotion from Ligue 2 and reach the Coupe de France final where they were beaten by FC Metz. Paille had been the division's top scorer that season with 18 holding the accolade jointly with Jean-Pierre Orts of Olympique Lyonnais. It was sufficient for him to be voted France's Player of the Year.

It was a huge gamble by the club's president Louis Nicollin. He had invested a substantial amount of money and that was expected to earn reward. After a mid-table finish he wanted honours to be won or at the very least a spot in Europe if not both which was possible should the previous season was to be built on. There was no financial incentive to join the club in fact Eric's wages were almost cut in half by the deal but his recruitment came with baggage. In addition to the well documented travails Nicollin had heard stories about missed training sessions and fall outs.

Montpellier looked unlikely to gain a European place having slipped to the foot of the league following defeat at Lille on 27 September 1989 and, after hearing team-mate Jean-Claude Lemoult suggest that this was the fault of attackers (Cantona and Paille) a red mist descended and Eric threw his boots into his face. The midfielder responded in kind and a dressing room punch-up ensued. Eric bore the brunt and a 10 day suspension was handed down by the club. Just over a week later Cantona and Lemoult were publicly photographed together. It turned out that Lemoult, along with Laurent Blanc and Columbian Carlos Valderrama, were instrumental in mitigating the punishment having approached the club hierarchy. Cantona returned to training at the beginning of November and results instantly improved. What seemed certain was that the brawl cleared a bad atmosphere and the improvements could be seen on the pitch.

With a mid-table finish the likeliest outcome Montpellier were able to concentrate on the Cup; Cantona scoring a hat-trick as Montpellier advanced to the last eight. His treble consisted of a right foot volley, a looping header and a precise low finish following a run down the left. A further two were scored in the quarter-finals with another disallowed. In the semis he scored the goal which beat St Etienne 1-0, volleying home a Kader Ferhaoui centre though it was his partnership with Valderrama that was capturing the imagination. In the final on 8 June 1990 Matra-Racing, who had beaten Marseille in the last four, were beaten 2-1 after extra-time. It was a tense battle between evenly match teams with Cantona the inspiration.

Meanwhile, Michel Platini was rewarded for bringing Eric back into the international fold with five goals in three games. Added to the two against Sweden, was another in his first appearance at the Parc des Princes in a World Cup qualifier against Scotland on 11 October 1989. Platini had opted to retain Cantona as a striker despite Montpellier preferring to use him as a creative midfielder in domestic games. Those goals against Sweden had given him a more than respectable average of a goal every other game and there was little point arguing with the selection policy. Yugoslavia's defeat of Norway meant that only Scotland or France could now join them at the World Cup finals. Les Bleus 3-0 win featured goals from Didier Deschamps and Jean-Phillipe Durand and came despite the loss of Eric Di Meco to a red card early in the second half. Cantona's goal, rounding Jim Leighton before rolling the ball into an empty net, turned the tide when the Scots looked likely to draw level.

Yet despite defeat, the Scots still held a two-point lead over France and qualified ahead of them for Italia 90. In one of the many warm-up games arranged in the months running up to the championship, France played eventual world champions West Germany at

Montpellier, Cantona scoring in a 2-1 win. The frustration at not going to Italy was evident after this performance. Jean-Pierre Papin equalised the visitor's early goal just before the break. Four minutes from the end Cantona showed real power in the air placing a diving header beyond Bodo Illgner. The attraction of the international game was clear to him as it brought him up against the best and there was often every indication he was up to the test.

RETURN TO MARSEILLES

ON THE BACK of his form for Montpellier and a run of nine goals from 11 games for Les Bleus, Bernard Tapie insisted Cantona return to Marseille. Had he stayed with Montpellier he would have met Manchester United, eventual victors in the European Cup Winners' Cup, who overcame their French counterparts 3-1 on aggregate in the quarter-finals.

Eric returned to the Stade Vélodrome reluctantly. In politics and business Tapie was used to dealing with 'yes men'. Cantona could not bring himself to do that. The pair tolerated one another but as Eric was still under contract and with no loan or transfer on offer he had no choice. However, with West Germany's successful manager Franz Beckenbauer now installed at OM there was at least the chance of a clean slate and perhaps some success.

Despite being part of the side which displayed ruthless efficiency rather than élan in beating the Holland team Cantona idolised in 1974, Beckenbauer was someone Eric respected and it showed in a sensational run at the beginning of the 1990-91 season. Chris Waddle had been brought in from Tottenham Hotspur at a cost of £4.5 million to provide some flair down the flanks. Dragan Stojkovic had been added from Red Star Belgrade to act as playmaker and the exciting Ghanaian international Abédi Pelé had returned after a spell with Lille. Meanwhile Eric's old friend Jean Tigana, who was now nearly 35, still moved about the field like a gazelle. Tapie's desire to become the first French team to win the European Cup had clearly been backed with all the resources at his disposal.

Cantona was encouraged to utilise his size, strength and striking instincts and after a dozen games he had scored seven goals. His partnership with Papin taking off immediately. The Cantona/Papin axis was also important for France. The European Championship qualifying group for the 1992 competition began without a hitch and though Papin was the one getting his name on the score sheet, Cantona was instrumental in many of the successful moves.

Clearly happier as an international, he only once displayed a fit of pique and that came following a late substitution in a game with Iceland. With France 2-0 up, manager Michel Platini thought he was doing Eric a favour by giving him a rest and allowing the small number of travelling fans to give him an ovation for his exploits which included a goal. With a face like thunder he stormed away from the pitch and into the dressing room. A member of staff was sent to check on him when Platini and Houllier sensed there could be a problem. Their envoy found Cantona storming around the dressing room throwing things. Though he was quickly placated and his team-mates didn't even know what had happened, the manager decided there would be no more substitutions. Eric would play the full 90 minutes unless forced off by injury.

Back at Marseilles however Beckenbauer proved to be another who failed to see eye-to-eye with Tapie. Used to having unfettered access to all areas of the club, the German excluded the chairman from the inner-sanctum of the dressing room and refused to give the owner any say over team matters. In December, while Cantona was recovering from knee ligament injured suffered following a tackle from behind by Brest's Racine Kane during late October, Beckenbauer accepted the post of technical director, stepping aside for Belgian Raymond Goethals to become manager. The excuse Tapie found for moving Beckenbauer 'upstairs' was a poor run of results.

Performances initially improved under Goethals. However when Cantona returned from injury he couldn't find a way back into the team. Abédi Pelé was now partnering Papin with Waddle playing just behind. Results picked up to such an extent that Marseilles won Le Championnat with ease. Despite the celebrations, Cantona played only a minor role, making just two substitute appearances for a combined total of just 47 minutes. His only appearances after that came following injuries to either Pelé, Papin or Waddle and it became clear that his place in the side was on the bench. Having picked up just a single goal since his return from injury he asked to leave.

The animosity between Tapie and Cantona persisted with Goethals making up an unhappy triangle. Cantona was sure the Belgian was no more than Tapie's yes-man. There was a championship medal courtesy of the dozen and a half appearances made - a first national title - but no desire to stay with the club any longer.

NIMES

*"Now I am accursed, I detest my native land. The best thing
is a drunken sleep, stretched out on some strip of shore"*
ARTHUR RIMBAUD – "A SEASON IN HELL" (1873)

A £1 MILLION switch to Nimes Olympique was arranged and his fifth club surprisingly made him captain. With France matters continued to improve. Qualification for Euro 92 in Sweden was more or less assured with a win over Spain in October. However, Eric remained a magnet for trouble and found things were not going well on the field in Nimes. He later stated that the game and the club he was now playing for gave him no pleasure. Nimes were limited. He wanted to give a discontented public more but simply couldn't. He scored just two goals in 17 games and the frustration was clear in early December when he disputed a referee's decision in a game against Saint-Etienne.

Having jumped to reach a cross and brought it down perfectly with his chest he heard the official's whistle. He was told the use of an elbow had been spotted. Cantona could not tolerate the incompetence and asked for an explanation but got a brusque gesture in return. Outraged at the decision Eric picked up the ball and hurled it at the referee, hitting the official on the back of his thighs before walking from the field. The four match ban imposed by the tribunal was doubled when Cantona approached each member of the panel individually and hissed the word "idiot" in their ears.

Cantona's temper had got him in trouble so often that he had become known in the press as 'L'Enfant Terrible'. His lengthy charge sheet included fights with team-mates, altercations with fans, officials and administrators. Handing down his judhement the President of the commission, Jacques Riolaci, asserted, "Behind you there is the smell of sulphur. You cannot expect anything from an individualist like you."

Cantona's immediate response was to retire and he made his decision public on 12 December 1991 - he was just 25 years old. He agreed to buy out the remainder of his contract with Nimes. At first he seemed to have retired from the game entirely, spending a month in the Provence countryside. But, incomplete without football, he soon sought guidance. During a visit from Michel Platini Eric relented saying that his decision would be reversed if an offer from a club outside France was received. However, a player with Eric's record of attracting trouble meant that this was unlikely. Most assumed he would not have the discipline for Italian league football, nor would he be suited to Spain where niggling fouls and diving were common. In early 1989 he was said to have presented himself to Barcelona director Joan Gaspart to enquire about the possibility of joining up with manager Johan Cruyff, Gaspart sent him away without referring to Eric's Dutch idol.

There were other options including Germany but one place more than any other sprang up as a likely place to rebuild his career. Platini and his assistant Gerard Houllier believed Eric could adapt to the particular demands of English football. The pair were desperate for Cantona to get playing again as both believed that they would have a very good chance of winning the European Championships with him in the squad, but without club football he simply could not be selected. English football would present Eric with a fresh challenge and a clean slate. As yet no clubs had shown an interest, nor was there any real clue how leaving the French game he had known so well would affect the player in the short or long term but the pair trusted their instincts.

Houllier was a student of world football and something of an obsessive who knew English clubs well. While studying for a degree at Lille University he had a spell teaching in a Liverpool comprehensive during the late 1960s where he became a regular at Anfield. He kept an interest in that particular club but also in the English game in general. Many inside and outside the game had suggested England may be a good place for Eric to ply his trade. Platini approached Liverpool boss Graeme Souness about a move as early as November 1991. The Frenchman was a figure Souness respected and he knew any player he recommended would be worthy of consideration but, after being told Cantona would perhaps like to play for Liverpool, Souness turned it down. There was some dressing room antipathy within the club and there was little desire to risk worsening things.

Meanwhile Nimes, who had cancelled Eric's contract on the understanding that his career was over, now protested that they had been excluded from a lucrative transfer fee for the problematic forward. Eric's lawyer Jean-Jacques Bertrand and Jean-Jacques Amorfini, vice-president of the French Players' Union, were despatched to negotiate and the player promised to pay Nimes compensation of 10 million francs (£1 million) should he find a new club - the same sum which Nimes had paid to Marseille just a few months earlier.

Eric also got himself an English agent, Dennis Roach, who had bagged Dutch star Johan Cruyff as his first client and more recently had brokered the deals which took Chris Waddle to Marseilles and Glenn Hoddle to AS Monaco. Roach quickly received interest from Sheffield Wednesday manager Trevor Francis for whom he had negotiated moves to Italy as a player. But the complex negotiations with Nimes seemed to put the Hillsborough hierarchy off Cantona. A meeting to hammer out these details took place in late January 1992 at the offices of the Mayor of Nimes and it seemed that a loan could be arranged. A further meeting was arranged at the headquarters of the Cacharel fashion house with representatives of Nimes Olympique, Sheffield Wednesday, Eric Cantona and his advisers. Jean Bousquet, who was part of the Nimes delegation, had founded the Cacharel label in the early 1960s.

The meeting broke up with an apparent understanding that a medical needed to be passed but Francis, who had not been present, was under the assumption that a trial would also take place. He wanted some degree of protection for the club after contacting Waddle for the inside track on the player. The England winger was adamant about his former colleague's skill and vouched for his disposition. Still, Francis thought Cantona too big a risk for the club. Cantona, who had already travelled to South Yorkshire, was equally resolute that a trial was never part of the deal and that, as an established international, he should not be expected to have to audition.

He arrived on 25 January 1992 during a typically unwelcoming cold snap. The harsh Yorkshire weather made a conventional training session impossible so the work moved indoors complex where basic fitness was looked at and some five-a-sides played. There was an opportunity to see what Eric had to offer in an indoor match against Baltimore Blast at the Sheffield Arena. The six-a-side clash included the likes of Graham Hyde, Nigel Worthington, Chris Bart-Williams and Gordon Watson and allowed Eric the chance to show his skills but the standard of football left him looking forlorn. No further training could be arranged outdoors and Francis, unwilling to take a risk without at least a practice match, suggested another week's stay but Eric turned it down.

In total Cantona spent four days with Wednesday and, having swallowed some pride to be on trial for a week, he felt anything more would be too much. There were already a host of strikers on the Hillsborough books and the Owls withdrew. The interest and the provisional £800,000 deal fell through.

The decision not to stay at Hillsborough was reported by many sections of the British and French press as a 'walk out', which only reinforced Eric's reputation as a highly strung character. Leeds United manager Howard Wilkinson had been interested weeks earlier but as his club refused to deal with agents who charged commissions this alternative had not been mentioned. Wilkinson found making contact difficult and when it appeared a deal was ready to be struck he withdrew until the Wednesday bid collapsed. In a bid to get something for his time and effort Roach finally raised the prospect of a move to Leeds...

ENGLAND

Howard Wilkinson remembered Eric Cantona from an under-21 tournament in Toulon some years. As part of the England youth coaching set-up, Wilkinson had scouted most of Europe's top teams, in that role he also took in a number of games in the European under-21 championship that France won in 1988.

Meanwhile, Platini had also been doing more canvassing around the upper echelons of the English game. Lawrie McMenemy, an assistant to then England boss Graham Taylor, was one who had been buttonholed. He was enthusiastic that the player come to England. Further homework was done by Wilkinson who contacted Glenn Hoddle following his return from a spell with Monaco to manage and play for Swindon Town.

Gerard Houllier, an old friend from countless UEFA conferences and someone he knew had mentored Cantona, offered the Leeds boss a candid assessment but added that, if handled correctly, Eric's recklessness would disappear and matters on the pitch would take care of themselves. He cited the international match against Iceland as a prime example. He also alluded to the usefulness Eric would have by pointing to the archetypal English role he had in the new and potentially very successful French side as proof that he suited the English game.

Eric Cantona was not the type of player Wilkinson would normally consider for his team. His success at Sheffield Wednesday and Leeds had been built on dourness and functionality. This formula had lifted the Whites out of Division Two and into a realistic fight for the title. There were good players in the side and some, such as Gary McAllister and Gordon Strachan, had plenty of skill but operated within a strict system. On the face of it, Leeds didn't look like a natural home for Cantona.

Nevertheless, an official approach was made on 31 January 1992 as Cantona prepared to fly home, his retirement now seemingly unavoidable. Wilkinson's intervention, provoked by Leeds downturn in form, forced Eric to re-think. The Leeds boss bolted across to a hastily arranged meeting in Sheffield and found Cantona lying on his hotel bed when he arrived. The player looked a little forlorn but quickly became interested in Wilkinson's offer. Leeds had topped the table at the end of October and remained serious challengers for the title. Now neck and neck with Manchester United they were now just a couple of points adrift. Free of the burden of chasing two domestic cups (they had been knocked out of each competition by the Reds) they seemed in pole position, particularly as United were beginning to tire after a long time as front runners and with the weight of 25 years of expectation weighing them down.

An injury crisis amongst the forwards, particularly that suffered by spearhead Lee Chapman who had fractured a bone in his wrist, meant Wilkinson was keen to bring Eric in as a stop gap or even on loan. There was also a hope that a new player could provide some momentum during the run-in. No one could deny Eric had the game to do just that but the risk was whether he could adapt to the English game and whether that infamous temperament, which many domestic players would seek to exploit, would re-surface. Taking the bull by the horns the player told Wilkinson he cared little for the past and was only looking to the future which, if it involved Leeds, would be successful for both parties.The manager also felt that he had a strong enough dressing room which Cantona wouldn't disrupt.

Basing his decision solely on football Wilkinson took the plunge and paid a £100,000 loan fee with a £900,000 permanent deal possible should things work out. Each man impressed the other and the tales of Elland Road's past and present enchanted Cantona. They shook hands on personal terms which would see a significant wage along with accommodation in a semi-detached house near Roundhay Park.

A day later he was presented to the media and fans after Leeds 3-0 victory over Notts County had put them top following United's draw at Arsenal. There was plenty to impress Cantona, notably an impressive solo effort from David Batty. Leeds had made a series of purchases since being promoted just over a season earlier and the successful blending of these players was perhaps Wilkinson's greatest acheivement. He would clearly need to employ the same skills with his latest acquisition.

When Cantona reported for training early the following week he was keen to get a ball at his feet following a six week lay-off.

He quickly impressed as the team went through training routines that concentrated on movement and passing rather than set plays. His team-mates and Howard Wilkinson were sure they had got themselves a gem if his talent could be harnessed.

OLDHAM ATHLETIC 2 LEEDS UNITED 0
DIVISION ONE - 8 FEBRUARY 1992

THERE WAS GOOD news for Cantona who on the eve of his much awaited debut was informed that he had retained his place in the national side for a friendly with England at Wembley Stadium in just over a week's time. Howard Wilkinson, worried about the fitness of his new charge after almost two months without a first team game, erred on the side of caution deciding very early in his preparations that Eric could only start on the bench, the theory being that his pace, passing and vision would favour Leeds as gaps opened later in the game.

It failed to work here as Oldham tripped up the ambitions of their guests on a day when victory would have consolidated pole position. Instead Leeds could not make the most of Manchester United being held to a draw by Sheffield Wednesday. The Latics utilised the offside trap well which neither Gary Speed nor Rod Wallace able to breakthrough. Both spent more time on the ball but that just allowed Oldham to hustle them out of possession. Rick Holden had the measure of Mel Sterland all afternoon and set up the opener for Paul Bernard on 18 minutes from a corner. A far post cross for Andy Barlow with just three minutes left secured victory although the full back needed two attempts.

Cantona came on as a substitute for the injured Steve Hodge and almost scored with his second touch in English football. Though he displayed a number of smart flicks, his efforts came to nothing and he looked understandably out of touch at times, over-hitting a number of passes. As his manager feared, fitness was an issue and a vital commodity for any player at the business end of the season as quickness of mind didn't match quickness of thought.

WITH NO CUP commitments there would be no Leeds game for just over a fortnight giving Cantona the chance to improve his sharpness in the international game with England before his new club next took to the field.

France had never scored at Wembley but were in good shape having gone 19 games without defeat since March 1989. Basil Boli showed there was steel as well as silk to this side making some bone-shattering challenges, particularly on Neil Webb and Gary Lineker minutes after his introduction from the bench at half-time. Just prior to the break Alan Shearer notched with a shot on the turn. The visiting side rarely looked like making a breakthrough and should have been behind when Lineker put Geoff Thomas away in acres of space. The Crystal Palace midfielder accelerated past defenders then tried to chip Giles Rousset. The ball ballooned embarrassingly off his foot and so high and wide that it was closer to the corner flag when it crossed the byline.

Lineker showed greater control when put through by Shearer, his effort grazing the bar. Shearer then linked with Rob Jones on the right and crossed for Nigel Clough, whose effort was parried by Rousset, Lineker hit the rebound onto the bar before heading home to make it 2-0. Like the rest of the French attack Eric Cantona was largely anonymous. He had three goal attempts and sent in a cross from either side of the field but neither were capitalised on although substitute Amara Simba hit the foot of the post in the dying minutes.

EVERTON 1 LEEDS UNITED 1
DIVISION ONE - 23 FEBRUARY 1992

MANCHESTER UNITED SEEMED to be making a decisive dash for the title as Leeds' progress stalled. The Reds now had a three point lead having beaten Crystal Palace 24 hours before this clash at Goodison Park. Leeds spurned far too many chances in the first half. The most glaring from Eric Cantona who played from the start but seemed off the pace.

While he looked stylish on the ball and beat opponents with ease there was little end product so that he looked at times to be more of a showboater than a top class footballer. It was a performance that justified Trevor Francis's caution. When opportunities were not wasted Neville Southall proved a considerable obstacle, saving from from Gordon Strachan twice and Gary McAllister. Both midfielders were outstanding but when the latter had a shot rise up off John Ebrell's legs the keeper could only parry to Carl Shutt who netted despite Martin Keown's attempts to clear.

Howard Kendall immediately introduced Peter Beagrie and Andy Hinchcliffe and within nine minutes Everton were level. A Beagrie corner caused confusion as Gary Ablett flicked on for Matthew Jackson to score his first for the Toffees. Peter Beardsley thought he had won the game with a late goal but it was ruled out. Manchester United played Chelsea at Old Trafford the following Wednesday. A draw was rescued by a Mark Hughes goal which allowed the gap to grow to four points but both teams had now played 29 games.

LEEDS UNITED 2 LUTON TOWN 0
Division One - 29 February 1992

MATTERS AT THE top changed once more when Manchester United recorded a second successive draw at Coventry while Leeds won at home to Luton halving the gap to two points. Lee Chapman returned with Cantona back on the bench. Rod Wallace's leg injury was not as bad as first feared and he kept his place. Luton were struggling to avoid relegation and gave the hosts few favours. It wasn't until the final quarter that Leeds secured the points. Play was tentative as both sides seemed unwilling to take a chance, this only changed when Cantona came on for the injured Tony Dorigo after 30 minutes.

It was the first time he had played with Chapman outside training and as the pair's understanding grew, Leeds began to look the more likely to score. Cantona could have opened his account within minutes of coming on after reaching a long ball just inside the penalty area, his attempted lob over the advancing keeper landed just over but that long awaited goal fell for Cantona soon after when he converted a straightforward chance and was mobbed by his team-mates. Lee Chapman's late volley erased any hope of an equaliser leaving Leeds on 60 points compared to United's 62.

LEEDS UNITED 0 ASTON VILLA 0
Division One - 3 March 1992

Leeds wasted the chance to take pole position as they were held at Elland Road by Aston Villa. The score was made all the more galling by Gordon Strachan missing a second half penalty. His tame shot in the 58th minute, after Mark Blake had handled, was saved by Nigel Spink. Once again Eric Cantona was on the bench from the start – his first goal apparently not enough to guarantee a berth in the starting XI.

Tony Agana, who had been selected for his pace, had a chance after three minutes from a Lee Chapman cross but the man signed on loan from Notts County snatched at the opportunity and sent it wide. Mel Sterland and Chris Fairclough clashed heads soon after with the centre back going off for treatment before being replaced after 34 minutes due to concussion. Sterland was off the field for almost a quarter of an hour to have six stitches in a facial wound. When he did return to the fray it was in midfield as protection against opening the cut up again. John McClelland came on as a like for like replacement but after that start Leeds were more than content to go in on level terms. Blake, Dalian Atkinson and Cyrille Regis were all a threat and each drove good opportunities wide.

Sterland returned to his more accustomed defensive role in order to help stem Villa's growing momentum. Chapman posed a danger but Agana, who was belatedly replaced by Cantona, couldn't use his speed across the ground to any great effect. Manchester United missed out on their opportunity to pull clear at the top, drawing at Middlesbrough 24 hours later.

TOTTENHAM HOTSPUR 1 LEEDS UNITED 3
DIVISION ONE - 7 MARCH 1992

ERIC CANTONA REMAINED a substitute with his fitness still an issue. Howard Wilkinson remained convinced that he should not change his team, especially the forward line, just for the sake of fitting in the new man. Yet Leeds remained tentative and played without conviction which made the final score all the more unlikely. Errors from the hosts led to the first after 36 minutes when Steve Sedgley could only find Rod Wallace with a defensive header. He easily beat an exposed Erik Thorstvedt from 15 yards. Spurs levelled when Paul Allen met a Paul Stewart centre just after the break and but for John Lukic, who denied Stewart a few minutes later, Leeds would have trailed.

When Thorstvedt failed to catch a Gordon Strachan corner substitute Newsome nodded in. With 14 minutes on the clock Cantona came on and within 30 seconds set up Gary McAllister for the third with an exquisitely timed and weighted pass.

QUEENS PARK RANGERS 4 LEEDS UNITED 1
DIVISION ONE - 11 MARCH 1992

JUST WHEN IT seemed the twists and turns of the championship run in could not get any more tortuous, Leeds went down to a large defeat at Loftus Road while Manchester United advanced to the final of the League Cup after an extra-time victory over Middlesbrough in the 2nd leg of their semi-final. United had been routed by Queens Park Rangers by the same margin at Old Trafford on New Year's Day but that didn't erase the pain for Howard Wilkinson's men. The gap remained at two points but with three games in hand it was United's title to lose rather than Leeds' to win.

The team cut a sorry state on the long journey back to Yorkshire. Two errors in 60 seconds by the normally secure John Lukic were crucial. The keeper managed to fluff an attempt to cut out a through ball from Ray Wilkins to Bradley Allen. Though the angle was tight Allen finished with aplomb. Then, in the next attack, Andy Sinton sent a shot through his legs. Those goals wiped out a tenth minute lead established by Gary Speed who had headed in during a period in which Leeds seemed in total control. But an eye injury to Rod Wallace saw Leeds temporarily down to 10 men and QPR took advantage, Les Ferdinand levelling the score from a corner.

Chasing the three points proved costly for Leeds, those goals in the 62nd and 63rd minutes leaving them floundering. The introduction of Eric Cantona for Gary McAllister couldn't turn things around and with the away side stretched Chris Whyte tripped Sinton in the area. He was dismissed and Clive Wilson converted the spot kick eight minutes from time.

LEEDS UNITED 5 WIMBLEDON 1
DIVISION ONE - 14 MARCH 1992

BOTH LEEDS AND Manchester United may have won but the Reds owed their victory by the odd goal in three to keeper Peter Schmeichel and when Lee Chapman nodded in the final goal of his hat-trick on 80 minutes it seemed a draw at Bramall Lane would round off an almost perfect afternoon for Howard Wilkinson. Brian Deane gave Sheffield United a lead but second half goals by Brian McClair and Clayton Blackmore kept things as they were at the start of play.

At Elland Road a comprehensive win ended a seven game unbeaten run for the Dons. Attacking flair down the flanks was something Joe Kinnear's side had no answer to and it allowed Leeds to effectively win the game within an eight minute period of the opening half. Chapman grabbed two, meeting crosses from David Batty and Rod Wallace before Wallace beat Hans Segers from 12 yards. Paul Miller pulled one back but a fairly simple goal for Eric Cantona and the completion of Chapman's treble gave the hosts a comprehensive win.

ARSENAL 1 LEEDS UNITED 1
DIVISION ONE - 22 MARCH 1992

MANCHESTER UNITED HAD been denied a chance of returning to the top after a midweek defeat at Nottingham Forest. Alex Ferguson was scathing in his criticism and things got little better 24 hours before Leeds took to the field at Highbury as United staggered to a goalless draw at home to Wimbledon. It seemed that the title momentum was once more swinging towards Elland Road but there was still a tricky tie with reigning champions Arsenal to be negotiated. Paul Merson, who had scored goals to secure The champions seemed to have played a decisive role in deciding their successors with a stunning, late equaliser. Leeds looked certain to hold on to an advantage provided by ex-Gunner Lee Chapman to open up a four point gap - the biggest margin they had been able to establish all season. Yet Merson foxed the visitor's static backline, latching on to his own chip forward before steering the ball past John Lukic to deny them all three points.

Cantona, making his second successive start, was a virtual spectator as both sides successfully sprang well drilled offside traps. Leeds had taken the lead when Nigel Winterburn was too busy complaining to officials after a challenge from David Batty to notice Rod Wallace taking the ball down his vacated flank. The referee urged the left back to play on but it was too late. Steve Bould tried clearing the danger but only succeeded in letting Chapman in from close range at the near post. Once ahead Leeds pulled everyone behind the ball. Even when level Howard Wilkinson continued to be cautious and held out for a point even though three could have proved decisive.

LEEDS UNITED 0 WEST HAM UNITED 0
DIVISION ONE - 28 MARCH 1992

QUEENS PARK RANGERS followed up their defeat of Manchester United at Old Trafford by holding them to a draw in the capital but this was a score Leeds could only match to ensure things remained tight at the top. Lee Chapman, whose goalscoring exploits left many wondering why he didn't fit into England's plans, missed a sitter that threatened to prove costly at the season's end. A cleverly played reverse pass by Eric Cantona on 20 minutes caught the Hammers defence, David Batty ran in on goal on the right as defenders retreated and the midfielder's square ball for Chapman at the far post was a gift.

The striker failed to trouble Miklosko who put in a desperate dive to divert the ball around the post. Though a disappointing miss, the build up included the first flash of the true genius of Eric Cantona.

The entire team appeared affected by the miss and only the chance to regroup at the break seemed to remedy that but Miklosko was able to repel efforts from Cantona, Newsome and Chapman with supreme agility. The title was often won or lost on such errors. It was just a question of who would make the fewer in the half dozen games that remained.

MANCHESTER CITY 4 LEEDS UNITED 0
DIVISION ONE - 4 APRIL 1992

HOWARD WILKINSON WASN'T exactly waving a white flag after this 4-0 hammering at Maine Road but now he could only hope that his side won each of the last five games to maintain some semblance of pressure on Manchester United. Leeds were not four goals worse than City on this showing but couldn't put away any of the chances they created whereas the home side converted all theirs. Possession flowed well, so well that even when 2-0 behind at the break the visitors appeared confident that something could be rescued from a torrid afternoon but Tony Coton rarely looked like he would be beaten. The keeper denied each and every forward player including Cantona after his introduction but his best saves were reserved for Gary Speed, Chris Fairclough and Rod Wallace. Meanwhile City were clinical in front of goal: Andy Hill headed in a Mark Brennan corner, Mike Sheron beat John Lukic to a Steve McMahon ball which beat the offside trap before Niall Quinn drove in from just outside the area and Brennan added the fourth in the last minute.

City played Manchester United in the following week so had a chance to return the favour. A draw at Old Trafford left the Reds two points ahead with a game in hand. Ryan Giggs scored an early goal before Neil Pointon was dismissed for a foul on the Welshman. However, ten man City rescued a point thanks to the blistering pace of David White who earned a penalty following a Steve Bruce lunge - Keith Curle converting. Fitzroy Simpson missed a sitter in the last minute that could have sunk the Reds.

LEEDS UNITED 3 CHELSEA 0
DIVISION ONE - 11 APRIL 1992

WHEN ERIC CANTONA rose from the bench, Leeds were dourly defending a 1-0 lead courtesy of Rod Wallace. With Manchester

United pre-occupied with the Rumbelows Cup final there was no pressure from another result on the day yet Chelsea were pushing for an equaliser. Throwing on a forward in those circumstances was not typical of Howard Wilkinson's philosophy. He would normally look to close the game out but with Jon Newsome already on in place of Steve Hodge, Cantona came on for Wallace. By full-time he had given the game, and the title race, a completely different look.

In the half dozen minutes remaining he created a comfortable looking win - scoring one and making another. Within moments of his introduction, Gary McAllister found Eric in the penalty area. Dave Beasant and his defenders expected a shot but instead he rolled the ball to Lee Chapman and two touches later the ball was in the net.

In the closing seconds Cantona scored the most sublime goal of the season. Collecting a Gordon Strachan throw-in he lifted the ball over an oncoming defender, charged through an attempt to tackle from another Chelsea player before driving the ball into the top corner just yards from the touchline. From his first touch the ball hadn't touched the floor until it hit the net. Leeds had been far from convincing but that injection of flamboyance had put them back on top and, with United struggling due to a lack of the same flair, it seemed that Eric's six minute burst had tilted the title Leeds way.

LIVERPOOL 0 LEEDS UNITED 0
Division One - 18 April 1992

Despite his cameo the previous week there was still no place in the starting line-up for Cantona as Rod Wallace and Lee Chapman were preferred for the trip to Liverpool. The Merseysiders were without a full-time manager as Graeme Souness continued to recover from heart by-pass surgery. Caretaker Ronnie Moran, who had guided the Anfielders to Wembley during the week, remained at the helm. Many wondered just how much that tense FA Cup semi-final with Portsmouth had taken out of the hosts but this proved no walk in the park for Leeds and John Lukic performed heroics to ensure a share of the points.

All too often a keeper's contribution can go unnoticed and outfield players have a tendency to grab the headlines. Lukic's contribution was all too obvious. Leeds were anonymous up front and regularly caught out by Liverpool's well-drilled offside trap. When someone finally got beyond the last line Chris Fairclough was thwarted by Ray Houghton on the line and £1.6 million striker Rod Wallace missed a glaring opportunity when put clean through on the half hour. Rather than take a shot on himself, he tried to find Chapman but the ball ran too far ahead of his partner and although Steve Hodge reached the loose ball he could only manage a weak shot which dribbled wide of Bruce Grobbelaar's goal.

At the other end Lukic dealt with shots, crosses and all manner of other efforts making crucial stops from Dean Saunders, Ian Rush and Michael Thomas. The latter two were denied by an incredible double save. Rush was thwarted again with a top drawer block. Mike Marsh also brought out the best in the keeper and John Barnes had a screamer kept out by a finger tip. There was some assistance from the referee who waved decent penalty appeals away on the hour when Chris Whyte appeared to pull Rush off the ball but Whitley Bay official Ken Redfearn decided it was a fair challenge.

Eric Cantona came on for the latter stages but failed to alter the course of the game, volleying a decent injury time chance over. Liverpool proved far too good in every area and Leeds had to view this as a point won rather than two lost. Fortunately for the Elland Road side, Manchester United could not take advantage. A 1-1 draw at Kenilworth Road against relegation candidates Luton Town kept Alex Ferguson's side top.

LEEDS UNITED 2 COVENTRY CITY 0
Division One - 20 April 1992

LEEDS RECEIVED A boost prior to kick-off as Manchester United unexpectedly lost to Nottingham Forest, a late Scott Gemmill winner stunning the Old Trafford crowd. Leeds, kicking off 15 minutes later, had Eric Cantona on the bench again. A cautious opening from both sides was cast aside as the game opened up.

Frustrated by a goalless first half, a Leeds goal arrived soon after the resumption. Mel Sterland's high free-kick was flicked on by Whyte, Brian Borrows' sliced clearance was headed past Steve Ogrizovic by Chris Fairclough. Eric Cantona was brought on with little time to influence matters but helped earn a penalty ten minutes from time. He was first on the scene when the ball ran free after Ogrizovic denied Gary Speed on the left and shot at an unguarded net, Lloyd McGrath handling on the line - McAllister converted from the spot.

The performance mattered little as three points put Leeds top by a point with two games remaining while their rivals had a game in hand but their clash with West Ham at Upton Park was never likely to be straight forward. In the event the Hammers won courtesy of a goal from full back Kenny Brown which put Leeds back in control and meant the title could be decided at the weekend. Manchester United were at Anfield while Leeds made the short if testing journey to Bramall Lane.

SHEFFIELD UNITED 2 LEEDS UNITED 3
DIVISION ONE - 26 APRIL 1992

MARK WALTERS' LATE goal secured all three points for Liverpool in a match which had seen United hit the woodwork three times. Leeds win secured by Brian Gayle's own goal and United's third defeat in a week, saw Leeds crowned champions. The Sheffield skipper had done well to keep the Whites out but all three away goals on the day owed something to fate. Across the field every Leeds player looked tense which almost allowed the Blades in on a number of occasions before Alan Cork netted an opener. The striker capitalised on defensive jitters at a corner, Chris Whyte blocked even though he knew little about it and the ball rebounded to the former Wimbledon man after flicking off Glyn Hodges and Gordon Strachan. Ironically Cork was only in as Bobby Davison was not allowed to play as part of his loan agreement with the visitors.

A lucky goal just before half-time squared affairs. Gayle cleared a Strachan free-kick but hit Gary Speed. A kind bounce saw the ball ricochet in off Rod Wallace. Goalkeeper Mel Rees came out for the second half with his knee heavily strapped. Speed gave him an early test, striking the post within a minute of the resumption. Lukic tipped two efforts from Brian Deane over before Gary McAllister exploited the Blade's keeper's lack of mobility with a cross which Jon Newsome converted at the far post. Though in a winning position, nerves returned during the next Sheffield United attack which concluded with Lee Chapman turning John Pemberton's cross past his own keeper.

A draw was not quite enough as a win would still be needed in the last game and Leeds went looking for the decisive strike which came when a through ball was attacked by Wallace and substitute Eric Cantona. Gayle was always favourite to reach it but under pressure he allowed it to bounce up off his knee. He looked to head it back to Rees but the keeper, who had hobbled closer to the ball expecting a deft touch back, saw the ball loop over his arms outstretched and roll slowly over the line.

Just three weeks earlier Leeds had looked anything but potential champions having been soundly thrashed 4-0 by Manchester City but now that's exactly what they were.

At a civic reception to honour the triumph a day later Eric had the microphone thrust in his hand and was told to say something. He simply said of the Leeds fans: "Why I love you, I don't know why, but I love you." The statement and its pigeon English was later mixed into a record produced by a couple of Leeds fans.

LEEDS UNITED 1 NORWICH CITY 0
DIVISION ONE - 2 MAY 1992

LEEDS, THE FINAL winners of Division One under the Football League's old structure, played the last game of a triumphant season in a strange atmosphere. There was non-stop singing and chanting and the champions remained unbeaten at Elland Road courtesy of Rod Wallace's strike. The former Southampton forward seemed to be enjoying his football now the tension had disappeared and took the ball inside his own half, beating three players on his way to the area before dispatching a low finish from 15 yards. Eric Cantona made his first start since late March and showed a range of tricks Norwich struggled to deal with. He also contributed to some memorable moves but was withdrawn for Steve Hodge.

1991-92

Although Leeds' style was not suited to Eric Cantona, he was delighted to be back playing with the admiration of supporters and the respect of his fellow professionals - it seemed the manager would be more than happy to exercise his option to make the transfer permanent. Howard Wilkinson seemed reluctant to fit Eric into his side and later claimed that the Frenchman's contribution to Leeds title victory was negligible. Nevertheless he felt there was an opportunity for the player and club to help one another. Cantona brought much to the table and it was felt the player could benefit from the side's disciplined approach.

Cantona agreed to remain though something of a illusion built up around his contribution to the title win and just how crucial his arrival was. The bald facts are that when Eric was in the starting line-up results were not good enough and from his six starts he managed just one goal. Two of those games ended in victory with three drawn - anything but championship form. Leeds' faultless finish to the season came with Cantona on the bench. Nine substitute appearances brought him two more successful efforts on target but none, except his opener against a struggling Luton Town, were actually pivotal.

Though not wholly instrumental in the title win his arrival provided some momentum at a crucial stage and, as it coincided with Manchester United's dismal closing form, many thought that it tipped the balance towards the Yorkshire team. In some of those outings he had seemed anonymous but there were enough flashes to suggest that with a full pre-season the Frenchman would have something substantial to offer the champions. He would also share the creative burden with Gary McAllister who, along with Lee Chapman, spoke a bit of French having had a brief spell at Chamois Niortais towards the end of the 1987-88 season. Both had gone out of their way to make their new team-mate feel welcome and showed signs of having a decent rapport on and off the field.

As for Leeds' chances in the European Cup - it would be difficult given that English teams would be making their return following the six year ban handed down in the wake of the Heysel Stadium disaster final, but anything was possible.

SWEDEN 1 FRANCE 1
European Championship Finals Group A - 10 June 1992

FRANCE OPENED THE championships with a match against the hosts who were set to make a winning start when central defender Jan Eriksson converted an Anders Limpar corner on 25 minutes after making a late charge from half way. The muscular approach of Sweden contrasted greatly with the finesse displayed by their opponents who based their game around feeding the front two of Eric Cantona and Jean-Pierre Papin but the ball rarely found its way through. With the Scandinavians holding on, the French passing game bemused the Swedes who looked uneasy. It was a case of athletes against artisans but Jonas Magnus Thern and Stefan Schwarz just about managed to block out the usually productive Didier Deschamps and Franck Sauzée.

Pascal Vahirua looked dangerous early on but without much support from Manuel Amoros it made the task of containment easier for Roland Nilsson. Eriksson eased Papin away from a dangerous cross to the far post by Jocelyn Angloma on the right but none of the officials saw anything untoward. France deservedly levelled when Papin was released by a diagonal ball which made the task of finishing all too easy for the prolific marksman. After the goal Cantona and Papin combined again only for a resolute Swedish defence to resist them - Thomas Ravelli in particular was in top form but no save was better than the one he made from his own colleague Klas Ingesson.

FRANCE 0 ENGLAND 0
European Championship Finals Group A - 14 June 1992

ENGLAND ALMOST MADE France's job of qualifying from the group stage impossible. Just six minutes remained when Stuart Pearce thundered a free-kick against the crossbar with Bruno Martini beaten by its pace. On the basis of the first 84 minutes Les Bleus would have failed to come back. Both sides lacked ingenuity or a creative spark to support their front pairings though Chris Woods made the only meaningful save of the match when a clearance was seized upon by Jean-Philippe Durand. Papin had enough room to put in a deft flick towards goal, Woods tipped the ball aside.

Martin Keown kept tabs on Eric Cantona as he had done at Wembley four months earlier, ensuring he remained quiet until the final whistle and although Andy Sinton cleared a header from Jocelyn Angloma off the line, England were better in the first half but the sterility on the pitch spread to the fans. It was only when Basile Boli performed a head butt on Pearce that matters became more animated. Both left backs had uncompromising reputations and not just in their approach to legitimate tackling. Marquis of Queensbury Rules may have been employed to settle the matter had such an incident occurred anywhere other than a football field but the chance for revenge came within a minute when Boli, who somehow escaped punishment, grounded Alan Shearer just outside the area. Pearce was only allowed to lash the ball at goal after his bleeding face was cleaned up. UEFA promised to look at the incident.

FRANCE 1 DENMARK 2
European Championship Finals Group A - 17 June 1992

A Lars Elstrup goal 13 minutes from time changed the course of a game which Michel Platini's side seemed to have in the bag. The 2-1 win gave the unfancied latecomers, who were only invited to take part following Yugoslavia's withdrawal due to civil war, a place in the semi-finals. A draw would have been enough for France to join Sweden in the last four. Jean-Pierre Papin had earlier equalised Henrik Larsen's half volley to keep the French on course for the semis.

Papin's goal deserved to win any match let alone tie it. Jean-Philippe Durand was found by an Eric Cantona cross. Durand took the ball down before dabbing a delicate through ball for Papin to accelerate before rifling home a right foot shot from the angle. However, hopes were dashed when a low cross aimed at Brian Laudrup was prodded past Bruno Martini.

HAVING EXCELLED IN the qualifiers with eight straight wins in a difficult group and piecing together a 19 game unbeaten run, France's failure was a surprise as they finished joint bottom of their group with England who were sunk by Sweden on the same night. Denmark finished second to the hosts courtesy of their defeat of Cantona's side in the final game and went on to astound the continent by beating Holland on penalties in the semis and Germany 2-0 in the final.

Following France's poor showing, Michel Platini stood down with Gerard Houllier taking over. There were all kinds of theories about why France went out so easily. Despite holding a chance until the closing stages of their final group game, there should not have been such a dependence on the last chance saloon. Some pointed to unrest in the camp though there was very little evidence to back that up. It was also suggested that a good side simply peaked too soon and even if it had managed to squeeze past Denmark they would probably have gone out at the next stage. A theory that carried more logic was that having found qualifying so easy and having strung together an impressive run of results, complacency had crept in.

LEEDS UNITED - PREMIER LEAGUE 1991-92

DATE	OPPONENT	VENUE	SCORE	ATTD	1	2	3	4	5	6	7	8	9	10	11	
8-Feb-92	Oldham Athletic	Boundary Park	0-2	18,409	Lukic	Sterland	Dorigo	Batty	Fairclough	Whyte	Strachan	Wallace	Hodge	McAllister	Speed	Cantona (Hodge), Whitlow (Sterland)
23-Feb-92	Everton	Goodison Park	1-1	19,248	Lukic	Sterland	Dorigo	Batty	Fairclough	Whyte	Strachan	Wallace	Cantona	McAllister	Speed	**Shutt**[1] (Wallace)
29-Feb-92	Luton Town	Elland Road	2-0	28,231	Lukic	Sterland	Dorigo	Batty	Fairclough	Whyte	Strachan	Wallace	**Chapman**[1]	McAllister	Speed	**Cantona**[1] (Dorigo), Agana (Wallace)
3-Mar-92	Aston Villa	Elland Road	0-0	28,896	Lukic	Sterland	Whitlow	Batty	Fairclough	Whyte	Strachan	Agana	Chapman	McAllister	Speed	McClelland (Fairclough), Cantona (Agana)
7-Mar-92	Tottenham Hotspur	White Hart Lane	3-1	27,622	Lukic	Sterland	Whitlow	Batty	Fairclough	Whyte	Strachan	**Wallace**[1]	Chapman	**McAllister**[1]	Speed	**Newsome**[1] (Sterland), Cantona (Whitlow)
11-Mar-92	QPR	Loftus Road	1-4	14,641	Lukic	Newsome	Whitlow	Batty	Fairclough	Whyte	Strachan	Wallace	Chapman	McAllister	**Speed**[1]	Cantona (McAllister)
14-Mar-92	Wimbledon	Elland Road	5-1	26,760	Lukic	Newsome	**Cantona**[1]	Batty	Fairclough	Whyte	Strachan	**Wallace**[1]	**Chapman**[3]	McAllister	Speed	Shutt (Strachan)
22-Mar-92	Arsenal	Highbury	1-1	27,844	Lukic	Cantona	Dorigo	Batty	Fairclough	Newsome	Strachan	Wallace	**Chapman**[1]	McAllister	Speed	
28-Mar-92	West Ham United	Elland Road	0-0	31,101	Lukic	Cantona	Dorigo	Batty	Fairclough	Whyte	Strachan	Wallace	Chapman	McAllister	Speed	Hodge (Wallace)
4-Apr-92	Manchester City	Maine Road	0-4	30,239	Lukic	Cantona	Dorigo	Batty	Fairclough	Whyte	Strachan	Wallace	Chapman	McAllister	Speed	
11-Apr-92	Chelsea	Elland Road	3-0	31,363	Lukic	Hodge	Dorigo	Batty	Fairclough	Whyte	Strachan	Wallace	Chapman	McAllister	**Speed**[1]	Newsome (Hodge), Cantona (Wallace)
18-Apr-92	Liverpool	Anfield	0-0	37,186	Lukic	Newsome	Dorigo	Batty	Fairclough	Whyte	Hodge	Wallace	Chapman	McAllister	Speed	Cantona (Hodge)
20-Apr-92	Coventry City	Elland Road	2-0	26,582	Lukic	**Newsome**[1]	Dorigo	Batty	**Fairclough**[1]	Whyte	Strachan	Wallace	Chapman	**McAllister**[1]	Speed	Shutt (Strachan), Cantona (Chapman)
26-Apr-92	Sheffield United	Bramall Lane	3-2	32,000	Lukic	**Newsome**[1]	Dorigo	Batty	Fairclough	Whyte	Strachan	**Wallace**[1]	Chapman	McAllister	Speed	Cantona (McAllister), **Gale og**[1]
2-May-92	Norwich City	Elland Road	1-0	32,673	Lukic	Newsome	Dorigo	Batty	Fairclough	Whyte	Cantona	**Wallace**[1]	Chapman	McAllister	Speed	Hodge (Cantona), Strachan (Chapman)

SALE OF THE CENTURY

LIVERPOOL 3 LEEDS UNITED 4
CHARITY SHIELD - 8 AUGUST 1992

LEEDS AND LIVERPOOL served up one of the best Charity Shield games in recent memory but it was the champions and particularly Eric Cantona (playing at what would turn out to be his favourite venue against the team which would become his favourite opposition) who were celebrating at the close. Howard Wilkinson reacted to Graeme Souness' decision to field a 3-5-2 formation as he had done throughout pre-season by asking Cantona, Rod Wallace and Lee Chapman to act as forwards. Friendlies before the traditional pre-season curtain raiser had convinced the manager that his theory about the growing relationships between his front players could well be right and gained further credence from events at Wembley.

Wilkinson had added central midfielder David Rocastle and left sided winger Scott Sellars to his squad in the close season. Rocastle was on the bench to accommodate the tactic of playing three forwards and Gordon Strachan. The absence of both players left Leeds' midfield weaker than the manager would like but it mattered very little as for the first time in many seasons Liverpool looked toothless in that area. The Merseysiders were not helped by the absence through injury of Rob Jones, John Barnes, Steve McManaman, Steve Nicol, Michael Thomas and Jan Molby. It meant a key player was missing in every area of the field, most notably in defence, as Cantona made the most of his freedom by claiming the first hat-trick of his career and became the first player to hit three in the traditional season curtain raiser since Manchester United's Tommy Taylor in 1957.

Midway through the first half Leeds claimed their opener. David Batty found Rod Wallace on the left and after a dart down the flank he cut the ball back for Cantona who beat Bruce Grobbelaar from eight yards via a substantial deflection from David Burrows. Liverpool attempted to make an instant recovery and went close through Ian Rush and Paul Stewart, the former levelling within nine minutes

- Ronnie Rosenthal conjuring a cross for the Welshman which he nodded past John Lukic. From that point on Liverpool made most of the running but fell behind again when a Tony Dorigo free-kick flew past Grobbelaar after hitting Rosenthal who was the last body in the wall.

Liverpool started where they left off after the resumption with Mark Walters giving Jon Newsome a torrid time. Lukic, who had already denied the winger, parried another shot but couldn't stop Dean Saunders converting from close range. Wallace was then denied by Grobbelaar as Saunders and Burrows threatened to give Liverpool a lead for the first time but, having worked good positions, they pulled their efforts wide. Liverpool were favourites to go on and win until Cantona put the game beyond them in the final dozen minutes. A Gary McAllister free-kick sent long into the area was nodded to Chris Fairclough who chested the ball back to the Frenchman. A low shot before Grobbelaar missed a Wallace cross and Cantona nodded into an empty net. Mark Wright set up a tense finale with an effort Strachan should have blocked on the line but the ball slipped between his heels on the line.

The match eased some of Howard Wilkinson's doubts about Cantona and particularly the effectiveness of his collaboration with Chapman. The two sides met again in a testimonial for Jim Beglin who had been forced to retire recently after failing to fully recover after breaking his leg while at Liverpool in 1987. He was just 27 when the decision to quit was taken. Almost 8,500 fans attended the match at Elland Road which Liverpool won 4-1.

LEEDS UNITED 2 WIMBLEDON 1
PREMIERSHIP - 15 AUGUST 1992

ENGLISH FOOTBALL'S BRAVE new world kicked off with few obvious changes at Elland Road or for that matter any other football ground in the country. The game and teams looked very much the same, the First Division had merely been re-branded as The Premier League. That was certainly true of Leeds despite Howard Wilkinson's summer spending which brought midfielders Scott Sellars and David Rocastle to the club. Sellars was making a return to the club after six years at Blackburn Rovers while Arsenal midfielder Rocastle, a two time title winner and England international, was brought in for £2 million, a Leeds record. However, both were left out in favour of the players who landed the final Football League championship under its old structure.

Apart from the Premiership's formation there was another change to the game and Wimbledon's Roger Joseph became one of the first players to be undone by the new back-pass law after a quarter of an hour when trying to decide how he should deal with a Gary McAllister cross which Rod Wallace had flicked on. Unable to simply touch it back to his keeper as he would have done last term and worried about making a clearance he would have little control over, he did neither. Lee Chapman nipped in to dribble past a helpless Hans Segers.

Leeds remained dominant throughout the first half but exerted little pressure until after the break. It was a feature of their game that had almost handed the title to Manchester United the previous season and may have done so if the latter's season had not imploded. It almost cost a couple of points as Wimbledon managed to level with a Warren Barton cross-cum-shot which sailed over John Lukic's head 15 minutes from time. Cantona thought he had doubled Leeds' lead early in the second period after turning a Steve Hodge cross in but was flagged for offside. He also converted a McAllister corner but was once more pulled up when the linesman spotted the same transgression.

The equaliser inspired Leeds to pursue a winner and lay seige to the Dons goal. But it took until four minutes from time for Chapman to strike again to earn all three points – Cantona nodding down for his strike partner to drill in from 20 yards. Though David Batty's belligerence in midfield provided plenty of possession while Eric, as he had done to such devastating effect at Wembley, decided to look towards his flair as a route to link with Chapman. Despite often appearing less effective against a combative side, his delicacy of touch contributed much.

ASTON VILLA 1 LEEDS UNITED 1
PREMIERSHIP - 19 AUGUST 1992

LEEDS WERE DISCOVERING that defending a title was harder than winning it in the first place. Excepting Liverpool, no side had achieved that feat since Wolverhampton Wanderers in 1959 and it took an 83rd minute equaliser from Gary Speed to earn a point at Villa Park.

Aston Villa were expected to be one of the serious challengers to Leeds' crown and offered a thorough examination of their credentials via the searing pace of Tony Daley and Dalian Atkinson. Ron Atkinson's men looked to have secured the points when the latter put the home side ahead 13 minutes from the close. A Kevin Richardson corner was headed on at the near post by Cyrille Regis, who had come on as an early substitute for the ineffective Dwight Yorke. Regis' introduction changed the game and saw Villa dominate, going close with his first touch, an effort that reared up steeply off a length and clipped the bar. Daley, who gave Newsome a severe test, would have provided a goal had his crossing been anywhere near as impressive as his ball skills and dribbling. The game would have been irretrievable had the unmarked Ray Houghton converted a simple chance just two minutes into his home debut. Lukic had already denied Dalian Atkinson after another link with Regis just past the hour but the Leeds keeper got close enough to the through ball and managed to smother.

At the other end Villa were hard to break down. Spink was forced to parry a 25 yard drive from Eric Cantona before the interval, it was his first save of any note. There was a huge slice of fortune about the Leeds equaliser. Speed took a pass from Steve Hodge then delivered a decent shot but the ball slipped through the legs of an embarrassed Nigel Spink. Cantona, who was effectively being accommodated in the line up by Howard Wilkinson utilising a 4-3-3 formation rather than 4-4-2, was a peripheral figure.

MIDDLESBROUGH 4 LEEDS UNITED 1
PREMIERSHIP - 22 AUGUST 1992

AN INEPT DISPLAY saw Leeds receive exactly what they deserved at Ayresome Park. Newly promoted Boro were rampant from the start and within eight minutes Paul Wilkinson had made it 2-0 converting a couple of Tommy Wright crosses from the left - first with his foot then his head. The goals were 57 seconds apart and Leeds never recovered. They were never allowed to with Wright and former Elland Road winger John Hendrie darting towards a backline that looked short of confidence. Chris Fairclough, who had been given the slip for both goals, looking particularly vulnerable.

When Wright headed in a Jimmy Phillips corner two minutes after the break, Eric Cantona became the scapegoat for a laconic style which appeared at odds with the previous season's blood and guts approach. In reality he was one of the few Leeds players to apply himself when the going got tough. With Leeds hustled out of their preferred passing style, Cantona's contribution remained unconvincing although if he had taken either of two excellent chances before Boro's third, it could well have changed the complexion of the game. Cantona did score in the 68th minute with a well executed volley but the game was already lost and Hendrie made it 4-0 with just over thirty minutes remaining. In truth the Leeds midfield was just not producing the goods, neither assisting the backline nor creating chances for attackers who were had little support. There seemed a need for change yet close season signings David Rocastle and Scott Sellars remained sidelined.

LEEDS UNITED 5 TOTTENHAM HOTSPUR 0
PREMIERSHIP - 25 AUGUST 1992

BOTH ERIC CANTONA and Leeds United snapped back into form in spectacular fashion, the game was played just three hours after Eric had been told that he had been left out of the French squad to take on Brazil in Paris 24 hours later. For Eric it was a huge blow to miss the tie against the storied South Americans. New manager Gerard Houllier was a friend and confidante to Eric but after the nation's disappointing opening round exit in the European Championships he decided to take a look at alternatives.

It would have been easy for Howard Wilkinson to follow that example and wield the axe but he kept faith with the same side humiliated at Middlesbrough. They repaid him handsomely. Leeds were on the front foot very early on and could have scored before the opener. Neil Ruddock almost diverted Gary McAllister's free-kick into his own net, David Howells was forced to stop a Chris Whyte shot on the line and Cantona came close with a spectacular bicycle kick.

Then David Batty played Cantona in behind Spurs' backline. Only Ruddock was able to track back and though he made an interception the ball put Eric Thorstvedt under pressure. The keeper, who had done so much to ensure his side remained level, forgot that he could no longer handle from a backpass until the last second. His attempted clearance only found Rod Wallace who stuck the ball straight back past him from an angle.

Then Cantona stepped forward to steal the show. He got on to the end of a weak Justin Edinburgh header and despatched an angled drive with his right foot from 18 yards before Thorstvedt had moved. Next he connected perfectly with a David Batty cross on the half hour from close range only missing out on a hat-trick when slicing the ball wide following an accurate McAllister centre.

A minute after the resumption Cantona secured his second treble of the season, thumping a shot through a crowd of defenders after a Lee Chapman nod down. It looked a simple goal but the first time strike took some execution. There could have been a fourth on 66 minutes but Cantona returned the favour for Chapman who converted an easy chance after Eric had drawn a beseiged defence and keeper out of position.

LEEDS UNITED 2 LIVERPOOL 2
PREMIERSHIP - 29 AUGUST 1992

LEEDS PERFORMED A smash and grab raid to claim a point courtesy of Lee Chapman's late equaliser but all three would have been won had an injury time goal from the same player stood. It was ruled out for pushing and despite struggling with injuries Liverpool, who were weaker than when the teams met in the Charity Shield just three weeks earlier, followed Middlesbrough in forcing doubts about Leeds' ability to retain their crown. David James had put in a remarkable display but potential championship winning sides would be expected to put an ailing team like Liverpool to the sword with few problems.

That looked likely when Gary McAllister put his side into an early lead with a spectacular right foot volley after David Batty's throw-in was lobbed into the area. Every member of the Leeds side had their tails up after the savage demolition of Spurs, none more so than Eric Cantona who was not only at the heart of everything but more often than not was a catalyst for Leeds attacks. Liverpool rode their luck, especially when Lee Chapman and Rod Wallace missed by no more than a yard or so. McAllister fired over when he may have done better and Cantona failed by inches to divert a Wallace cross-shot.

James made the save of the game from Cantona and a couple more from Chapman. It seemed Leeds would net sooner rather than later but a minute from half-time Liverpool found their feet and equalised. Mark Wright beat Chapman to the ball in defence before flicking play to the left from where Paul Stewart found Ronnie Whelan with a reverse pass which the Irishman curled past John Lukic.

Liverpool dominated the second half - Gary Speed making a

goal-saving tackle from fellow Welsh international Ian Rush and Chris Whyte came within a yard of putting through his own goal. Leeds had chances to regain their advantage but were repelled by James. It appeared the Merseysiders could end a 25 game unbeaten run when Jan Molby stuck away a debateable penalty for a foul on Mark Walters by Jon Newsome.

Leeds were determined to preserve their home record and got their rewards following a double substitution - James failing to collect a Gordon Strachan corner, Chapman netting with a near post header. A Cantona shot set up what appeared to be the late winner but referee Roger Dilkes ruled that Chapman had pushed David Burrows, with whom Cantona had enjoyed a series of conflicts, in the process of scoring.

OLDHAM ATHLETIC 2 LEEDS UNITED 2
Premiership - 1 September 1992

BOUNDARY PARK HAD been the scene of Eric Cantona's introduction to English football and on his return he seemed to have ratcheted up an already prominent reputation as a match winner by notching a brace. His second came just 14 minutes from time and appeared to have brought Leeds a win but Ian Olney, Latic's £700,000 record signing, enhanced his reputation with a brace of his own. If his first restored a little pride, the second, an equaliser deep in injury time, sunk the visitors.

Leeds made a point of driving down the centre via Lee Chapman. The striker won the ball three times in a minute via the tactic and Leeds were able to get numbers forward but failed to benefit from this advantage. Cantona was more subtle and drifted across the line. A cross from the left was his first meaningful contribution although again nothing came of it. Gary McAllister, who had come through a fitness test in the morning, was another refined presence to compliment Cantona and the pair released Rod Wallace who took one touch too many and failed to test Jon Hallworth.

For the hosts Gunnar Halle shot wide when he should have done better as should Ian Marshall who headed Neil Adams's free kick wide. Leeds ratcheted up the pressure during the early phases of the second half with McAllister's crosses a particularly potent weapon. Chris Fairclough went close before playing a part in the opening goal on 54 minutes, winning Tony Dorigo's lob forward which, following a melee, fell for Cantona to finish easily. The Frenchman then took a pass from McAllister for the second.

Olney's late intervention proved decisive however, a left footed volley on 85 minutes was followed by a header from a Graeme Sharp corner two minutes into time added on to deny Leeds victory.

MANCHESTER UNITED 2 LEEDS UNITED 0
PREMIERSHIP - 6 SEPTEMBER 1992

LEEDS NEVER LOOKED likely to win their first encounter with Manchester United in nine attempts and the home side triumphed thanks to the dominance of Paul Ince in midfield. David Batty and Gary McAllister could not contain the England international or the driving force of Brian McClair.

The Old Trafford side had risen to fourth on the back of four successive wins after a poor start. Yet the hosts began sluggishly and there would have been few complaints if Leeds had taken advantage. They may have done so but for Rod Wallace's withdrawal 13 minutes in due to a pulled hamstring. The stinging runs mounted by the former Southampton man were missed, his replacement, Gordon Strachan, had many attributes but pace wasn't one of them. Leeds attacks met with scant reward. Eric Cantona looked towards the exceptional and despite the acrimonious relationship between the two sets of fans, he drew a sporting round of applause for a couple of volleys from the home supporters who instantly recognised his quality. It was a rarity for Leeds players to obtain too much acclaim at Old Trafford, although when he failed to net with a close range header the howls were louder than the acclaim.

Jon Newsome, who had been troubled by pace before, received some measure of protection, swapping with Chris Fairclough, although his anticipated duel with Ryan Giggs didn't materialise as Alex Ferguson had already taken the decision to swap his wingers over with Giggs on the right and Andrei Kanchelskis on the left. No matter which flank they were on the pair were always likely to unsettle Leeds and tore at Fairclough and Tony Dorigo throughout.

Giggs outpaced the left back to set up the first on 30 minutes crossing for Kanchelskis to head in at the far post. Strachan came close to equalising on 42 minutes following an enterprising thrust by Gary Speed but Peter Schmeichel smothered his effort from a dozen yards. It was a chance Leeds were left to rue when Steve Bruce scored just before the interval, scrambling the ball in from five yards after John Lukic lost the flight of a Denis Irwin corner.

LEEDS UNITED 1 ASTON VILLA 1
PREMIERSHIP - 13 SEPTEMBER 1992

ONLY A LATE goal by substitute Steve Hodge spared home blushes. Villa, who came within minutes of beating Leeds for the second time in a month, dominated but the late equaliser wouldn't have mattered if debutant Dean Saunders hadn't spurned a chance after a Kevin Richardson pass on the hour. The £2.3 million signing from Liverpool was sent clear but John Lukic stuck out an arm to divert the ball out for a corner. Paul McGrath, despite dodgy knees which meant he couldn't train during the week, remained Villa's rock at the back. On 18 minutes Ray Houghton won the ball in midfield and cut a swathe through the Villa defence before finding Garry Parker unmarked inside, the midfielder beating Lukic with a firm shot. The Villains should have doubled their advantage, Earl Barrett wasting a free header late in the opening period.

Again Leeds missed the pace of Rod Wallace which left Eric Cantona and others far too much to do. Nevertheless Speed had a header cleared by Parker from under the bar, Scott Sellars, had a shot saved by Nigel Spink who also denied McAllister and Cantona. The hosts continued to push but other than a goal line clearance from Lee Chapman, had nothing to show for their pressure and were always vulnerable to Villa counters.

There were three home penalty shouts directed at referee Joe Worrall. Two for fouls on Cantona while Gary McAllister was thought to have been brought to ground, however the official waved them away. Hodge, who had appeared late to supply an equaliser against his former employers in the second league game of the season, now rose from the bench with a quarter of the game remaining and repeated the feat, controlling a Cantona flick before beating Spink from 10 yards. Buoyed by squaring matters Leeds had chances in the time remaining but found Spink far too alert.

VFB STUTTGART 3 LEEDS UNITED 0
EUROPEAN CUP 1ST RD 1ST LEG - 16 SEPTEMBER 1992

AS CHAMPIONS, LEEDS became England's first representatives in the European Cup since the Heysel ban was lifted. However, 17 years after the Whites last took on teams from the continent it appeared that a hasty exit would be made as Howard Wilkinson's men were totally outclassed by VfB Stuttgart.

The first half was an open affair which Leeds shaded in terms of possession but just a few minutes of madness cost them dear. Leeds began brightly, Rocastle shooting into the side netting from close range before Eric Cantona attempted to chip Eike Immel from the edge of the 'D', the German keeper tipping over the bar. Strachan took the resulting corner from which Chris Whyte flicked to Cantona whose downward header was bundled off the line via a post by Fritz Walter. Immel made another full stretch save this time from Strachan who drilled in a low shot from 25 yards, the host's keeper again diverting the ball to safety. Believing that the German champions were there for the taking, Chris Fairclough was pushed forward to lend height to moves and the shedding of a little more caution was reflected by the introduction Hodge.

Stuttgart looked a different side following the break and three minutes after the resumption John Lukic made a save from Thomas Strunz. Leeds, perhaps believing that they could ride out any storm their hosts able to muster, remained positive but had their plans ruined by one lax moment from Cantona on 63 minutes although there was mitigation in that he appeared to grab his hamstring when attempting to deliver a 70 yard cross-field pass intended for Gary Speed. Michael Frontzeck intercepted and in turn found Kogl. The midfielder had the beating of Batty and crossed for an unmarked Walter to chip the advancing Lukic from 12 yards to underline his class.

Soon after Cantona, who just minutes before the goal had gesticulated towards the bench, was replaced. Given that he was already carrying the injury, trying to make such a difficult pass was fraught with danger. Wilkinson, who saw exactly what was crossing his player's mind, screamed at him to play safe or knock the ball out. His comments after the goal were caught by a pitch side microphone, it proved to be a turning point in Cantona's Leeds career.

Walter, the Bundesliga's leading scorer the previous season with 22 goals, registered his second after a corner fell for Eyjolfur Sverrisson whose parried shot fell to the striker. Close to the end Andreas Buck appeared to end Leeds' European adventure with a third against a now demoralised side. Maurizio Gaudino headed on for Buck who charged from halfway past Fairclough and Tony Dorigo before slotting home an angled shot from 20 yards.

LEEDS UNITED 2 EVERTON 0
PREMIERSHIP - 26 SEPTEMBER 1992

THERE WAS NO better way to bounce back from disappointment in Europe than recording a well-deserved victory which ended a five game run without a league win. Everton matched Leeds over the first half-hour but once the Toffees' initial energy sagged the hosts imaginative edge saw them dominate.

Watching Stuttgart officials may not have seen the best of Eric Cantona in the opening leg of their European Cup meeting but couldn't help but be impressed by him here. The French forward was at his best throughout directing play with accurate passes. Only an inability to time his runs to beat Everton's offside trap robbed Cantona of the chance to cap his performance with a goal.

After just seven minutes he seemed to have set Lee Chapman on a familiar trail towards the posts but Dave Watson managed to intervene. The Cantona/Chapman axis seemed to be developing game by game and, fitness allowing, would be important when Stuttgart came to Yorkshire. Yet there remained a defensive vulnerability. David Batty looked ill at ease - Jon Newsome's inability to settle had forced Howard Wilkinson to use the midfielder at right-back. David Unsworth attempted to benefit but with the diminutive Tony Cottee up against giants Chris Fairclough and Chris Whyte, Unsworth's crosses were wasted.

Once Batty ended the threat from Unsworth, Leeds controlled the game. Andy Hinchcliffe denied Chapman on the line and Gary Ablett nearly put through his own goal. A Gary Speed volley was diverted by Neville Southall before the Welsh keeper was beaten by McAllister who rattled an upright from 35 yards. A second effort from range from the Scot sailed whistled just over but a 61st minute penalty proved pivotal. Gary Ablett seemed to win the ball cleanly off McAllister but referee Ken Redfearn decided the Scottish midfielder had been impeded, the Scot sending Neville Southall the wrong way from the spot.

Two minutes later Speed and Strachan sent McAllister to the byline and his low cross was converted by a diving header from Lee Chapman on the six yard line.

LEEDS UNITED 4 VFB STUTTGART 1
EUROPEAN CUP 1ST RD 2ND LEG - 30 SEPTEMBER 1992

FEW FANCIED LEEDS to pull off the 4-0 victory they required, a pessimism reflected by a disappointing attendance of just over 20,000. No English side had ever recovered from a first leg deficit of three goals. If their absent support thought the task beyond Leeds, Gary McAllister had other ideas – he tore towards goal at every opportunity and sent three efforts close in the opening minutes. So vicious was the assault that the aggregate score could have been levelled within five minutes. Two efforts whistled just past the posts while another forced an exceptional stop from Eike Immel.

Scott Sellars raided dangerously down the left but a breakthrough came down the opposite flank 17 minutes in - Gary Speed converting a chance crafted by Eric Cantona who laid off Strachan's lobbed pass to tee-up a sweet left footed volley which sent Elland Road wild. The atmosphere fell flat moments later when Andreas Buck equalised - Fritz Walter wriggling clear and scoring from the rebound after Lukic had saved. Yet Leeds had demonstrated the Germans vulnerability and their continued pressure paid off in the 38th minute when Guido Buchwald barged into Lee Chapman, McAllister converting the spot kick.

The break interrupted Leeds' flow, but Cantona roused things, going close with a couple of headers while Chapman was disappointed to find the side netting with a close range header. On the hour Strachan added a third, Cantona beating Gunther Schafer to the ball and passing for the Scot to beat Immel with a precise lob. Chapman thought he had forced the ball in moments later when he jumped with Slobodan Dubajic but his header struck the underside of the crossbar. When, with ten minutes remaining, Chapman levelled the tie - leaping unopposed to meet a Strachan corner - Leeds went after the crucial fifth and Stuttgart were delighted at the final whistle having apparently progressed on away goals.

Yet controversy followed the next day when it became clear that the limit of three non-German players had been breached. Fans of a rival Bundesliga club spotted that Jovo Simanic, a Yugoslav defender, had exceeded UEFA's quota when he came on as an 82nd minute substitute for Maurizio Gaudino barely a minute after the Germans had introduced the Swiss Adrian Knup. With the Serb Slobodan Dubajic and Iceland's Eyjolfur Sverrisson already on the pitch, Stuttgart had fielded 4 'non-nationals'.

After five hours of deliberation in Zurich the result was annulled and Leeds awarded the match 3-0 leading to a tie on aggregate and a one off replay was ordered. Barcelona's Nou Camp Stadium was selected as the neutral venue.

IPSWICH TOWN 4 LEEDS UNITED 2
PREMIERSHIP - 3 OCTOBER 1992

As A SPECTACLE there had been few finer showings in the Premiership
- the match ebbed and flowed from first to last and though Leeds
were eventually over-powered they played their part and may have
fancied a draw having almost retrieved a 3-0 first half deficit.

Inspired by veteran John Wark, enjoying a third spell at Portman
Road, the hosts capitalised on defensive lapses from Leeds. The first
came when Chris Whyte conceded possession in his own half which
allowed Jason Dozzell to release Paul Goddard. The striker got a shot
in from the edge of the penalty area which John Lukic tipped over the
bar. Neil Thompson took the resulting corner but Chris Kiwomya
converted from just six yards. A second came when Fairclough
gave away a cheap free-kick. Wark beat Lukic despite the keeper
getting a hand on the ball. Minutes later David Batty, performing as
a makeshift right-back once more, brought down Goddard when he
was certain to score - Wark fired the penalty high into the net.

Leeds were showing signs of tiredness after their exertions
against Stuttgart during the week yet 10 minutes after the restart
Gary McAllister and Lee Chapman combined to get them back in
the game. When, with 25 minutes remaining, Craig Forrest was
beaten for a second time following a Gary Speed header from a
corner, Leeds looked likely to complete a remarkable comeback. Yet
it was Wark who put Ipswich back in control, crossing perfectly for
Dozzell to glance home.

A continuing problem for Leeds was the inability to get men
forward in support of Cantona and Chapman. It meant the forwards
were isolated figures for lengthy periods and coming back to link play
may have suited Cantona but was not something Howard Wilkinson
encouraged and with Phil Whelan shadowing the Frenchman's every
move, he had little space in which to operate.

LEEDS UNITED 2 VFB STUTTGART 1
EUROPEAN CUP 1ST RD PLAY-OFF - 9 OCTOBER 1992

CARL SHUTT CELEBRATED his 31st birthday by sending Leeds through
from this play-off with Stuttgart just a minute after replacing Eric
Cantona in the cavernous, thinly populated, Camp Nou. Leeds
progress was deserved as, but for an aberration during the second
half in Stuttgart, they had been comfortably the better side over the
three games.

Howard Wilkinson had seen enough in the two games played to decide on a little more insurance at the back - Jon Newsome was drafted in to the centre of defence. Jovo Simanic was an absentee and Stuttgart, fearing the influence Cantona had exerted in the second game, recalled Uwe Schneider who had watched the Frenchman so successfully in the opening game and did so once more. No number of flicks, tricks, dummies or feints - and there were plenty of them – could yield an end product.

Leeds went close to opening the scoring in the first quarter of an hour, David Batty's cross was almost turned into his own net by Thomas Strunz but cleared the crossbar by inches. The same player then almost gave a penalty away blocking Gary McAllister inside the area but Italian referee Fabio Baldas decided no offence had been committed. A free-kick was awarded when Gary Speed went down under a heavy challenge from Gunther Schafer. McAllister tested Eike Immel who parried and was relieved as Chris Fairclough sliced the rebound wide.

On 34 minutes Gordon Strachan cracked home a 25 yard drive after Andrei Golke could only half clear. Immel did well to get something on it but couldn't do anything more than deflect the ball in off an upright. At the other end Golke made up for his error after Slobodan Dubajic and Alex Strehmel linked down the right - his diving header beating Lukic. Fritz Walter threatened to add a second against the run of play but was thwarted by an excellent tackle from Newsome.

Leeds were outstanding after the break though there was little end product until Shutt replaced a frustrated Cantona. Sellars wriggled clear on the left, found Shutt who drifted passed Gunther Schafer before firing in from 12 yards to send Leeds through to a 'Battle of Britain' meeting with Glasgow Rangers in the next round.

FRANCE'S EURO 92 hangover continued into World Cup qualification. Something of an experimental side lost a friendly against Brazil in Paris. Cantona, who had been able to turn out for Leeds, was not in Houllier's plans for the opening game in the group when his side travelled to Bulgaria and fell to a couple of first half goals. Things changed dramatically upon Cantona's return, as he created a goal for Jean-Pierre Papin within three minutes of their home tie with Austria. Eric then secured the win with a well taken strike 13 minutes from time.

LEEDS UNITED 3 SHEFFIELD UNITED 1
PREMIERSHIP - 17 OCTOBER 1992

A COUPLE OF late goals gave Leeds the perfect fillip ahead of a testing trip to Ibrox but this game was no classic with both sides contributing to the lack of spectacle. Leeds had the better of the early exchanges and but for a little more sharpness from Lee Chapman would have grabbed a two goal start. Gordon Strachan was outstanding at that stage, presenting the striker with chances he would usually expect to snap up. Chapman finally netted following a perfectly delivered Cantona cross. The Blades equalised from a John Gannon corner, Paul Beesley rising highest to touch the ball past Lukic.

Leeds regained the initiative following an end-to-end passage of play that saw a Cantona header saved by Alan Kelly before Gary Speed blocked a Carl Bradshaw volley on the line at the other end. However, the most telling demands were on the away side who were finally beaten 16 minutes from time when a Newsome free-kick wasn't cleared before a long punt upfield reached Speed who fired in. Chris Whyte smacked against an upright before Speed mopped up and forced the ball in for a deserved third.

RANGERS 2 LEEDS UNITED 1
CHAMPIONS LEAGUE 2ND RD 1ST LEG - 21 OCTOBER 1992

CARL SHUTT, HERO of the Nou Camp, got just six minutes in the weekend victory over Sheffield United, replacing Eric Cantona who had been booked for a harsh foul on Tom Cowan and was walking a disciplinary tightrope as a result. Shutt came into contention for a place in Howard Wilkinson's plans due to fitness concerns over Rod Wallace. However, as the winger came through a reserve game on the same day as that match against the Blades, he remained on the sidelines.

As a European tie this match may not have excited the majority of Europe but it certainly lived up to the hype in the British press. It was more like an FA Cup clash than the measured approach continental encounters produced. Leeds made a sensational start. Just 64 seconds had gone when Gary McAllister scored a contender for goal of the season. Richard Gough could only clear a Gordon Strachan corner a yard or so outside the area from where McAllister sent a first time volley arcing past Andy Goram into the top right hand corner. If there was one drawback to the sensational start it came in Leeds' response to the early goal. Rangers were always likely to pursue an equaliser and with 88 minutes left, time was on their side as Leeds sat back.

The visitors continued to craft openings before the hosts settled. Jon Newsome had a chance at the far post but with Goram stranded on the other side of goal could only find the upright. Strachan burst into the penalty after a one-two with Gary Speed but was wrongly flagged offside. The tide only turned when Leeds keeper John Lukic punched an Ian Durrant corner into his own net after 15 minutes. Tony Dorigo attempted to clear off the line but couldn't get enough of his head onto the ball. Just after the half hour Trevor Steven and Dave McPherson combined to flick the ball towards goal. Lukic looked certain to gather but didn't get there quickly enough allowing Ally McCoist to nip in to give the Scots a lead.

With Rangers now dominant, Howard Wilkinson was relieved to reach half-time just a goal in arrears. Leeds improved after the break, a Cantona cross fired in from the left was almost touched in by a diving Lee Chapman. Rangers replied in kind with McCoist forcing Lukic to save a well directed header from 12 yards. Though the same player should have scored after Pieter Huistra sent David Robertson down the left. At the byline he dragged the ball back but McCoist ballooned over. The result left the tie on a knife edge for the second leg in a fortnight's time.

Yet all was not sweetness and light in Leeds' dressing room. Cantona had been substituted following some tightness in his hamstring with 12 minutes left at Ibrox. He should have been fit for the trip to Queens Park Rangers three days later but on the morning of the game was told he had been dropped. As the players trooped towards the borrowed London training pitch each squad member was handed a bib to signify which role they would perform. Red meant you were out of the frame and when coach Mick Hennigan proferred that colour to Cantona he may as well have been flashing it at a bull. Eric remained professional, seeing out the session for his colleagues benefit, but was visibly seething.

Wilkinson had been livid with Cantona's decision to head straight for the showers rather than take a seat on the Ibrox bench after he came off in Glasgow. He attempted to talk to him at the hotel but gained no joy. Cantona, who had been unhappy at being replaced in such a vital and delicately poised game, would not exchange a word and refused to attend the pre-match lunch, remaining in his room.

Lee Chapman, his regular roommate, found Eric dressed in

garish colours rather than the club regulation shirt and tie. It seemed to be a deliberate move to provoke a reaction and met with instant success. He was told to leave immediately and from some accounts was handed his passport in front of team-mates, although this may have been an overly dramatic interpretation as Eric had already been granted a few days' leave following the match.

Despite going ahead at QPR, Leeds lost the game after conceding two late goals. Cantona spent most of the week in France. Coming off at Ibrox provided cover for missing out at the weekend and a Coca-Cola Cup match with Scunthorpe United. The papers reported that the hamstring injury suffered north of the border was the problem but were oblivious to the bust up. The back pages were predicting a return at home to Coventry even while Eric was still across The Channel.

LEEDS UNITED 2 COVENTRY CITY 2
PREMIERSHIP - 31 OCTOBER 1992

THOUGH FAR FROM cowed, Eric Cantona returned to Elland Road and made peace with Howard Wilkinson who, without word from his striker for a significant number of days, wondered if he might see him again. Though named in the squad, Eric was kept on the bench as Rod Wallace, a scorer in the 2-2 draw with Scunthorpe, retained his place in the starting XI. Tony Dorigo was also available following a mild groin strain.

It being Halloween perhaps Leeds were expecting a fright and trailing Coventry well into injury time they certainly got that. It threatened to end an 18 month, 30 game unbeaten league run at home. It took a late Chris Fairclough leveller gained a point.

Gordon Strachan and Gary McAllister, who scored an early own goal, did all they could to rescue things but when Peter Ndlovu popped up to give the Sky Blues a lead 12 minutes from time their prospects looked bleak. McAllister provided Coventry with their head start in attempting to clear a Lee Hurst corner but could only send it in at the far post. The loss of David Batty, after he had clipped heels with Stewart Robson, was also a damaging blow particularly as the 2nd leg of the European Cup clash with Rangers lay just ahead.

David Rocastle proved a good replacement but the substitute spurned all three chances he received. Eric Cantona came on for Rod Wallace with 32 minutes left and Leeds levelled soon after, Rocastle finding Strachan on the right whose cross was nodded across goal by

Gary Speed allowing Lee Chapman to convert from close in.

Leeds initially felt that the build-up to the Ndlovu goal was offside when Robson put Phil Babb through. Fairclough had failed to respond as his colleagues tried to spring forward but the 21 year-old Babb didn't look for a flag and his curled effort came back off a post for the Zimbabwean to volley in from 15 yards. Coventry withstood the onslaught until 90 seconds of time added on had elapsed, Fairclough heading a Strachan free-kick past Steve Ogrizovic.

LEEDS UNITED 1 RANGERS 2
European Cup 2nd Rd 2nd leg - 4 November 1992

It took just three minutes for Rangers to all but settle this tie, cancelling out the precious away goal Leeds had scored at Ibrox to ensure progression to the financially lucrative group stages of the newly created Champions League. A long kick from Andy Goram was nodded on by Ian Durrant for Mark Hateley who turned and shot in the same movement from 20 yards out - Lukic couldn't get near the ball as it arrowed inside the right hand post.

David Batty's replacement, David Rocastle, had a torrid time. Rangers domination of midfield was such that he was replaced by Steve Hodge with 28 minutes remaining. Eric Cantona, who had found the system employed at Ibrox difficult due to the small amount of time he had on the ball, got an unexpected start but the Glasgow club's directness overwhelmed sorry Leeds.

Durrant's imperious control of midfield allowed him to master fellow Scot Gary McAllister. Had McCoist found the net with another early chance, the game would have been over as a contest before the half hour. The Gers continued to press but when called upon Richard Gough and John Brown were outstanding in defence while Andy Goram made a number of crucial saves. The keeper was unquestionably the best player on the pitch, producing a top drawer effort to divert an excellently struck 20 yard Cantona strike. Chris Whyte then almost converted a Gordon Strachan corner but Stuart McCall cleared off the line.

Having gained a foothold in the game, the break came at the worst time for Leeds. Then, just prior to the hour, Ally McCoist sealed Rangers their passage with a diving header from a Hateley cross. The hosts, facing the prospect of needing four goals to progress, made a double substitution on 62 minutes with Fairclough sacrificed for Rod Wallace who almost scored within a minute of his introduction. His clipped effort was pushed on to a post by Goram. Roared on by the Elland Road crowd Leeds continued to press but by the time Cantona scored five minutes from time the stands had thinned out. That didn't stop the hosts attempting the impossible in the time remaining – Goram denying Wallace and Gary Speed in quick succession. Cantona had been asked to do far too much by colleagues who turned to him at virtually every point but failed to match his level of performance or drive.

FRANCE COACH GERARD Houllier travelled to Elland Road to discuss various matters with Eric and take in the game. The French were under pressure following a 2-0 defeat in Bulgaria in their latest World Cup qualification match. Eric hadn't made that game but did grab a goal in the subsequent group match – a comfortable 2-0 home win over Austria. Finland would be next at the Parc de Princes in just over a week's time. Unfancied as the Finns were the coach needed all his best players at their sharpest and was concerned with reports about Cantona's recent absence.

Following meetings with Andy Roxburgh, who attended in his role as the Scots' manager and Alex Ferguson, Houllier met with Jacques Amorfini, the head of the French players' union. Amorfini was deeply concerned that Eric was headed for an unavoidable crisis which would require him to move on once more. Houllier later recalled that his chat with Alex Ferguson involved the Scots recent failed bids for the likes of David Hirst and Alan Shearer. He contacted him the following afternoon to suggest his quest for a centre forward include Eric Cantona. Like many other club bosses Ferguson had heard rumours on the managerial grapevine but had not yet contacted Leeds.

MANCHESTER CITY 4 LEEDS UNITED 0
PREMIERSHIP - 7 NOVEMBER 1992

GERARD HOULLIER'S COMMENTS were mulled over intently by Howard Wilkinson who, after a meeting with Eric Cantona, tried to iron out the problems which threatened the dressing room atmosphere and dropped Lee Chapman in an attempt to find the right blend for the visit to Maine Road. It had been the latest of a series of discussions during which Eric had revealed his difficulty playing alongside Chapman. Cantona was far happier playing as a link man but the system Leeds used didn't allow for that. It was affecting his game and, though he shared the passion of the fans, he was once again falling out of love with the game. Chapman was in great goalscoring form and was already approaching double figures for the season.

Leeds, fresh from a European exit at the hands of Rangers, looked totally dispirited. Veteran Mervyn Day came in for the injured John Lukic and though the 37 year-old was making his first appearance since an outing in the League Cup two seasons earlier, he looked solid and made one or two smart saves early on but was given little protection. City had been in good form, winning each of their last two league games and scored after a dozen minutes when Chris Whyte headed back to Chris Fairclough expecting his partner to clear. An alert Mike Sheron poked a foot in to score. It undid a good start at the other end where Cantona was partnering Rod Wallace with the latter passing up a good opportunity to score. Tony Coton's smothering save denied him.

After that Sheron goal the match changed, Day was Leeds' man of the match denying Niall Quinn, Sheron and Rick Holden with saves. He was only beaten again when another defensive lapse occurred. A Sheron cross was allowed to reach David White who converted at the far post. Day made another save from Fitzroy Simpson but Andy Hill picked up the loose ball to score before an Ian Brightwell effort ten minutes from time completed the rout.

Chapman came on but only once Leeds had resorted to Route One football which City found easy to defend. Only Gordon Strachan was able to bother Coton who made a comfortable save. Gary Speed's switch to midfield from the wing had helped Leeds at various points of the season and provided some solidity at Maine Road but the team's problems were manifest. Without David Batty, Tony Dorigo and John Lukic the team was fatally weakened. In the event the scoreline flattered Leeds. Wilkinson couldn't let matters go unaddressed. Though he considered omitting Cantona from the Coca-Cola Cup game with Watford he relented and included his mercurial French talent in the XI for the trip to Vicarage Road.

WATFORD 2 LEEDS UNITED 1
Coca-Cola Cup - 3rd Round 10 November 1992

Watford lay mid-table and a division below the champions and the Hornets took delight in inflicting a third successive defeat on their esteemed guests. Cup shocks were a theme for life in the lower leagues at Vicarage Road and that record was continued courtesy of two second half goals. Leeds tried to claw a way back. Eric Cantona spurned three good chances and if just one had gone in Gary McAllister's curling finish six minutes from time may have set up more than just a tense finale. David Batty's continued absence was most keenly felt, Watford massed their ranks behind the ball whenever possible and without an enforcer like Batty, Leeds never looked likely to break them down.

Lee Nogan was the hub of Watford's forward thrusts and cut a decent Cantona impression, combining with Andy Hessenthaler's pace and Gary Porter's work rate the Hornets were at times an irresistible force. Watford's first came come nine minutes after the restart when Trevor Putney sent in a high free-kick which David Holdsworth headed past a helpless Lukic. Jason Drysdale created the second after testing the backline with a cross. Chris Whyte, who had struggled all night, fouled Paul Furlong and Drysdale converted the spot-kick.

David Rocastle was brought on to give Leeds an extra body upfront for the 17 minutes left and high balls were targeted at Chapman but apart from that McAllister strike Watford, who were the better team on the night and played consistently better football, survived. Cantona showed his frustration as the minutes ticked down kicking Furlong's legs from underneath him when with just seconds remaining the young striker nut-mugged him close to the right hand touchline. It was Eric Cantona's first taste of knock-out football in England. Considering his later impact on cup competitions it came as a surprise that this occasion seemed to pass him by.

CLEARLY WILKINSON HAD reached breaking point in his attempts to mould a team around Eric Cantona. Soon after the game Eric flew out to Paris to gain additional preparation time before the crucial match with Finland which was won by the odd goal in three. Cantona and Jean-Pierre Papin again on target for the hosts.

If Eric could not fit in he was short of options other than to bench him or leave him out but both were tricky options for a manager who had spent £1 million on the fans favourite just months earlier. However, Eric didn't train well. He turned up every day but refused to obey certain instructions or undergo specific drills. Leeds, it seemed, were now just another club on the list Eric Cantona had fallen out with and usually these rows only ended one way. Wilkinson couldn't let matters go unaddressed. He omitted Cantona from the Coca-Cola Cup game with Watford, who sprung a shock 2-1 win at Vicarage Road. Eric flew out to Paris to gain additional preparation time before the crucial match with Finland which was won by the odd goal in three. Cantona and Jean-Pierre Papin again on target for the hosts.

LEEDS UNITED – PREMIER LEAGUE 1992-93

DATE	OPPONENT	VENUE	SCORE	ATT'D	1	2	3	4	5	6	7	8	9	10	11	
15-Aug-92	Wimbledon	Elland Road	2-1	25,795	Lukic	Newsome	Dorigo	Batty	Fairclough	Whyte	Cantona	Wallace	Chapman[2]	McAllister	Speed	Hodge (Batty) Strachan (Newsome)
19-Aug-92	Aston Villa	Villa Park	1-1	29,151	Lukic	Newsome	Dorigo	Batty	Fairclough	Whyte	Cantona	Wallace	Chapman	McAllister	Speed[1]	Hodge (Batty) Strachan (Cantona)
22-Aug-92	Middlesbrough	Ayresome Park	4-1	18,649	Lukic	Newsome	Dorigo	Batty	Fairclough	Whyte	Cantona[1]	Wallace	Chapman	McAllister	Speed	Strachan (Newsome) Hodge (Batty)
25-Aug-92	Tottenham H	Elland Road	5-0	28,218	Lukic	Newsome	Dorigo	Batty	Fairclough	Whyte	Cantona[3]	Wallace[1]	Chapman[1]	McAllister	Speed	Hodge (Batty) Strachan (Fairclough)
29-Aug-92	Liverpool	Elland Road	2-2	29,597	Lukic	Newsome	Dorigo	Batty	Fairclough	Whyte	Cantona	Wallace	Chapman[1]	McAllister[1]	Speed	Hodge (Cantona)
01-Sep-92	Oldham A	Boundary Park	2-2	13,848	Lukic	Newsome	Dorigo	Batty	Fairclough	Whyte	Cantona[2]	Wallace	Chapman	McAllister	Speed	Strachan (Wallace) Hodge (Newsome)
06-Sep-92	Manchester Utd	Old Trafford	0-2	31,296	Lukic	Newsome	Dorigo	Batty	Fairclough	Whyte	Cantona	Wallace	Chapman	McAllister	Speed	Hodge[1] (Newsome)
13-Sep-92	Aston Villa	Elland Road	1-1	27,817	Lukic	Newsome	Sellars	Batty	Fairclough	Whyte	Cantona	Wallace	Chapman	McAllister	Speed	
26-Sep-92	Everton	Elland Road	2-0	27,915	Lukic	Sellars	Dorigo	Batty	Fairclough	Whyte	Cantona	Strachan	Chapman[1]	McAllister[1]	Speed[1]	Rocastle (Sellars)
03-Oct-92	Ipswich Town	Portman Road	2-4	21,200	Lukic	Sellars	Dorigo	Batty	Fairclough	Whyte[1]	Strachan	Cantona	Chapman[1]	McAllister	Speed[1]	Shutt (Cantona)
17-Oct-92	Sheffield Utd	Elland Road	3-1	29,706	Lukic	Newsome	Dorigo	Batty	Fairclough	Whyte[1]	Strachan	Cantona	Chapman[1]	McAllister	Speed[1]	Rocastle (Batty) Cantona (Wallace)
31-Oct-92	Coventry City	Elland Road	2-2	28,018	Lukic	Newsome	Dorigo	Batty	Fairclough[1]	Whyte	Strachan	Wallace	Chapman[1]	McAllister	Speed	Chapman (Hodge)
07-Nov-92	Manchester C	Maine Road	0-4	27,255	Day	Newsome	Wetherall	Hodge	Fairclough	Whyte	Strachan	Cantona	Wallace	McAllister	Speed	

LEAGUE CUP

DATE	OPPONENT	VENUE	SCORE	ATT'D	1	2	3	4	5	6	7	8	9	10	11	
10-Nov-92	Watford	Vicarage Road	2-1	18,035	Lukic	Newsome	Kerr	Wallace	Fairclough	Whyte	Strachan	Cantona	Chapman	McAllister[2]	Speed	Rocastle (Newsome)

EUROPEAN CUP

DATE	OPPONENT	VENUE	SCORE	ATT'D	1	2	3	4	5	6	7	8	9	10	11	
16-Sep-92	VfB Stuttgart	Neckarstadion	0-3	38,000	Lukic	Rocastle	Dorigo	Batty	Fairclough	Whyte	Cantona	Stachan	Chapman	McAllister	Speed	Hodge (Rocastle) Shutt (Cantona)
09-Oct-92	VfB Stuttgart	Nou Camp	2-1	10,000	Lukic	Newsome	Dorigo	Batty	Fairclough	Whyte	Strachan[1]	Cantona	Chapman	McAllister	Speed	Shutt[1] (Cantona)
21-Oct-92	Rangers	Ibrox	1-2	44,000	Lukic	Newsome	Dorigo	Batty	Fairclough	Whyte	Strachan	Cantona	Chapman	McAllister[1]	Speed	Wallace (Cantona) Rocastle (Strachan)
04-Nov-92	Rangers	Elland Road	1-2	25,118	Lukic	Newsome	Dorigo	Rocastle	Fairclough	Whyte	Strachan	Cantona(1)	Chapman	McAllister	Speed	Hodge (Rocastle) Wallace (Fairclough)

CHARITY SHIELD

DATE	OPPONENT	VENUE	SCORE	ATT'D	1	2	3	4	5	6	7	8	9	10	11	
08-Aug-92	Liverpool	Wembley	4-3	61,291	Lukic	Newsome	Dorigo	Batty	Fairclough	Whyte	Cantona	Wallace	Chapman	McAllister	Speed	Strachan (Newsome) Hodge (Chapman)

A MATCH MADE IN HEAVEN

BACK IN ENGLAND Eric pulled out of preparations for the visit of Arsenal, sustaining an injury in one of his final training sessions for the club but without Cantona Leeds scored an impressive 3-0 victory over the Gunners. Wilkinson felt his position was augmented but wasn't prepared for the events of 23rd November 1992.

That morning a fax came through at Elland Road from Jean-Jacques Bertrand which stated that his client wished to be transferred. There was a list of three teams Eric would consider - Liverpool, Arsenal and Manchester United. On reporting to the club late in the day Cantona submitted his own written request. Wilkinson took the situation seriously and gave matters some considerable thought but he didn't want to strengthen a rival. Attempts were made to gauge interest back in France and when that proved fruitless other destinations on the continent were tried.

Then fate intervened. On Wednesday 25th November Manchester United chairman Martin Edwards took a call from Bill Fotherby, Leeds United's financial director. Leeds were looking to strengthen at the back and with Tony Dorigo likely to be out for some time enquiries were made about the availability of Denis Irwin who had started his professional career at Elland Road. It was obvious that such a request would be rejected but out of courtesy the proposition, along with an opening bid of £1 million, was formally raised.

Alex Ferguson was sat next to Edwards in the chairman's office preparing a bid for Everton's Peter Beardsley. Having rejected Leeds' enquiry for Irwin, Ferguson, recalling his conversation with Gerard Houllier, wondered if the Cantona situation had deteriorated to a level at which business would be considered and passed on a note requesting Edwards enquire about him. Even though he was aware of some unrest Ferguson knew nothing of the transfer request. When no flat refusal was forthcoming it was obvious that Leeds were prepared to sell.

United had remained under a cloud following the disappointing run-in to the previous season. The team were failing to live up to the high standards expected and autumn 1992 had seen a dearth of goals. Defeat at Bramhall Lane and a 0–3 reverse at home to Everton was followed by a 1–1 home draw with Ipswich Town but successive wins over Southampton, Nottingham Forest, Crystal Palace, Leeds and Everton had pulled Alex Ferguson's men from 17th to 3rd.

An early exit on penalties at the hands of Torpedo Moscow in the UEFA Cup had added to United's woes. Their form was sporadic at best – it took a last gasp volley by Mark Hughes to rescued a point at home against Liverpool before the Reds made a League Cup exit at the hands of Aston Villa. United had managed just 17 goals in 16 league games and that total included a 3–0 win the previous Saturday at home to lowly Oldham. The urgent meeting between chairman and manager followed a final rejection of a bid of almost £5 million by Sheffield Wednesday for striker David Hirst. The pair had reached something of an impasse – with the form of Brian McClair and Mark Hughes faltering, the attack needed a new spark. United now lay sixth, nine points adrift of leaders Norwich City.

Ferguson knew that a shortage of goals had cost United the previous term. They had managed just 22 goals from the final 22 games during the previous campaign and floundered as a result. Leeds had hit 36 in the same period and though they suffered a few heavy defeats it proved crucial to their championship success. Hughes and McClair performed well separately but failed to gel when fielded together. McClair had arrived a season after Hughes had left for Barcelona and completed his first season for Manchester United with 24 league goals, becoming the first Old Trafford player to manage more than 20 in the top flight since George Best's stellar 1967–68 campaign but following the Welshman's return he had struggled.

Rebuffed by Wednesday for Hirst and having lost out to Blackburn for the services of Alan Shearer, who went to Ewood Park in a £3.6 million British record deal, Edwards and Ferguson faced a dilemma. With few strikers of quality in England there seemed no other option than to await Dion Dublin's return. The huge striker had broken his leg in his sixth game and wasn't expected to return until late spring at the earliest by which time any title challenge might be dead in the water. Cantona was almost the last hope - his performance during Leeds defeat at Old Trafford in September a reminder of his quality.

Following the telephone call, Fotherby approached Howard

Wilkinson said any deal for Cantona had his blessing if the £1 million fee could be recovered and be used to reinforce his squad. The basics of a transfer were agreed between the two clubs within 30 minutes of the initial phone call. In an ideal world Wilkinson would not have wanted to sell the player but the current season's statistics were revealing – Eric had already struck the net 10 times in just 20 appearances that season. Leeds remained functional rather than inspiring and Eric, who may have been considered a luxury by some, offered something different. Wilkinson feared that the same situation encountered by Nimes could arise at Leeds in which case the club would have been out of pocket for a substantial sum of money which they could probably only retrieve via the courts. As cautious in business as he was on the field, the Elland Road boss felt he had to accept any reasonable offer.

Cantona was contacted at home to discuss events and an agreement about the decision being a mutual one was made but later reneged upon when details of the written application to leave were leaked. The parties met the following day and a deal was concluded in quick time. Both sides were happy with the selling price of £1.2 million and the personal terms were more than acceptable to the player who had now signed for his ninth club in less than a decade. Alex Ferguson was dining with Manchester City counterpart Peter Reid when everything went through. He was called away from his table to take a call confirming that the paperwork had been completed. On returning he casually dropped the signing into conversation. Liverpudlians are rarely at a loss for words but Reid was stunned, managing no more than a couple of words to signify his disbelief. His side had played Leeds just 72 hours earlier and he had seen Cantona as the focal point of that side.

Reid was not the only one taken aback. When the transfer was announced it shocked the game. Experienced hacks on the national and local newspapers were left stunned at the thought of the league champions allowing the man they perceived had swung the title their way to join a direct competitor. Howard Wilkinson explained the switch to his own fans by suggesting that the player had better prospects on the other side of the Pennines and could not be assured of a place every week at Elland Road as demonstrated by the time he spent on the bench and his omission over the past few weeks.

There were also suggestions that Cantona could not gel with his strike partner Lee Chapman although the latter had hit 11 goals in just over a dozen games. Cantona had bagged a hat-trick in the second league game against Spurs plus another five in all competitions. In addition he had created plenty of chances in his four other games plus a treble at Wembley in the Charity Shield against Liverpool.

Most felt that Cantona's move to United would end in tears. The combustible nature of the player and his new manager was sure to explode at some point. Yet Ferguson backed himself to tame the wild beast and Eric settled well into the United dressing room, striking up an immediate rapport with his new colleagues. Reputation apart a valid question asked was whether Cantona was the man to propel Manchester United to the top. He had briefly helped Leeds overcome the Reds the previous season and had lifted the French title in his last year with Marseilles, so had a history of success on his side but whether he was the man United needed remained to be seen.

Eric watched United's 1-0 victory at Highbury that weekend from the comfort of the Directors' box, the new signing drawing acclaim from the travelling fans before he had even kicked a ball. A trip to Benfica's famed Estádio da Luz, the same arena George Best had illuminated to devastating effect for Manchester United just over 25 years earlier, gave the chance for a debut away from the high pressured English game. United were the opposition for a friendly to commemorate the 50th birthday of Portuguese legend Eusebio.

The new man was paired with Brian McClair and Mark Hughes separately to see how he would perform with each. There was also a suggestion that he may play deeper just behind a front two who could be energised by their new team-mate. Rui Costa scored a late winning goal although it could have been nothing more than an equaliser had William not managed to block a Cantona effort on the line. Goalscoring was only one feature of the Frenchman's game however and he did more than enough in this match and during training to show he had the skill, vision and passing ability to fill a yawning gap at Old Trafford. Another side of Cantona's persona was the accrual of a booking for a heavy challenge. It was a strange environment in which to make his bow but in completing the full 90 minutes he at least improved his match sharpness after almost a month out.

MANCHESTER UNITED 2 MANCHESTER CITY 1
PREMIERSHIP - 6 DECEMBER 1992

ERIC CANTONA'S FIRST competitive game in a red shirt came against the same side he last faced as a Leeds player, Manchester City, but the two matches proved a huge contrast to one another. Amongst other attributes there could be no greater test of a player's temperament than a derby and no better stage on which to make a competitive debut but any contribution from Cantona would have to wait as he was selected on the bench.

The atmosphere was hot, even if the conditions were predictably cold and wet. The game was won in midfield an area in which Robson and Ince held sway against Steve McMahon. Over 20 fouls were awarded in the first half hour. Some of the more robust challenges came from City but the most telling led to the free-kick from which Bryan Robson found Mark Hughes. His header on to Ince via Steve Bruce allowed the midfielder to beat Tony Coton and register his fourth of the season. United went on to enjoy the better of the exchanges until the break but Ince had to dispossess David White and Fitzroy Simpson would have been disappointed not to level with the goal at his mercy.

The home fans got their first sight of the new signing when Cantona came on at half-time for Ryan Giggs who had picked up an ankle injury. At least one of the pair would have laid on a goal had it not been for profligate finishing. City enforcer Steve McMahon let the French international know that he could expect as warm a reception on the pitch as he received from the stands. Within five minutes of his introduction there was a chance to score from a Lee Sharpe cross but Eric had yet to attune himself to the frenetic pace and allowed Keith Curle to whip the ball off his toes. One reverse ball for Brian McClair which bisected Phelan and Curle had the home crowd drooling with anticipation even if a lack of match fitness told towards the close.

Any sceptical home fans who hadn't already realised they had landed themselves some player realised his true worth when his next meaningful touch was a whipped cross from the right which Hughes disappointingly put over. The game remained in the balance and even though Hughes scored with a dipping shot 17 minutes from time after collecting a pass on his chest and taking a rebound off Curle, City were able to hit back within a minute. Holden made his way down the left and sent in a cross which fooled both Peter

Schmeichel and Steve Bruce allowing Niall Quinn to stroke the ball home. In the time that remained Schmeichel made an astounding double save from Andy Hill and David White to preserve a third win in a row and set up a clash with leaders Norwich City the following weekend.

It was United's third successive victory and lifted Alex Ferguson's men into fifth place in the league though still nine points behind Norwich City at the top. On the same weekend Leeds suffered a 4-1 home defeat to Nottingham Forest.

MANCHESTER UNITED 1 NORWICH CITY 0
PREMIERSHIP - 12 DECEMBER 1992

THE CANARIES, PRE-SEASON relegation favourites with the bookmakers, had built an eight point advantage over second place Aston Villa. However their meteoric rise had recently been halted following defeats to Manchester City, Liverpool and Blackburn Rovers who administered a 7-1 thumping.

An evenly contested game was shaded by United who deserved the win earned by Mark Hughes's opportunism after a lapse by the usually sure Daryl Sutch who failed to control a Lee Sharpe cross. Hughes moved in to volley past Bryan Gunn from six yards. Eric Cantona, who many fancied to take the Welshman's place, delighted the home fans in his first start. Everything that he did so eloquently at Leeds seemed to look silkier in his new team and with a host of excellent players able to exploit his vision and skill, Cantona's signing already looked to have given United's title challenge added impetus.

Mark Hughes had struggled to find the net before Cantona's arrival but with goals in successive games he immediately looked a different player. As it transpired Mark Robins, making a first return to Old Trafford since his £800,000 transfer in August, was the catalyst for a frenzied few minutes. The striker, who had netted 12 goals from 19 league games, went close following a melee, Robins' low shot seemed to have the beating of Peter Schmeichel as it arced towards the far post but the Dane made a crucial intervention with his legs and the ball rose over the bar.

United could have built a two goal lead in the time remaining before the interval. Hughes made his way round Gunn but couldn't manoeuvre either his body or the ball into a position to find the net. Cantona almost brought the stadium to its feet when put through by

Ryan Giggs but his shot was too close to the keeper. That promise of flair the French international brought with him was evident in some of the delightful touches he made in the second half. However, it was a deft flick from Giggs which almost brought reward. Cantona had acres of space down the right flank as a result but was thwarted by some quick thinking by Ian Culverhouse. Eric almost returned the favour later in the half but Giggs was also denied by the full-back.

CHELSEA 1 MANCHESTER UNITED 1
Premiership - 19 December 1992

Eric Cantona netted his first goal in a red shirt and provided a rare shaft of light in a poor game played in sodden conditions. With Bryan Robson still missing and Ryan Giggs joining him on the casualty list, Cantona started and made sure of a vital point against an uncompromising Chelsea team. The Pensioners were riding high in the league thanks to the tireless running of Dennis Wise, Robert Fleck and Graham Stuart allied to Andy Townsend's graft in midfield.

Yet United were happy to soak up attacks for long periods and neither keeper was troubled during the first period. Peter Schmeichel readied himself when Fleck received the ball inside the penalty area not long after the restart but the Scotsman showed a leaden first touch and a goalless draw looked inevitable.

The game was finally brought to life after Mick Harford's introduction from the bench. It gave the previously unruffled Gary Pallister and Steve Bruce something to think about as the pair were bombarded. When Pallister fouled Harford 25 yards out, Eddie Newton slid the resulting free-kick to David Lee who beat Schmeichel with a deflected drive. It was the least their attacking intent deserved.

Yet United were level within four minutes. Lee Sharpe broke through the Chelsea defence and rolled a ball into the area which Mike Phelan touched towards Cantona whose swift turn and shot beat Kevin Hitchcock. It was a finish of the highest quality, as he beat defenders with speed of thought and accurate shooting. Amid the blood and thunder, Cantona stood out showing his full range of tricks, long range passes, and deft control that had yielded so little at Leeds.

SHEFFIELD WEDNESDAY 3 MANCHESTER UNITED 3
PREMIERSHIP - 26 DECEMBER 1992

IN TERMS OF league position there was a huge gulf between Sheffield Wednesday and Manchester United. The Owls had won just five games and exited the UEFA Cup at the second round stage at the hands of Kaiserslautern. Yet it took David Hirst just two minutes to prove his quality to long-term admirer Alex Ferguson. The Cudworth born forward had gone five games without finding the net prior to this match but looked back in form here making the most of a Carlton Palmer run into the area. Ince initially won possession with a well timed tackle but he fell in the process and the ball squirted out to Hirst just inside the area, from where he slotted home.

Another telling feature of the striker's play was an appreciation of his fellow forwards. A headed pass into Mark Bright's path from Chris Waddle's cross on the right saw Wednesday double their lead with just six minutes gone. The home side were in total control and the game looked over when Hirst beat Parker in the air to set up Stretford born United fan John Sheridan for the third.

United tried to get back into it, forcing Chris Woods to produce two fine saves from Brian McClair. And it was McClair who got United back into the game scrambling home following a goalmouth melee. Sharpe's thrusts down the left and the midfield pairing of Ince and McClair started to unsettle a tiring and nervous Wednesday. The trio changed the focus of the game. Wednesday looked there for the taking but even when McClair arrived late in the area to bag a second with another header from close range after a Sharpe cross, so little time remained that the odds still favoured a win for the home side.

Schmeichel kept hopes alive by turning aside a Hirst drive that was as good a save as he had made all season before United, urged on by their fans at the Leppings Lane End, found inspiration thanks to Eric Cantona. The Frenchman applied the finishing touch in a goalmouth scramble six minutes from the close. It was a scuffed effort forced in at the second attempt but many thought that it would prove priceless by the season's close. Afterwards Cantona paid tribute to the visiting fans and the scenes as he ran to the crowd who joyously engulfed him supported that claim.

Ince might have snatched all three points with a snap shot from distance in stoppage time but the game as well as the honours justifiably ended equal.

MANCHESTER UNITED 5 COVENTRY CITY 0
PREMIERSHIP - 28 DECEMBER 1992

UNITED PICKED UP where they had left off at Hillsborough 48 hours earlier, thrashing a Coventry side who had climbed up to seventh after a good first half of the season that included a 5-1 win over Liverpool at Highfield Road. Jonathan Gould, the son of manager Bobby, had recently taken over from Steve Ogrizovic in goal and had been beaten just once in the top flight so far. It took just six minutes for that tally to be doubled and over the remaining 84 minutes he was humbled as another four went past him. In truth, it could have been far worse.

The first came when Lloyd McGrath's clearance fell to Ryan Giggs who smashed the ball in off the post from an angle. Paul Ince and Brian McClair bossed midfield while Cantona, Giggs and Lee Sharpe created havoc in the Sky Blues rearguard who only remained in touch thanks to the Reds profligate finishing. It wasn't until the final stages of the first half that the lead was increased through Mark Hughes who benefited from a neat move between Cantona and Giggs. The former then cracked in a penalty after Phil Babb handled Paul Parker's cross. Lee Sharpe rounded off an excellent end to the year by claiming his first goal in over eight months from a mis-hit effort following a Cantona knock-down 12 minutes from the close. Denis Irwin, always a danger to a defence from set pieces or open play, bagged the final goal of the game.

Mick Quinn, who had been accruing goals for Coventry as proficiently as a squirrel collects nuts, was bereft of service and barely touched the ball. Peter Schmeichel seemed more concerned with keeping out the cold rather than the Sky Blues attack. The two chances sent his way: a Robert Rosario header and a shot from Lloyd McGrath caused him no worry. Leaders Norwich had faltered, being held to a second successive goalless draw at Leeds which put United just a win away from the summit should other results go their way.

MANCHESTER UNITED 2 BURY 0
FA CUP 3RD ROUND - 5 JANUARY 1993

BURY WERE 83 places lower than the Reds in the pyramid and hoped to make up a huge gulf in class at Old Trafford. A win over Witton Albion at the first hurdle may not have been spectacular but the Shakers had got past Wigan Athletic in the previous round who were a division higher to earn this money-spinning tie.

Just over 30,000 saw teenage winger Keith Gillespie make a debut to remember. Andrei Kanchelskis, Paul Ince and Ryan Giggs were missing through injury although there was a return for Bryan Robson who was able to take a place on the bench. Brian McClair continued in central midfield partnering Lee Sharpe. Bury had all hands to the pump during a demanding opening in which they defended six corner kicks in as many minutes. However, even when that job was done United came straight back at them after the ball was cleared up field to score. Mark Hughes found Gillespie on the right and the young Irishman's centre found Phelan who headed in despite Gary Kelly's best efforts.

For a brief period, Bury delighted the 5,000 or so away fans with a spell of pressure and clung to the dream of at least another lucrative game at Gigg Lane. Steve Bruce was forced to clear when Schmeichel found himself beaten on the edge of his area. Hulme and Darren Lyons then tested the keeper's concentration after a lengthy period of inactivity, but their efforts presented little danger. Bury held out until the final 14 minutes when Gillespie capped his debut with a weak shot that somehow slipped through Kelly's hands.

MANCHESTER UNITED 4 TOTTENHAM HOTSPUR 1
PREMIERSHIP - 9 JANUARY 1993

A HOME WIN seemed a forgone conclusion from early in the game, the only surprise being that it took United most of the first half to find the opening goal. It wasn't a case of possession not being turned into goals on this occasion more that Eric Thorstvedt was in superb form keeping out efforts from Brian McClair and Ryan Giggs with saves of the highest order. Having said that Spurs made a bright opening - Teddy Sheringham, Nick Barmby and Paul Allen carving out chances.

However, the Spurs storm soon blew out. Eric Cantona, who had notched a hat-trick against the North Londoners earlier in the season while at Leeds, operated in a free role and his skills and speed of thought quickly had Tottenham on the back foot. Yet Eric was still wasteful in front of goal; when Lee Sharpe sent him clear a few seconds' dalliance allowed Thorstvedt time to close him down. The Norwegian also darted from between his posts to perform a tackle on Cantona when he decided to go through alone rather than find a colleague. Yet Cantona gave United the lead on the stroke of half-time when his header from a Denis Irwin cross floated over the giant

Spurs stopper and all resistance was broken within 13 minutes of the resumption. Cantona returned the favour to Irwin who knocked a square ball to the Frenchman's feet and continued his run into the left side of the penalty area. Cantona's chipped pass with a casual flick of the boot back to the Irish full-back was inch perfect, as was Irwin's finish.

Spurs looked to go on the front foot soon after but were caught in possession and could only watch as Brian McClair thundered a shot in from 25 yards. Paul Parker, who had failed to score in over 50 games for the Reds, claimed the fourth after a one-two with McClair. Cantona's crowd pleasing efforts were stymied by a hamstring injury which saw him withdrawn to a standing ovation but as both substitutes had been used, United finished the game with ten men. Barmby grabbed a consolation two minutes from time nodding home a Paul Allen cross but it couldn't stop United reaching pole position ahead of Aston Villa and Norwich.

Norwich were always going to be playing catch-up on United with their game at Sheffield Wednesday played on Sunday for the TV cameras. A 1-0 defeat ensured they would remain third.

MANCHESTER UNITED 2 NOTTINGHAM FOREST 0
PREMIERSHIP - 27 JANUARY 1993

ERIC'S PRECAUTIONARY REMOVAL from the field following the hamstring tweak against Spurs proved a prudent measure and there was no temptation to risk him on the long trip to London for a meeting with Queens Park Rangers. Even without the mercurial Frenchman, who had swiftly become a firm favourite amongst United fans, the Reds eased to a 3-1 victory. Though the early loss of in-form Mark Hughes threatened to be a further blow at an important stage of the title campaign. The striker had been felled by a robust challenge from Alan McDonald who received a booking when a stiffer sanction seemed more just. Hughes left the field and had six stitches in a calf wound.

Both Cantona and Hughes then sat out the FA Cup 4th round tie with Brighton and Hove Albion which was settled with a late goal from Ryan Giggs but were declared fit for the visit of Nottingham Forest. the Reds were little short of magnificent against Brian Clough's side who were bottom of the table and struggling to make headway. Neil Webb, who had found himself surplus to requirements at Old Trafford, and Roy Keane were overrun in midfield. The future United captain was substituted when his frustration got the better of him.

Keane's pangs of exasperation began as early as the opening quarter of an hour when Mark Crossley was forced into action five times. The two times European Cup winners managed to produce a couple of useful counters but Gary Bannister, who got on the end of both meaningful breaks, planted a header wide before hitting a shot straight at Peter Schmeichel.

There was no denying the excellence of Crossley when he turned a Gary Pallister header over but for all United's enticing skills, Forest held out until the break, ably assisted by wasteful finishing by the home side. On the restart Forest's resistance was broken by a deflected goal from Paul Ince. His 30 yard effort took a wicked nick off Carl Tiler inside the area. Mark Hughes threatened to burst the ball with a spectacular shot before he extended United's lead as the game entered its final stages with another picture book goal. Steve Bruce won the ball just inside the Forest half and found Eric Cantona with a clever chipped pass, a deft flick sent Hughes through to volley past Mark Crossley and in off the bar. The keeper was grateful to Brian Laws for intervening when beaten by a Pallister header late on.

IPSWICH TOWN 2 MANCHESTER UNITED 1
PREMIERSHIP - 30 JANUARY 1993

NORWICH HAD KEPT their title hopes alive but were now two points adrift of United and Aston Villa. This was no mean feat considering Alex Ferguson's side had collected 26 points out of 30 thanks to a run of eight wins and two draws. Cantona's impact on United's attack had been instant with a run of four wins on the bounce featuring 17 goals. At the other end United rarely looked stretched and had the best defensive record in the top flight but too few teams were able to exploit their weakness against pace.

Yet Ipswich Town had that in abundance with striker Chris Kiwomya a key figure in the East Anglian club's march to the Second Division title the previous term. It seemed the Suffolk side's top flight odyssey would not be ending any time soon as they now sat sixth in the Premiership.

However it was Ipswich who began nervously, goalkeeper Clive Baker's poor kicking putting the home side under pressure, enticing United forward. He redeemed himself with a fine save from Mark Hughes who saw his chip pushed over while Brian McClair and Lee

Sharpe spurned chances arising from those weak punts upfield.

Ipswich manager John Lyall, who had guided West Ham United to two FA Cup wins in the 1970s, proved he was still capable of plotting an upset by successfully stifling the twin threats of Lee Sharpe and Ryan Giggs on the wing. Losing the battle in that key area for attack, combined with Kiwomya's pace had United on the back foot for most of the afternoon. Peter Schmeichel needed to turn Vlado Bozinoski's shot over before Kiwomya pounced on an uncharacteristic error from the Dane to open the scoring. Schmeichel's slip, following a long pass by Boncho Genchev, saw him miss the ball allowing Kiwomya to slide the ball into an unguarded net.

Kiwomya's pace continued to trouble United's defence and the hosts faced few threats before the break, although Baker restored his confidence by palming aside a Denis Irwin shot. Kiwomya hit a post with a rising drive after outpacing Steve Bruce within seconds of the restart before Canadian international Frank Yallop scored with a deflected effort. The defender was an infrequent visitor into opposition territory but had notched against Spurs in midweek and was quick to latch onto Jason Dozell's pass.

United enjoyed the lion's share of possession after that but with their flair players strangely out of sorts they failed to make any impression until the closing stages when Brian McClair pulled one back from a Cantona cross. Baker made an excellent save from Mark Hughes during injury time to secure all three points for Ipswich. Although the pitch was in a sorry state, United could not use that as an excuse for this surprise reverse. In the event, Aston Villa's unexpected loss at Southampton and a 1-0 Norwich win at Everton saw Ipswich's East Anglian neighbours return to the top of the league.

MANCHESTER UNITED 2 SHEFFIELD UNITED 1
PREMIERSHIP - 6 FEBRUARY 1993

THE REDS WOULD meet Sheffield United twice in a week having been paired with them in the FA Cup 5th round and the visitors stunned Old Trafford, grabbing an early lead following a mix-up between Eric Cantona and Paul Ince. On loan Franz Carr chased a hopeful punt and, ignoring Brian Deane's calls from the centre, poked the ball past Peter Schmeichel.

It appeared that it might be the only goal of the afternoon as Cantona, having possibly his worst game since joining United, persisted with fanciful tricks his colleagues failed to read. At times he was infuriating, producing the lacklustre play that hallmarked his final weeks at Leeds. He wasn't alone, but in the absence of Bryan Robson, he failed to provide the spark that had been so evident thus far in a red shirt.

However, as great players often do, he got it right in the end, scoring the goal that sent the Reds back top of the Premier League. The Blades could have gone further ahead before Brian McClair found an equaliser, capitalising on a Denis Irwin centre to convert from a few yards out.

So many of the good positions United squandered came as a result of Giggs' poor distribution. The teenage sensation was replaced by Andrei Kanchelskis who made the difference in the final 20 minutes. The Blades couldn't cope with his pace, close control or his ability to pick out forwards with perfectly timed crosses. With ten minutes on the clock Cantona made the most of Mitch Ward's stretched effort to clear by volleying home. The win returned the Reds to the summit with Norwich having to wait until midweek to reclaim the position. Though by that time United would have played again.

Following the game Sheffield United manager Dave Bassett, who was without four regulars and lost Chris Kamara early in the game, suggested that the match winner would not be his first choice signing if he had a blank cheque book and the pick of any Old Trafford players. He suggested Eric was "nothing special" and went on to claim that Cantona was no more difficult to play against than any other United man.

LEEDS UNITED 0 MANCHESTER UNITED 0
PREMIERSHIP - 8 FEBRUARY 1993

JUST THREE MONTHS previously Eric Cantona had been idolised by all at Elland Road but nobody would have known judging by the reception which greeted his return. A couple of hundred Leeds fans surrounded the United coach on arrival screeching "Judas" at their former darling with insulting banners and T-shirts aimed at the Frenchman the order of the day.

Visibly nervous prior to kick off, Eric commented on events after the game saying: "I knew I was going to get a hot reception tonight. If I was a Leeds fan I would have reacted the same way." United fans made up a sizeable portion of the 34,166 gate and rallied to his aid but the occasion fell flat for Eric who was booed at every touch and missed two gilt edged chances to take all three points. Irritation at that and other matters seemed to take its toll on the Frenchman, who picked up a yellow card for attempting to rectify matters, nudging Jon Newsome over in an attempt to win the ball.

Champions Leeds were languishing just six points off the bottom with no chance of retaining their crown. They were also without a host of regular first-teamers and stopping United in any way shape or form seemed to be the order of the day. The tough midfield battle ended in a stalemate as did the final score. Gary Speed and David Batty got through a number of bone-crunching challenges while the rapier skills of Gary McAllister threatened only briefly. More often than not Leeds resorted to long range shots and, other than a chance for Speed when Scott Sellars sent him charging through the middle, United had little to worry about.

Lee Sharpe played Cantona in with 20 minutes gone but his attempted chip over John Lukic fell just over the crossbar cueing catcalls. Later, former United trainee Rob Bowman blocked from Sharpe on the goal line, while Brian McClair's effort soon after took a deflection off Chris Whyte but Lukic proved equal to it with an agile one-handed stop. Peter Schmeichel then saved Tony Dorigo's 30 yard free-kick while Batty fluffed a shot before the ball fell kindly for an unmarked Lee Chapman who only found Schmeichel's chest from 10 yards.

A £1,000 fine was handed down by the FA a month after the game when Cantona was found guilty of misconduct on the final whistle. Leeds fans close to the players' tunnel claimed he spat at them. Cantona admitted he spat but said it was at the wall not at any person. It was alleged Steve Bruce was the victim of a spitting incident from the home supporters and it may have been an act of retribution for his team-mate.

UNITED MISSED the presence of Eric Cantona, who was away on World Cup duty, during a 2-1 defeat in the FA Cup 5th round tie with Sheffield United. Steve Bruce had missed a penalty five minutes from the end which would have brought an undeserved replay. Meanwhile Cantona was in Tel Aviv helping his nation record an important victory over Israel and grabbing the first in a 4-0 win. Defenders Alain Roche and Laurent Blanc were the other scorers.

THE COMPLETE ERIC CANTONA

MANCHESTER UNITED 2 SOUTHAMPTON 1
PREMIERSHIP - 20 FEBRUARY 1993

FOR ALMOST 80 minutes of this game United were ponderous. Southampton could and should have led courtesy of Matt Le Tissier whose display was to a standard Cantona would have appreciated but unfortunately he lacked the same quality of support. Iain Dowie was one of those to spurn opportunities while Micky Adams, saw his volley cannon to safety off Paul Ince. Jason Dodd dragged an effort well wide when Le Tissier launched his next perceptive through ball and Neil Maddison fared little better after an Ince lapse presented him with a sight of goal

Peter Schmeichel made one of his rare errors early in the second period when he lost an Adams cross and then his footing but managed to stick out an arm to grab the ball before it hit the ground. Ironically it was Le Tissier's replacement, Nicky Banger, who gave the Saints a deserved lead, escaping the attentions of Gary Pallister to force a low shot past Schmeichel with only 10 minutes remaining.

Stunned by the reverse, United, who had looked lacklustre to that point, roused themselves. Ryan Giggs picked the Saints' pockets with a break down the left which put him one-on-one with Tim Flowers, the 25 year old keeper stood up well but fell for the Welshman's dummy, allowing the winger to whip the ball home. Just 60 seconds later Giggs repeated the dose with a drive that caught Flowers off balance to win the points.

Aston Villa had crammed a couple of games in following their FA Cup exit to Wimbledon on penalties after a 4th round replay. Both were won by the only goals of the game at Crystal Palace and Chelsea. A home win over Everton allowed them to establish a two point lead at the top. Though they had played a game more the gap could have been more but for Giggs.

MANCHESTER UNITED 3 MIDDLESBROUGH 0
PREMIERSHIP- 27 FEBRUARY 1993

AROUND THIS STAGE in the previous season, United had developed a bad case of the yips. It seemed the same syndrome may well come back to haunt them for a second term as, despite the margin of victory, United were far from fluent.

The win was only secured late on and once more it was Ryan Giggs, deployed in a roving role, who frightened the Boro defence witless. He set United on the road to victory with an early strike, getting the better of Chris Morris close to the byline, beating the defender and former Old Trafford apprentice keeper Stephen Pears with a shot from an acute angle.

Giggs had earlier carved out a chance for Mark Hughes but his effort was chalked off for a foul. Later, Lee Sharpe applied two disappointing finishes while Giggs proved not quite everything he touched turned into gold by squandering a one-on-one with Pears.

A series of free-kicks allowed Denis Irwin some shooting practice but it was only during the last 11 minutes that he managed to make one count, this time with the aid of a post. United, seeking to boost an already impressive goal difference, set up camp in the Boro half and only luck seemed to stop at least one more crossing the line. Pears, who had denied Eric Cantona so adeptly with two fantastic saves, couldn't stop the Frenchman netting from point blank range five minutes from the whistle.

A further booking took Eric to 21 disciplinary points for the season, meaning he would be suspended for Premier League matches at Liverpool and Oldham although, as he had also picked up a one game international ban, he would now be available for a home game with Arsenal on 24 March rather than be required by France for a World Cup qualifier in Austria 72 hours later.

MANCHESTER UNITED 1 ASTON VILLA 1
Premiership - 14 March 1993

In the two matches Cantona had missed United had enjoyed mixed fortunes. They were buoyed by a 2-1 win at Anfield which saw the Reds overhaul Aston Villa who didn't play that weekend. Now the teams were separated by a single point, both having played 31 games. However, they suffered an unexpected reverse at Boundary Park against bottom of the table Oldham Athletic courtesy of a Neil Adams strike.

Cantona's return coincided with what was predictably billed as a title decider. And, had Steve Staunton's opener on 54 minutes not been cancelled out within minutes the title runes may have fallen in Villa's favour. The visitors were under intense pressure for lengthy spells but defended well and proved themselves to be an effective counter-attacking side.

Australian keeper Mark Bosnich, who enjoyed a spell at Old Trafford under Alex Ferguson, had managed to oust long term number one Nigel Spink and displayed the form which had seen him claim five clean sheets from eight games in keeping efforts from Cantona, Irwin and Giggs out. The Frenchman was denied just seven minutes in by an athletic save following a pass from Paul Ince. Not long after Lee Sharpe shook the crossbar from 10 yards.

Goalscoring chances came at the other end but with less regularity. Only the pacy Dean Saunders caused Peter Schmeichel any trouble, forcing the Dane into a full length save while Kevin Richardson and Ray Houghton went far closer with efforts later in the first half.

Ron Atkinson gambled at the start of the second period, replacing Garry Parker with Tony Daley. It was a decent ploy given the worries Saunders' pace had caused. He reasoned two quick men would increase his chances and his courage paid dividends when Staunton picked up the ball close to the touchline from Richardson and drifted in before unleashing an angled drive which flew in just inches below the crossbar.

Moments later Bosnich was powerless to deny Mark Hughes from close range. Brian McClair back-heeled the ball to Denis Irwin whose cross was deflected to Cantona. An adroit cushioned header back across goal allowed the Welsh striker to pounce. Throughout Paul McGrath, who had been shown the door at Old Trafford in the summer of 1989, gave the kind of display that would see him nominated PFA Player of the Year. The sides were now level at the top with just nine games remaining. Although Norwich, who had beaten Oldham at Carrow Road 24 hours earlier, must have been the happiest with events at Old Trafford.

MANCHESTER CITY 1 MANCHESTER UNITED 1
PREMIERSHIP - 20 MARCH 1993

IF ANY CLUB was motivated to halt United's title challenge, it was Manchester City. The Blues were still last team from the city to win the league and were determined that their 26 year run was continued. As it turned out City were let off the hook by some profligate finishing from two of United's most dangerous and consistent performers – Ryan Giggs and Eric Cantona. The former's delivery was poor and Tony Coton in City's goal was relieved not be stretched further. Cantona could and should have had a hat-trick, seeing a header scooped off the line by a low dive while a second effort, a lob from no more than six yards, was straight at the City keeper.

City took the lead, tough play in midfield creating space for Rick Holden on the wing. His cross was met by the towering Niall

Quinn who sent a header past Peter Schmeichel. With 22 minutes left Cantona levelled matters. Hughes made his way past Michel Vonk on the halfway line and played in Lee Sharpe on the left. His cross found Cantona who had been afforded too much space in a central position, a deft header clipped the far post before hitting the net.

City regained the levels of possession which had allowed them to control the game and came close to a winner when Mike Sheron struck an upright. They caused more than a little panic in the United rearguard, winning three corners in the closing minutes. Nevertheless this would have been seen as two points dropped, a view re-inforced by Aston Villa's win against Sheffield Wednesday the same afternoon which appeared to scupper the Reds title ambitions for a second successive season.

MANCHESTER UNITED 0 ARSENAL 0
Premiership - 24 March 1993

United may have been spluttering up front but at least they had a rock at the back where Peter Schmeichel maintained not only a clean sheet but his club's title ambitions. Though with just four points from five games in March it seemed United's title bid may have to wait another year. They had netted just four times this month and had fallen to third.

Arsenal, now unbeaten in nine games, selected a team with more than a hint of attacking intent and this was on show in the opening minutes. Schmeichel bravely denying Kevin Campbell and making a sprawling save to thwart Ian Wright with his knees. There could be few criticisms of Alex Ferguson who had gambled on a top heavy forward line with out and out wingers serving them. Paul Ince was the only permanent member of midfield relying on others to get back and support if Arsenal got the ball. The system had a poor track record having been employed in the FA Cup defeat to Sheffield United but Eric Cantona had not been available on that day. It was reasoned that the system may be worth another look with the Frenchman present.

It played to his strengths and Cantona was the most dangerous threat for United although his contributions were sporadic and David Seaman proved equal to anything hurled at him. There was only one effort which seemed to have the England international beaten but he was able to make a block with his body. In truth Seaman was rarely troubled due to Tony Adams' resilience.

Campbell was denied again late on by Gary Pallister who managed to get a foot to the ball. Only the woodwork came to United's aid when Paul Merson sent in a drive from fully 30 yards that thudded back off the crossbar. The introduction of Bryan Robson for Hughes was crucial in balancing the side and stemming the Gunners' flows forward.

Aston Villa's unexpected loss at home to Norwich courtesy of a late John Polston goal was followed by a win at Nottingham Forest 24 hours before United travelled to East Anglia. Villa now led by four points meaning the Carrow Road clash was a must-win for both sides, the loser would almost certainly be out of the title picture.

NORWICH CITY 1 MANCHESTER UNITED 3
PREMIERSHIP - 5 APRIL 1993

NORWICH HAD PROVED to be one of the most erratic and unpredictable sides amongst the elite. They could post victories against top sides but lose to teams their league position suggested they would brush aside. With a place in the UEFA Cup up for grabs and the title still not settled, they needed a win as badly as the visitors. Villa knew that they just had to keep on winning in order to become inaugural winners of the Premiership but as United had proved the season before, an extended stay at the top brought its own pressures.

By contrast the pressure could be said to have been shed by United and the outstanding players they had amongst their ranks could concentrate on their game rather than grinding out results. It certainly seemed to be the way at Carrow Road. Three goals in eight minutes were enough to break Norwich's slim title chances and haul the Reds back into contention, leaving them a point behind Villa.

Ryan Giggs owed much to Eric Cantona for his opener. His pass split the home defence allowing the winger to go clean through on Bryan Gunn. The keeper was always second favourite as Giggs rounded him to slide home. To their credit Norwich had started in an attacking mood and had a penalty for a Gary Pallister body check on Mark Robins denied in the opening minutes, looked for a quick reply but this proved to be their undoing when Pallister broke up an attack and found Brian McClair. His pass to the pacy Andrei Kanchelskis sent the Ukrainian past Norwich's ragged defenders into the area where he comfortably beat Gunn at the near post.

Within a minute it was 3-0. Paul Ince broke up another desperate Canaries move, beat three defenders and slipped the ball to Cantona who had taken a wide position, his shot flew past the keeper like a missile and into the net off an upright.

A stunned home side managed to pull one back via a Mark Robins header just past the hour before introducing new signing Efan Ekoku. He at least showed he had the potential to revive a faltering title push and gave Steve Bruce and Pallister plenty to think about but the Reds were rarely troubled in the time which remained. The only blemishes on United's performance were cautions for Bryan Robson (following a two footed lunge at Ian Crook) and Ince (during the squabble which followed).

Alex Ferguson picked out Eric Cantona for specific praise following the game describing his performance as "quite marvellous" but his brave decision to opt for pace and all out attack rather than the security of Robson played a huge part. The manager's recent bold decisions, no doubt shaped by the failures of his attack the previous season, had finally borne fruit. In Giggs, Sharpe and Kanchelskis he had one of the quickest attacks English football had ever seen.

MANCHESTER UNITED 2 SHEFFIELD WEDNESDAY 1
PREMIERSHIP - 10 APRIL 1993

IF THE WIN at Norwich was crucial, events at Old Trafford the following weekend have gone down in football history. When United fan John Sheridan converted a Sheffield Wednesday penalty following a crude tackle on Chris Waddle by Paul Ince, only a quarter of the game remained. Wednesday were good value for their lead especially as they had more than matched United despite the absence of key figures such as David Hirst and Paul Warhurst. With the Reds in dire need of leadership, Robson was summoned from the bench.

United had struggled throughout. The few chances at the other end were wasted through over-elaboration. With Carlton Palmer man-marking Cantona effectively and former United man Viv Anderson shackling Hughes and McClair, United looked short of a cutting edge. On the few occasions their cover was broken, Chris Woods proved unbeatable - Giggs and Sharpe working a position for the latter to centre but the keeper blocked Hughes's shot. He also denied McClair but was otherwise untroubled until the game changing substitution.

Robson's introduction immediately invigorated the home side. A more direct style ensued, forcing Wednesday to defend more than they had previously. Not long after Woods had turned a Hughes shot aside, Steve Bruce headed home a Denis Irwin corner to equalise. Seven minutes into an extended period of injury time (played because linesman Michael Peck had to be replaced) and with United laying siege to the Wednesday goal, Gary Pallister, sent forward for a corner, retrieved the ball on the right wing. His deflected cross fell perfectly for Bruce to nod beyond Woods. The stands around Old Trafford went into raptures with Alex Ferguson and assistant Brian Kidd cavorting on the pitch, it felt like the hangover from the previous season had finally disappeared and fans could finally see the light at the end of a 26 year long tunnel.

To add to the euphoria, Aston Villa lost their grip on top spot after a goalless draw at home to United's next opponents Coventry City. The Reds now led by a point – five wins would guarantee a first title in over a quarter of a century.

COVENTRY CITY 0 MANCHESTER UNITED 1
PREMIERSHIP - 12 APRIL 1993

UNITED WERE ONCE more grateful to a defender for winning three precious points. It had been a demanding 48 hours and to some extent that showed with a number of tired performances yet the Reds got exactly what they required with a Denis Irwin goal just before the break.

Lee Sharpe pushed the ball through to Irwin who had made an overlap and bypassed a crowded penalty by thrashing a shot past Jonathan Gould. There were few other goal mouth incidents. Eric Cantona, nursing a wrist injury, looked subdued although he did show a few superb touches including one drive forward which gave Lee Sharpe a chance.

When the Frenchman was withdrawn for Robson, United looked to close the game down. It proved a dangerous game. Coventry had already gone close through Micky Quinn and Roy Wegerle. With nine minutes to go the latter managed to round Robson and slide the ball past Schmeichel from 18 yards. His shot struck the upright and trundled defiantly across goal before it was cleared.

The headlines following the game surrounded the dismissal of Quinn who raised a hand to Schmeichel with time almost up. The Liverpudlian was assumed to have allowed his frustration to show and pushed the keeper during a brawl caused by Lee Hurst's high challenge on Steve Bruce. Paul Ince was quickly on the scene as were Quinn and Schmeichel. After consultation with his linesman, referee

Roger Gifford decided Quinn, who had already been booked for a challenge on Bruce, had to go.

The home side thought Schmeichel had gone to ground too easily and although the official admitted that he had got the decision wrong after viewing TV replays there remained concern that the keeper could be missing for the run-in. Fortunately the official took a view that Schmeichel had been knocked off balance. Aston Villa maintained their challenge by defeating Arsenal at Highbury courtesy of a Tony Daley goal.

MANCHESTER UNITED 3 CHELSEA 0
PREMIERSHIP - 17 APRIL 1993

UNITED HAD NEGOTIATED Easter in far better fashion than they had the year before and continued their improved form here against a beleaguered Chelsea. The gifts forthcoming from Chelsea's backline allowed United to see off potentially tricky opponents and heap yet more pressure on Villa who would entertain Manchester City 24 hours later.

Dave Beasant, who had been 'sacked' as goalkeeper by former Pensioners manager Ian Porterfield, was back in the Chelsea goal a matter of weeks after Porterfield's dismissal. His return had gone well until this, the ninth game since his return, when with just 23 minutes gone he allowed a tame Mark Hughes shot to slip through his fingers to hand United a precious lead.

Cantona dominated thereafter, constantly pulling the Chelsea defence out of position and generally bossing the game. The Londoners, rattled by their misfortune, created few openings, although John Spencer forced Schmeichel to save from close range and Graham Stuart shot straight at the keeper. Chelsea survived at the other end until the final minute of the opening period when Steve Clarke, attempting to divert a Lee Sharpe cross to safety, put the ball through his own goal.

Both Sharpe and Cantona were congratulated but United were comfortable despite barely having to get out of first gear. Matters got worse for the visitors on a warm afternoon when Cantona applied a simple finish to a Giggs centre that Beasant had failed to catch just three minutes after the resumption. Chelsea rarely looked likely to beat Peter Schmeichel who was fiercely protected by his defenders.

When Niall Quinn gave Manchester City a lead at Aston Villa it seemed the Blues would do their rivals a favour but a second half revival by the home side gave Villa a 3-1 win to maintain the pressure.

CRYSTAL PALACE 0 MANCHESTER UNITED 2
PREMIERSHIP - 21 APRIL 1993

THE TITLE COULD be decided within the next fortnight after Blackburn Rovers, who were looking set to complete their first season back amongst the elite, hammered Aston Villa 3-0 at Ewood Park - Rovers would be United's next opposition. A win over Crystal Palace meant that either a victory at Old Trafford against Kenny Dalglish's side or Villa's failure to beat Oldham at home would hand United their first title for 26 years.

Clearly sensing the historic occasion, more than 15,000 people watched this game on CCTV back at Old Trafford, while Selhurst Park was a sea of red. That said, Palace were better than the scoreline suggested. Manager Steve Coppell deployed Eddie McGoldrick as a sweeper to counter the roving threat of Eric Cantona. It proved tricky to find a way through for long periods during which Palace were unlucky not to take a lead. Peter Schmeichel's errant throw towards Ryan Giggs allowed Eric Young to nip in and feed Gareth Southgate who played in Chris Armstrong. The striker clipped the foot of a post and the visitors breathed a sigh of relief. Ricky Newman also went close from 25 yards before Armstrong placed a John Humphrey cross wide of the far post on the hour. It was Palace's last chance to gain the lead.

Andrei Kanchelskis, replacing flu victim Lee Sharpe on the right, made way for Bryan Robson a minute before the opening goal. Cantona finally picked the Palace lock on 64 minutes sending in a cross that was met by Mark Hughes who applied the type of flying volley that was his trademark. It was some way to bring up his 100th league goal for the club but it looked unlikely to be the winner when ten minutes from the end a Chris Coleman shot was spilled by Schmeichel. Armstrong was quickly on the scene but with a decent part of the goal at his mercy the highly rated striker put his shot wide.

A minute from time Cantona's ball through the middle allowed Paul Ince to break through the cover and round off a perfect night and put United a win away from glory. It wasn't just the fact that Hughes and Cantona were regularly finding the net that was propelling the Reds closer and closer to the title. The two were combining well despite having similar traits and the Welshman was the first to admit that another player taking responsibility for goalscoring was the big difference from previous seasons.

MANCHESTER UNITED 3 BLACKBURN ROVERS 1
PREMIERSHIP - 3 MAY 1993

OLDHAM'S VICTORY AT Villa Park the day previously had finally clinched the title for United whose fans came from far and wide to join in the long and lengthy celebrations outside the famous stadium. For 24 hours before this game fans had been toasting the end of a 26 year wait for the league title and tickets for this 'lap of honour' were worth more than their weight in gold.

Blackburn offered the champions generous applause prior to the game but their determination to post notice of their ambitions ended at the whistle. United's players, who had clearly been celebrating just as hard as the fans, got a shock when Kevin Gallagher steered the ball in after just eight minutes, a lead that should have been doubled when Paul Parker sent Jason Wilcox tumbling in the area for what appeared to be a cast iron penalty, the referee waved it away.

United levelled midway through the first half when Ryan Giggs blasted home a free-kick that beat Bobby Mimms all ends up. Lee Sharpe had a shot turned over the bar which suggested it was only a matter of time before the party was allowed to step up. The noise rose a level with the introduction of Bryan Robson from the bench for Sharpe.

Paul Ince was set free by a defence splitting ball from Cantona on the hour to give United the lead and the game was rounded off almost on the stroke of time by Gary Pallister's first goal of the season from a free-kick. He was the only member of the outfield squad not to hit the target that term and Bobby Mimms possibly took the threat a little less than seriously. However, a scramble across his line saw him miss the low drive by no more than a yard. Players swamped the popular central defender who had done so much at the other end to bring the ecstasy of this evening to fruition.

It seemed appropriate that Bryan Robson help Steve Bruce lift the inaugural Premiership trophy in the presence of Sir Matt Busby, the last United manager to win the English league title. Robson's substitute appearance ensured he would also qualify for a much-deserved medal.

WIMBLEDON 1 MANCHESTER UNITED 2
PREMIERSHIP - 9 MAY 1993

BRYAN ROBSON MADE his first start since early December for a game which brought the contrasts of the modern game together on the pitch. Wimbledon were a team who adopted a physical approach and regularly looked to spoil the party of more illustrious opponents. Vinnie Jones planted his boot onto Paul Ince's thigh within the first five seconds and threatened to set a record for the fastest sending off in football history but remained on the field to see his victim turn in Eric Cantona's carefully directed header following a Ryan Giggs corner just past the hour to open the scoring.

The England midfielder should have grabbed a goal far earlier when intercepting a Jones pass but Hans Segers, who had already turned a Lee Sharpe effort away, held out. The Reds were fairly prosaic in the first period but managed to respond to a huge away following that took over nearly every corner of Selhurst Park. Strangely their record was exactly the same as that which had been set the last time United won the title in 1967. Goals for and against excluded.

Cantona was revelling in both the sleek football and the vigorous nature of the contest. A host of Wimbledon players attempted to intimidate him only to be shown that for every ounce of silk in his game there was more than an equal amount of steel. Vinnie Jones applauded one stiff challenge on his colleague John Fashanu by the Frenchman. Bryan Robson, the epitomy of United's work ethic and a totem during United's long wait for the this sort of glory, rounded off the season with a superb left footed finish from a chipped Steve Bruce free-kick. Cantona and others had been trying to set him up all game. Dean Holdsworth grabbed a consolation when he nodded in a Warren Barton centre eight minutes from the close, although the hosts rarely looked like conceding.

As the whistle sounded the crowd spilled on to the pitch in celebration and new hero Eric Cantona was engulfed within seconds, emerging from the throng without his shirt. There was an attempt by police to clear the scene but further surges occurred. Alex Ferguson told reporters that these events meant that any prospect of giving fans a glimpse of the gleaming new trophy had to be abandoned. The attendance of 30,115, the overwhelming majority of them away fans, brought Wimbledon's record gate receipts of £303,000 - double the previous mark.

1992-93

Twelve months ago Leeds fans argued that the introduction of Eric Cantona won them the title and though it was rare for United fans to see eye-to-eye with their rivals from Elland Road they had to agree that the mercurial Frenchman was the difference between despair and triumph. Eric operated differently at Old Trafford but he looked born to perform there and after a few games he himself described as mediocre, everything just seemed to click - his surroundings, colleagues, manager and fans - and he didn't look back after netting the equaliser at Chelsea in mid-December.

United already had a strong team and one capable of a championship challenge but as in the previous season they proved they lacked inspiration when it mattered. Cantona was the missing link, walking into Old Trafford with a certainty his colleagues lacked, giving them confidence and an instant aura of success. Not only that but his work ethic shone through - he had been a mere player under Wilkinson at Leeds. At United he was given responsibility and shone as a result. Alex Ferguson recognised that Eric was different but also had more to offer away from a match day.

On the pitch he brought guile and perception, seeing the early pass was a key weapon in his armoury. He played a fundamental part in 22 of the 46 league goals scored after his mid-season arrival. 13 of those were direct 'assists'. Over the 20 games Cantona played with Mark Hughes 39 goals were scored between the pair. Their relationship however was strictly professional, Hughes later admitting that, while they respected one another, they rarely socialised. That said, there's little doubt that Cantona saved Hughes Old Trafford career, even if it ended the striking role of former first choice Brian McClair. Hughes and Cantona were immense, the strength, skill and understanding a key compenent in United's success. McClair, shorn of his earlier pace, reverted well to midfield duties or, in extremis, a role as an auxiliary attacker.

At Elland Road Cantona had been asked to play in a more structured and rigid way - Alex Ferguson reasoned that this limited his effectiveness and allowing him a freer role in a side which preferred passing rather than direct play brought the best out of him. He essentially did the same thing with both clubs but alongside better players at Old Trafford and within a more open style he prospered.

It was a responsibility he basked in. Nobody connected with Manchester United had a bad word to say about him on or off the field. That included George Best who identified many similarities between himself and the Frenchman. Whether they could be held as kindred spirits or not Best was in the company of many of his team-mates from the last side to win the title.

Alex Ferguson was fulsome in his praise saying: "Cantona has done very well. He has brought something extra which we haven't had in my time here. He is capable of creating all manner of things with his vision and touch on the ball. A lot of players come here and find it all too much for them, but he has lifted everyone around him."

Doubts from critics outside Old Trafford were swept away by his commitment to games and training. He would often return after training drills to perfect his skills and was an example to the youngsters who would assist him practising dribbling, passing and shooting. Through these acts he changed the club's approach as the manager recognised the usefulness of working on technique as an exercise rather than just as add-ons to the physical work.

Some still wondered if the powder keg would explode but that became less and less of a worry with every day that passed. Not that he was always a paragon of virtue. He would opt out of some minor disciplines such as dress codes. When Ferguson was asked why such foibles were allowed, he would tell even senior colleagues that Eric was a special player and some latitude was called for.

The signing of Cantona has gone down in history as perhaps the greatest coup Ferguson has pulled off during his time at Old Trafford. From Howard Wilkinson's point of view the deal made sense, as he struggled to fit the Frenchman into his plans. There's little doubt that but for the transfer, Eric would have quickly found himself back in the same situation he was following his retirement from Nimes. The £1.2 million Wilkinson recouped allowed him to concentrate on the rest of his squad. But for Ferguson he got a lot more than he bargained for – arguably Cantona's impact can still be felt at Old Trafford today.

The players Cantona joined were freshly invigorated - Giggs, Sharpe, Ince, and Kanchelskis were accused of lacking an edge at the crucial time the previous season. Now they fizzed about at the Frenchman's prompting ending that long wait for a league title. United fans had been used to the sublime skills of so many great players over the years. Even those who could hark back to memories before the war and in the decades which followed including the days of George Best, Denis Law and Bobby Charlton in the 1960s. Now they finally had a team that could compare with the greats.

More than that the Reds never say die approach, typified by the two games against Sheffield Wednesday when they came back from 3 down on Boxing Day to snatch a draw and, even more spectacularly, from a goal down in injury time to beat them at Old Trafford, ended any lingering doubts. However, as so many managers can attest winning the title was one battle, retaining it an even bigger feat.

MANCHESTER UNITED - PREMIER LEAGUE 1992-93

DATE	OPPONENT	VENUE	SCORE	ATT'D	1	2	3	4	5	6	7	8	9	10	11	SUBSTITUTES
06-Dec-92	Manchester C	Old Trafford	2-1	35,408	Schmeichel	Parker	Irwin	Bruce	Sharpe	Pallister	Robson	Ince¹	McClair	Hughes¹	Giggs	Cantona (Giggs)
12-Dec-92	Norwich City	Old Trafford	1-0	34,500	Schmeichel	Parker	Irwin	Bruce	Sharpe	Pallister	Cantona¹	Ince	McClair	Hughes¹	Giggs	Kanchelskis (Phelan)
19-Dec-92	Chelsea	Stamford Bridge	1-1	34,464	Schmeichel	Parker	Irwin	Bruce	Phelan	Pallister	Cantona¹	Ince	McClair	Hughes	Sharpe	Kanchelskis (Giggs)
26-Dec-92	Sheffield Wed	Hillsborough	3-3	37,708	Schmeichel	Parker	Irwin	Bruce	Sharpe	Pallister	Cantona¹	Ince	McClair²	Hughes¹	Giggs	Kanchelskis (Giggs)
28-Dec-92	Coventry City	Old Trafford	5-0	36,025	Schmeichel	Parker	Irwin¹	Bruce	Sharpe¹	Pallister	Cantona¹	Ince	McClair¹	Hughes¹	Giggs¹	Phelan (Bruce) Kanchelskis (Giggs)
09-Jan-93	Tottenham H	Old Trafford	4-1	35,648	Schmeichel	Parker¹	Irwin¹	Bruce	Sharpe	Pallister	Cantona¹	Ince	McClair¹	Hughes	Giggs	Phelan (Bruce) Kanchelskis (Giggs)
27-Jan-93	Nottingham Forest	Old Trafford	2-0	36,085	Schmeichel	Parker	Irwin	Bruce	Sharpe	Pallister	Cantona	Ince¹	McClair	Hughes¹	Giggs	
30-Jan-93	Ipswich Town	Portman Road	1-2	22,068	Schmeichel	Parker	Irwin	Bruce	Sharpe	Pallister	Cantona¹	Ince	McClair¹	Hughes	Giggs	Kanchelskis (Sharpe)
06-Feb-93	Sheffield United	Old Trafford	2-1	36,156	Schmeichel	Parker	Irwin	Bruce	Sharpe	Pallister	Cantona¹	Ince	McClair¹	Hughes	Giggs	Kanchelskis (Giggs)
08-Feb-93	Leeds United	Elland Road	0-0	34,166	Schmeichel	Parker	Irwin	Bruce	Sharpe	Pallister	Cantona	Ince	McClair	Hughes	Giggs	
20-Feb-93	Southampton	Old Trafford	2-1	36,257	Schmeichel	Parker	Irwin	Bruce	Sharpe	Pallister	Cantona	Ince	McClair	Hughes	Giggs²	
27-Feb-93	Middlesbrough	Old Trafford	3-0	36,251	Schmeichel	Parker	Irwin¹	Bruce	Sharpe	Pallister	Cantona¹	Ince	McClair	Hughes	Giggs¹	
14-Mar-93	Aston Villa	Old Trafford	1-1	36,163	Schmeichel	Parker	Irwin	Bruce	Sharpe	Pallister	Cantona	Ince	McClair	Hughes¹	Giggs	
20-Mar-93	Manchester City	Maine Road	1-1	37,136	Schmeichel	Parker	Irwin	Bruce	Sharpe	Pallister	Cantona¹	Ince	McClair	Hughes	Giggs	
24-Mar-93	Arsenal	Old Trafford	0-0	37,301	Schmeichel	Parker	Irwin	Bruce	Sharpe	Pallister	Cantona	Ince	McClair	Hughes	Giggs	Robson (Hughes)
05-Apr-93	Norwich City	Carrow Road	3-1	20,582	Schmeichel	Parker	Irwin	Bruce	Sharpe	Pallister	Cantona¹	Ince	McClair	Kanchelskis¹	Giggs¹	Robson (Kanchelskis)
10-Apr-93	Sheffield Wed	Old Trafford	2-1	40,102	Schmeichel	Parker	Irwin	Bruce²	Sharpe	Pallister	Cantona	Ince	McClair	Hughes	Giggs	Robson (Parker)
12-Apr-93	Coventry City	Highfield Road	1-0	24,429	Schmeichel	Parker	Irwin¹	Bruce	Sharpe	Pallister	Cantona¹	Ince	McClair	Hughes	Giggs	Robson (Cantona)
17-Apr-93	Chelsea	Old Trafford	3-0	40,139	Schmeichel	Parker	Irwin	Bruce	Sharpe	Pallister	Cantona¹	Ince	McClair	Hughes¹	Giggs	Robson (McClair)
21-Apr-93	Crystal Palace	Selhurst Park	2-0	30,115	Schmeichel	Parker	Irwin	Bruce	Kanchelskis	Pallister	Cantona	Ince¹	McClair	Hughes¹	Giggs	
03-May-93	Blackburn Rovers	Old Trafford	3-1	40,447	Schmeichel	Parker	Irwin	Bruce	Sharpe	Palliste·¹	Cantona	Ince¹	McClair	Hughes	Giggs¹	Robson (Sharpe) Kanchelskis (McClair)
09-May-93	Wimbledon	Selhurst Park	2-1	30,115	Schmeichel	Parker	Irwin	Bruce	Sharpe	Pallister	Robson¹	Ince¹	McClair	Hughes	Cantona	

FA CUP

DATE	OPPONENT	VENUE	SCORE	ATT'D	1	2	3	4	5	6	7	8	9	10	11	SUBSTITUTES
05-Jan-93	Bury	Old Trafford	2-0	30,668	Schmeichel	Parker	Irwin	Bruce	Sharpe	Pallister	Cantona	Phelan¹	McClair	Hughes	Gillespie¹	Blackmore (Irwin) Robson (McClair)

AT THE DOUBLE

ARSENAL 1 MANCHESTER UNITED 1
CHARITY SHIELD - 7 AUGUST 1993

ONE OF THE better pre-season curtain raisers at a venue used to staging enthralling matches got the new campaign underway as United sought to continue their success. The second period, by contrast, was somewhat lethargic and the destination of the silverware was decided by spot-kicks for the first time, the FA having decreed that teams could no longer share the trophy.

Peter Schmeichel looked edgy for much of the game and may have been beaten had it not been for the strength and organisation of his backline. Andrei Kanchelskis troubled the Gunners for lengthy periods but United had the busier defence. The Reds found their danger men isolated by George Graham's smothering tactics although David Seaman still had to make a smart stop from debutant midfielder Roy Keane. That effort 14 minutes from time should probably have decided this tie but a sprawling save by the keeper denied the former Nottingham Forest man.

Mark Hughes opened the scoring, the Welsh forward hitting a stunning scissor kick following a precise lob from Eric Cantona on the right. Ian Wright equalised, capitalising on a smart headed pass from Paul Davis to net from the edge of the area just before the break.

Irwin and Wright were the somewhat surprising players to miss their penalties - Wright taking the fifth and final chance with the United left back having bobbled his effort wide just moments earlier. Bryan Robson converted United's first in sudden death. Schmeichel denied his opposite number Seaman whose run up seemed half-hearted. The Dane's save low to his left won the shield - a second on the trot for Cantona.

SOUTHAMPTON 1 MANCHESTER UNITED 3
PREMIERSHIP - 28 AUGUST 1993

DURING INTERVIEWS AFTER the game Matt Le Tissier, Southampton's playmaker and the man many credited with keeping the Saints in the top flight, suggested any of his colleagues would trade places with their Manchester United counterparts. The Channel Islander, coveted by a range of clubs, had stayed loyal to the one he had joined as a 16 year old. Eight years later many felt he was ready for a change and the fact he had given this game his all yet still ended up on the losing side, added to their argument. His input was overshadowed by a rampant side and in particular Eric Cantona who returned after missing the first four league games of the season. Andrei Kanchelskis was the man to sit out this trip to The Dell but Alex Ferguson's faith was justified.

There had been little wrong with United in Cantona's absence as three wins and a draw testified. Though a tinge of disappointment came at allowing a good position against Newcastle United to slip at home, Andy Cole bagging a late equaliser. Alex Ferguson justified his decision to give Cantona an immediate recall saying: "I always think with Eric playing the team is going to win the game. He either scores a goal or makes one."

In the event Southampton got off lightly as a crowd of just over 16,000 were privileged to witness the number seven's full repertoire including a sublime chip over Tim Flowers for United's second. Eric's contribution extended to the other strikes - Lee Sharpe, a two goal hero at Aston Villa five days earlier, hooked in after five minutes following a Cantona dummy and back-heel. Denis Irwin's inch perfect centre was struck home by the United winger.

Le Tissier set up an equaliser for Neil Maddison with a back heel of his own which put the midfielder in on Peter Schmeichel after a dozen minutes. Cantona didn't take long to re-establish the lead. In plenty of space after Ince emerged from a midfield battle with the ball, Eric took a couple of steps towards the angle of the penalty area before sending in the most delicious lobbed shot over Flowers.

Despite Cantona looking like he could just drift through the gears in order to find another, Southampton refused to accept defeat and forced Schmeichel to save from Iain Dowie and Neal Bartlett while Le Tissier packed so much power into one effort that the Dane required treatment after making the save. The game was all but over minutes into the second half when Irwin latched onto a Cantona and Giggs move to beat Flowers.

MANCHESTER UNITED 3 WEST HAM UNITED 0
Premiership - 1 September 1993

UNITED EXTENDED THEIR early lead at the top to three points with a scintillating performance over West Ham. When Lee Sharpe hit his fourth goal in three matches it seemed a rout was in the offing, as the Reds, orchestrated by the imperious Eric Cantona, played with flair and incredible movement. The avalanche never came but at least when a penalty was converted by the French forward just before the break it was some kind of true reflection of United's dominant play. Cantona played a small role in the opener, taking a Gary Pallister header out of defence but, just when he seemed to be moving forward, Roy Keane whipped the ball off his toes and drove on. A pass to Andrei Kanchelskis began the second phase of the move. The Ukrainian delayed his cross and floated it to the far post where Sharpe arrived late to score.

Ludek Miklosko was the difference between the Hammers and humiliation. He dived bravely at Sharpe's feet, made a decent stop from Kanchelskis and then a sprawling save from Cantona but had no chance with the spot kick. Keane took a Pallister pass and streaked inside the area rounding Miklosko before being brought down as he was about to pull the trigger. Alex Ferguson gave Ryan Giggs a run out at centre forward, bringing him in for Mark Hughes before United's European Cup game the following week. The latter would be serving a suspension against Honved and this seemed the likely combination with Cantona given the results so far. Steve Bruce headed in a third at close quarters late in the second period to give the scoreline some deserved credibility. A three goal victory was certainly a more accurate reflection on the balance of play.

CHELSEA 1 MANCHESTER UNITED 0
Premiership - 11 September 1993

ONCE MORE ALEX Ferguson seemed to make a conscious decision to look at different systems and test his plans for Hungary in midweek. Mark Hughes was omitted again with Andrei Kanchelskis sitting on the bench with 36 year-old Bryan Robson preferred.

A heavy price was paid however with a first defeat since a reverse to Oldham Athletic six months earlier. The Champions League and its riches of £1 million plus £250,000 a point in the group stages threatened to be huge diversion for United. Hughes and Kanchelskis seemed to be the most likely victims of UEFA's three foreigner rule as they were omitted from the starting line-up.

Glenn Hoddle's subtle methods as a player seemed to be successfully adopted by his charges at Stamford Bridge. Their defensive resolve was sturdy enough to withstand Ryan Giggs and Eric Cantona - something that few other rearguards had managed over recent times. Late in the game Lee Sharpe did provide Cantona with a headed opportunity and, though he was under little pressure at the far post, he uncharacteristically guided the ball wide. Yet most of the after-match talk revolved around a chance much earlier in the game. 15 minutes in Dimitri Kharine dashed out of his area to head clear when Roy Keane seemed set to go through the middle after a long ball out of defence from Pallister. The ball fell to Robson who nodded it to Cantona who attempted a lob from 40 yards that bounced inside the area but rose steeply to clip the bar before settling in the grateful arms of the Russian keeper as Cantona stood in the centre circle with his head in his hands.

United invited far too much pressure and when Steve Bruce's poor clearance found Steve Clarke, Schmeichel could only parry his shot to Gavin Peacock who tipped the loose ball high into the net. This defeat reduced United's lead at the top to four points

HONVED 2 MANCHESTER UNITED 3
CHAMPIONS LEAGUE 1ST RD 1ST LEG - 15 SEPTEMBER 1993

A 24 YEAR ABSENCE from Europe's premier competition was ended in the Hungarian capital city of Budapest. Although the victory was thorough and the margin should have been larger, the three away goals scored looked more than enough ahead of the second leg at Old Trafford. A slippery pitch was no excuse, nor was the relatively stilted atmosphere, especially as United dominated with Eric Cantona pulling the strings in a display full of quick movement and slick passing. However, the direct style of Honved, along with their effective methods of moving the ball, presented a threat.

The hosts' forwards were surprisingly inventive in the final third which often caught Gary Pallister and Steve Bruce out. Attila Plokai and Stefanov were only thwarted by the magnificence of Peter Schmeichel at times. The keeper saved early from Bela Illes in the 4th minute after a Pallister error gave him the chance to bear down on goal. Yet by half time it seemed that United would run away with matters as once they got their act together the game appeared easy. The power of Roy Keane was a crucial factor, netting a brace. After

Illes had denied the Irish midfielder, Keane combined with Ryan Giggs to drag the sweeper Janos Banfi out of position, before taking a return pass which he hammered past Istvan Brockhauser.

At the other end Paul Parker fluffed his attempt to clear a centre from Illes which presented Szabados with a gift he gratefully accepted with a cracking finish past Schmeichel to level. United responded immediately regaining their advantage within minutes. Lee Sharpe took a Giggs throw-in on the left, crossed low and Keane was on hand to apply the finishing touch. Minutes before the break Plokai miscontrolled an attempted interception, the ball falling for Cantona to score from close range. Honved closed the gap again. A long ball from Banfi matched Stefanov's perfectly timed run which took him beyond a square United backline. Schmeichel came out but was lobbed by the striker.

MANCHESTER UNITED 1 ARSENAL 0
Premiership - 19 September 1993

The top two met at Old Trafford and a predictably close game was decided by one man - Eric Cantona. Not just in terms of his performance but a crucial strike eight minutes from the break.

United surged forward and the skilled ball work and artistry of Cantona and Ryan Giggs allied to the power of Hughes threatened to blow Arsenal away. Cantona had a shot deflected wide and grazed the post with a header from a Giggs corner. Yet it was a foul by David Hillier on Hughes that gave Eric his chance. Paul Ince tapped the ball to the Frenchman who drove an unerring shot past Seaman.

Arsenal's cautious start suggested they had would be happy with a point and this extended to the deployment of Eddie McGoldrick in a sweeper role. After the goal McGoldrick went out to the right with Martin Keown taking over behind Tony Adams and Andy Linighan. The switch allowed Arsenal to stay tight at the back but attack with more vigour.

Yet the Gunners remained quite light upfront despite Paul Merson's industry. They did pose more of a threat in the second half but the Londoners couldn't find a way through. Gary Pallister and Steve Bruce were just too solid. Regardless of some of the heavy artillery thrown at them and Bruce's absence for 17 minutes following a gash on his head, Arsenal refused to press. Peter Schmeichel was only called on once to make any kind of meaningful stop - a double save on the hour from Wright and Campbell.

MANCHESTER UNITED 4 SWINDON TOWN 2
Premiership - 25 September 1993

REGARDLESS OF THIS being a top versus bottom clash Alex Ferguson decided against making too many changes. He had a useful lead over Honved and both that game and the one at hand were at home. Andrei Kanchelskis came in for Ryan Giggs although there were, as expected, many changes from the youth/reserves side which had exited the League Cup at Stoke City during the week.

Swindon had suffered some heavy defeats and had gleaned just three points so far - all from draws - but could have had a couple of early goals here. If Jan-Aage Fjortoft had applied himself a little more the Robins would have taken the lead. In the event United gathered their thoughts and eased two ahead by the break. Eric Cantona swept a pass to the flank which allowed Kanchelskis to tear down the field from close to half way and beat former Reds' apprentice keeper Fraser Digby to open the scoring. Cantona's pivotal role was in full evidence here as he linked with Lee Sharpe to score the second on 40 minutes. When Mark Hughes scored just after the break, the manager felt it was time to utilise his bench with the Honved game foremost in his thoughts.

The increasingly influential Sharpe came off immediately but there was still more than enough talent to see things out. Only 12 minutes remained when Andy Mutch converted a cross and although Paul Bodin hit a penalty two minutes from time after Steve Bruce had brought down Steve White, United always seemed able to make another on the break. And so it proved as Hughes added a fourth late on.

MANCHESTER UNITED 2 HONVED 1
Champions League 1st Rd 1st leg - 29 September 1993

WITH UNITED ALWAYS likely to progress, two headed Steve Bruce goals within eight minutes confirmed their passage into the next round. Yet the Hungarians made a spirited opening which earned them a couple of corners. Otherwise they were happy to sit back and see how the game progressed and even though Istvan Brockhauser made a host of fine saves it wasn't enough to stop United.

When the Hungarians conceded United routinely had 70% of the pitch to themselves. Ryan Giggs put two good chances wide at either end of the first half. Eric Cantona was one of many figures who seemed anonymous until brought in to play by the livewire Giggs. Cantona burst through the defence to reach a cross from the

Welshman but knocked the ball over. He then put Sharpe in but the shot was deflected wide. Bryan Robson was denied by the keeper but that save led to the corner from which Bruce headed home with Denis Irwin's assistance. Another dead ball, this time a free-kick taken by Sharpe, presented the centre-half with his second.

Istvan Salloi reduced the aggregate margin to two goals, beating Schmeichel to a through ball and rolling it into an empty net. In truth the margin of victory could and should have been bigger.

SHEFFIELD WEDNESDAY 2 MANCHESTER UNITED 3
PREMIERSHIP - 2 OCTOBER 1993

ARSENAL'S DRAW AT Anfield and a win by the odd goal in five in Sheffield saw United extend their lead at the top to five points. The Reds already looked imperious with a common observation that they had yet to hit a peak. Though the score looked tight at Hillsborough, victory was far more comprehensive than it looked. Despite a little early fragility after their European exploits.

Wednesday had an early penalty shout when Lee Sharpe appeared to foul John Sheridan in the 10th minute but play was waved on. It wasn't until shortly after the break that the hosts opened the scoring. Andy Sinton was halted in full flow by Gary Pallister. The winger got to his feet and his quickly taken free-kick found Chris Bart-Williams who beat Schmeichel.

United's goals came in a magical 20 minute spell - the Reds roaring back within minutes of falling behind. Sharpe, running on to a Keane through-ball, centred for Hughes to flick the ball up before stroking home. Eric Cantona, quiet until the break, came to the fore on the restart. He rolled a perfectly weighted pass to Hughes who grabbed the second before the Frenchman did the same for Ryan Giggs who ghosted past Phil King before finishing low to Chris Woods's left.

Chris Waddle forced Schmeichel to scramble and Bart-Williams headed over before Mark Bright nodded in a Waddle free-kick four minutes from the end but the Owls never looked likely to grab a draw in the time remaining.

*

THE INTERNATIONAL BREAK saw the final matches of World Cup qualification take place. The situation in Europe was interesting with one of England or the Netherlands certain to miss out but France seemed likely to qualify. They led Group 6 with 13 points and needed just one more from the two games that remained - both at home - to book a place in the finals. Having been so disappointing in recent years, there was some trepidation that it could all go wrong.

Israel had kissed goodbye to their chances of making it through a tough group some months ago. While they could not be described as whipping boys and gave a very good account of themselves early on, they were certainly one of UEFA's weaker sides as emphasised by France's comfortable 4-0 win in Tel Aviv back in February.

France were noticeably tense but built a 2-1 lead. The pitch was almost waterlogged and at times the puddles helped Israel break down attacks. Frequent goalmouth scrambles were survived until Franck Sauzée netted with a low effort from 20 yards. Ginola, who had created room for the equaliser with a short square ball, then curled in an effort from the left hand side of the area to make it two. It was a wonderful goal following an excellent piece of control on his chest then a touch which took him inside the right back.

Ginola, who formed part of a three pronged attack which saw him and Cantona flank Jean-Pierre Papin, came off for the final half hour. France attempted to kill the Israelis off in the time that remained. Sauzée fired straight at the keeper and Papin should have done better with a half volley from a swirling cross Cantona sent in from the left. Papin also missed when a ball threaded through the centre of defence after a burst from the centre circle put him up against the keeper with defenders trailing in his wake. His shot dribbled disappointingly wide of the left hand post.

As the match entered its final ten minutes it seemed Les Bleus had qualified. However, strikes from Eyal Berkovic who came on as a substitute and Reuven Atar who netted in the third minute of injury time shocked the home side. Berkovic was in the right place to convert after a palm out by Bernard Lama, the ball defeating Desailly's vain attempt to clear it off the line. Atar volleyed in after Rosenthal streaked down the flank and crossed. Gerard Houllier could only watch on helplessly as his side capitulated. Meanwhile England were beaten by the Netherlands, the 2-0 reverse in Rotterdam virtually ensuring they would not be going to the USA.

MANCHESTER UNITED 2 TOTTENHAM HOTSPUR 1
PREMIERSHIP - 16 OCTOBER 1993

AN ANKLE INJURY picked up on international duty saw Paul Ince ruled out as a precaution for the midweek clash with Galatasaray.

Bryan Robson came in. Minds seemed to drift to the upcoming European tie rather than the task at hand.

Yet United deserved the points and were the better side for most of the game as Spurs only came to the fore for a brief period. The visitor's job was made harder by the withdrawal of Teddy Sheringham midway through the first half. The 18 goal striker emerged from a tackle from behind by Robson second best. After feeling his knee and receiving treatment, he opted to carry on but collapsed soon after. Paul Moran came on to partner Nick Barmby in attack but it made the Londoner's attacking line too lightweight.

It took a switch of flanks between Giggs and Sharpe to change the game. Eric Cantona's quickness of thought, characterised by an impudent back-heel, created a chance for Mark Hughes with the help of Giggs. The keeper parried and Sharpe put the rebound into the stands with the goal gaping. He was able to make amends when one of his subsequent crosses was only half cleared by Gary Mabbutt. Roy Keane hammered the ball into the small gap between Thorstvedt and his left post from the edge of the box. Four minutes later David Howells failed to control a Cantona pass. Sharpe made further recompense for his earlier profligacy with a cool finish. Spurs pulled one back quickly through Darren Caskey after a Justin Edinburgh pull back. Nevertheless a ninth Premiership win lengthened United's lead over Norwich City and Arsenal to seven points.

MANCHESTER UNITED 3 GALATASARAY 3
European Cup 1st Rd 1st leg - 20 October 1993

It took a late goal from Eric Cantona to preserve United's unbeaten home record in Europe, one that stretched back 36 years and 52 games but, while the result may have kept pride intact, it didn't bode well for the return leg in the Turkish Champions' Ali Sami Yen Stadium.

United began very promisingly, carving out a 2-0 lead within 13 minutes. Cantona's ball for Mark Hughes deflected off a Turkish defender for Bryan Robson to power home. Then Hakan tried to clear a Giggs corner flighted for Gary Pallister but only managed to head the ball past his own keeper.

Galatasaray took control of midfield soon after and built swift, penetrating attacks, countering well and taking advantage of United's open style. A solid defence managed to hustle the ball away from the home strikers then turn play quickly to Arif and Tugay who had a speed of thought which matched the burning pace of striker Hakan. The game turned on its head when Gala pulled one back after Arif linked with Hakan 25 yards out. There seemed little danger until a dipping shot was hammered past Peter Schmeichel.

Cantona and Hughes saw little of the ball after that, as Robson and Ince were swamped in midfield. United were missing Denis Irwin after Alex Ferguson opted to use Roy Keane as one of his foreign players. Lee Martin came in but struggled to handle Kubilay and on one of the increasingly regular occasions the winger ran at the full back he caused sufficient confusion to find an equaliser.

Stumpf began a move which concluded with Arif attempting to find Kubilay. Martin got to the ball first but his under-hit backpass was intercepted by the Turkish international who saw his goal bound shot turned in by Kubilay who made sure before a defender could get a block in. Another burst from deep led to the third. Arif was thwarted by the post but once again Kubilay was on hand to finish off.

Lee Sharpe was required to track back and posed little threat as a result. When Mike Phelan replaced Robson just past the hour United steadied themselves, and Cantona, who had had a poor game, levelled matters late on by stabbing in a Giggs cross at the far post to spare some blushes.

EVERTON 0 MANCHESTER UNITED 1
PREMIERSHIP - 23 OCTOBER 1993

DESPITE BEING HOSTS, Everton showed little adventure having lost forwards Maurice Johnston to Hearts and Paul Rideout to injury. The Merseysiders tactic of launching long balls at the diminutive forward pairing of Stewart Barlow and Tony Cottee gave Steve Bruce and Gary Paillister an easy afternoon. The duo were more concerned by the raids made by Peter Beagrie but Peter Schmeichel was rarely troubled after an initial burst.

Following the poor display against Galatasaray, Bryan Robson and Ryan Giggs were omitted, Brian McClair returning on the right hand side of midfield while Denis Irwin's re-introduction brought more solidity to defence. Those who expected United to make a domestic foe pay for European embarrassment were left surprised at their tentative opening.

The Reds claimed a win through Lee Sharpe's superb volley from an astute Cantona pass early in the second half which Neville

Southall had no chance of stopping. Everton's style didn't lend itself to an open game and United were happy to maintain their lead and pick off what they could should the chance arise. Beagrie had just one opportunity a dozen minutes from the end. Faced by Schmeichel with plenty of time he rushed and his effort was blocked. The win was much needed as it opened up a nine point gap over Norwich City in second.

MANCHESTER UNITED 2 QUEENS PARK RANGERS 1
PREMIERSHIP - 30 OCTOBER 1993

THE VISITORS HAD enjoyed a decent start to the campaign but were not expected to trouble the runway leaders at Old Trafford. However, they held a deserved lead for much of this game and were only denied by two quick fire goals that extended United's lead at the top to 11 points.

Paul Parker, appearing against his former employers, filled in for Gary Pallister at centre-half but was out-muscled early on by Les Ferdinand who forced Peter Schmeichel into an excellent save, the same player flicking a David Bardsley cross on for Bradley Allen to drive in after beating Steve Bruce. This time not even United's normally solid keeper could keep the ball out.

Towards the end of the half Mark Hughes and Lee Sharpe struck a post, although Ray Wilkins and Trevor Sinclair had the better of the midfield exchanges until the break. It paid off quickly with Eric Cantona and Ryan Giggs at the centre of the revival. The first United goal came when Cantona took the ball in his own half and beat Alan McDonald before venturing deep into the Rangers' half. Defenders backed off until Cantona unleashed a shot across Jan Stejskal to level matters. A few minutes later Roy Keane nodded on a Sharpe corner. The ball fell for Hughes at the far post who crashed it in from close range. It might have been 3-1 moments later had Bruce not hit the post with a header. Giggs was wreaking havoc down the left often beating a host of defenders in the process. On one glorious dribble he beat Bardsley, Darren Peacock and Ian Holloway within the space of just a few yards. The end product was a cross which Sharpe narrowly failed to steer on target.

GALATASARAY 0 MANCHESTER UNITED 0
EUROPEAN CUP 2ND RD 2ND LEG - 3 NOVEMBER 1993

FROM THE MOMENT United touched down in Turkey, their life was made a living hell. The 24 hour din outside the team's hotel continued the theme while the demonic flares and firecrackers inside the ground bore a passable imitation of Hades. 'Welcome to Hell' indeed as the missiles tumbled out of the sky and United tumbled out of Europe.

A rush of blood to Eric Cantona's head near the close seemed sure to rule him out of a large proportion of the club's next continental campaign. On the whistle he hurried towards referee Kurt Rothlisberger of Switzerland to remonstrate with the official about his handling of proceedings before gesturing. One or both led to a red card.

Then, as Bryan Robson tried to guide him away from the cauldron, a brawl broke out with riot police. One over-enthusiastic officer seemed to crash a baton against his head which further incensed the player who squared up to what he perceived to be the aggressor. A group of officers replete with weaponry came towards Cantona who not only stood his ground but looked like he expected further confrontation, Robson was struck and needed two stitches for a hand wound.

Alex Ferguson provided detail to the press stating: "A policeman punched Cantona in the back - we have filmed evidence of that. Another one hit Robson with a shield and cut his hand." Formal protests to UEFA were promised but one of their observers stated he saw no strike by a policeman but claimed Cantona had knocked an officer down some steps. There were also accusations that the referee had been called a cheat and sworn at. However, Cantona insisted neither version was true and that he had merely gone to shake hands. Only after the pleasantries were complete did he indicate his disgust at the official's performance. Just how the bookings for Paul Ince, Steve Bruce, Roy Keane and Paul Parker would be addressed was another matter. Most were incurred due to frustration but few could be attributed to decisions made on the night, United had simply left themselves too much to do after drawing the home leg 3-3.

Mark Hughes was left out in favour of a five-man midfield and the visitors missed the Welshman's ability to hold the ball up in attack while there was a lack of firepower elsewhere. Galatasaray, set up to thwart United, were swift to counter and rarely looked threatened. The Reds failed to soil 'keeper Hayrettin's gloves, Cantona was often isolated and surrounded by Gala defenders. Without adequate support his job was impossible and with limited personnel available there were few tactical options open to Ferguson.

By contrast Peter Schmeichel kept his side in the game. The Turks were preoccupied with time wasting which often came in the form of diving or feigning injury but when they broke forward they possessed huge menace. One save close to the break to deny Hakan when played in by Tugay was brave and brilliant in equal measure. The next soon after was little short of miraculous as Hakan was denied just inside the six yard area by Schmeichel's superb reflexes.

In the event Cantona's actions triggered a four match European ban. Mr Rothlisberger pressed for a longer suspension after reports that Cantona had told French journalists that he believed the referee had been bribed. However, UEFA were content to leave matters as they were after representations from United.

As a postscript the official later received a lifetime ban from the game after being found guilty of attempting to influence a game between Grasshoppers of Zurich and Auxerre in October 1996. He was found to have approached the Swiss club's general manager Erich Vogel who in turn alerted UEFA although there was no evidence of corruption at any other point in his career.

MANCHESTER CITY 2 MANCHESTER UNITED 3
Premiership - 7 November 1993

THERE COULD HAVE been no worse time for Manchester United to visit Maine Road than on the weekend following their European Cup exit to Galatasaray. Sales of Turkish Delight chocolate bars went through the roof in Moss Side and the players were greeted by a hail of the sweets as they left the tunnel.

The atmosphere, seemingly every bit as red hot as Istanbul, affected United as they struggled to come to terms with City who quickly established a 2-0 lead. Denis Irwin made a mistake on the edge of City's area which didn't seem vital at the time but Mike Sheron sped 60 yards downfield before crossing for Niall Quinn to nod past Peter Schmeichel. The left flank proved a fertile area for the Blues on half an hour when Steve McMahon crossed for Quinn once more who repeated the dose. The keeper then denied David White when he seemed guaranteed to score a third.

That save proved vital as the second half saw a complete turnaround. The Reds improved and made sure their superiority told, yet the goal that got them back into the game was a gift. Defender Michel Vonk sold Tony Coton short with a header which dropped to Eric Cantona. There was still work to do and Coton made a decent attempt to close down the angle but the Frenchman's finish was unerring.

Time seemed set to be the biggest enemy for Alex Ferguson and less than 15 minutes remained when Ryan Giggs replaced Andrei Kanchelskis. The winger had been on just seconds when he found Cantona, the Frenchman showed a couple of deft touches before floating the ball to Giggs whose return ball across the face of goal allowed Cantona to equalise. Just minutes remained when Lee Sharpe worked an interchange with Irwin. The full-back's cross evaded Mark Hughes but fell instead for Roy Keane whose belly first slide along the Maine Road pitch celebrated United's sensational comeback.

THE SHOCK HOME defeat to Israel just over a month earlier had not quite dealt a fatal blow to French hopes of qualifying for the World Cup as they still needed just a point from their final group game at the Parc des Princes against Bulgaria. The Bulgarians were two points adrift of leaders Sweden and one behind France following a 4-1 defeat of Austria, although their chances of taking the last remaining qualification place looked hopeless to most as only a win would see them qualify.

As a result Gerrard Houllier erred on the side of caution. David Ginola dropped to the bench and was informed of this well before kick-off. Crucially the news came before the player spoke to the press. Among his comments were remarks about players with strength of character. A furious Cantona stormed into his hotel room demanding an explanation for what he felt to be an unwarranted and more to the point false attack on himself and Jean-Pierre Papin. Ginola insisted he had mentioned no names when speaking to journalists. It was an inauspicious start to what would turn out to be a disastrous evening for French football.

Cantona seemed to have calmed nerves, rifling in a volley after Papin nodded down a Didier Deschamps cross just past the half hour to give the hosts the lead. They had enjoyed the better of the game, even if they looked understandably cagey, attempting to ensure that a goal was not conceded. However, their lead proved short lived. Emil Kostadinov equalised in the 37th minute but try as they might Bulgaria failed to gain a lead in the second half and with time running out, the French walked the ball towards Mikhailov's goal.

With so little time left the natural instinct was to head towards the corner flag but that didn't appeal to Ginola, a second half replacement for Papin. Ginola won a free-kick by the corner flag, with less than 30 seconds of normal time remaining. Vincent Guerin played possession short to Ginola who he expected to shepherd the ball towards the byline. Rather than run the clock down the PSG man spotted Cantona lurking in the area and crossed but the ball was headed clear and Bulgaria's Luboslav Penev broke at pace.

As blue shirts frantically back-pedalled the Bulgarian surged down the wing before crossing for Kostadinov who somehow controlled an awkward cross before powering a shot beyond Bernard Lama. The ball billowed high into the roof of the net. There was no way back for France.

Gerard Houllier, normally a placid character regardless of the circumstances, was visibly outraged afterwards at having failed to steer his side to the World Cup and resigned on the spot. His assistant Aime Jacquet was quickly installed as successor.

Though initially careful in his choice of words he singled out Ginola in post-match comments saying: "The adventure is over all too soon. With only 30 seconds remaining we were there but we got stabbed in the back and at the worst possible time. The referee still had his whistle to his mouth when Ginola won that free kick near the corner flag, but then he goes and sends in a huge 60-metre cross instead of hanging on to the ball. That allowed Bulgaria to go and hit us on the counter." The next part of his comment was a little more prickly: "The fact that one player cracked up was like a drop of acid," he added. "David Ginola is the murderer of the team. He sent an Exocet missile through the heart of French football and committed a crime against the team. I repeat a crime against the team."

Ultimately Ginola made the mistake of looking to secure a win. If his cross had reached its target he may well have been a hero but the players who should have been alert when the visitors broke were not and allowed a much easier route to goal. Unfortunately the French team remained a far from effective unit and without that vital ingredient, they were doomed to failure. Most thought that this was the reason they had failed to do well at major championships.

Unfancied Bulgaria took France's place at the 1994 World Cup in the US and despite a 3-0 defeat to Nigeria in the opening game somehow found a formula that took them all the way to the semi-finals, accounting for World Champions Germany in a memorable quarter-final along the way before losing to Italy in the semis.

MANCHESTER UNITED 3 WIMBLEDON 1
PREMIERSHIP - 20 NOVEMBER 1993

WIMBLEDON WERE THEIR usual combatative selves as they sought to inflict a first defeat in seven games on the reigning champions. 13 months earlier they had been the last away team to win at Old Trafford, yet despite the absence of Roy Keane, the Dons never appeared likely winners here as once more United came through a severe test with three top quality goals.

Defensively Steve Bruce looked particularly worried by the threat posed by Dean Holdsworth. Eric Cantona displayed moments of sublime skill while Gary Pallister's solidity at the back restricted the visitors to just one goal. Even centre backs with prowess in the air often succumb to lofted balls but on this occasion the England international was faultless and for good measure grabbed his first goal of the campaign nodding in United's tenth corner of the game on 53 minutes to grab the lead.

Wimbledon committed numbers forward in pursuit of a leveller which came when Holdsworth teed up John Fashanu just after the hour. Schmeichel had to make a couple of good saves to preserve parity.

A little bit of guile restored the Reds advantage. Cantona was predictably involved in both efforts. A quick free-kick by Paul Parker caught the Dons unaware, Cantona's perfect cross was converted by a Mark Hughes bicycle kick. Then, from an apparently benign position, Cantona worked the ball to Kanchelskis who turned Brian McAllister before sending in a blistering effort from distance which left a diving Hans Segers clutching at thin air.

MANCHESTER UNITED 0 IPSWICH TOWN 0
PREMIERSHIP - 24 NOVEMBER 1993

UNITED'S REGAL PROGRESS, following eight successive wins, was halted by a well-drilled Ipswich side. Like Wimbledon they relied on organisation even if they showed little ambition in attack. It resulted in United's first home blank since the March visit of Arsenal. Yet Aston Villa's defeat meant their lead at the top was extended by a point.

Prior to the game much was made of the fact that United would have been facing Barcelona in the 3rd round of the European Cup. Yet in Eric Cantona and Ryan Giggs United should have had the players to cope with Ipswich's rearguard. Fifteen minutes from time Giggs hit the bar after Ipswich keeper Craig Forrest had made a pair of superb saves before the break to preserve the deadlock. Lee Sharpe and Paul Ince were both denied when getting on the end of Eric Cantona crosses. Gary Pallister rifled an effort at goal from the edge of the area but the Canadian stopper proved equal to it. He also kept out a low Lee Sharpe free-kick.

When the chance of a break fell to the away side the nippy Chris Kiwomya and more lumbering Ian Marshall posed a threat, although the clearest chance fell to Noel Whelan who managed to rise above United's defence to reach a floated ball into the area from veteran John Wark. Mickey Stockwell almost set up Mason late on but the midfielder sent his shot sliding across the face of goal.

COVENTRY CITY 0 MANCHESTER UNITED 1
Premiership - 27 November 1993

Eric Cantona celebrated the anniversary of his signing by scoring the only goal of a tense encounter to extend the gap at the top to a commanding 14 points. It was a victory which the Reds didn't deserve and over recent weeks Alex Ferguson must have wondered what had happened to the free-flowing team that had started the season.

The hosts would have secured victory had it not been for the woodwork. The permanent appointment of Phil Neal to the hotseat at Highfield Road certainly seemed to be popular with the players who performed superbly with Micky Quinn, Peter Ndlovu and Roy Wegerle superb in attack. The American, breaking through from deep positions, often left United defenders looking flat footed. Fortunately Peter Schmeichel was in superb form and executed three instinctive saves while United made the most of the their best spell of the game.

United created just two chances but Cantona was good enough to grab the one that mattered. Following a sustained spell of pressure Steve Ogrizovic could only push a Denis Irwin shot to the side. Mark Hughes saw his follow up bounce off David Rennie and fall to Cantona whose shot from a narrow angle was partially cleared towards the corner flag. Ryan Giggs was quickly on the scene and his whipped cross was helped on by Irwin to Cantona who headed in from eight yards to notch his tenth of the season. Ogrizovic, who had just managed to get back, was left helpless as the ball zipped across him.

Schmeichel had kept the score goalless in the first half, thrusting up a hand to prevent Quinn from scoring at point-blank range. The same player then saw a drive which seemed destined for the roof of the net diverted round the post. Those efforts were bettered after the break when Sean Flynn finally appeared to have beaten the Dane who, although off balance still managed to jab out his left hand to divert the ball. Chris Marsden smashed a late volley against the underside of the bar before Ndlovu struck a post not long after United scored.

EVERTON 0 MANCHESTER UNITED 2
COCA-COLA CUP 4TH RD - 30 NOVEMBER 1993

UNITED'S CONTINUING HUNGER for domestic silverware now extended to the much maligned League Cup. It offered an opportunity to make alterations to the side which had beaten Coventry City with Bryan Robson coming in for Darren Ferguson while Andrei Kanchelskis replaced the injured Lee Sharpe. With the club now out of Europe Ferguson set his sights on a possible domestic treble with Everton, a team the Reds had never beaten in the competition, providing a tricky first hurdle.

An early goal from Mark Hughes set United on their way to victory. On 13 minutes Paul Ince floated the ball over Dave Watson and Hughes chased it down the channel. The Welshman chested the ball into his own path before whipping a volley high past Neville Southall from outside the area. There were few worries until half-time while Southall handled all other tests put his way. A minute after the interval Ryan Giggs doubled the lead - his interchange with Eric Cantona, after Everton were caught on the break, allowed Andrei Kanchelskis to be played in. The winger cut in and saw his shot parried by Southall fall to Giggs who rounded matters off from close range. Peter Schmeichel protected the lead with a superb penalty save from Tony Cottee just six minutes later.

MANCHESTER UNITED 2 NORWICH CITY 2
PREMIERSHIP - 4 DECEMBER 1993

NORWICH PROVIDED FURTHER evidence that they may be more than just early season surprise packages. With their forthcoming UEFA Cup second leg tie in mind against Inter Milan, The Canaries were trailing 1-0 from the home leg and this successful visit to another world famous stage must have further bolstered the Norfolk side's confidence. Norwich dominated the first hour, United hardly touching the ball. All this despite losing captain Ian Butterworth at the break and trailing twice at Old Trafford. With Mark Robins, Efan Ekoku, Ian Crook and John Polston absent through injury Norwich could consider themselves unlucky not to have claimed all three points.

Their confident passing game forced Denis Irwin into action on his own line to deny emergency striker Chris Sutton early on. Peter Schmeichel also had to make an early save from Lee Powers' hooked volley and on a couple of occasions was indebted to other members of his defence for maintaining a clean sheet.

By contrast United's chances were far more isolated. That owed much to a five man defence and sweeper system which required more than just a ram-raid approach if it was to be breached. As a result Cantona often dropped deep to force defenders out of position which gave others an opportunity to make runs. Cantona's passing and deft flicks saw United take a measure of control and a through ball for Andrei Kanchelskis threatened to provide an opening before Ryan Giggs burst through a gap between Ian Butterworth and Rob Newman to finish a Cantona cross.

Norwich hit back immediately - Schmeichel blocking a Ruel Fox shot, the ball falling kindly for Chris Sutton who steered it in from just outside the area. More magic by Giggs and Cantona helped the home side regain the lead just before half-time. The pair linked with Cantona nodding across goal, Brian McClair gave Bryan Gunn no chance. Norwich were level again minutes after the re-start but the damage was self inflicted - Pallister pushed and pulled at Sutton in the box and Fox converted from the spot. There was a chance Norwich could have fallen behind for a third time. Directed by Cantona and Giggs United poured forward but failed to make anything of the chances created.

SHEFFIELD UNITED 0 MANCHESTER UNITED 3
Premiership - 7 December 1993

SHEFFIELD UNITED WERE plucky but never seriously in the hunt as United's quality told at a rain swept Bramall Lane. In the event the score flattered the hosts as United cantered to a commanding away win. All of a sudden the champions, who had recently scraped good results from poor performances, now hit the high notes.

Mark Hughes opened up the scoring with a trademark spectacular after 13 minutes when Paul Parker found Brian McClair. The Scot ran beyond the defence spotting Hughes in the middle, his perfect ball was hammered acrobatically past Republic of Ireland international Alan Kelly by the striker's left foot. The scorer then flicked on for Paul Ince who sent Lee Sharpe haring through on Kelly to beat the keeper once again. Eric Cantona's goal on the hour added gloss to United's victory. Released by Giggs he raced half the length of the pitch before finishing inside the near post.

The Yorkshire club tried to launch the odd counter via the flanks but this approach required far more accurate crosses than the hosts could provide. In truth this was a canter for United against a poor Blades team.

NEWCASTLE UNITED 1 MANCHESTER UNITED 1
PREMIERSHIP - 11 DECEMBER 1993

AFTER THIS MATCH Kevin Keegan suggested he had seen this season's champions play at St James Park and although he was proud of his own team's efforts, his post-match remarks were reserved for the visitors. Newcastle provided a stern test and gave their all before a vociferous home crowd. If their passion and that of their manager had been the decisive factors, the Magpies would have been comfortable winners but the hosts were fortunate to grab a share of the spoils on an afternoon when United dominated for long spells.

Strong icy winds and a slippy pitch meant this match was never going to be a classic but both sides managed to pass the ball accurately. Newcastle looked useful for spells in the first half forcing Steve Bruce and Gary Pallister to be watchful. Peter Beardsley was in convincing form, proving he had lost none of his work ethic or natural ability. Beardsley was at the centre of the Magpie's best play - thrashing a couple of shots at Peter Schmeichel - the first from 15 yards saw the keeper parry, the second was saved at full stretch by the Dane. The England international then brushed a header inches beyond the far post from a Lee Clark centre.

United rode out the first half storm and took the lead through Ince. Substitute Andrei Kanchelskis ran at the home defence and his cross from the right was nodded back by Ryan Giggs for Ince who drilled home from 20 yards.

Newcastle deserved a share of the spoils. Beardsley's craft engineering several openings for Andy Cole but the scorer of 35 goals in just 33 games in a black and white shirt conspired to waste all but one. 18 minutes from time a piece of guile put Rob Lee through down the right and his centre was nodded home from six yards. Cole seemed on his way to becoming a legend on Tyneside. His rate of scoring was the same as Hughie Gallagher who finished with 143 goals from 174 games. Many felt Cole would do better so long as he remained at the club.

Newcastle took their foot off the gas once level which allowed United to finish the stronger. Eric Cantona's contribution was more fitful than usual although his glancing header put Sharpe through only for the winger to be denied by an acrobatic Mike Hooper save.

MANCHESTER UNITED 3 ASTON VILLA 1
PREMIER LEAGUE - 19 DECEMBER 1993

THIS TOP OF the table clash guaranteed a fascinating 90 minutes and the action at Old Trafford continued almost until the last kick. United seemed to be heading for a narrow victory before adding a couple of late goals. Villa, who had chased continuously after going behind midway through the first half, contributed to an open game.

Ron Atkinson added an extra midfielder to contain Cantona, Ray Houghton making way for Earl Barrett. After the whistle Eric suggested "it was an honour to be so closely marked" though restricted himself to any comments about the tactic's effectiveness merely stating: "It is the first time I have been man- for-man marked in this country. It happens in France and Europe and it's all the same to me. I'll change my game to counter it. Today it worked for me, maybe next time it won't."

When a man was tight the emphasis of any United attack could be altered and with the inexperienced Bryan Small deputising at left back there was, as far as Andrei Kanchelskis was concerned, a licence to charge down the wing. Neil Cox attached himself to Lee Sharpe with a better measure of success but Barrett couldn't grip the leash as tightly as intended. Kanchelskis's flank always seemed a likely source of goals and Cantona got his head to an early cross and hit the post. A goal finally came when Paul Parker found Roy Keane. There were attempts to divert his low centre but Cantona arrived late to slide it past Mark Bosnich. Further saves from the Australian kept the score down, particularly when Paul Ince was denied from close range.

Another ex-United man, Paul McGrath, was just as impressive and the pair allowed Villa to have some kind of security at the back which allowed the visiting forwards to push for an equaliser. In that mode the Midlands side were committed to flowing football which may have brought rewards had Gary Pallister and Steve Bruce not made crucial interceptions. It also took a solid save from Peter Schmeichel to deny Kevin Richardson.

Cantona ran on to a Keane pass before sliding the ball home to suppress any lingering Villa hopes in time added on. Then Ince's charge from the centre saw the midfielder add a third before a free-kick scored almost directly from the restart gave Villa some consolation.

MANCHESTER UNITED 1 BLACKBURN ROVERS 1
Premier League - 26 December 1993

United's unbeaten home record was always likely to be tested by Blackburn Rovers. The Lancashire millionaires were fancied as the team to push United all the way in the title race. Dalglish's side were formidable and a win would have hoisted them up to second, albeit ten points behind the Reds.

For 88 minutes of this contest they looked like worthy winners. Tim Flowers, one of Rovers' expensive summer signings, didn't have a save to make until the final quarter and so desperate was United's plight that Peter Schmeichel came up for a late corner. As it turned out the Dane's presence didn't prove crucial but it may have been enough to divert attention from Gary Pallister who was able to flick the ball goalwards. Brian McClair tried to force it in but failed to get a clean contact before Paul Ince thrust the ball past Flowers for a last-gasp leveller.

Kevin Gallacher had given Blackburn a deserved lead on 16 minutes after David Batty had emerged from midfield having ridden challenges from Roy Keane and Paul Ince. Gallacher latched on to Batty's through ball, beat off the attentions of Pallister and Steve Bruce before driving the ball beyond Schmeichel. Tim Sherwood also went close with a drive and had a fiercely volleyed effort saved at the second attempt. Shearer struck the woodwork with a header to keep the deficit at one while a Jason Wilcox cross saw the player rattle the crossbar with just a minute of normal time left.

Even the early loss of Mike Newell had failed to upset Rovers' rhythm. By contrast United's attempts to find a leveller looked in vain. There was a touch of controversy about the award of the crucial corner. Sharpe had tried to roll the ball across the face of goal, Colin

Hendry claiming Ryan Giggs had applied the final touch and his side should have had a goal kick. He was booked for his protestations and TV replays proved inconclusive. Eric Cantona was the biggest threat but his star shone only briefly in the December gloom. Nevertheless United were relieved with the point that maintained their impressive lead.

OLDHAM ATHLETIC 2 MANCHESTER UNITED 5
PREMIER LEAGUE - 29 DECEMBER 1993

THOUGH THE HOSTS equalised twice after falling behind, there was never much prospect of Oldham repeating the win they had enjoyed in the corresponding fixture last season. That had been one of many unlikely results that saved the Latics from the drop. Their inability to defend against forward lines of United's quality suggested they would be need more last ditch heroics if they were to spend another season in the top flight.

Andrei Kanchelskis proved impossible to contain. The Ukrainian scored an early opener after a one-two with Eric Cantona before winning a penalty. Then Graeme Sharp equalised following a slip by former Latic Denis Irwin. Cantona, who made up for his quiet game against Blackburn by grabbing a goal and creating three others, punished Tore Pedersen's challenge with his usual accuracy from the spot. Rick Holden levelled matters once more with an excellent free-kick after Irwin had fouled Richard Graham near the corner flag. The acute angle might have persuaded the keeper to expect a cross yet Holden's shot rasped in just under the angle of post and bar.

Six minutes before the break United re-established their lead for good when Steve Bruce nodded the ball home from an Irwin corner conceded following an excellent Jon Hallworth stop to deny Giggs. The winger then latched on to an angled pass with an equally well timed run to add a fourth and the keeper was beaten again when Cantona crossed for Lee Sharpe who in turn set up Giggs to finish from close range. Cantona came off with less than half an hour remaining to keep him fresh for the visit of Leeds in a few days time. Had he stayed on the damage to Oldham may have got far worse. That it didn't in any case was down to some good defending and goalkeeping. A few slices of luck. As well as a touch of wayward finishing. The year ended with a host of centuries for the Reds. 100 points for the calendar year and 100 goals scored across all competitions.

MANCHESTER UNITED 0 LEEDS UNITED 0
PREMIERSHIP - 1 JANUARY 1994

LEEDS LAY SECOND as a result of United's late equaliser against Blackburn Rovers a week previously but were far from the side that had pipped their hosts to the league title two seasons ago. Howard Wilkinson denied he had a cautious approach, suggesting his side liked to pass and play but couldn't find a final ball. All the same he wasn't unhappy with a goalless draw here. His side dominated possession for lengthy periods but seemed disinclined to attack. Any side shorn of Rod Wallace, Gary Speed and Noel Whelan was going to suffer, although they didn't even thrust forward when Steve Bruce went off to have stitches put in his lip after a clash with Brian Deane's elbow.

United, without Ince, Sharpe and Hughes, lacked some of their usual swagger. All the statistics favoured the hosts but going forward a wall of white made things difficult. Eric Cantona was closely watched by Chris Fairclough, the defender only occasionally breaking free and almost nicking an unlikely victory when he met a Tony Dorigo cross but his firm header struck the bar.

Villa had tried to man-mark Cantona just a couple of weeks earlier which only served to incite the Frenchman to grab a couple in a comfortable 3-1 win. But on this occasion Cantona almost always received the ball with his back to goal and couldn't turn. His irritation was marked by a second half booking for a cynical foul on Gary McAllister. Two minutes from time the Frenchman managed to get his only shot on goal, meeting a Ryan Giggs centre with a volley that struck Andrei Kanchelskis before Mark Beeney gathered.

At the other end new signing David White, a shock £2 million capture from Manchester City, was the only Leeds player to force Peter Schmeichel to lay a glove on the ball when trying his luck from the edge of the area.

LIVERPOOL 3 MANCHESTER UNITED 3
PREMIERSHIP - 4 JANUARY 1994

FOR THE OPENING 24 minutes it looked as if Manchester United would cruise to an emphatic win that would bruise the pride of the vast majority of a capacity 43,000 Anfield crowd. Yet Liverpool somehow recovered from three goals down to escape with a point leaving the Merseyside supporters in ecstasy at a home draw, something that would have been considered unthinkable just a few seasons before. Already 12 points clear at the top, the Reds could have effectively ended the title race in January with a win at their fiercest rivals, yet the opportunity eluded them in a thrilling contest. Liverpool created the first chance of the game just 50 seconds in. Robbie Fowler, without a goal in his last three games, snatching at Nigel Clough's clever flick to sky the ball over. It seemed the home team would pay for that profligacy eight minutes in after a weak header from Jamie Redknapp sold John Barnes short. Barnes' attempted clearance only found Eric Cantona, the Frenchman picked out Steve Bruce at the far post and a perfectly timed cross allowed the centre back to nod in.

Fowler had another chance as Liverpool roared back but couldn't find the direction to beat Peter Schmeichel. Ryan Giggs was over-indulgent in another threatening move for the visitors but made up for that when he intercepted a feeble Jamie Redknapp backpass and beat Mark Wright before lobbing Bruce Grobbelaar from 20 yards. On 24 minutes a Neil Ruddock foul on Roy Keane gave away a free-kick just inside the 'D' - Denis Irwin curled the ball beyond Grobbelaar into the top right-hand corner to make it 3-0. As it turned out United's early goals forced Liverpool into a gung-ho approach. Their unbeaten run at Anfield stretched back 11 games since Blackburn's visit in September and within minutes the hosts were back in it through Nigel Clough. The former Forest man picked up the ball 30 yards out before drilling a low shot into the bottom left hand corner of the Kop goal to provide some relief. Seven minutes before the break Clough reduced the deficit further, reaching a loose ball in United's area to prod home.

Having got their breath back at the break, United looked to extend their lead on the resumption but Bruce Grobbelaar made a stunning save from Giggs, somehow managing to fist the ball away despite going in the wrong direction. Peter Schmeichel was less spectacular but just as sure when denying a Redknapp 25 yard curler. The momentum may have been with Liverpool but time was not. Graeme Souness withdrew Steve McManaman for Stig Inge Bjornbye and within minutes the Norwegian's introduction was justified. His swirling cross from the left was met squarely by Ruddock's head as the defender attacked the ball. Incredible!

Afterwards Alex Ferguson complimented the home side on their efforts. The Kop played a huge part in the comeback and the 'devil may care' attitude of the players endured simply because they had nothing to lose.

SHEFFIELD UNITED 0 MANCHESTER UNITED 1
FA CUP 3RD ROUND - 9 JANUARY 1994

MARK HUGHES MAY have scored the winner which saw United through a topsy-turvy opening FA Cup tie but his dismissal three minutes from time for aiming a hack at David Tuttle cast a shadow on an otherwise outstanding contribution. Referee Gerald Ashby was given no option after earlier cautioning the striker for stamping on Chris Kamara.

Events provided a huge contrast to the encounter at Anfield in midweek. The Reds were majestic against Liverpool early on but stunned by a forceful comeback. At Bramall Lane, scene of a shock 2-1 defeat the previous season, they were simply pulled down to their host's level and often reduced to hitting high balls with their true quality only rarely emerging. Sheffield's five-man midfield were physical and worked tirelessly. Some aspects of their game deserved plaudits but the general style was to disrupt their opponents play. Alex Ferguson, anticipating such a game, countered by positioning Roy Keane and Paul Ince in the middle with Eric Cantona handed a free role as support Hughes.

It took one piece of genius from Hughes, who exchanged passes with Ince and Cantona in the middle, to break clear. He played another one-two with Ince before beating Alan Kelly with an effort that rolled in off the far post. Kelly had earlier only been tested by a Ryan Giggs effort fired straight at his legs after Carl Bradshaw could only clear a lobbed ball forward to the young Welshman.

Sheffield United created few chances. Glyn Hodges had a fine game but his promptings only brought limited reward. Dane Whitehouse headed a lofted free-kick just over while Jamie Hoyland's pea-roller from distance presented no problem for Peter Schmeichel although Jostein Flo saw a header cleared off the line just before the interval by Irwin.

MANCHESTER UNITED 2 PORTSMOUTH 2
LEAGUE CUP - 12 JANUARY 1994

TWO-GOAL HERO Paul Walsh denied United a semi-final place but the Reds would have been disappointed about twice losing the lead at home to a mid-table First Division team. Pompey, who just a week earlier had taken Blackburn Rovers to an FA Cup replay after a 3-3 draw at Ewood Park, simply couldn't be shaken and it could have been worse. At 1-1 the visitors thought they had won a penalty when one time Old Trafford apprentice Alan McLoughlin was unceremoniously brought down by Paul Parker. Portsmouth manager Jim Smith was irate at the time but after the whistle became quite philosophical when discussing two more spot-kicks he believed had been wrongly denied.

Giggs linked with Brian McClair to score the opener, the Welshman taking the Scot's flick to slide home. Just three minutes later the visitors were level - a McLoughlin corner found Walsh unmarked and although Peter Schmeichel got a hand to the header its flight beat the Dane. Knight denied Bryan Robson and Eric Cantona with fine saves - the latter being one of the best ever witnessed at Old Trafford as it seemed to defy the laws of physics. Eric seemed to have his arms in the air before realising he had been denied. Half-time came at the worst point for United who emerged sluggish and almost conceded a lead. Only some fortune, poor shooting and moments of excellence stopped the South Coast outfit grabbing what would have been a deserved goal. Jim Smith suggested his side missed out on at least three penalties though only the claim against McLoughlin seemed to have much merit.

On the hour Eric Cantona headed an inch-perfect Parker cross in and this settled United nerves if not the game. Again Portsmouth's reply was timely. Mark Stimson outfoxed the home defence, delaying a through-ball for Darryl Powell. Schmeichel saved but Walsh, an unlikely choice for captain, lunged forward to nod the bouncing ball into an unguarded net. The remaining 19 minutes saw chances for both sides - mostly for United - who came closest at the death when McClair struck the bar.

TOTTENHAM HOTSPUR 0 MANCHESTER UNITED 1
PREMIERSHIP - 15 JANUARY 1994

ALTHOUGH THE FINAL score would suggest a close match it doesn't fully reflect the Reds' superiority at White Hart Lane. Two goals were disallowed for offside and though the one which counted just a few minutes in to the second half may have gone in off Colin Calderwood's shins, Mark Hughes' instinct when he flicked a right foot at Roy Keane's low cross deserved the ultimate reward.

Eric Cantona was in his pomp and enjoyed every second strolling around midfield rebuffing each attempt to halt or hinder him. In the process he also slighted George Graham. The Arsenal boss may usually have delighted in a Tottenham defeat but with his side on the wrong side of a double digit lead he decided to use the press to launch an attack on the United number seven saying in an interview, "he [Cantona] will let you down at the very highest level . . . he's a cry baby when the going gets tough."

France's failure to qualify for the World Cup was cited as an example. So too was Cantona's nomadic career. Yet not even a muddy pitch could upset the smooth rhythm he set in North London. Eric even produced an array of trickery, quick passing and cunning which his colleagues appreciated. It created a multitude of chances and the game should have been won by a huge margin.

One move was typical of United's style. Giggs finding Cantona in the centre circle before sprinting over 60 yards to offer himself for the return which he took on for just a few yards before unleashing a shot which Walker, seemingly involuntarily, kept out with his legs. In the final quarter of an hour Cantona's eagerness to get on the scoresheet saw him stray offside.

Ossie Ardiles kept his faith in youth - Nick Barmby and Darren Caskey were prominent in the prolonged absence of Jason Dozzell and Teddy Sheringham. The Spurs manager had tried to bring in reinforcements but his players had recently been told that their usual allocation of tickets for games would be cut drastically - a relief on this evidence - and there was even a drive to reduce the milk consumed at White Hart Lane to save an estimated £100,000 per year.

Alex Ferguson confessed to journalists that in recent weeks he had rested players to freshen them up a little but would be doing no such thing with Cantona. An early end to his afternoon at Oldham late the previous month was as close as he came to a rest, the boss admitting "I've been looking to give him a break but he doesn't want it and it seems he doesn't need it. He has showed he has the resilience to cope with the unique demands of the English game."

MANCHESTER UNITED 1 EVERTON 0
PREMIERSHIP - 22 JANUARY 1994

JUST 48 HOURS after the death of Sir Matt Busby aged 84, football took second place to the moving tributes paid to the Godfather of Manchester United. A lone piper led the players of Manchester United and Everton on to the field with a minute's silence impeccably observed. The seat he had occupied in the director's box was poignantly left vacant. The holy trinity of his great 1960s side - George Best, Bobby Charlton and Denis Law were on hand as were luminaries such as Paddy Crerand, Willie Morgan, and Wilf McGuinness along with the Busby family.

Before the sombre elements of the day were over there was an attempt to raise the mood although the PA announcer couldn't mask his emotions when reading out a message from the Busby family: 'Matt always had a smile on his face even during the last few days in hospital. For champions past and present, please sing the roof off the stadium today.' Many tried to do that but the atmosphere, though lifted, seemed to have the usual raucous edge removed. Only the winning goal broke the sobriety.

Fittingly it was Ryan Giggs, the type of homegrown superstar that Sir Matt would always be synonymous with, who provided the game's only goal - connecting forcefully with a cross from Roy Keane. Another player who gave Matt an awful lot of pleasure was Eric Cantona who could have scored three or more goals in the second half but for Neville Southall's excellence between the posts and a John Ebrell clearance. His most eye-catching opportunity after an hour's play saw him take a centre from Giggs, control it on his chest and, while still in the air, pirouette before smashing a shot against the foot of an upright. Kanchelskis hit the crossbar and 15 minutes from the end Giggs ran past three defenders only to be thwarted by his international colleague Southall.

The Everton keeper's performance and the visitor's general contribution only added to the spectacle. It was perhaps an unfair reflection of play that the Goodison Park club only forced one save out of Peter Schmeichel albeit an outstanding stop just inside the post from full debutant Neil Moore.

PORTSMOUTH 0 MANCHESTER UNITED 1
LEAGUE CUP 5TH ROUND REPLAY - 26 JANUARY 1994

ALEX FERGUSON GUIDED his side to a third League Cup semi-final in four seasons courtesy of Brian McClair's winner. They would now meet Sheffield Wednesday in the last four with the prospect of a domestic treble hoving in to view. Portsmouth, bolstered by £500,000 signing Gerry Creaney, had few responses to United either before or after the goal. The dismissal of John Durnin extinguished all hope of an equaliser.

Kit Symons' return helped the home defence resist the promptings of Ryan Giggs and Eric Cantona for long periods. At the other end Creaney, a purchase from Celtic, just a day earlier came straight into the Pompey side to partner Paul Walsh but found Gary Pallister and Steve Bruce tough opponents. He got just two chances but put his first effort wide then saw the next cleared by Keane at the far post. The new man also set up Alan McLoughlin but Peter Schmeichel made an unhurried save to thwart his soft effort. Walsh was full of good touches and clever play but got little change this time out.

McClair, in for the suspended Mark Hughes, spearheaded the attack, Giggs and Keane combined to play him in, the Scot's shot was parried to Andrei Kanchelskis whose shot was blocked by Alan Knight's legs. The goal came after Cantona nodded on a Giggs' corner. McClair, always looking to profit from that type of ball, lost his marker and gave the keeper no chance from just a few yards. He could have had a second soon after following work by Cantona and Keane but sent the ball well wide from a good position.

NORWICH CITY 0 MANCHESTER UNITED 2
FA CUP 4TH ROUND - 30 JANUARY 1994

UNITED HAD NOT lost at Carrow Road since exiting the same competition two seasons earlier yet their progress to the 5th round was imperious against a home side who stood eighth in the Premier League. Until an hour had been played Peter Schmeichel had barely touched the ball let alone made a save.

Norwich had scored few goals at home in the league and looked to keep things tight. Manager John Deehan deployed Ian Culverhouse as a sweeper with John Polston told to stick to Cantona - a job he carried out to the letter even if it left the forward line short of support when Norwich looked to break. Despite remaining on the back foot the plan worked for the most part and it took a set piece to deliver the breakthrough, ironically following a Paul Ince foul on Culverhouse. Ryan Giggs intercepted the ball and sprinted out of defence covering two thirds of the pitch before playing in Andrei Kanchelskis. The winger's pace gave the home defence no chance, Roy Keane converting the Ukrainian's cross shot. A minute later Kanchelskis thought he had scored again but for a second successive weekend one his efforts thudded off the bar.

The hosts settled in to a tempo which provided them with an attacking edge in the second half. Within a minute Schmeichel had parried shots from Jeremy Goss and John Polston, the latter spurning a second chance to score from the rebound when it finally seemed the Dane had been beaten. Norwich's most fertile and as it turned out brief period of control ended when Mark Bowen fired wide.

At the other end Bryan Gunn came out to thwart Kanchelskis and then Hughes although his efforts proved fruitless with little more than a quarter of an hour left. Cantona may have been shackled by the attentions of his marker but three cross-field passes sent out to Kanchelskis, which alone were worth the admission money, stretched the hosts before he seized on Newman's attempt to play his side out of trouble, lost Polston before flicking the ball past Gunn.

Unfortunately Cantona provided his critics with further ammunition late on. Already on a caution for a late challenge on Jeremy Goss just before the interval he aimed a back-heeled flick at John Polston's shoulder as the pair slid along the touchline during a challenge with just 13 minutes remaining. Neither the referee nor his linesman saw it as play carried on although the incident was replayed on live TV.

Those post-match comments about Cantona and the incident with Polston rankled with Alex Ferguson. When told Jimmy Hill had described the actions as "despicable" the Old Trafford boss immediately rallied to his star's defence accusing the pundit of writing United off during the warm-up. Suggesting Cantona did no more than react to intimidation saying, "I'm not interested in Jimmy Hill, neither are my players," before adding "the BBC are dying for us to lose. Everyone is from Liverpool with a supporter's badge. They will be at our games every week until we lose. That mob - Bob, Barry, Hansen, the lot of them. That's what will drive us on and you can quote me if you like." Little has changed since it seems.

QUEENS PARK RANGERS 2 MANCHESTER UNITED 3
PREMIERSHIP - 5 FEBRUARY 1994

QUEENS PARK RANGERS' open approach underlined their belief that United's defence had a soft centre. Les Ferdinand, identified as a possible Old Trafford target, was charged with the task of finding it and enjoyed no small measure of success. But for all their testing moments United were able to seize enough chances to win the game.

A Ryan Giggs goal on the hour was the pick of the five seen at Loftus Road. He won the ball inside the opposition half after a wayward Rangers pass, before cutting inside to avert attempts to check him. He danced around two further challenges veering right and left before hammering the ball past Jan Stejskal. Schmeichel's ability to turn defence into attack made him not only United's last line of defence but their first line of attack and his quick, accurate clearances were the difference between the teams. Andrei Kanchelskis, collecting a long Schmeichel throw as the QPR defence switched off, opened the scoring with a solo run finished by a low shot. Clive Wilson equalised with a penalty awarded when Gary Penrice was judged to have been upended by Roy Keane. But just a minute later the host's inability to clear the ball on the stroke of half-time allowed Denis Irwin to retrieve the free-kick he had struck and then swing in a cross for the late arriving Eric Cantona to grab a second before Giggs' wonder effort put United two clear.

At times QPR looked dead and buried but even with the Dane in superb form they pulled to within a goal and could have grabbed a point had it not been for Schmeichel. Ferdinand had chances to level with one effort saved and another missed from six yards. He achieved some reward for a fine afternoon's work with a low shot which Schmeichel did his best to avert. A quiet game for Cantona almost concluded with a sensational goal in the dying seconds. He beat three defenders on a mesmeric run which ended with a shot which drifting less than a foot wide. An unbeaten run of 30 games was established by virtue of this win.

MANCHESTER UNITED 1 SHEFFIELD WEDNESDAY 0
COCA-COLA CUP SEMI-FINAL 1ST LEG - 13 FEBRUARY 1994

ONLY A ROLAND Nilsson mistake separated the sides although Ryan Giggs' ability to profit from it had to be applauded. Wednesday would have been good value for a draw after resisting their hosts for much of the game courtesy of a solid midfield and defence. Des Walker lived up to his reputation while Carlton Palmer and Graham Hyde got to grips with matters in midfield.

Roy Keane's method of finding a way through involved charging from box to box while urging the flair players surrounding him to weave their usual magic. A dynamo in central midfield, the Irish international threatened to find at least one goal. He was inches away from converting crosses from both Giggs and Andrei Kanchelskis.

Wednesday, with Chris Waddle back after a six week absence, coped well. One time United target David Hirst, back after five months out with an Achilles problem, showed some rustiness when presented with a gilt-edged chance, the striker had space and time to chest the ball down but his trundling effort didn't worry Peter Schmeichel. Swedish defender Nilsson, who had headed over while in a state of confusion over signals from his goalkeeper, made his lapse when trying to play the ball back to Kevin Pressman but failed to see Giggs lurking. One side-step later the the ball was nestling in the goal.

Giggs was otherwise disappointing and with Cantona below his best the attack was only sparked when Andrei Kanchelskis had possession. He laid on three crosses that Roy Keane just failed to convert. The aerial threat of Gary Pallister produced only one header which Walker cleared off his line on the hour.

Cantona missed the second leg played just over a fortnight later through injury. His former Marseille teammate Chris Waddle, an important figure in attack, was also missing which hampered the hosts who had to attack. United recorded a sound 4-1 victory at Hillsborough to reach Wembley and maintain their domestic treble hopes.

BETWEEN THIS COCA-COLA Cup tie and meeting Wimbledon in the FA Cup Eric Cantona was appointed national skipper on Aimé Jacquet's succession. The honour came at a point in his career when Eric was a respected elder statesman of the team, a player Jacquet knew others looked up to. He was the natural choice to take the armband and his tenure started with a 1-0 win over a very capable Italy side in Naples, Youri Djorkaeff scoring the goal just before half-time.

WIMBLEDON 0 MANCHESTER UNITED 3
FA CUP 5TH ROUND - 20 FEBRUARY 1994

WIMBLEDON WERE THEIR usual combative selves but even at Selhurst Park they couldn't resist United's quality. Eric Cantona underlined their supremacy with a breathtaking goal that knocked the wind out of the host's sails. Had it not been for Warren Barton United could well have earned a quick-fire lead. The full-back blocked a Cantona cross which Mark Hughes could not have failed to convert, Barton then diverted a Roy Keane shot off his own line. Cantona gave Barton no chance with his first chance but placed his header narrowly wide. Then came his touch of genius which lifted the match into another dimension.

When a Denis Irwin cross was headed out by Gary Elkins the ball fell to Cantona who controlled it deftly with his right instep before unleashing a volley in to the top left hand corner of the net from 20 yards to give the visitors the lead. After that the pace of Ryan Giggs and Andrei Kanchelskis tore the Dons apart. There was little resistance although Vinnie Jones, keen to assert some authority on the game, ploughed through Cantona midway through the opening period earning a booking in the process.

Cantona, his sense of injustice heightened, appeared to stamp on Jones and Scott Fitzgerald had his name taken when clattering into Giggs. Once United scored it always seemed sure to be enough although Giggs hit a post when he met a Roy Keane pass and soon after the advantage was doubled by Paul Ince who nodded home the Welshman's corner. Had Cantona not executed his opener so perfectly the final goal – a 15 pass move which took the Reds from a deep position to the edge of the area – would have been the pick of the three. The move ended with Irwin and Ince performing a one-two. The left back glided past Barton and Fitzgerald before sliding the ball past Segers.

WEST HAM UNITED 2 MANCHESTER UNITED 2
PREMIERSHIP – 26 FEBRUARY 1994

As MANCHESTER UNITED had done just over a month previously, West Ham paid their respects to a club icon. Bobby Moore, who had passed away almost a year to the day earlier, was honoured by having a new 9,000 seat stand named after him. However, it was one of West Ham's least popular figures who proved pivotal on the day. Paul Ince, who left the Boleyn Ground early in the 1989-90 season on a note of controversy after being pictured wearing a Manchester United shirt before he had signed, salvaged a point just three minutes from time. It was a just reward for a performance which became increasingly influential despite the abuse received.

There had been similar exhibitions of revulsion at the home of his former club on each occasion Ince returned but there were some increasingly unsavoury aspects to this display including the hurling of bananas at the player. On the field West Ham gave a distinguished exhibition and came back admirably from going a goal behind by notching a couple of their own in just three minutes as the game ticked towards its final quarter. It would have inflicted only a second league defeat of the season on Alex Ferguson's men but Ince and others were able to recover from a moribund period to grab a deserved share of the points.

There was a fair argument that the late rally shouldn't have been needed. Eric Cantona prompted a goal in the sixth minute when he fed Roy Keane down the right. A low centre was put past Ludek Miklosko by Mark Hughes who nipped in behind Alvin Martin. West Ham rallied within minutes, a Trevor Morley header was gloved against a post by Peter Schmeichel but Cantona maintained his side's ascendancy co-ordinating a host of threatening moves as he loitered with intent in midfield. Had Andrei Kanchelskis and Hughes not been so poor in completing the chances which came their way the home side could have been playing for little more than pride by the break.

Cantona's old striker partner Lee Chapman netted from close quarters after he had beaten Denis Irwin to a Matty Holmes cross before Gary Pallister seemingly gifted the three points to the Hammers after fluffing a pass-back to Schmeichel. Chapman got a toe to the ball setting Holmes away. A centre was fumbled by Schmeichel and Trevor Morley just a yard out seemed to have won the game. Yet Ince beat Miklosko from a similar distance after Keane's cross couldn't be held to earn the Reds a point.

MANCHESTER UNITED 3 CHARLTON ATHLETIC 1
FA Cup 6th Rd - 12 March 1994

In Cantona's two week absence Chelsea had ended the Reds' 34 match unbeaten run with a 1-0 win at Stamford Bridge. United progressed to the last four of the FA Cup here but at some cost. Peter Schmeichel was dismissed and although the ten men proved no handicap in this game, his prospective suspension was a huge blow as it would coincide with the Coca-Cola Cup final. The keeper had raced from his area to thwart a Kim Grant break. When they tangled outside the area and Schmeichel appeared to handle, the referee felt he had no option but to dismiss him.

Les Sealey came off the bench with Paul Parker the outfield player sacrificed. Roy Keane covered at right back with Mark Hughes asked to deputise in midfield albeit in a more advanced position than the Irish international would occupy. Having returned to bolster the side Eric Cantona remained up front and despite being a man down, Cantona's roving brief allied to Hughes' support was more than Charlton could handle.

Credit must be given to the Addicks who were ambitious enough to push Darren Pitcher and Carl Leaburn high up field. Their presence was a threat as was Alan Pardew's distribution and

Schmeichel was called upon to make a couple of saves before United got out of the blocks.

Ryan Giggs' corner found Hughes whose effort was thwarted by Vaughan's reflex save but the reserve keeper was helpless with the rebound. Then Ince crashed a header on to the crossbar with little more than an hour gone. Soon after Kanchelskis and Cantona fashioned the second. A touch from the French star in a central position brought a roar of approval from the crowd. Kanchelskis's pace took him through on the keeper and though he placed a hand on the resulting shot it was hit so hard that there was no hope of stopping its course to the net. The Ukrainian added the third latching on to another pass – this time from Ryan Giggs. Again there was no answer from Charlton's defence and Vaughan was once again helpless. Leaburn pulled one back but it was a mere consolation.

MANCHESTER UNITED 5 SHEFFIELD WEDNESDAY 0
PREMIERSHIP - 16 MARCH 1994

THE TOTAL DEVASTATION wreaked on poor Sheffield Wednesday suggested only United could deny themselves their second successive league title. Hillsborough manager Trevor Francis was bold enough to suggest Manchester United were the best team in Europe after his side were eliminated from the Coca-Cola Cup and on this form and with Eric Cantona in such glorious shape, he had a point.

That Cantona was in the right back position when United grabbed the first also spoke volumes of his work ethic. An extravagant 50 yard pass from that position teed up the rampaging Ryan Giggs who gained a yard on Roland Nilsson before applying a cool finish past an advancing keeper. A minute later the advantage was doubled courtesy of Mark Hughes who volleyed low past Kevin Pressman from outside the area following a Cantona flick.

The two goals gave United confidence and with only a quarter of an hour gone Wednesday wore the look of defeated opponents. By contrast United were buzzing – Paul Ince spinning on to a pass from Andrei Kanchelskis before drilling another past the keeper for the third. Just before half-time the enigmatic Cantona fittingly grabbed the fourth to cap a first period performance Alex Ferguson described as 'the best opening 45 minutes of the season'. Racing on to a through ball from Ince, Eric beat Des Walker for pace before finishing past poor Pressman.

When Cantona hit a fifth within ten minutes of the restart it seemed United could notch double figures - a slick move down the right full of intricate passes (nine in total) reduced the Wednesday rearguard to spectators by the time the move was rounded off by the man himself. It was some goal - finished with a dummy that sent the crowd the wrong way before a finish which cannoned in off a post. After that United declared and seemed happy to play out time.

SWINDON TOWN 2 MANCHESTER UNITED 2
PREMIERSHIP - 19 MARCH 1994

MOST FEARED THAT the hosts would be humiliated with something approaching a rugby score widely predicted. Swindon had been walloped 7-1 by Newcastle United a week previously while United had knocked in five against Sheffield Wednesday. Yet the hosts could thank Cantona for the point they earned as he was dismissed for the first time in 25 months in English football. The incident came after an apparent stamp on the chest of John Moncur following an effort to ensure the ball ran harmlessly over the touchline.

Following Peter Schmeichel's dismissal seven days earlier headlines suggested a disciplinary problem at Old Trafford but manager Alex Ferguson suggested referee Brian Hill (famous in Old Trafford circles for disallowing a Brian McClair goal in the FA Cup some years earlier) never oversee another game involving his side. There was little dispute that the 65th minute incident changed the course of the game. Referee Hill claimed, "he [Cantona] stamped on John Moncur and caught him in the chest. I saw it, my linesman saw it. Alex Ferguson did not say anything to me after the game."

Roy Keane gave United the lead following a Mark Hughes through-ball. The Irish midfielder shimmying past Kilcline before netting. Swindon, who seemed to think their only chance to gain anything from the afternoon lay in physicality, gradually brought United down to their level. Veteran scrapper Laurie Sanchez was the first to see yellow and Denis Irwin followed the former Wimbledon man soon after. With that job done Swindon's tactics bore fruit with a goal coming via a slice of luck. Luc Nijholt chanced his arm from distance. His shot taking a huge deflection that beat Schmeichel. Paul Ince's effort gave United the lead once more, the midfielder firing in from outside the area.

United's inability to make the game safe saw Cantona flick a boot at Kilcline and Laurie Sanchez either side of half-time. Added to that Keane seemed to have a number of quarrels with Nijholt that threatened the peace. In the stands there was just as much spite as on the pitch. Mark Hughes seemed to be struck with a punch when his momentum took him into the tight hoardings around the pitch and had a missile aimed at him minutes later.

Cantona's dismissal gave Swindon space and Fjortoft's equaliser seven minutes from time after Adrian Whitbread's cross rescued a point for the home side. Eric would now be suspended for the crunch meeting with Blackburn Rovers who were now just five points behind courtesy of a win at Hillsborough by the odd goal in three. He would also miss a league meeting with Oldham Athletic along with the FA Cup semi-final encounter with the same opponents.

ARSENAL 2 MANCHESTER UNITED 2
PREMIER LEAGUE - 22 MARCH 1994

ONCE AGAIN POST-MATCH discussion centred around Eric Cantona as he was dismissed for the second time in four days. With a three game ban already likely for his dismissal at Swindon, there was a possibility that the suspension could now be doubled meaning he would miss the return fixture at Elland Road which would comprise the fourth game of an extended suspension. Clearly Eric was a marked man following his actions at Swindon and he should have avoided any type of confrontation before his disciplinary hearing but there were many who thought this latest red card was a miscarriage of justice.

The flashpoint came following a tense game United controlled for long periods. Referee Vic Callow issued a caution to Cantona four minutes from the end for a two-footed tackle on Ian Selley. Just over sixty seconds remained when Eric missed Tony Adams with another lunge but followed through and caught Nigel Winterburn. The official wasted no time in ending the French striker's participation.

Lee Sharpe, returning following a hernia problem, opened the scoring after just 10 minutes, following up when David Seaman failed to hold a swerving effort from Mark Hughes. Arsenal equalised via a Gary Pallister own goal following a Paul Merson free-kick. Steve Bruce and Paul Ince produced heroics to stem the Arsenal tide before Lee Sharpe finally saw off this concerted period of pressure with a goal line clearance.

United took control at the start of the second half. Cantona gliding down the left before crossing towards Sharpe. Winterburn got something on it but Sharpe was in the right place at the right time to convert. Merson took the opportunity to grab a point after

Lee Dixon's lob caught the United backline in two minds. A cross-shot beat Schmeichel. Ian Wright thought he had scored a winner two minutes from time. He was celebrating with the crowd before realising his effort had been chalked off following Smith's nudge on Schmeichel. The forward had earlier come close to equalising with a delicate chip and Steve Bould was also just inches away with a towering header.

At no point before the initial flash point with Selley did Cantona look close to finding his name in the referee's notebook. A display full of flair and skill was somehow allowed to degenerate and skew a contribution which played a full part in United gaining a winning position. Roy Keane, booked for a foul on Paul Davis which took him beyond 21 disciplinary points, was now also ruled him out of the FA Cup semi-final. Paul Ince was walking a similar tight-rope after a high tackle brought Selley down clutching his thigh.

With a game in hand and United out of action until a clash with Liverpool the following midweek, Blackburn could now have a share of the Premiership lead before the Reds completed the league programme's 34th game having at one stage enjoyed a 16 point advantage. A record of one win in five games was as worrying as the loss of key personnel.

ASTON VILLA 3 MANCHESTER UNITED 1
LEAGUE CUP FINAL - 27 MARCH 1994

THE FIRST LEG of a possible treble ended in failure with a United player dismissed for the third successive game. Andrei Kanchelskis was the man to take an early bath this time and was now also suspended for the forthcoming FA Cup semi-final with Oldham Athletic. It meant Ron Atkinson had led a side to League Cup victory over his former club for the second time in three years after guiding Sheffield Wednesday to a win in 1991. In truth it was a triumph for Big Ron, as his side outplayed and outthought United throughout.

Villa's five-man midfield dominated the game while Dean Saunders tireless efforts in a lone striking role and Dalian Atkinson and Tony Daley's pace had the Reds on the back foot all game. Yet it was United who made the better start. Cantona finding Ryan Giggs with a raking cross but the youngster's header flew wide of the far post. Mark Hughes was next to trouble Mark Bosnich after being teed up by Giggs on one rare occasion when he evaded his markers. Earl Barrett, who had failed to shackle Cantona earlier in the season, enjoyed greater success with the Welshman who came off midway through the second half.

After almost being caught out Villa concentrated their efforts on the flanks. Villa looked comfortable once Atkinson rounded off a slick move involving Andy Townsend and Saunders. It was Villa's first attack of any real significance and while far from the last it seemed Ron Atkinson was happy for his side to hold on to their lead. At the other end United plugged away trying to take half chances. Paul Parker was forced to take a punt from outside the area which caused minor concern. So too did Gary Pallister from inside the box while Shaun Teale made a tackle on Kanchelskis just before it seemed the trigger would be pulled. Richardson then produced a last ditch tackle to stop substitute Lee Sharpe before taking the free-kick that effectively settled the game. Daley was fouled by Parker on the edge of the area and his low shot was converted by Saunders.

United still had hope when Keane sent a half cleared Denis Irwin corner back into the area for Mark Hughes to blast past Bosnich with seven minutes still remaining. Brian McClair came on as a replacement for Steve Bruce as United searched for an equaliser. It would have come had Bosnich not made a dramatic one-handed save from Hughes. The pressure continued but Daley led a counter attack and after striking a post Atkinson hit the rebound toward goal, Kanchelskis handling on the line. Keith Cooper had no option but to dismiss the winger. Saunders converted the spot kick to finally put the tie beyond United's reach.

While United were bidding for glory at Wembley Blackburn Rovers cut the lead at the top of the Premiership to three points making the midweek visit of Liverpool vital. It would be Cantona's last before his ban kicked in. The first game of that suspension would be the equally crucial clash between the top two at Ewood Park.

MANCHESTER UNITED 1 LIVERPOOL 0
PREMIERSHIP - 30 MARCH 1994

As THE NUMBER of suspensions continued to grow and confidence dipped, United knew the run-in had turned into a tense affair. A home fixture with Liverpool provided further frayed Old Trafford nerves. A United defeat would see the Reds go into the crunch tie with Blackburn Rovers without Eric Cantona and leave them three points ahead of the Lancashire outfit who had suffered a shock defeat to Wimbledon 24 hours earlier.

In the event United prevailed, even if they rode their luck when Andrei Kanchelskis hauled Michael Thomas down in the box. Referee Keith Hackett awarded a penalty but reversed his decision after seeing his linesman flag for offside. After a brief consultation to ensure the order of events, a free-kick was awarded to United.

Liverpool opened brightly, Michael Thomas and Neil Ruddock seeing early chances before Jamie Redknapp rippled the side netting. Those three efforts came before United had got going, when they did a tame effort from Eric Cantona failed to trouble David James. Eager to make an impact prior to a five game absence, Cantona pulled off the spectacular, including a back-heel which almost put Sharpe away. His next touch was to spray a ball out for Andrei Kanchelskis who seemed to have the beating of Ruddock before the defender thrust a leg out.

Redknapp forced Schmeichel into an athletic save while Mark Hughes looked bright at the other end but failed to get much service. Instead Liverpool's more measured pace set the dominant tone in the first 30 minutes. Rush missing a presentable chance before Peter Schmeichel flapped at McManaman's corner providing Ruddock with a gift he passed up from eight yards, Redknapp's effort from a tight angle only found the side netting a few minutes later.

Eight minutes before the interval United took the lead, Sharpe hustling Rob Jones into a poor lay off which forced James to push the ball wide. The initial corner was cleared but only at the expense of another inswinger which Paul Ince glanced in.

Liverpool improved in the second half, Redknapp forcing Schmeichel to scramble to his left, before John Barnes' deflected shot also brought the best out of the Dane. Liverpool left the United midfielders largely unattended as they continued to get the better of exchanges using the ball effectively but missing the killer finish. United countered down the wings - Kanchelskis and Sharpe made some headway but were stopped by Ruddock and then James. Kanchelskis shot just wide before Giggs missed a gilt edged chance to wrap matters up. Still with results all-important, few home fans left complaining.

ON THE EVENING of 10 April 1994 a little piece of history was made when the Professional Footballers' Association Awards honoured a foreigner as their Player of the Year for the first time. Eric Cantona was a worthy recipient and also became the first player to receive the award at the same time as serving a five-match suspension. Resplendent in bow tie and dinner jacket Cantona displayed a few nerves as he stooped to talk into the microphone.

"Thank you. I would like to thank Manchester United, my manager Alex Ferguson, my coach Brian Kidd, all the players – even those who did not vote for me – for giving me the pleasure to play in English football. Thank you."

Despite his recent problems he was an obvious choice, his performances in 1993-94 were sublime.

IN ERIC'S ABSENCE United had lost two league games, won another and beaten Oldham Athletic (after a replay) to reach the FA Cup Final. Defeat at Blackburn looked like a savage blow – a couple of goals from former transfer target Alan Shearer seeing Rovers move within three points of the lead. There followed three matches against Joe Royle's Oldham, United winning the home league game 3-2. They then trailed late in extra-time during the Wembley semi-final. A late, stunning Mark Hughes volley saved the day and United overran Latics in the Maine Road replay 4-1. That same weekend Blackburn drew level at the top with a win over Aston Villa. The Ewood Park side had played a game more but everything became equal after a 1-0 reverse at Wimbledon which marked the last of Eric Cantona's enforced five match lay off.

In their talisman's absence United looked no different to the side which had blown away their title chances in 1992, before his return to a sunlit Old Trafford for the derby.

MANCHESTER UNITED 2 MANCHESTER CITY 0
PREMIERSHIP – 23 APRIL 1994

ERIC CANTONA'S IMPECCABLE timing was to be a feature of his Old Trafford career and his return from suspension here in time for the 120th Manchester derby proved decisive to United's title fortunes. City, enjoying a seven game unbeaten run, were no match for the rejuvenated Reds who now held a three point advantage over Blackburn. The Lancashire side would play QPR 24 hours later. Cantona was one of three changes along with Lee Sharpe and Roy Keane. Brian McClair, Ryan Giggs and Bryan Robson made way.

Prior to the game Terry Phelan had suggested City's players

would try to wind Cantona up and the left back along with Steve McMahon were as good as their word but Eric simply walked away from intimidation. He teed up Andrei Kanchelskis, the Ukrainian winger's burst down the right drawing defenders before squaring for the Frenchman to tap in from no more than a few yards. A simple finish but a good goal nonetheless. Deep into first half injury time Hughes and Cantona exchanged passes. Once again Eric benefited, concluding a flowing move by sliding the ball past Andy Dibble.

Despite the hype both sides were keen to let the match be remembered for the football and the visitors were lively up front with Uwe Rosler and Paul Walsh a threat. Cantona was one of those front men eager to get back and assist. The numbers were needed as Peter Schmeichel was called upon although never stretched.

At 2-0 up flair replaced graft and the lead could have been extended. The best chance started with Cantona deep on the left and the ball worked along the flank with assistance from Kanchelskis and Hughes. Cantona took the ball back inside the penalty area and after selling two dummies laid on a chance for Kanchelskis who dwelt on the ball allowing City to clear.

Cantona seemed intense in all areas of the game and at one stage hurried back to dispossess Rosler in the United area. He also launched attacks from deep with one pass from left-back being a perfect 40 yard ball allowing Keane to burst through. The match was passionate and following the second goal settled into a tense but not seething midfield battle between Keane, Paul Ince, McMahon and David Rocastle. However, matters were fought out in the right sense of the word with bookings only picked up in the closing minutes. Cantona was shown a yellow card following a rash tackle on Rosler.

LEEDS UNITED 0 MANCHESTER UNITED 2
Premiership - 27 April 1994

With Blackburn held to a draw at home by QPR, this win at Leeds put United within touching distance of back-to-back titles. The Yorkshire side were without a win against one of their bitterest rivals in the last dozen attempts. At his old stomping ground Eric Cantona, the freshly named PFA Player of the Year, was for once little more than a support act to Mark Hughes.

Talk of trouble for Cantona's return proved to be hot air but there was still a vocal minority intent on attacking the Frenchman. A minder crossed the Pennines with the United team to ensure any threats of violence were not acted on. On the pitch Eric was closely watched by Chris Fairclough marshalling him as well as he had at Old Trafford earlier in the season.

Leeds had the first chance of a cagey affair 40 minutes in when Gary Speed beat Steve Bruce to a Gordon Strachan cross at the far post. Peter Schmeichel met the challenge of a solid header with a good if unspectacular save. Having slipped his marker Cantona had the first United chance holding off three defenders to meet a Denis Irwin cross. John Lukic matched his opposite number's dexterity, plucking a hooked volley out of the air.

The first goal arrived two minutes into the second half. Kanchelskis rounded off a move he started by sending Hughes charging down the left. David Wetherall was beaten on the edge of the penalty area and as Kanchelskis had kept pace with the Welshman he was able to convert. The match was rounded off six minutes from time with a second, this time Giggs supplying Hughes with the ball before racing for the return and converting ten yards out.

IPSWICH TOWN 1 MANCHESTER UNITED 2
PREMIERSHIP - 1 MAY 1994

DESPITE INCHING TO within a point of the title following this edgy win a blow was suffered with Peter Schmeichel now a doubt for the FA Cup final with ankle ligament damage. Alex Ferguson blamed a poor end of season pitch. Another injury to Ipswich's Phil Whelan, who broke an ankle with no one around him, supported his claim.

Relegation battlers Ipswich were expected to provide a stiff challenge and so it proved and despite a rare Schmeichel howler, United always had something to spare in East Anglia. A spilled Ian Marshall shot allowed Chris Kiwomya to gobble up the rebound from a couple of yards. Gary Walsh replaced Schmeichel on 28 minutes after a collision with the goalscorer.

An Andrei Kanchelskis cross allowed Eric Cantona to level at the far post just prior to the substitution and the match turned around very quickly. The hosts were pegged back for most of the time that remained. When Ryan Giggs prodded a Roy Keane cross in from the right at close range there seemed no way back. It could and possibly should have been more. Denis Irwin hit a post, while Kanchelskis, Steve Bruce and Mark Hughes could also have provided a more emphatic flourish as the Reds powered through the second half with Ipswich powerless to resist.

Within 24 hours United were crowned champions without kicking a ball when Blackburn were beaten 2-1 at Coventry City, it was United's first back-to-back title win since the Busby Babes double in 1955-56 and 1956-57.

MANCHESTER UNITED 2 SOUTHAMPTON 0
PREMIERSHIP - 4 MAY 1994

WITH THE PRESSURE off, the Reds seemed to lose some of their earlier drive. Eric Cantona missing four presentable opportunities, the first in the opening minute. Ryan Giggs fizzed his way past Jeff Kenna but Roy Keane saw his effort blocked, the ball falling to Cantona inside the six yard area but he fired wide. Eric looked bemused as to how he had managed to miss. Southampton's tactic of blocking off the wings worked for the most part but they were helpless on a number of occasions only for the profligacy of Hughes, Cantona and Keane to spare them.

The opener came just past the hour. A Denis Irwin pass from deep played Kanchelskis in and although Dave Beasant made a half block, the ball went through him and flew just inside the post. A Le Tissier free-kick almost levelled, Walsh making a sprawling save. The lead was only doubled during the closing minutes. A Hughes drive which powered in to the roof of the net gave the scoreline some gloss.

MANCHESTER UNITED 0 COVENTRY CITY 0
PREMIERSHIP - 8 MAY 1994

MANCHESTER UNITED PAID tribute to a talismanic figure's final game in a red shirt. Bryan Robson, who had accepted the post of player/manager at Middlesbrough, would qualify for another Premiership winners medal with this appearance and the setting for his farewell could not have been better.

On a glorious late spring day a capacity crowd paid its respects for 13 seasons endeavour. The club captain joining Steve Bruce to lift the Premiership trophy into a perfect blue sky after a seven day wait. It was the ideal preparation for the FA Cup final at Wembley despite the absence of seven players and a nil-nil scoreline. Youngsters Gary Neville (20) and Colin McKee (19) came in for their full debuts and linked well down the right flank. The pair set Dion Dublin up for what seemed to be a long awaited opener 20 minutes from time but the effort was ruled out for handball in the build-up. They also provided Cantona and Dublin with further opportunities but neither could take advantage.

Coventry, who had beaten Blackburn to confirm United's title, were given a good reception. Julian Darby, the scorer of the goals against Kenny Dalglish's side, came closest to breaking the deadlock with a shot which pinged off the angle of bar and post. Peter Ndlovu caused problems with a live wire performance.

Robson, who knew he had little hope of being selected for the cup final, could have rounded his Old Trafford career with a perfect finish and his 100th goal for the club two minutes from time. On taking the ball from Brian McClair on the right hand side of the area he shaped to test the keeper but his effort curled a yard wide. The club captain, who had been United's best player for well over a decade before the arrival of Cantona, left the team on top of the tree and with two league championship medals, a prospect that seemed unlikely just 18 months previously.

CHELSEA 0 MANCHESTER UNITED 4
FA CUP FINAL - 14 MAY 1994

HAVING DOMINATED THE league programme to such an extent that runners-up Blackburn Rovers trailed home eight points behind, United now attempted to become just the third team to complete the League and Cup double. The last time the Reds had such a gilt edged chance was 37 years previously when the title was captured but the cup final was lost to Aston Villa after keeper Ray Wood was forced to play on the wing following an horrific challenge from Peter McParland. Chelsea were not well fancied but were capable of pulling off an upset on the biggest stage.

Heavy rain and a greasy pitch threatened to disrupt an excellent passing side like United but under former England midfielder Glenn Hoddle, who named himself as a substitute, the Pensioners were equally slick. There was only one decision for Alex Ferguson to make relating to the dozen men he would like to call upon. Bryan Robson was omitted from not only the starting XI but the bench with Brian McClair handed the number 12 jersey.

A dull first half saw cautious Chelsea take control. Mark Stein and John Spencer proved dangerous and when Gavin Peacock struck the bar with a volley which beat Peter Schmeichel it seemed to wake United from their slumbers. The champions finally came into the game in the second half using their much heralded wingers to full effect. Denis Irwin and Paul Parker provided more support for Giggs and Kanchelskis who exploited the space.

A combination on the left between the pair led to a penalty following a clumsy Frank Sinclair challenge on Irwin. Eric Cantona, whose excellent record from 12 yards out was widely known, ignored Denis Wise's offer of a £100 wager to miss, before slotting calmly past Kharine. Chelsea, striving to get level immediately, were caught on the break six minutes later. Speed merchant Kanchelskis broke upfield before most defenders had a chance to react. With only Eddie Newton back an awkward attempt to win possession was punished by another penalty. There was a debate whether Newton had merely collided with him in a desperate attempt to prevent a shot being unleashed. The linesman seemed unmoved but referee David Elleray was adamant over the issue. All the furore was of little consequence to Cantona who produced a carbon copy of his first penalty to double the lead.

Minutes later United made sure of the cup when the hapless Newton misjudged the ball allowing Mark Hughes to take possession and fire past Kharine from the edge of the area. Chelsea's pluck was still evident but their pressure yielded few rewards and no goals. United were happy to play out time but in the last minute another break saw Paul Ince advance on Kharine. He could have gone for glory but squared for McClair to prod into an empty goal.

1993-94

Following a first championship in almost three decades and now a league and cup double United, from looking like perpetual bridesmaids just 18 months before, took their place among the greats of the English game. The decisive factor had to be Eric Cantona, a player central to United's approach, as demonstrated by the poor results suffered during his lengthy suspension.

Nevertheless United's pursuit of Roy Keane as a direct replacement for Bryan Robson was equally vital to their double success. Following Nottingham Forest's relegation from the top flight and the departure of legendary manager Brian Clough, they were unable to resist United's bid. Clough had publicly stated that the player had sought high wages during his last contract negotiations and that a clause allowing him to move on in the event of relegation had been inserted. All the top clubs were circling around the midfielder and it seemed big spending Blackburn Rovers had got in first after agreeing a record £4 million fee and personal terms. That was until an intervention from Old Trafford just a day before he was due to sign, Ferguson getting his man for £3.75m. An understanding with Ince seemed instant and a couple of goals on his debut plus the winner in the Manchester derby was a start few could match. Keane certainly seemed to have no regrets about his choice during the summer.

For Eric Cantona, the virtuoso skills which had earned him the PFA Player of the Year award also saw a return of the petulance that had always been a factor in his career. The ban which ensued enabled Eric to recharge his batteries and return with a bang against Manchester City to put United's title bid back on track. Nevertheless, Eric's contribution wasn't all about swashbuckling play, there were plenty of battling performances and his commitment to defence was a feature throughout. Faced with similar tests, the Ewood Park side crumbled when they had the chance.

An FA Cup win rounded the season off with Cantona scoring twice from the spot. Resplendent in a red and white wig he was pictured kissing the cup and on the back pages of every paper in Britain as the Wembley hero. At Wembley or elsewhere Eric was a catalyst for moves bringing everyone into play and he was often the first man his colleagues would look for. He really did make United tick and was the reason they were now head and shoulders the best team in the country.

Whether it be a short pass, long ball, quick one-two, a brief touch, a pause for thought or just a flash of genius Cantona instinctively seemed to be one step ahead. He was also a joy for United's trio of pacy wingers – Giggs (17 goals), Kanchelskis (11) and Sharpe (10) were always a threat on the break and Cantona's habit of finding them in space proved critical. Cantona, with 25 goals from 49 games in league and cup competitions, was the club's top scorer which was some achievement when one considers he played in a withdrawn role. Mark Hughes was just four behind his teammate.

The sole disappointment was the team's early exit from Europe at the hands of unfancied Galatasaray. While it's true that UEFA's foreigner rule restricted United's ability in the Champions League, there could be few excuses for underestimating the talented Turks, especially as they were 2-0 up during the home leg.

Besides his PFA award, Eric had also been named as France's international captain. This was some turnaround from the time just a few years ago when he had walked out on Marseilles and Nimes following disagreements. Unfortunately he would also be absent from the World Cup, France taking part in the Kirin Cup alongside Australia and hosts Japan instead. Les Bleus met the Socceroos for the first time in Kobe, Eric scoring the only goal, a looping header, just before half-time. France won the Kirin Cup after a heavy defeat of Japan and topped the three team table with a 100% record. Japan and Australia drew their head to head meaning the trophy was won by five points.

MANCHESTER UNITED - PREMIER LEAGUE 1993-94

DATE	OPPONENT	VENUE	SCORE	ATTD	1	2	3	4	5	6	7	8	9	10	11	SUBSTITUTES
28-Aug-93	Southampton	The Dell	3-1	16,189	Schmeichel	Parker	Irwin[1]	Bruce	Sharpe[1]	Pallister	Cantona[1]	Ince	Keane	Hughes	Giggs	McClair (Giggs) Kanchelskis (Keane)
01-Sep-93	West Ham	Old Trafford	3-0	44,613	Schmeichel	Parker	Irwin	Bruce[1]	Sharpe[1]	Pallister	Cantona[1]	Ince	Keane	Kan'skis	Giggs	Robosn (Kanchelskis) McClair (Ince)
11-Sep-93	Chelsea	Stamford Bg	0-1	37,064	Schmeichel	Parker	Irwin	Bruce	Sharpe	Pallister	Cantona	Ince	Keane	Robson	Giggs	McClair (Robson)
19-Sep-93	Arsenal	Old Trafford	1-0	44,009	Schmeichel	Parker	Irwin	Bruce	Sharpe	Pallister	Cantona[1]	Ince	Keane	Hughes	Giggs	McClair (Hughes)
25-Sep-93	Swindon Town	Old Trafford	4-2	44,583	Schmeichel	Parker	Irwin	Bruce	Sharpe	Pallister	Cantona[1]	Ince	Keane	Hughes[2]	Kan'skis[1]	McClair (Sharpe) Giggs (Kanchelskis)
02-Oct-93	Sheffield Wed	Hillsborough	3-2	34,548	Schmeichel	Parker	Irwin	Bruce	Sharpe	Pallister	Cantona	Ince	Keane	Hughes[2]	Giggs[1]	Kan'skis (Giggs)
16-Oct-93	Tottenham H	Old Trafford	2-1	44,655	Schmeichel	Parker	Irwin	Bruce	Sharpe[1]	Pallister	Cantona	Robson	Keane[1]	Hughes	Giggs	McClair (Robson)
23-Oct-93	Everton	Goodison Pk	1-0	35,455	Schmeichel	Martin	Irwin	Bruce	Sharpe[1]	Pallister	Cantona	Ince	McClair	Hughes	Keane	
30-Oct-93	QPR	Old Trafford	2-1	44,663	Schmeichel	Parker	Irwin	Bruce	Sharpe	Phelan	Cantona[1]	Ince	Keane	Hughes[1]	Giggs	
07-Nov-93	Manchester C	Maine Road	3-2	35,155	Schmeichel	Parker	Irwin	Bruce	Sharpe	Pallister	Cantona[2]	Ince	Keane[1]	Hughes	Kan'skis	Giggs (Kanchelskis)
20-Nov-93	Wimbledon	Old Trafford	3-1	44,748	Schmeichel	Parker	Irwin	Bruce	Sharpe	Pallister[1]	Cantona	Ince	Robson	Hughes[2]	Kan'skis[1]	Phelan (Robson)
24-Nov-93	Ipswich Town	Old Trafford	0-0	43,300	Schmeichel	Parker	Irwin	Bruce	Sharpe	Pallister	Cantona	Ince	Robson	Hughes	Kan'skis	Giggs (Kanchelskis) Ferguson (Robson)
27-Nov-93	Coventry City	Highfield Rd	1-0	17,009	Schmeichel	Parker	Irwin	Bruce	Sharpe	Pallister	Cantona[1]	Ince	Ferguson	Hughes	Giggs	Sharpe (Hughes)
04-Dec-93	Norwich City	Old Trafford	2-2	44,694	Schmeichel	Parker	Irwin	Bruce	Kan'skis	Pallister	Cantona	Ince	McClair[1]	Hughes	Giggs[1]	Keane (McClair)
07-Dec-93	Sheffield Utd	Bramall Ln	3-0	26,744	Schmeichel	Parker	Irwin	Bruce	Sharpe[1]	Pallister	Cantona[1]	Ince	McClair	Hughes[2]	Giggs	Kanchelskis (Hughes) Keane (McClair)
11-Dec-93	Newcastle Utd	St James	1-1	36,332	Schmeichel	Parker	Irwin	Bruce	Sharpe	Pallister	Cantona[1]	Ince[1]	McClair	Hughes	Kan'skis	Giggs (Sharpe)
19-Dec-93	Aston Villa	Old Trafford	3-1	44,499	Schmeichel	Parker	Irwin	Bruce	Sharpe	Pallister	Cantona[1]	Ince[1]	Keane	Hughes	Giggs	McClair (Parker) Ferguson (Hughes)
26-Dec-93	Blackburn Rvrs	Old Trafford	1-1	44,511	Schmeichel	Parker	Irwin	Bruce	Sharpe	Pallister	Cantona[1]	Ince	Keane	Hughes	Giggs	McClair (Cantona) Robson (Ince)
29-Dec-93	Oldham Athletic	Boundary Pk	5-2	16,708	Schmeichel	Parker	Irwin	Bruce[1]	Sharpe	Pallister	Cantona[1]	Ince	Keane	Kan'skis[1]	Giggs[2]	
01-Jan-94	Leeds United	Old Trafford	0-0	44,724	Schmeichel	Parker	Irwin	Bruce	Robson	Pallister	Cantona	Keane	McClair	Kan'skis	Giggs	
04-Jan-94	Liverpool	Anfield	3-3	42,795	Schmeichel	Parker	Irwin[1]	Bruce[1]	Keane	Pallister	Cantona	Ince	McClair	Kan'skis	Giggs[1]	
15-Jan-94	Tottenham H	Wt Hart Ln	1-0	31,343	Schmeichel	Parker	Irwin	Bruce	Kan'skis	Pallister	Cantona	Ince	Keane	Hughes[2]	Giggs	McClair (Hughes)
22-Jan-94	Everton	Old Trafford	1-0	44,750	Schmeichel	Parker	Irwin	Bruce	Kan'skis	Pallister	Cantona	Ince	Keane	Hughes	Giggs[1]	
05-Feb-94	QPR	Loftus Road	3-2	21,267	Schmeichel	Parker	Irwin	Bruce	Kan'skis[1]	Pallister	Cantona[1]	Ince	McClair	Hughes[2]	Giggs[1]	
26-Feb-94	West Ham	Upton Park	2-2	28,832	Schmeichel	Parker	Irwin	Bruce	Kan'skis	Pallister	Cantona[1]	Ince[1]	McClair	Hughes[2]	Keane	
16-Mar-94	Sheffield Wed	Old Trafford	5-0	43,669	Schmeichel	Parker	Irwin	Bruce	Kan'skis	Pallister	Cantona[2]	Ince[1]	Keane	Hughes[2]	Giggs[1]	McClair (Giggs) Robson (Kanchelskis)
19-Mar-94	Swindon Town	County Gd	2-2	18,102	Schmeichel	Parker	Irwin	Bruce	Keane[1]	Pallister	Cantona	Ince[1]	McClair	Hughes	Giggs	

Date	Opposition	Venue	Score	Att.	1	2	3	4	5	6	7	8	9	10	11	Subs / Scorers
22-Mar-94	Arsenal	Highbury	2-2	36,203	Schmeichel	Parker	Irwin	Bruce	Sharpe[2]	Pallister	Cantona	Ince	Keane	Hughes	Giggs	Robson (Sharpe)
30-Mar-94	Liverpool	Old Trafford	1-0	44,751	Schmeichel	Parker	Irwin	Bruce	Sharpe	Pallister	Cantona	Ince[1]	Keane	Hughes	Giggs	Giggs (Sharpe) Robson (Cantona)
23-Apr-94	Manchester C	Old Trafford	2-0	44,333	Schmeichel	Parker	Irwin	Bruce	Sharpe	Pallister	Cantona[2]	Ince	Keane	Hughes	Kan'skis	Giggs (Sharpe)
27-Apr-94	Leeds United	Elland Road	2-0	41,127	Schmeichel	Parker	Irwin	Bruce	Kan'skis[1]	Pallister	Cantona	Ince	Keane	Hughes	Giggs[1]	
01-May-94	Ipswich Town	Portman Rd	2-1	22,478	Schmeichel	Parker	Irwin	Bruce	Kan'skis	Pallister	Cantona[1]	Ince	Keane	Hughes	Giggs[1]	Walsh (Schmeichel) Sharpe (Giggs)
04-May-94	Southampton	Old Trafford	2-0	44,705	Walsh	Parker	Parker	Irwin	Keane	Sharpe	Pallister	Cantona	Ince	Kan'skis[1]	Hughes[1]	Giggs
08-May-94	Coventry City	Old Trafford	0-0	44,717	Walsh	Parker	Neville G	Irwin	Bruce	Sharpe	Pallister	Cantona	Robson	McKee	Dublin	McClair
FA CUP																
09-Jan-94	Sheffield Utd	Bramall Ln	1-0	22,019	Schmeichel	Parker	Irwin	Bruce	Kan'skis	Pallister	Cantona	Ince	Keane	Hughes[2]	Giggs	McClair (Hughes)
30-Jan-94	Norwich City	Carrow Rd	2-0	21,060	Schmeichel	Parker	Irwin	Bruce	Kan'skis	Pallister	Cantona[1]	Ince	Keane[1]	Hughes	Giggs	McClair (Hughes) Dublin (Cantona)
20-Feb-94	Wimbledon	Selhurst Pk	3-0	27,511	Schmeichel	Parker	Irwin[1]	Bruce	Kan'skis	Pallister	Cantona[1]	Ince[1]	Keane	Hughes	Giggs	Sealey (Parker)
12-Mar-94	Charlton Ath	Old Trafford	3-1	44,347	Schmeichel	Parker	Irwin	Bruce	Kan'skis[2]	Pallister	Cantona	Ince	Keane	Hughes[2]	Giggs	McClair[1] (Kanchelskis) Sharpe (Irwin)
14-May-94	Chelsea	Wembley	4-0	79,634	Schmeichel	Parker	Irwin	Bruce	Kan'skis	Pallister	Cantona[2]	Ince	Keane	Hughes[2]	Giggs	
LEAGUE CUP																
30-Nov-93	Everton	Goodison Pk	2-0	34,052	Schmeichel	Parker	Irwin	Bruce	Kan'skis	Pallister	Cantona	Ince	Robson	Hughes[2]	Giggs[1]	Ferguson (Robson)
12-Dec-93	Portsmouth	Old Trafford	2-2	43,794	Schmeichel	Parker	Irwin	Bruce	Kan'skis	Pallister	Cantona[1]	Robson	McClair	Hughes	Giggs[1]	Keane (Hughes) Dublin (McClair)
26-Jan-94	Portsmouth	Fratton Park	1-0	24,950	Schmeichel	Parker	Irwin	Bruce	Kan'skis	Pallister	Cantona	Ince	Keane	McClair[1]	Giggs[1]	
13-Feb-94	Sheffield Wed	Old Trafford	1-0	43,294	Schmeichel	Parker	Irwin	Bruce	Kan'skis	Pallister	Cantona	Ince	Keane	Hughes	Giggs[1]	
27-Mar-94	Aston Villa	Wembley	1-3	77,231	Sealey	Parker	Irwin	Bruce	Kan'skis	Pallister	Cantona	Ince	Keane	Hughes[1]	Giggs	
CHAMPIONS LEAGUE																
15-Sep-93	Honved	Bozsik Stad	3-2	9,000	Schmeichel	Parker	Irwin	Bruce	Sharpe	Pallister	Robson	Ince	Cantona[1]	Keane[2]	Giggs	Phelan (Giggs)
29-Sep-93	Honved	Old Trafford	2-1	35,781	Schmeichel	Parker	Irwin	Bruce[2]	Sharpe	Pallister	Robson	Ince	Cantona	Hughes	Giggs	Martin (Irwin) Phelan (Ince)
20-Oct-93	Galatasary	Old Trafford	3-3	39,346	Schmeichel	Martin	Sharpe	Bruce	Keane	Pallister	Robson[1]	Ince	Cantona[1]	Hughes	Giggs	Phelan (Robson) Hakan o/g[1]
03-Nov-93	Galatasary	Ali Sami Yen	0-0	40,000	Schmeichel	Parker	Irwin	Bruce	Sharpe	Phelan	Robson	Ince	Cantona	Keane	Giggs	

RECKLESS ERIC

BLACKBURN ROVERS 0 MANCHESTER UNITED 2
CHARITY SHIELD - 14 AUGUST 1994

BLACKBURN, WEAKENED BY illness and injury, counted Alan Shearer among their casualties, the striker having fallen victim to food poisoning contracted from a Portuguese seafood cocktail. Also absent were David Batty, Kevin Gallacher, Mike Newell, Paul Warhurst and new £5 million signing Chris Sutton meaning that Kenny Dalglish was unable to call on £16 million worth of talent.

Just as it had in the Reds' last visit to Wembley, an Eric Cantona penalty set United on the way to victory. Ince grabbing a well deserved goal late on to settle matters. New FIFA edicts about tackles gave referee Philip Don plenty of work with seven bookings made - four to Blackburn - yet the game was never as unsporting as the number of cautions suggested. Ironically one of the players who should have found himself protected by the new laws on tackling, Ryan Giggs, was the first to be cautioned. From then on the standard was set and anything remotely dangerous was punished.

Blackburn may have enjoyed at least a share of the spoils if their finishing had been more clinical and, for all his flicks and tricks, Eric Cantona was below par. Only a handful of his efforts came off. Though that didn't stop the United fans present standing and singing his name. With a Premiership and Champions League ban ruling him out until the end of August it would be their only chance to venerate the Frenchman for a few weeks.

United took the lead from the spot. A Cantona ball into the area was latched onto by Ince, Colin Hendry's leg felling the midfielder. Cantona's finish from the penalty was definitive. Ten minutes from the end a corner was only cleared as far as Cantona who headed back across goal for Ince to hit a spectacular overhead kick to wrap things up.

MANCHESTER UNITED 3 WIMBLEDON 0
PREMIERSHIP - 31 AUGUST 1994

ERIC CANTONA RETURNED to the first team following his three match ban during which United had beaten QPR at home (2-0) and Spurs away (1-0) but were held to a draw at Nottingham Forest (1-1). Alex Ferguson confessed he felt the team had been missing that vital something without him and it didn't take Eric long to remind Old Trafford of his importance as his goal five minutes from half-time helped break Wimbledon's spirited resistance.

Cantona's perplexed the visitors, as he ghosted past defenders in a roving brief. From almost every deep lying position of the field he peppered the ball at the Wimbledon backline. The only surprise was that it took so long for the ball to hit the net again.

With less than 10 minutes left and the visitors threatening a comeback a Vinnie Jones error allowed Brian McClair to blast in from distance. Soon after Giggs got himself into a closer position after an exchange of passes with Mark Hughes to add a third. Alex Ferguson's praise afterwards was deserved, "Eric at his brilliant best is a calming influence for us. He gives us an extra dimension and has an aura that all great players possess."

THAT EXTRA DIMENSION was also present with France who got their qualifiers for Euro 96 underway against Slovakia in Bratislava. This was an international tournament Cantona valued highly with the finals due to take place in England. He would not tolerate anything that distracted his team from success and that included the press. As a result the French media were not supportive of their captain. They saw his actions and comments as an attempt to marginalise their role especially when Cantona told reporters he expected to see them around the squad no more than a couple of times, informing them: "If it was up to me I would shit on you."

FFF President Claude Simonet decided not to show much support when asked for a reply saying: "I regret his attitude and some of his comments which were out of place. I will have to have a meeting and talk with Eric." Simonet also suggested Cantona only got the role of on-field leader as no one else wanted it and added to the insult by commenting, "Eric certainly deserves the captaincy as far as talent goes but I'm not sure about his cultural knowledge."

Cantona's reply was somewhat pithy but left no room for

doubt about his intent, "I don't care what Simonet says. Whether a president is good or not has no influence on the game." Whether this disagreement had much impact on the team's 0-0 draw with Slovakia is hard to say but it was a disappointing start nevertheless.

LEEDS UNITED 2 MANCHESTER UNITED 1
PREMIERSHIP - 11 SEPTEMBER 1994

FOR ALL THE criticism Howard Wilkinson had endured throughout his career over the style his teams adopted, his judgements were usually sound and a perceived weakness at right back, where David May was standing in for the injured Paul Parker, was exploited to perfection here. Leeds probed the left wing often and could have gone ahead well before finally taking the lead when David White's corner was missed by Gary Speed and somehow fell for David Wetherall whose bobbling shot beat Peter Schmeichel.

Ryan Giggs had a great chance to level soon after courtesy of an elegant lobbed pass from Cantona but John Lukic anticipated well. The real thrust behind Leeds attacks came from Gary McAllister and Speed who out-battled Paul Ince and Brian McClair. United missed Roy Keane's ability to dictate the pace and direction of the game while Giggs and Kanchelskis failed to spark. Cantona, full of flair as usual, seemed to be on a different wavelength to his colleagues, although one glorious chance was created by the French international after he juggled a difficult pass from Pallister between his feet, evaded Carlton Palmer's challenge with a quick change of balance but shot wide. The ugly side of Eric's game crept in a little later and he was lucky not to at least be cautioned for a two-footed lunge at McAllister.

Substitute Brian Deane could have increased the lead just before the break but spooned over. However the striker made up for his weak finish within a few minutes of the resumption. Whelan beat May and Pallister before squaring for the striker to force the ball in from a few yards out. The double substitution of McClair and Giggs for Nicky Butt and Lee Sharpe for the final 27 minutes helped maintain pressure. But the penalty which gave Cantona a chance to pull one back owed something to David Elleray's generosity. The Harrow schoolmaster held that a foul by Deane on Ince was inside the box when replays suggested otherwise. Cantona, ignoring the predictable abuse, made no mistake. The closing stages were far more tense than anticipated and Leeds were grateful that Mark Hughes volleyed over and Bruce missed a good headed chance in injury time.

MANCHESTER UNITED 2 LIVERPOOL 0
PREMIERSHIP - 17 SEPTEMBER 1994

ERIC CANTONA RETURNED after his midweek European suspension that saw United begin their Champions League campaign with a 4-2 home win over Gothenburg, Yet it was Paul Ince who proved the difference between the sides as United and Liverpool served up one of their better encounters of recent years. The game looked destined to be a draw until John Scales' back header to Liverpool keeper David James fell short allowing Andrei Kanchelskis to get a toe on the ball and lob the prone keeper.

The visitors based much of their attacks from the wings with Steve McManaman a constant threat causing Denis Irwin and David May all manner of problems. John Barnes and Jan Molby marshalled Liverpool's fluid passing which stretched Bruce and Pallister who were grateful to the excellence of Peter Schmeichel. One particular save from a Neil Ruddock header looked unspectacular but relied on finely honed instinct. Stig Inge Bjornebye and McManaman also tested the stopper. At the other end James was far less stretched. Only an effort from Cantona looked likely to cause any trouble. Sharpe, Ince and Giggs had presentable opportunities but made nothing of them.

Once Molby was replaced by debutant Phil Babb Liverpool's thrusts became less frequent but the move was prompted by Alex Ferguson throwing Brian McClair on to act as a link between midfield and attack. Mark Hughes made way allowing Cantona, who had only shown occasional glimpses of his class, to push up and unsettle the Liverpool backline.

The United manager had little choice. His team were on the rack and looked close to slipping behind. Babb, English football's costliest defender, looked uncomfortable in midfield. Following the Scales slip Liverpool had to chase the game and left gaps which United exploited. Brian McClair worked a neat interchange of passes with Cantona a few minutes later to double the lead.

Cantona was booked for a two footed challenge on Ruddock. The centre-back, who had tampered with Eric's upturned collars, was fouled at the first available opportunity afterwards. Gestures regarding waistline were deemed suitable retribution for the cockney's sartorial interference. The Bury St Edmunds official waved a yellow card but it could so easily have been red and would have triggered Cantona's second three game ban of the season.

IPSWICH TOWN 3 MANCHESTER UNITED 2
PREMIERSHIP - 24 SEPTEMBER 1994

UNITED WERE IN such disarray at half-time at Portman Road that Alex Ferguson had to totally rethink his tactics and formation. There had been wholesale changes from the side which had beaten Port Vale in the Coca-Cola Cup during midweek. Ipswich had lost in the same competition fielding the best XI John Lyall had available to him.

Each of the Old Trafford big guns were back including Roy Keane who was able to start his first match of the season. United were expected to beat struggling Ipswich Town but the home side ran rampant and led courtesy of a Paul Mason brace - he converted a Claus Thomsen cross before a side-step and shot doubled the lead.

The Ipswich goals had been punctuated by a Giggs header which Forrest put over but otherwise United struggled to compete. Ferguson re-organised at half-time, switching Keane to right back following a testy first half during which the Irishman was lucky not to be dismissed following a studs-up lunge at Palmer. Now Keane retained his cool and helped keep Ipswich at bay while his overlapping sent in crosses for Eric Cantona and Paul Scholes to convert within a couple of minutes of one another.

Having gained parity United were favourites to finish off the job yet the hosts grabbed the winner with ten minutes left. Steve Sedgely netting a low Frank Yallop cross to give his side a first home win since February.

MANCHESTER UNITED 2 EVERTON 0
PREMIERSHIP - 1 OCTOBER 1994

EVERTON CAME TO Old Trafford rock bottom of the table. As a result under pressure manager Mike Walker played Daniel Amokachi as a lone striker and strung five across midfield. It worked for most of the first half and Eric Cantona was kept quiet by Joe Parkinson's attentive marking. But United, as ever, found joy on the flanks and it was Lee Sharpe's burst down the left that set up Andrei Kanchelskis who nodded home at the far post.

United rarely touched the heights here. Cantona's contribution may have been more subdued than usual but he provided more angles than any of his team-mates had in that week's goalless draw with Galatasaray. Roy Keane and Paul Ince toiled to gain control in midfield but frequently found themselves outnumbered.

Everton, in dire need of a point, relied on Vinny Samways and Graham Stuart to support Amokachi and had it not been for the excellence of Peter Schmeichel, who denied Andy Hincliffe twice and Stuart from free-kicks, they may have earned a point. Fittingly it was Sharpe who had the last word, scuffing in a shot from close range two minutes from time after an Ince throw in. It continued a sorry tale of woe for the Merseysiders who now stood two points adrift of the field and without a Premiership win all season.

An INTERNATIONAL BREAK saw Old Trafford players disappear to various points of the continent. Cantona would be in Saint Etienne where his side faced Romania in a Euro 96 qualifier. The Stade Geoffroy-Guichard had not hosted an international since 1984 and though this match ended goalless there was plenty to admire in some aspects of play - mostly those Cantona was involved in which revolved around slick passing and movement. Unfortunately the remainder of the team were little more than average. The French papers laid into the team and captain afterwards and pulled few punches.

MANCHESTER UNITED 1 WEST HAM UNITED 0
PREMIERSHIP - 15 OCTOBER 1994

THERE WAS A worry that Eric Cantona was going off the boil due to his European ban. Alex Ferguson may have been tempted to play him in the shadow team fielded for the 2nd leg of the League Cup tie with Port Vale but his call up for France ruled him out of that game and the league defeat at Sheffield Wednesday three days later. A midweek meeting with Barcelona in the European Cup was thought to be taking up the thoughts of many United players. Yet Cantona, still banned from Europe, didn't have this excuse and without him few doubted that United would have failed to win all three points.

West Ham copied recent visitors to Old Trafford by packing midfield. As a result the Hammers showed little ambition. Cantona's deft touches allied to Paul Ince's presence at the heart of midfield meant that although United bossed the game the visitors' goal was rarely threatened until Alvin Martin's intervention near half-time. A Kanchelskis cross was not cleared by the Scouser who thought he had heard a call and allowed the ball to run. Giggs took possession at the near post and found Cantona who steered home from four yards.

Some of the finishing which followed didn't do justice to the build-up play. Cantona sent a soft shot wide from a good position and Giggs struck a post after surging through the Hammers resistance. At the other end Martin Allen set up Cottee, Joe Moncur and Matthew Rush for chances that were wasted. Barcelona assistant coach Bruins Slot, watching in the stands, was no doubt relieved Cantona would not play in the Champions League game on Wednesday at Old Trafford.

BLACKBURN ROVERS 2 MANCHESTER UNITED 4
PREMIERSHIP - 23 OCTOBER 1994

DESPITE PLAYING WELL, United were held to a draw courtesy of a late Lee Sharpe back-heel against Barcelona. United looked leggy following their European exploits, until they were dealt a helping hand by referee Gerald Ashby.

The Reds had fallen behind when Paul Warhurst chipped the ball over Peter Schmeichel from 30 yards following an attempted clearance from a Graeme Le Saux free-kick. The Dane's punch landed straight at the feet of the midfielder who executed the shot perfectly. Blackburn looked confident that they could add to their lead and with Warhurst and Alan Shearer going close plus Gary Pallister nearly putting through his own goal the home side were well on top until Mr Ashby intervened on the stroke of half-time.

The official had booked Henning Berg ten minutes earlier and when he judged that the Norwegian had fouled Sharpe in the area he awarded a penalty, giving Berg his marching orders. There was some doubt over whether either decision was correct but Cantona had no qualms and coolly dispatched the spot-kick. Blackburn had little choice but to abandon their attacking ambitions and withdrew forward Chris Sutton into defence and Warhurst to right back. Yet the home side re-took the lead just six minutes after the resumption - Colin Hendry heading home a Jason Wilcox centre.

However, the Scot was called into action minutes later and, though he did his best to cut out a testing Andrei Kanchelskis cross he could only divert the ball back into the Ukrainian's path who drilled it past Tim Flowers to level. With the best part of 40 minutes left the Reds looked to land the knock-out blow. Paul Ince took total control and a slip by Le Saux, who tried to find Hendry rather clear the ball, allowed Mark Hughes behind the backline. From an acute angle the Welshman sent a delicate lob over Flowers. Blackburn pushed hard for an equaliser and only the agility of Schmeichel denied Stuart

Ripley. United made the game safe eight minutes from time, a break from a rare Blackburn corner saw Kanchelskis race 50 yards before rounding Flowers and sliding the ball through Wilcox's legs. Earlier in the day Eric Cantona had been announced as one of the faces that would be used to advertise Euro 96 ticket sales.

MANCHESTER UNITED 2 NEWCASTLE UNITED 0
PREMIERSHIP - 29 OCTOBER 1994

VICTORY AT EWOOD Park pulled the Reds to within seven points of Premiership leaders Newcastle United and this game represented a chance to narrow the gap further. In between those two league games United had played the Magpies in the 3rd round of the Coca-Cola Cup at St James Park. Alex Ferguson's inexperienced side going down 2-0 to a full strength home team.

The tables were turned in the league encounter as Newcastle had their 18 game unbeaten run brought to a shuddering halt. United became the first side to stop the Magpies scoring that season although first choice strike partners Andy Cole and Paul Kitson were missing. Despite their absence Kevin Keegan refused to be cautious but for all the excellent approach play of Peter Beardsley and Rob Lee there was no one capable of providing a finish.

Newcastle started brightly, Philippe Albert blasting a chance wide before Beardsley and Lee were denied by Schmeichel. United were just as creative with Paul Ince loading the bullets for Eric Cantona and Andrei Kanchelskis. Yet it was a set-piece which gave United the 11th minute lead. Steve Watson brought Ince to ground on the left and from the resulting free-kick Ryan Giggs found Pallister just six yards out.

Newcastle had a couple of chances to level prior to the break. Scott Sellars had a shot blocked before he mis-timed a volley that went wide of the left post. Pavel Srnicek repelled Kanchelskis, Giggs and Hughes before denying the Welsh striker again with an outstanding reflex save. Keith Gillespie, one of those promising youngsters granted a chance in midweek, replaced Giggs ten minutes before netting his first league goal. The 19 year-old took a pass from Cantona, cut inside Watson and Steve Howey before hitting a low shot from the edge of the area that beat Srnicek's left hand to settle matters.

ASTON VILLA 1 MANCHESTER UNITED 2
PREMIERSHIP - 6 NOVEMBER 1994

UNITED, SHELL-SHOCKED by Barcelona's bravura 4-0 performance at the Nou Camp in midweek, got back on track immediately with a fine win at Villa Park. Forced to play without Cantona in Spain, United, who also had to field a nervous Gary Walsh in goal against the likes of Romario and Stoichkov, returned to full strength here. Schmeichel was still out, meaning Walsh could make amends for the previous Wednesday and with just under a minute on the clock he blocked a poor backpass but could only knock the ball to the feet of Steve Staunton who missed the target.

There was little fluency about the visitors, especially in midfield where players stood around once possession was lost. Eric Cantona was as guilty as anyone for that lax attitude. Villa sensed their chance and a Dalian Atkinson long range shot ended up in the net after Steve Bruce's toe diverted it over Walsh's head. Own goals were swiftly becoming the keeper's bugbear but he did at least do his confidence no harm with a fine save from Staunton's drive.

Villa switched off minutes from half-time - an Andrei Kanchelskis cross headed out by Ehiogu saw Andy Townsend hesitate. The ball ran away from the Republic of Ireland international allowing Ince to lash an effort past Nigel Spink. Within six minutes of the second half the Reds hit the front, Denis Irwin's cross from the left was dummied by Cantona, Kanchelskis shot flying through Phil King's legs and past the unsighted Spink.

Walsh made a fingertip save from Dwight Yorke and was relieved when Referee Philip Don ruled that Paul McGrath hadn't been impeded when Bruce put an arm across his chest late on.

MANCHESTER UNITED 5 MANCHESTER CITY 0
PREMIERSHIP - 10 NOVEMBER 1994

THE SKETCHY PERFORMANCES leading up to this game were forgotten in the Manchester Derby with United registering their biggest margin of victory in the past 121 fixtures and exacting sweet revenge for one of their most infamous defeats just five years earlier. Victory was built on the towering midfield presence of Paul Ince who drove his side forward allowing Eric Cantona and Andrei Kanchelskis to test on-loan keeper Simon Tracey. Rocked by the absences of Tony Coton, Andy Dibble and Keith Curle, City were on the back foot from the start.

Cantona opened the scoring with a finish which bordered on arrogance. The ball from Kanchelskis was inch perfect but Cantona flicked it in to his own path with his heel then blasted in. Tracey did well to deny Roy Keane, enjoying an extended run at right back, when he met a Cantona pass sweetly, City's stand-in producing a fine save. Eric set up the second a few minutes before the interval, Ian Brightwell and Terry Phelan backed off allowing the French international to saunter past them before finding Kanchelskis whose shot deflected off Phelan's heels.

Two minutes after the break a back header from Cantona fell to Kanchelskis who hit Tracey with his initial shot but was able to gather the rebound and make no mistake. Peter Schmeichel had little to do, City enjoyed few chances though Gary Pallister managed to deflect a Paul Walsh effort over the bar. It took until the 70th minute for United to add a fourth. Keane's searching cross saw Michel Vonk outmuscle Mark Hughes but fail to clear, the Welshman was on to the loose ball first and lashed home.

Cantona and Kanchelskis rounded off the scoring two minutes from time with another rapier like move after City had lost possession deep inside United territory. Within seconds the ball was at the other end, Eric cut inside and squared for Kanschelskis who completed his hat-trick when the rebound ran kindly.

FRANCE WERE HELD to a third successive goalless draw in Euro 96 qualification against Poland. The media soon turned on the team, particularly its captain. This time League President Noel Le Graet told journalists: "There are doubts over whether Eric will remain as captain or even retain his place."

Meanwhile manager Aimé Jacquet said he felt his skipper was disappointing. From that point on the dye was effectively cast. At some stage Eric Cantona's international career would come to an end and it came quicker than expected. The events of January 1995 provided the excuse needed. Just before Christmas France met Azerbaijan in Trabzon, Turkey. Due to security issues all Armenia's qualifiers were staged there and just 4,000 spectators turned up to witness John-Pierre Papin and Patrice Loko score goals in either half. It was a win which took some heat out of the campaign but it met with further fault finding.

Just seven days before Manchester United were due to take on

Crystal Palace at Selhurst Park France journeyed to Utrecht for a friendly with the Netherlands. It was a patchy game won by a Loko strike. It was the 45th and last time Eric Cantona wore his country's colours.

MANCHESTER UNITED 3 CRYSTAL PALACE 0
PREMIERSHIP - 19 NOVEMBER 1994

VICTORY OVER MANCHESTER City had drawn United to within a couple of points of the summit and another win combined with Newcastle's defeat at Wimbledon edged them ahead of Blackburn Rovers who registered a convincing win at Ipswich. Even the loss of Peter Schmeichel after just eight minutes failed to disrupt United. Eric Cantona, his European ban now expired, marshalled this victory over Palace just in time, it was hoped, to resurrect the Reds ailing Champions League campaign.

Denis Irwin provided an eighth minute lead with a free-kick which deflected off the wall past Nigel Martyn but was lucky not to reduce his side to ten men when he pulled Chris Armstrong back with the striker bearing down on Kevin Pilkington. The rookie goalkeeper was also fortunate not to receive his marching orders when he handled outside the area. The visitors were irked by two of their players being booked for offences which seemed far less serious. United extended their lead before the break, Kanchelskis crossing for Cantona to convert. United's thrusts continued – Cantona and Kanchelskis combining five minutes into the second half, this time the winger did the finishing.

Alongside the illustrious names which usually peppered an Old Trafford teamsheet were some of the youth products often referred to as 'Fergie's Fledglings'. Gary Neville was outstanding at right back, Simon Davies looked industrious on the left flank and was replaced 19 minutes from time by Paul Scholes. A little earlier Keith Gillespie also made an outing from the bench.

IFK GOTHENBERG 3 MANCHESTER UNITED 1
CHAMPIONS LEAGUE GROUP A - 23 NOVEMBER 1994

THE RETURN OF Eric Cantona bolstered United's European ambitions which hung by a thread going into this winner-take-all tie in Sweden. In the event poor defending and indiscipline from Paul Ince wrecked the Frenchman's happy return. Cantona could only watch as his colleagues imploded around him. Gothenberg had provided the opposition for the opening game of the group stage and were well beaten at Old Trafford. Following successive draws with Galatasaray away and Barcelona at home, the 4-0 hammering in Camp Nou was a serious setback. Remarkably United could still qualify with a win in Gothenberg.

The Swedes looked to defend in depth and hit on the break a plan that took just ten minutes to pay dividends when Denis Irwin played Stefan Rehn onside, Jesper Blomquist converting the former's cross. Andrei Kanchelskis almost levelled on 16 minutes but saw his shot smothered by Thomas Ravelli. In midfield Brian McClair and Paul Ince were lacking their usual authority and there were few chances to stretch the Swedish defence.

Cantona risked further problems with UEFA when he was booked early in the second half for a foul on Joachim Bjorklund. But just when it seemed all hope was slipping away David May floated a ball into the box which Cantona flicked down for Mark Hughes to shoot past Ravelli. Though he had played a significant part in clawing the Reds back into contention within a minute May was cursing his limitations at the other end. The defender was comfortably beaten down the right by Blomquist who squared for Magnus Erlingmark to knock past Gary Walsh.

Gary Neville, replacing the shell-shocked May, slipped when confronted by the ever threatening Blomquist. Pallister tripped the winger and Pontus Kamark tucked the resulting penalty away. Ince was dismissed for a particularly dreadful foul on Blomquist. There was an unexpected twist in Turkey where Galatasaray beat Barcelona 2-1 with a late goal. It seemed unlikely at the beginning of the night but it offered a lifeline meaning there was still a slim hope of qualifying if United beat Galatasaray and Barca lost to Gothenberg. Either result was a possibility.

ARSENAL 0 MANCHESTER UNITED 0
Premiership - 26 November 1994

BOTH CLUBS WERE out of form with United having suffered a setback in the Champions League and Arsenal on a run of two defeats. As a result George Graham reverted to a containment policy while United looked happy with a point.

Yet this game, despite ending goalless, was full of action although for the most part it came in the form of the settling of personal greivances. As usual in these fixtures there was a sending off. This time Mark Hughes was the player to take an early bath while others believed that Paul Ince was fortunate to stay on. Arsenal were without Paul Merson (whose recent confessions to a newspaper took him out of George Graham's plans for the rest of the season) and Ray Parlour. United had six names missing through injury and suspension and were most frustrated at not being able to call on the services of Roy Keane, Lee Sharpe and Ryan Giggs as Andrei Kanchelskis and Keith Gillespie struggled to make any headway against Lee Dixon and Nigel Winterburn.

Arsenal were quick out of the blocks but missed Merson's guile meaning Ian Wright saw little of the ball and got only a few half chances. The first came in the opening period when, after dispossessing Ince, he shot over the bar. The former Crystal Palace man was later denied by Pallister who cleared a volley from point blank range and then from close in again by Gary Walsh after Alan Smith nodded an Eddie McGoldrick cross goalwards. Substitute Paul Dickov was denied a penalty despite being upended by Ince. It took almost the entire first half for David Seaman to be brought into action and for most of that time Cantona was mired in a cluttered midfield becoming increasingly infuriated when his promptings came to nothing.

Hughes was sent off for a second foul 11 minutes from time having already received a harsh yellow following a first half tackle on John Jensen that was mistimed rather than malicious. Many thought Paul Ince should have gone for a bad challenge on the same player. Ince escaped a second caution when he clattered into the Dane who clutched his ankle and left the game soon afterwards.

This draw ended United's six match winning streak and forced them to cede leadership of the table, Blackburn taking over by a point following their 4-0 hammering of Queens Park Rangers.

MANCHESTER UNITED 1 NORWICH CITY 0
Premiership - 3 December 1994

Eric Cantona may have scored the winning goal but it was the spirit and motivation of Paul Ince which ultimately won the game. The Canaries were always a threat and came as close as any side had to scoring at Old Trafford since Graham Sharp's goal in a 3-2 defeat for Oldham Athletic eight months earlier.

Nevertheless United should have won by a significant margin. When Eric Cantona netted just past the half hour it seemed the floodgates would open. Yet over during the last half hour Norwich came close to nicking a draw. In fact had it not been for the referee's decisions they may well have done or even gained a better result. Former Old Trafford striker Mark Robins had a goal ruled out for offside and was then denied a penalty after he appeared to be hauled down by Gary Neville. Referee Tim Holbrook awarding a free-kick just outside the area.

Cantona finished off the first focussed United thrust after sending Brian McClair away down the right hand side with a back-heel. McClair looked up to see Cantona's charge into the area and a lobbed return ball saw the Frenchman convert.

McClair had earlier struck the post and failed to convert other chances as did Cantona, Keith Gillespie and Mark Hughes. Ince also struck the crossbar. Cantona would have doubled his tally in the dying seconds had it not been for a late crucial challenge by John Polston. Had he fallen Eric may have earned a penalty but he carried on only to stumble making Bryan Gunn's job easier. Norwich retained their open style of play throughout which allowed them to mount a late rally but their defenders could not keep up with the pace of United's breaks.

MANCHESTER UNITED 4 GALATASARAY 0
Champions League Group A - 7 December 1994

United bowed out of Europe after Gothenberg and Barcelona drew 1-1 but they did so with some style. The Reds were denied when Barcelona did just enough to deny them runners-up place in Group A behind the Swedes. The maths were simple. A win combined with a Barcelona defeat at the Nou Camp was all that would suffice. Barca scored late through Jose Bakero and even though Stefan Rehn equalised in the final minute a share of the spoils suited both sides. United finished level on points with the Spanish champions but went out due to their head-to-head record.

Before kick-off Alex Ferguson admitted his side needed something approaching a miracle to reach the next stage. United, hampered by the foreigners' rule, suspensions and the loss of Andrei Kanchelskis with a stomach strain, nevertheless produced a fine attacking display to gain a measure of revenge over their Turkish opponents following last season's disaster.

Injuries forced the manager to field some of his highly regarded 1992 Youth Cup winning side. Simon Davies and David Beckham found the net while Nicky Butt joined Roy Keane in midfield.

Gary Neville, who had endured some indifferent form domestically, settled his nerves when he linked with fellow fledgling Davies just two minutes in to give United the lead. His cross was intended for Brian McClair but fell instead for Davies to chest down and dispatch past Lithuanian keeper Gintaras Stauce.

Eric Cantona looked like he was dispensing on the job training throughout and each of the youngsters would have learnt much from the Frenchman. There was one lesson they would have been less wise to heed when Cantona lunged into a tackle on Bulent Korkmaz which earned him a yellow card plus a suspension from the club's next European tie but it could have been red. A tackle by the same player on McClair saw the ball break for Beckham, the midfielder hitting a shot of such pace and accuracy that Stauche couldn't get near. It was a quality strike from a player who looked more than comfortable on this stage.

Just as the Turks sensed they were getting a foothold, Cantona, eager to make up for his indiscretions in Turkey the previous season, crossed to Beckham who flicked on for Keane to net after dancing past a couple of challenges. United fans had welcomed their guests with a banner reading "Welcome to Heaven" but could only celebrate a pyrrhic victory - Bulent putting a Cantona cross into his own net to complete the Turks humiliation.

MANCHESTER UNITED 1 NOTTINGHAM FOREST 2
PREMIERSHIP - 17 DECEMBER 1994

ERIC CANTONA MISSED the tight 3-2 win at Queens Park Rangers but his return couldn't prevent the Reds going down to a first defeat at Old Trafford since late in the previous season. Forest's tactics came in for some justified criticism, especially the manner in which they played for time. There was also a row over a racial remark allegedly made to Paul Ince by Stuart Pearce but Frank Clark's men deserved their victory and in Stan Collymore, signed from Southend United, they had a match winner.

As expected United had most of the game while Forest relied on their strength at the back to resist. Only Ince stopped Collymore opening the scoring after a few minutes, the forward robbing Steve Bruce before bearing down on Gary Walsh but Ince's challenge saved the day. Alex Ferguson was said to have more than a passing interest in the exploits of Collymore having tried to sign the forward that summer.

Ryan Giggs, making his first appearance in five weeks, looked laboured throughout and was unable to get much change out of Des Lyttle or Steve Stone. Nevertheless United started brightly – Mark Hughes' effort cannoning back off the crossbar after just three minutes. Cantona, displaying his full range of tricks and flicks, was the next to take aim, though his back header from a Giggs corner was well saved.

Collymore, sent clear by Bryan Roy, beat Gary Pallister for pace before rifling past Gary Walsh from 25 yards. It was the first time an opposing player had scored at Old Trafford since April and he could have easily added to his strike with a header that hit the post before another effort was disallowed. Stuart Pearce increased the gap with a deflected effort just past the hour. Lax marking at a corner gave Pearce his chance yet despite the slice of luck involved, the visitors were good value for their advantage.

Eric Cantona looked isolated but managed to pull one back just after the second Forest goal, nodding in a Giggs corner. A quarter of the game remained but Alex Ferguson's side failed to find a way through which heightened the allegations of time-wasting.

Eight players were booked and Roy Keane, playing at right back against his former side, picked up the first yellow card. Most of the rest came in the frantic closing moments. Mark Crossley held out and was aided by some desperate defending. Stone cleared off the line from Giggs while Ince was denied a leveller by a last ditch intervention.

CHELSEA 2 MANCHESTER UNITED 3
PREMIERSHIP - 26 DECEMBER 1994

CHELSEA HAD BEEN the only team to perform the double over United the previous term and when the Reds conspired to let a two goal lead slip it seemed they may register a third successive league win. It would have been harsh based on the first half performance during which Eric Cantona was commanding. At times United looked untouchable - stroking the ball around with such nonchalance that the game had the appearance of a training exercise. It earned a reward before the first quarter was out. Mark Hughes rounded off a move Brian McClair had started with a ball down the flank for Ryan Giggs to chase. The winger outpaced Steve Clarke and crossed, Hughes nudging the centre past Dimitri Kharine. When Cantona converted a penalty following Frank Sinclair's mistimed tackled on Roy Keane the game appeared to be over.

Yet Chelsea got a penalty of their own just before the hour mark, after substitute Mark Stein was felled by Gary Pallister. John Spencer blasted the ball past Gary Walsh. The Scot could have had another chance from the spot soon after when Pallister clumsily barged into Paul Furlong but the referee waved away the claims.

Chelsea levelled 23 minutes from time when Furlong swung over a cross which Walsh failed to claim allowing Eddie Newton to head home. But they threw their initiative away within a minute after Keane charged into the area, his flick found Cantona who fed McClair to finish calmly.

MANCHESTER UNITED 1 LEICESTER CITY 1
Premiership - 28 December 1994

SINCE HITTING THE top Blackburn Rovers had matched United step for step but with the leaders lacking a game until New Years Eve, following the postponement of their match with Leeds United, the Reds had the chance to snatch back pole position. Second from bottom Leicester City came to Old Trafford having won just three games from the opening 20 and having picked up only one point away from Filbert Street. Foxes manager Mark McGhee, who had been Alex Ferguson's first signing as manager of Aberdeen, expected no favours.

Leicester would have been forgiven for doing nothing more than keep 11 men behind the ball but their manager's attacking philosophy won just reward even if Kevin Poole's goal was often under siege. United predictably dominated the opening exchanges, Eric Cantona should have done better from a Denis Irwin cross and was also denied by Simon Grayson who nodded a well measured chip off the line with Roy Keane bearing down upon him. However, those chances apart there was nothing to show until the hour mark when winger Andrei Kanchelskis plundered the ball and beat Poole from the angle.

Sloppy work at the back allowed Whitlow to equalise within a few minutes - Gary Walsh missing Lee Philpott's corner after Gary Neville seemed to get in his way. Mark Draper threatened a winner with a curling effort from 20 yards deep into injury time.

There was plenty of possession for United but they were let down by carelessness. Poole thwarted Kanchelskis and Gary Pallister and used a foot to deny Paul Scholes late on. Notwithstanding those early contributions Cantona was only a peripheral figure.

SOUTHAMPTON 2 MANCHESTER UNITED 2
PREMIERSHIP - 31 DECEMBER 1994

AT THE TURN of the previous year Manchester United had been 14 points clear of the field but this draw combined with Blackburn's win at Crystal Palace saw the Reds trail Rovers by three points having played a game more. Even earning a point proved hard work as United, minus Paul Ince and Andrei Kanchelskis, twice had to battle back from a goal down.

Southampton showed great industry and their attack made an early impact, Ronnie Ekelund heading just over in the opening stages. Yet it was defender Jeff Kenna who provided the opener just before the break, feeding the ball to Jim Magilton in space in the area. A low shot evaded Gary Walsh's grasp. Nicky Butt equalised seconds after the restart with a smart finish after a pass from Cantona. The young midfielder was all over the centre of the park, his ceaselessly running allowing the Reds some measure of control.

Alex Ferguson, who received a CBE in the New Year's Honours List, watched an improved United performance in the second half as Cantona imposed himself a little more. Nevertheless the hosts regained the lead 16 minutes from time after Neil Heaney's charge down the left teed up Hughes. It took just four minutes for Pallister to equalise. The centre back stayed up for a corner and though it came to nothing he was rewarded when the ball was quickly won back and Cantona found him with a perfect cross.

There was a little controversy caused by Cantona who celebrated the second goal perhaps a little too close to the home fans although there was no indication that he had goaded The Dell support.

MANCHESTER UNITED 2 COVENTRY CITY 0
PREMIERSHIP - 3 JANUARY 1995

UNITED, SEEKING TO put a poor festive period behind them, dropped Mark Hughes in favour of Paul Scholes. The Ginger Prince, who had scored twice on his last start against Queens Park Rangers, now partnered Eric Cantona and opened the scoring before earning the penalty that settled the game.

However, it could have all looked so different had a very familiar face at Old Trafford seized an early chance. Dion Dublin, who left United the previous September, had scored ten goals in 13 games for the Sky Blues until his injury jinx returned forcing him out for six games. The striker had a decent shout for a spot-kick when his header from a Mike Marsh free-kick hit Gary Pallister on the arm but the official waved Coventry protests away.

The incident proved to be the turning point. A low cross from Keith Gillespie gave Nicky Butt the chance to wrong foot Steve Ogrizovic with a clever back-heel. The keeper could only parry out to Scholes who scored from close range after a smart turn. After the game Alex Ferguson compared the youngster's strike to the type of poachers goals Denis Law was famed for.

Pressley feared that Scholes would score another when he was dispossessed 25 yards out but in chasing back only succeeded in pulling him down. The Scot was dismissed and Cantona tucked the ball away to settle the result. Blackburn still held an advantage of three points at the top and had a game in hand.

SHEFFIELD UNITED 0 MANCHESTER UNITED 2
FA Cup 3rd Rd - 9 January 1995

A game which featured the extremes of Eric Cantona's personality will ultimately be remembered for the sublime effort that finally saw off the hosts. The Blades displayed huge spirit despite being a man down for most of the game after Charlie Hartfield was dismissed for lashing out in the 14th minute. Sheffield dominated the opening period and withstood United for much of the second.

United, plagued by injury and illness following a bout of 'flu, were forced to bring in Peter Schmeichel ahead of schedule. Sheffield United made the most of the obvious discomfort felt by the Dane although the closest they came to beating him was a Nathan Blake effort which he parried, John O'Kane clearing. Carl Veart set up Blake again but Steve Bruce barged into the forward. There were inevitable appeals but no penalty was forthcoming. A few players exchanged words in the immediate aftermath of the incident which arguably triggered the red card. Hodges received a booking for dissent while both Steve Bruce and Denis Irwin were cautioned for separate fouls on Veart.

Paul Rogers showed his frustration with a solid tackle on Nicky Butt. A few players squared up to each other and Eric Cantona was seen to have flicked his boot at Hartfield on the restart causing the midfielder to retaliate and be dismissed. United, unbeaten in the FA Cup by a lower league team in over a decade, took some time to get forward.

It wasn't until the 80th minute that the man advantage told –

Hughes heading home from a Giggs cross. Butt was just off target with two long range efforts including an exquisite lob which went just inches over.

However it is the second goal that will live long in the memory. Giggs, finding more space as the game wore on, worked a position for Cantona with an astute pass to the edge of the area. Spotting Kelly advancing, Eric took a steadying touch before delicately lobbing the ball over the keeper and inches under the angle of post and crossbar.

NEWCASTLE UNITED 1 MANCHESTER UNITED 1
PREMIERSHIP - 15 JANUARY 1995

WITHIN HOURS OF United progressing to the 4th round of the FA Cup their squad was bolstered with the shock £7 million signing of Newcastle's leading goalscorer Andy Cole. There had been moves to tempt Stan Collymore away from Nottingham Forest but their manager Frank Clark had been lying low courtesy of a short illness and Alex Ferguson's call went unanswered. There was little time for delay and, believing that negotiations with Forest wouldn't run smoothly he took a lead from his audacious bid for Eric Cantona by raiding another rival club of their main goalscoring threat. When announced the signing of Cole made as many jaws drop as the Cantona signing had two years before.

United paid £6 million cash with young winger Keith Gillespie also going the other way as a makeweight. Magpies' fans were bewildered as to why the man who had scored 55 goals in just 70 league games, and broken Hughie Gallacher's 70 year old record for most goals in a league season, was allowed to leave just five days before the teams were due to meet at St. James' Park. From United's point of view and with recent failures in Europe in mind, the signing added another English forward to the squad.

Mark Hughes picked up a knee ligament injury that seemed likely to keep him out of action for the rest of the season. Rumours suggested this had only scuppered the Welshman's imminent move to Everton. Hughes had injured himself in the act of converting a Roy Keane cross. The sight of the scorer leaving the field on a stretcher was a huge blow. The problem seemed to have an effect on both teams and stalled a United performance that had looked convincing hitherto.

Shorn of Cole, Newcastle were also missing the crucial influence of Peter Beardsley. Nevertheless the hosts closed the first half on a high, Steve Howey miscueing an astute flick from Fox close to the penalty spot and Rob Lee lobbing a shot on to the bar. Newcastle continued in a similar vein after the restart with Kitson leading the line and grabbing a deserved equaliser following a Robbie Elliott cross from the left which struck Gary Pallister on the shoulder, Kitson netted after collecting the ricochet.

United finished the stronger with Keane going close late on, Cantona missing two chances. The Frenchman nearly won it for United in the final seconds, his shot bouncing along the line before being cleared. With Butt forced off with double vision and Keane picking up a hamstring problem as well as a yellow card to earn a two match ban, United were at full stretch and forced to field an ailing Steve Bruce, the latest victim of the flu bug which had been passed round the Old Trafford dressing room, until the close.

MANCHESTER UNITED 1 BLACKBURN ROVERS 0
PREMIERSHIP - 22 JANUARY 1995

THE DRAW AT Newcastle ensured that in-form Blackburn Rovers emerged from the weekend five points clear. It made the clash between the top two an even more important game. An eight point lead towards the beginning of February would be very hard to pull back. Andy Cole made his debut, replacing Mark Hughes who required more than a dozen stitches in his leg but was passed fit to play. However the new striker showed real nerves when presented with chances, the best of which came early and late in the game. It was left to Eric Cantona, who had been so integral to United's best play, to wrap up the points with a spectacular late header.

Cole spurned his first chance after 90 seconds when Brian McClair floated the ball beyond Paul Warhurst, but like a rabbit caught in the headlights, the debutant seemed to freeze and screwed the ball well wide. Despite this miss, Paul Ince and McClair were dominant in midfield - Cole, Giggs and McClair put further efforts wide and Flowers was forced into a number of saves.

Rovers held out until ten minutes from time when Ryan Giggs, who had been sent down the inside left channel by Cantona, beat Berg to the ball and quickly crossed to the far post where his provider was peeling away. The Frenchman was just a yard or so from goal when he met the ball - the resulting header flew into the corner just inches inside the angle of post and bar.

It seemed the match was won but with the clock ticking towards the 90 minute mark Berg nearly made up for his earlier error sending in a cross from the right which Alan Shearer flicked on for Tim Sherwood who headed in despite pressure from Steve Bruce. However, referee Paul Durkin ruled that Shearer had pushed Keane and seconds later the game was over. Blackburn were irate. Not only because it seemed both their games against United had ended in defeat as a result of refereeing decisions but also fully aware that despite having a game in hand their ambitions had suffered a huge psychological blow.

CRYSTAL PALACE 1 MANCHESTER UNITED 1
PREMIERSHIP - 25 JANUARY 1995

No ONE WAS talking about the game when the final whistle blew at Selhurst Park after one of the most remarkable events ever seen at a professional football match. If Eric Cantona being dismissed just three minutes in to the second half was not a big enough story what followed had an impact on the rest of the season.

Dismissed following a kick at Richard Shaw, who had earlier caught the striker with a tackle from behind on 48 minutes, Cantona left the pitch to a predictable barrage of insults. In among the home fans Matthew Simmons, who later claimed he was making his way down the steps to visit the toilet, was alleged to have held up his middle finger to the departing player and shouted one or two off colour remarks in the Frenchman's direction - a steward stepping in to calm him down.

Whatever the truth of the situation one thing is incontestable. Something snapped in Cantona who, though chaperoned by kit-man Norman Davies, turned sharply and squared up to Simmons demanding that he repeat the comments. He then launched himself feet first into the stands in what became referred to as a kung-fu kick into Simmons' chest. After leaping over the hoardings Eric then traded several punches once his abuser got back to his feet with Simmons floored by a right handed jab.

Paul Ince was also on the scene and both men were heavily involved before being pulled away from the incident by police, stewards and Palace fans who realised the gravity of this event. Peter Schmeichel came over to escort Eric away to the sanctuary of the dressing room. Manager Alex Ferguson could be seen lost for words, refusing to make eye-contact with his star player and unable to quite take in what had happened. Once Eric got to the dressing room he sat motionless for a while reflecting on his actions before having a shower and a cup of tea.

Eric's frustration wasn't helped by United's failure to gain a foothold in the game. Alex Ferguson could not have complained had his side trailed at the break. Palace had struggled for goals all season but were well organised enough to cause United problems. Andy Cole looked better than he had against Blackburn but continued to flounder in the penalty area.

As a result the game developed into a testy affair. Roy Keane was the first United player into the book after a foul on John Salako before Chris Armstrong fluffed a chance from a Salako cross at the far post. Salako could have scored himself on the stroke of half-time but drove wide. David May put United ahead not long after Eric's dismissal, nodding a Lee Sharpe's cross past Nigel Martyn and in the process getting his first goal since leaving Blackburn Rovers.

The game settled down after the tumultuous scenes. Sharpe hit the crossbar and Palace made the most of that reprieve and an error from May that allowed Salako to advance on goal. The midfielder had a shot blocked and amid the inevitable scramble Gareth Southgate proved the coolest head sliding in a shot with 11 minutes left to leave Blackburn Rovers still top by a point with two matches in hand.

THE AFTERMATH

WHEN HIS TEAM-MATES joined him in the dressing room Eric Cantona apologised to everyone present, although the matter was barely discussed. The question of whether Cantona's career had been building up to the night's events was posed by many in the weeks that followed. He had endured a number of run-ins with, referees, managers and team-mates. They had all irked the player for one reason or another, it just so happened that this time a supporter was the one struck.

The FA had rarely dealt with attacks on fans which were not initiated by other supporters. Their immediate statement left no doubt that they believed the incident was serious: "The FA are appalled by the incident that took place by the side of the pitch at Selhurst Park tonight. Such an incident brings shame on those involved as well as, more importantly, on the game itself.

"The FA is aware that the police are urgently considering what action they should take. We will, as always, co-operate in every way with them. And as far as the FA itself is concerned, charges of improper conduct and bringing the game into disrepute will inevitably and swiftly follow tonight's events. It is our responsibility to ensure that actions that damage the game are punished severely. The FA will live up to that responsibility."

What was perceived to be a poor disciplinary record did not help – this was the fifth red card Cantona had received in just 16 months. The immediate fallout was that he was fined £20,000 by the club and banned from the first team until the end of the season, meaning that he would be out of the game for almost eight months. It seemed a reasonable punishment and headed off some of the more outraged opinions which claimed he should be banned from professional football forever.

A measure of the harm it had done came from the financial markets. During the 48 hours after the incident, United's value fell from £79.6 million to £77.2m. That mattered little to Reds who knew that no matter what legal status it had and how money was made Manchester United was a football club.

United fans quickly ran to Eric's defence. While supporters of rivals, the authorities of the game and pundits continued to press for his summary execution, United fans honoured the Frenchman in song at that weekend's 4th round FA Cup tie with Wrexham. Meanwhile a police incident room was set up at the Met's Addington station in south London where seven officers did nothing but undertake reviews of reports and witness statements. Some serious crimes in the capital didn't get that level of resource.

Simmons sold his story to *The Sun* for a rumoured £20,000 under the headline: 'Cantona's boot studs slammed into my heart.' Of course they did no such thing and according to the medical examinations which took place when the complaint was lodged only caused a little bruising. Rival papers quickly sought to undermine Simmons' character. *The Sun* had been on an anti-Eric crusade for most of the season. Early in the campaign its front page was splashed with mock outrage at a Nike ad which was seen to condone Cantona's previous misdemeanours and was subsequently banned by the Advertising Standards Authority.

Alex Ferguson, who only realised the full gravity of the situation when he watched a recording of Match of the Day after arriving home, was silent on the matter but publicly backed Cantona's ban for the rest of season. Despite his usual keenness to support his players he felt unable to object to the board's decision.

He was unhappy with his player's stupidity, especially as at half-time he had instructed him not to get involved with Richard Shaw. He also blamed the referee for letting a number of fouls on his players pass without reprimand. However, one thing he would not agree to was any suggestion that the club either wash their hands of Cantona or place him on the transfer list.

It was mooted that Eric would still be able to turn out for the reserves although the FA issued an early comment suggesting that he wouldn't be allowed to do anything more than train. The decision was handed down two days after the incident hence the confusion and any action had to be evaluated by an FA tribunal after it was decided that a charge of disrepute was appropriate. There was a 14 day period for response in which he could play but the club's decision ended that prospect.

The French Football Federation also acted promptly, stripping Cantona of the captaincy. It went without saying that he would not be picked for the foreseeable future. Certainly as long as United's ban was in place and maybe longer depending on any sanctions the FA, UEFA or FIFA may impose.

French Federation President Claude Simonet met with the national coach Aime Jacquet and French league president Noel Le Graet after which he told reporters: "The seriousness of the situation forces me to consider this attitude as incompatible with what is expected of a captain in the national team's colours. Unfortunately I think he will have to be taken off the French team."

Criminal investigations by the Metropolitan Police were in process which would take in the actions of Cantona, Ince and Matthew Simmons who had his season ticket taken away by Crystal Palace for breaking ground rules.

Matthew Simmons had lodged an official complaint to officers present and spoke of an intention to sue. Ince's conduct was the subject of a report by another Palace supporter who alleged that he had been punched by the England international. Even Gordon Taylor, chief executive of the players' union, was unable to offer his backing saying: "He's the PFA player of the year, he's made a great contribution to the English game and I hope people bear that in mind. But he's obviously in deep trouble. We will do all we can to help him but we cannot condone what he has done."

Lengthy bans had been the norm for players involved in violent conduct towards opponents and referees with Rangers player Duncan Ferguson receiving a 12-match suspension imposed for violent conduct though due to his imprisonment for a separate matter the sentence had not been served at the time. When then Nottingham Forest manager Brian Clough struck two fans who were part of a mob which invaded the pitch in good humour, he was fined £5,000 and banned from the touchline for the rest of the season. This sentence was expected to dwarf them.

One issue which could not count against him was an accusation of attacking a television news reporter with a similar kick to that which had floored Matthew Simmons after ITN's Terry Lloyd had 'door-stepped' Cantona in Guadeloupe. The journalist claimed he and a two-man crew were trying to get an interview with Cantona after he had failed to report to a Croydon police station. Cantona was sat on a bench with his son and pregnant wife so was understandably aggravated. After asking some questions about his return Mr Lloyd said he was ignored until: "He grabbed me in a headlock and said 'Come with me, I'd like a chat with you'". He claimed those with the reporter were told to go "somewhere quiet". "Suddenly, without warning, he came running at me, launched into the air and kicked me in the chest." He then claimed that Cantona stood above him as he lay prostrate in the sand saying: "I'm going to kill you." ITN commented through a spokesman that police told them film they had confiscated would be passed to Mr Cantona. Lloyd sustained cracked ribs in the attack.

THE FA HANDED down its verdict on 24th February 1995 extending the ban already imposed by Manchester United until 30th September 1995 and as both FIFA and the French Football Federation would verify it, the suspension extended across the globe. It would run to 34 games when all competitions were taken into account and there would be a fine of £10,000 added to that already levied.

A life ban was available according to the statutes but it was never seriously considered by the three man panel of chairman Geoff Thompson, Oldham Chairman Ian Stott and Gordon McKeag, president of the Football League. In concluding their hearing and defining what would be a fair punishment they looked at all levels of disciplinary problems, the generally accepted fact that provocation was involved and the level of punishments already imposed.

Pleadings, apologies and a measure of regret shown on the part of the player as well as promises about future conduct were also taken into consideration.

The final statement read: "The members of the FA Commission are satisfied that the actions of Eric Cantona following his sending-off at Crystal Palace in the Manchester United match on January 25 brought the game into disrepute. Eric Cantona has therefore been in breach of FA rules.

"After taking into consideration the previous misconduct of Eric Cantona, the provocation he suffered, the prompt action taken by Manchester United, Eric Cantona's expression of regret to the Commission, the apologies he conveyed to those affected and the assurances he gave to his future conduct, the members of the Commission decided that Eric Cantona should be suspended forthwith from all football activities up to and including 30 September 1995 and fined £10,000." The decision left him free to train, coach and he was still able to take his basic salary but not bonuses.

Cantona, flanked by Alex Ferguson and club solicitor Maurice Watkins, held a press conference but never spoke. Regret was expressed on his behalf by Watkins who said: "We are disappointed the FA felt it necessary to increase our suspension but we have accepted it. We will not be appealing. Eric has never sought to justify his action or minimise its seriousness. He deeply regrets what he has done."

THE COURT CASE

CONCURRENT WITH THE punishments, there was the law of the land to contend with. Once the Department of Public Prosecutions decided there was a case to answer the legal processes were set in motion and a hearing before Croydon Magistrates Court set for 23 March 1995. Paul Ince was also charged and both men faced the prospect of imprisonment and decided to make what could conceivably be their last night of freedom an enjoyable one. They spent time at Brown's in Covent Garden leaving at 2.30am in order to decamp to the Emporium nightclub in Kingly Street where Prince was giving a private concert. There they chatted to Paul Gascoigne and Hollywood actor Mel Gibson before leaving at 4.50am. Their appearances would take place later that morning.

Ince was the first to enter a plea of not guilty and left court on unconditional bail to be tried in May. It was already known that

Cantona would admit his guilt which meant the events of 25 January would have to be gone through in court. Mr Jeffrey McCann, appearing for the prosecution, set out the crown's case starting with the sending off and the walk to the dressing room. There were conflicting stories of the interjection Matthew Simmons made during that walk. One person in the stand who described himself as a neutral said it was "You fucking cheating French cunt. Fuck off back to France you motherfucker. French bastard wanker."

This led to a moment of stilted hilarity in court. Not for the language used or to have it delivered in such a measured way. Had they been Simmons's precise words they would have harboured far more vitriol. The magistrate's clerk asked if Cantona understood what was being said to him. Given that was the whole reason he was there it seemed an odd question. In his account to the Metropolitan Police Simmons, who would face separate changes at a later date, said his words were: "Off, off, off. Go on Cantona. Have an early shower." What was beyond contention were the events that unfolded in view of the television cameras.

The court was read a statement from Cantona by his barrister, David Poole QC, which said his client was "angry and frustrated" about his dismissal and what this may mean for his team and in the process of leaving the pitch when he heard racist abuse being shouted by a man running down the stairs to mock him – his face "contorted with hatred" as he shouted.

He added that "This, with my additional frustration [at being sent off], caused me to react in a way I now deeply regret by jumping up and kicking out at the man's chest."

There were additional comments in mitigation including punishments from his club who had fined him two weeks' wages and imposed a ban which the Football Association had extended. However, the magistrates decided that from the powers they had ranging from a fine, community service up to imprisonment, a custodial sentence of two weeks would be appropriate. Their chair, Mrs Jean Pearch, selected because she had no interest in football and therefore would be beyond any tribal approach said: "You are a high profile figure with undoubted gifts and as such you are looked up to by young people."

Cantona was led away to the cells spending two and a half hours in the bowels of the court as an application for bail pending an appeal was rejected. This decision was reversed by a Crown Court judge later in the day with surety of £500 set and an appeal to be heard eight days later. He emerged from the building at 3pm to cheers from Manchester United fans who had been there since the early morning. More had since joined them in reaction to events.

The player's agent Jean-Jacques Amorfini was stunned telling French radio: "I can tell you, he won't stay in that country a lot longer. I think people are trying to make Cantona disgusted with England and, obviously, I believe he is going to have to leave the country. We are dumbfounded and absolutely shocked because Manchester United's English lawyers advised a guilty plea so English justice would show clemency."

Chairman Martin Edwards expressed surprise at events saying: "This is a shock. The whole thing has got out of hand. He has been punished three times for the same offence."

He would be punished again when the appeal was held but this time Judge Ian Davies on hearing defence counsel state that the sanction should reflect the offence and not the notoriety of those who had perpetrated it, concluded that the accused had been subject to the type of provocation which would irritate most men. Arguments about fame were also accepted.

The controversial two-week prison sentence was replaced with 120 hours of football community service, training youngsters from the Manchester area how to play. After leaving court to a tumultuous reception Cantona returned to the Croydon Park Hotel for an impromptu press conference to deliver his infamous comments to the assembled media, "When seagulls follow the trawler, it is because they think sardines will be thrown into the sea." As he rose he offered only, "thank you very much".

Questions and remarks were aimed his way but unlike his exit from Selhurst Park he made no further comment but made for the door and strode away. His metaphor caused confusion and laughter among the assembled pressmen whose newspapers and broadcast organisations used headlines revolving around fish. Some even carried quotes from psychologists.

Alex Ferguson was at Buckingham Palace the same day, collecting the CBE he had been awarded in the New Years' Honours List, so was unavailable for comment. The manager offered few thoughts on the matter prior to the final decision by the court and continued to hold his tongue as the season drew to its end but criticised the FA who had earlier indicated they would not increase the club's own punishment. "I think the commission went too far. You can't have people in charge of an organisation like the FA being dictated to by the media." Matthew Simmons later received a £500 fine and a year long ban from Selhurst Park for threatening behaviour.

1994–95

I F ERIC CANTONA had won successive titles for his respective clubs – Leeds United and Manchester United, it can be argued that his moment of madness at Selhurst Park cost the Reds a chance to retain their crown and claim unprecedented back to back doubles. A lack of silverware and a lack of Cantona seemed more than just coincidence. His craft was badly missed in the crucial last few months of the league campaign.

The season had started sluggishly but wins home and away against Blackburn looked to have tipped things United's way. However, this time they dashed for the line with their legs tied. The Reds only just failed in the event, as Rovers lost at Anfield while United failed to beat West Ham at Upton Park thanks to a number of incredible misses and an outstanding performance by Hammers keeper Ludek Miklosko. In the FA Cup Final a week later, a drained and dispirited United lost 1-0 to Everton.

To some surprise Eric was again short-listed for the Professional Footballers' Association Player of the Year award. Player's votes had been received before the Selhurst Park incident but the nomination was recognition from his peers across a wide spectrum of clubs and meant as much as being chosen the season's best a year ago.

A day before Blackburn beat United to the Premiership title Eric Cantona, with FIFA's permission, turned out for the Variety Club of France against an amateur club in Marly-le-Roi, scoring in the 2-2 draw. The match was played in aid of Action Michel Platini a charity set up by his friend and former national coach to help combat drug abuse and assist those recovering from addiction.

The governing body were happy to permit his participation in a couple more charity games though only in France where the football federation had no objection. Further moderation of the terms ultimately lay with the English Football Association. Without this he could not play in the UK or elsewhere. Any chance of Manchester United seeking to vary the conditions by way of non-competitive

THE COMPLETE ERIC CANTONA

matches such as pre-season friendlies was remote as they risked the wrath of the FA.

United seemed unlikely to test Lancaster Gate's flexibility and didn't want even the best of causes seeking the inevitable publicity boost such high profile patronage would provide. Assistant Secretary Ken Ramsden said: "It should be seen in the context of a one-off for a good cause that Eric wanted to play in and FIFA were happy to allow."

Cantona himself was content to keep things as low key as the circus which surrounded him at the time would allow commenting: "I have been authorised to play charity games. Playing again is fantastic and to do so for a humanitarian cause is even better."

Even after his sentence was commuted from custodial to community service, his agent suggested his views on his adopted country may have soured, saying "Eric is thinking very hard about his future. He still has the suspension by the Football Association, as well as the sentence of the court. Today is better, but it is still a sentence. Eric's love affair with England has been affected by all of this. It will never be the same again because of what has happened. Can you blame him? As for Italy, I know the answer to that, but I can not say what it is."

Inter Milan had offered a route out of the English game to both players involved in the incident. During late May Paul Ince was cleared of the charges and later in the close season joined the club which had been courting him for a fee in excess of £7 million. Nerazzurri club president Massimo Moratti had tried to land Cantona as well but later claimed that the player felt obliged to see out his ban and remain in England to restart his career once the punishment was served. Inter's first approach came in January 1995, before the events at Selhurst Park.

A meeting to discuss the prospect of signing Ince and Cantona was arranged for 26 January 1995 just 24 hours after United were to play Crystal Palace in the league. The club president and two of his aides watched the game at Selhurst Park and were far from deterred by the incident which involved both targets. They re-iterated as much when the parties sat across a table at the Royal Lancaster Hotel. A £10 million double swoop was suggested which Martin Edwards said he would discuss with Alex Ferguson, who would have the last say on squad matters.

The manager rejected both approaches saying each player was

vital to his plans and as an Englishman Ince, in particular, was at a premium. Cantona's situation was a little more delicate given events and the lengthy ban the FA were almost certain to impose. Something which Inter knew and one of the reasons they made it very clear that their offers remained on the table. For Cantona a £5.5 million transfer fee was offered with wages of £25,000 per week, a salary that was more than four and a half times the basic salary he currently received.

United had begun discussions over a new four year contract with Cantona that within a matter of days of the interest from Milan. Rumours about salary and the terms had emerged in the press. Further cursory discussions with Jean-Jacques Bertrand took place in April. United were rumoured to be offering a similar salary to that now offered by Inter, a move which threatened to break Old Trafford's wage structure.

United had used Cantona's name to sell all manner of merchandise and Eric and his agent now attempted to negotiate a fee for his 'image rights'. This was immediately rejected by Edwards but the substantial rise remained. The ball was in Cantona's court as to whether £15,000 per week plus significant signing on fees was sufficient reward for his services.

The rumours continued. Massimo Moratti, when asked if he was worried about taking a player who was gifted but volatile said, "my concerns are with the skill and brain of a player. Cantona is a cultured man and super class." The tabloids predicatably went over board with the *Daily Mirror* going as far as to say that deals were signed and the transfer would go through soon. Lengthy and detailed discussions took place between player and club after which matters were unresolved. A final offer was put to him and though no doubt some degree of fluidity remained Cantona wanted time to reflect and promised a decision at the end of that week.

He had already let the club know he was happy to stay when his contract came up for tentative discussions during early January. His community service was a punishment from the law courts for his misdemeanour at Selhurst Park but he enjoyed working with the youngsters he met who reminded him of his own love and excitement for football at such a tender age. There was also the matter of the loyalty which had been shown to him from the club and fans he had grown to love. Manchester United and Alex Ferguson had always supported him and the player recognised this.

On Friday 28 April 1995 Eric accepted United's deal. At a press conference that same afternoon the supposition of the week's back pages was replaced by fact. Sporting a red shirt with a pink and cream striped jacket, Cantona said, "Manchester United are the biggest club in England, maybe in Europe, maybe in the world. I'm very pleased to have the opportunity in the next three years to win many trophies with them. Everybody at this club deserves this – and the fans too. I have never thought about leaving Manchester United, but maybe some people thought so. We are bigger than the people who have been so hard and so wrong sometimes. I hope to spend the rest of my career here."

Martin Edwards said he had hoped Eric would make this decision but had taken nothing for granted adding that he was only sure the player would stay when he walked into his office at 9.35 that morning. "There have been other offers and it is no secret that Inter were very interested in him. He would have been financially better remunerated, but he has shown loyalty to us and we have shown loyalty to him. We're very delighted as a club, and we look forward to him playing for us again. It's been a long, traumatic period. Eric has had four punishments – he's been banned by the club, banned by the FA, he has received a court sentence and been banned by the French FA and he's now serving those punishments. We hope this brings it all to an end."

Alex Ferguson was also candid about matters. "I thought that he was almost certain to leave. There was so much pressure on him, and you get to the point where you have to think if you are doing right by the player. When you think what has happened to him since January, you wonder who else could have coped with it. The easier route would have been to go, but he has made the harder decision and put himself in the firing line. He has said to himself: 'They are not going to defeat me.' Obviously you worry what sort of effect all this has had on him inside, but outwardly he has reacted to everything very well. It's that which persuaded me he can handle it. He knows this is his last chance."

After telling the press that "you fear me more than I fear you" Eric had the last word saying: "I'm sorry, I must leave for training. I need to be fit for my next match." Then after a pause he uttered one more word: "October."

The Italians admitted defeat in their quest although only for the foreseeable future saying, "If one day Cantona and United decide to part, we could then consider signing him. There's always room at Inter for a champion, and he is one."

FOR THE FIRST time in three seasons Manchester United finished without a trophy. The weekend before his infamous night at Crystal Palace in January, Blackburn had been beaten by a Cantona winner. However, his suspension led to home league draws with Leeds, Chelsea and Tottenham to hand an advantage to Kenny Dalglish's side. Even in the last game, Cantona's composure in front of goal was missed.

Talk of Cantona leaving Old Trafford did rear its ahead again just before the new season began. This time it was not contract issues but intransigence from the game's authorities which almost saw Cantona move clubs. A transfer request was rejected by the Old Trafford board after the Football Association decided to investigate Eric's appearance in a behind closed doors friendly with Rochdale during late July. Cantona was incandescent at being punished twice for the offence he committed at Selhurst Park and not being allowed to play or even keep himself match sharp prior to returning in October.

He was permitted to play training matches and as games were organised at the club's training complex there was no consideration that the fixtures arranged against Rochdale, Bury and Oldham Athletic were anything but impromptu contests aimed at mirroring match conditions. The FA seemed to consider them friendlies which lay outside the rules of their ban.

Press whispers about money or a desire from his wife to leave England were given no credence although Jean-Jacques Bertrand issued a statement from his Paris office stating that his client would not return to England unless certain conditions were met by the FA. The statement issued on 8 August 1995 read: "Eric Cantona has left England and will not return if the English FA doesn't change, before midnight, 11 August, its decision banning him from taking part in closed-door training matches with his club."

The FA had accepted an account from the club as to the nature of the fixture which a dozen people watched at The Cliff but after a terse demand immediately after the game FA spokesman Mike Parry offered a fairly ambiguous comment saying: "The FA received a response from Manchester United in regard to our inquiry about Eric Cantona. We are entirely satisfied with their explanation and we have conveyed that to the club."

United, who had sought clarification, acknowledged that another club being involved complicated issues but contended there was no call to impose a new sanction. On the club's behalf press officer, Ken Ramsden, said: "Eric was very upset at the recent inquiry by the FA concerning his involvement in the training session of 25 July. He told [United chairman] Martin Edwards that he felt he had little future in the English game and that his career would be best served by a move abroad. The board has considered the request very carefully but is not prepared to agree to it, believing that it is in the best interests of both the club and player that he remains with United." Plans for five additional private games were scrapped.

Alex Ferguson was certainly confident that the situation could be smoothed out telling the BBC: "I had a chat with Eric yesterday, and then his lawyer appeared and we had a chat with the directors. I feel that we've settled him down a bit. The FA thing had got to him, but they're not taking any action against him or the club, so hopefully he'll be playing for us next season."

Ambiguity remained as Lancaster Gate's decision meant, by implication, permission that these games didn't contravene the terms of the ban. Rumours persisted that Cantona's lawyer was considering a legal challenge. Ferguson added: "Eric's told me it's all about the FA. The important thing is to resolve that one, and if we do that I'm sure he'll play for United. I'm determined about it and I want him in my team."

When asked to consider if it was possible United could regain the title if Cantona returned, the reply was typically forthright with Ferguson saying: "I'm absolutely certain of that." It took a trip to Paris, with the manager ferried to a make or break meeting with the player on the back of a motorbike, to persuade the Frenchman to stay.

The manager's keenness to keep Cantona was in stark contrast to his sale of several key figures during the summer of 1995. Paul Ince went to Inter Milan, Mark Hughes joined Chelsea and Andrei Kanchelskis, rumoured to be under pressure to move by the Russian mafia, eventually wound up at Everton. No replacements were sought as Ferguson believed he had enough quality coming through the club's youth ranks to fill any gaps.

DATE	OPPONENT	VENUE	SCORE	ATTD	1	2	3	4	5	6	7	8	9	10	11	SUBSTITUTES
31-Aug-94	Wimbledon	Old Trafford	3-0	43,440	Schmeichel	May	Irwin	Bruce	Sharpe	Pallister	Cantona¹	Kan'skis	McClair¹	Hughes	Giggs¹	
11-Sep-94	Leeds United	Elland Road	1-2	39,120	Schmeichel	May	Irwin	Bruce	Kan'skis	Pallister	Cantona¹	Ince	McClair	Hughes	Giggs	
17-Sep-94	Liverpool	Old Trafford	2-0	43,740	Schmeichel	May	Irwin	Bruce	Sharpe	Pallister	Cantona	Ince	Kan'skis¹	Hughes	Giggs	McClair¹ (Hughes)
24-Sep-94	Ipswich Tn	Portman Rd	2-3	22,553	Walsh	Keane	Irwin	Bruce	Sharpe	Pallister	Cantona¹	Ince	McClair	Kan'skis	Giggs	Scholes¹ (Sharpe)
01-Oct-94	Everton	Old Trafford	2-0	43,803	Schmeichel	May	Irwin	Bruce	Sharpe¹	Pallister	Cantona¹	Ince	Keane	Hughes	Giggs	McClair (Hughes)
15-Oct-94	West Ham	Old Trafford	1-0	43,795	Schmeichel	May	Irwin	Bruce	Sharpe	Pallister	Cantona¹	Ince	Kan'skis	Hughes	Giggs	Butt (May)
23-Oct-94	Blackburn R	Ewood Park	4-2	30,260	Schmeichel	Keane	Irwin	Bruce	Sharpe	Pallister	Cantona¹	Ince	Butt	Hughes¹	Kan'skis²	McClair (Butt)
29-Oct-94	Newcastle Utd	Old Trafford	2-0	43,795	Schmeichel	Keane	Irwin	Bruce	Kan'skis	Pallister¹	Cantona	Ince	McClair	Hughes	Giggs	Gillespie¹ (Giggs)
06-Nov-94	Aston Villa	Villa Park	2-1	32,136	Walsh	Keane	Irwin	Bruce	Butt	Pallister	Cantona¹	Ince(1)	Scholes	Hughes	Davies	
10-Nov-94	Manchester C	Old Trafford	5-0	43,738	Schmeichel	Neville G	Irwin	May	Kan'skis³	Pallister	Cantona¹	Ince	McClair	Hughes¹	Gillespie	Butt (Kan'skis) Davies (Gillespie)
19-Nov-94	Crystal P	Old Trafford	3-0	43,788	Schmeichel	Neville G	Irwin¹	May	Kan'skis¹	Pallister	Cantona¹	Ince	McClair	Hughes	Davies	Gillespie (Davies) Butt (Kan'skis)
26-Nov-94	Arsenal	Highbury	0-0	38,301	Walsh	May	Irwin	Bruce	Kan'skis	Pallister	Cantona	Ince	McClair	Hughes	Giggs	Butt (Giggs) Neville G (Kan'skis)
03-Dec-94	Norwich City	Old Trafford	1-0	43,789	Walsh	Keane	Irwin	Bruce	Butt	Pallister	Cantona¹	Ince	McClair	Hughes	Giggs	Neville G (Ince) Kan'skis (Butt)
17-Dec-94	Nottingham F	Old Trafford	1-2	43,744	Walsh	Keane	Irwin	Bruce	Kan'skis	Pallister	Cantona¹	Ince	McClair	Hughes	Giggs	Scholes (Hughes)
26-Dec-94	Chelsea	Stamford B	3-2	31,139	Walsh	Keane	Irwin	Bruce	Butt	Pallister	Cantona¹	Ince	McClair¹	Hughes¹	Giggs	Gillespie (McClair)
28-Dec-94	Leicester City	Old Trafford	1-1	43,789	Walsh	Neville G	Irwin	Bruce	Kan'skis	Pallister	Cantona¹	Keane	Scholes	Hughes	Giggs	McClair (Keane)
31-Dec-94	Southampton	The Dell	2-2	15,204	Walsh	Neville G	Irwin	Bruce	Butt¹	Pallister	Cantona	Keane	McClair	Hughes	Giggs	Scholes¹ (Hughes) May (Bruce)
03-Jan-95	Coventry City	Old Trafford	2-0	43,120	Walsh	Neville G	Irwin	Bruce	Sharpe	Pallister	Cantona¹	Keane	Scholes¹	Gillespie	Giggs	McClair (Keane)
15-Jan-95	Newcastle Utd	St James	1-1	34,471	Schmeichel	Butt	Irwin	Bruce	Sharpe	Pallister	Cantona	Keane	McClair	Hughes¹	Giggs	
22-Jan-95	Blackburn R	Old Trafford	1-0	43,742	Schmeichel	Keane	Irwin	May	Sharpe	Pallister	Cantona¹	Ince	McClair	Cole	Giggs	Kan'skis (Sharpe)
25-Jan-95	Crystal P	Selhurst Park	1-1	18,224	Schmeichel	Keane	Irwin	Bruce	Sharpe	Pallister	Cantona¹	Ince	McClair	Cole	Giggs	Kan'skis (Sharpe)

FA CUP

DATE	OPPONENT	VENUE	SCORE	ATTD	1	2	3	4	5	6	7	8	9	10	11	SUBSTITUTES
09-Jan-95	Sheffield Utd	Bramall Lane	2-0	22,322	Schmeichel	O'Kane	Irwin	Bruce	Butt	Pallister	Cantona¹	Keane	McClair	Hughes¹	Giggs	Sharpe (O'Kane)

CHAMPIONS LEAGUE

DATE	OPPONENT	VENUE	SCORE	ATTD	1	2	3	4	5	6	7	8	9	10	11	SUBSTITUTES
23-Nov-94	IFK Goteborg	Gamla Ullevi	1-3	36,301	Walsh	May	Irwin	Bruce	Kan'skis	Pallister	Cantona	Ince	McClair	Hughes¹	Davies	
07-Dec-94	Galatasary	Old Trafford	4-0	39,220	Walsh	Neville G	Irwin	Bruce	Keane¹	Pallister	Cantona	Butt	McClair	Beckham¹	Davies¹	Bufent o/g¹

CHARITY SHIELD

DATE	OPPONENT	VENUE	SCORE	ATTD	1	2	3	4	5	6	7	8	9	10	11	SUBSTITUTES
14-Aug-94	Blackburn R	Wembley	2-0	60,402	Schmeichel	May	Bruce	Pallister	Ince¹	McClair	Kan'skis	Cantona¹	Hughes	Sharpe	Giggs	

REDEMPTION

In Eric's absence United began the 1995-96 campaign poorly, losing 3-1 at Aston Villa before United's young (some critics said too young) team won won each of their next five games before a goalless draw with Sheffield Wednesday.

The Reds were second in the table behind Newcastle United prior to Cantona's return. The Geordies had won all their games apart from a defeat at Southampton. United fared less well in the cups. A reserve team were beaten 3-0 by York City at Old Trafford in the Coca-Cola Cup while Rotor Volgograd ended their UEFA Cup hopes at the first hurdle, a goalless draw in Russia followed by a 2-2 draw at home saw them go out on away goals, despite Peter Schmeichel's extraordinary header from a late corner.

MANCHESTER UNITED 2 LIVERPOOL 2
PREMIERSHIP - 1 OCTOBER 1995

248 DAYS, 18 hours and 57 minutes after he last kicked a ball professionally, Eric Cantona made his return to Old Trafford. 32 games after his Selhurst Park assault, Sky's cameras were present for a fairytale fixture that saw the Prodigal Son return against United's biggest rivals, the game being postponed for 24 hours to allow the player to take part.

Just 67 seconds in home fans were able to re-state their adoration when Eric set up Nicky Butt for the opener. And, later, when Jamie Redknapp brought Ryan Giggs to ground in the area, a penalty gave him the chance to score a late equaliser.

Cantona acknowledged the acclaim during the warm up and he was last out of the tunnel when the teams emerged to a deafening reception. The familiar figure with his collar up, chest out and trademark ramrod gait was the centre of attention. Liverpool kicked-off but lost the ball just inside their own half. Eric ventured down the left before centring for Butt who poked the ball past Phil Babb and then over David James. The midfielder was close to having a second a quarter of an hour in.

Yet this wasn't quite the fairytale the home supporters had hoped. Liverpool had plenty of chances and Robbie Fowler should have equalised before finally levelling in the 33rd minute. The striker broke down the left before cracking the ball over Peter Schmeichel close to the angle of post and bar in front of the Stretford End. In the 53rd minute Fowler grabbed the lead for the Merseysiders taking a sublime pass from Michael Thomas, beating Gary Neville before chipping Schmeichel.

Cantona looked rusty after an eight month lay off. He only made a few of the deft flicks that were his trademark and as he ran out of steam United's ideas slimmed too. Yet that late, controversial penalty awarded by David Elleray denied Liverpool victory. Cantona sending David James the wrong way from the spot after which the scorer dived joyfully into the crowd following a swing on the goal stantion.

YORK CITY 1 MANCHESTER UNITED 3
LEAGUE CUP 2ND RD 2ND LEG - 4 OCTOBER 1995

THE MINSTERMEN'S SHOCK 3-0 Old Trafford success had been the talk of football before Cantona's return and Alex Ferguson was keen to ensure pride was restored at Bootham Crescent, even if the Reds were likely to make an exit. Eric Cantona was amongst a number of stars who played when they would normally expect to sit things out. Just over 9,000 fans crammed into York's homely ground to see if the hosts could cling on to their advantage and score the biggest win of their history.

It was Cantona's first away game since returning and he faced 19 year-old goalkeeper Andy Warrington making a full debut in place of Dean Kiely, who had broken his nose during a 3-0 win at Hull City the previous weekend. The youngster was beaten the required three times but the visitor's efforts were in vain as York grabbed a crucial goal to grab a 4-3 aggregate win.

Cantona was at the heart of the first goal, recovering an Andy Cole cross which had evaded everyone as he scampered towards to the left flank. An ingenious pass released Scholes who took a touch then lashed in from the edge of the area. On 13 minutes Scholes, Cole and Ryan Giggs plundered a way down the same wing and Terry Cooke applied the scoring touch at the far post.

Later Alex Ferguson suggested his charges took their collective feet off the gas. Whatever the reason, York certainly started to see more of the ball. One attack reaped dividends just six minutes before the break meaning United had to score another two to get through. Paul Barnes, a two goal hero at Old Trafford, breezed past Gary Pallister and although Steve Bruce seemed to have made a vital intervention his sliding challenge did no more than push the ball into Scott Jordan's path. His shot gave Peter Schmeichel no chance.

United dominated after the restart but a resilient display kept York's noses ahead with a third goal only coming 10 minutes from time when Scholes made the most of Cole's shimmying dribble in the area.

IN ORDER TO gain extra sharpness and match fitness ahead of the Manchester Derby that would follow a break for international fixtures, Eric was included in a Pontins League match with Leeds United at Old Trafford. Lee Sharpe and Paul Scholes also played for United. Leeds had an all first team heavyweight attack of Phil Masinga, Rod Wallace, ex-Manchester City winger David White and Noel Whelan in opposition.

Eric's participation with the reserves lasted a mere 18 minutes. He had almost played Brian McClair in with a neat back-heeled flick but after a sliding tackle to deny his former side a chance to counter from the edge of their own area he failed to get up. An injury to his right knee was the obvious problem. He tested it a little but could only hobble. After limping to the sidelines and receiving treatment he was substituted. Moving down the touchline towards the dressing room those present rose to acclaim the star whose participation added to the massive 21,502 gate. At half-time an announcement was made on the public address system assuring all that the injury was not serious and the substitution was precautionary. "Eric," the throng were told, "sends his apologies to you all."

The crowd grew from its already large number at the start during the break as the 2pm kick-off was not widely appreciated by those who came to see Cantona. The latecomers must have feared the worst on spotting that their hero was not present as expected in the number seven shirt. However, they were able to cheer late Graeme Tomlinson and Terry Cooke goals in a 2-0 win.

France, who had drawn two of the four internationals Eric missed, had dented their chances of making Euro 1996. There is no evidence to suggest the tied games with Israel and Poland would have finished differently with the Manchester United man but Aime Jacquet decided it was too early to recall Cantona for a crunch meeting with Romania in mid-October.

In fact he didn't even invite Eric to join his party for training and was rumoured to have considered dropping Cantona prior to events at Crystal Palace. Though Jacquet never confirmed the player was no longer in his plans, his omission from a match with Israel in Caen during mid-November when he had built up a little more match fitness and shown good form, seemed to suggest there was no route back.

Claude Simonet, president of the French Football Federation, had already suggested that the incident at Selhurst Park would spell the end of his international career and there was now an excuse for the national side to wash their hands of him. With an eye on the 1998 World Cup Finals, which they would host, France had opted for youth rather than experience. No matter how well Eric performed the rebuffs continued as the season wore on although the general feeling was that France's loss could only be Manchester United's gain. There was also a touch of irony especially as Cantona was busy assisting and cajoling a young squad at Old Trafford. He was later to state that a huge disappointment in his career was not being able to represent his country at Euro 96.

CHELSEA 1 MANCHESTER UNITED 4
PREMIERSHIP - 21 OCTOBER 1995

MARK HUGHES IN Chelsea blue faced United for the first time in his career. The home side, suffering from injuries and suspensions, pushed Ruud Gullit back to act as a sweeper. The knee injury which had seen Eric Cantona miss the slender 1-0 derby win, had cleared up enough for him to start. Denis Irwin shook off a similar injury to play.

Newcastle United had established themselves as early favourites for the title and a 6-1 hammering of Wimbledon kept the Magpies four points ahead. Yet the Reds put together moves of such beguiling sophistication - a 21-pass opus brought the opener and typified the team's confidence, while the flamboyance of Giggs and Cantona thrived on the space provided, that they looked capable of mounting a challenge.

Following their opening day defeat, seven wins and two draws had critics reconsidering their words. The hosts had won four of their last five games so approached their task with confidence. Alan Wilkie, who had sent Cantona off against Crystal Palace moments before he launched himself into the stands, was the referee at Stamford Bridge. Possibly hoping to push buttons on Cantona's first return to the capital since his infamous night at Selhurst Park, boos and jeers rang around the stands every time he touched the ball, or at least until Paul Scholes notched the opener on three minutes. Gary Neville's cross flighted towards Cantona found the young midfielder who lashed in. Scholes then got a foot to Gullitt's attempt to start a move down the flank half a dozen minutes later to set up the second, Cantona flicking a return pass to the youngster who once again finished with aplomb.

Scholes hit the crossbar soon after the restart but there were few other chances until Paul Furlong, who had already given Peter Schmeichel concerns with two headers, nodded a John Spencer centre into Hughes' path 15 minutes from time.

If there was a danger United might throw away all their good work, that possibility was removed just three minutes later. Giggs raced down the left past Steve Clarke and Frank Sinclair before stroking the ball past Kharine. Cantona was instrumental in a nine pass move which substitute Brian McClair finished, executing an impudent switch of balance that helped him through a defence which attempted to close down any options. There was a late chance for Eric to add a fifth but he missed a late Neville cross.

MANCHESTER UNITED 2 MIDDLESBROUGH 0
PREMIERSHIP - 28 OCTOBER 1995

THERE WAS WARM applause on Bryan Robson's return to Old Trafford. His successor Roy Keane lasted half an hour before an apparently innocuous clash with Jan Aage Fjortoft ended with the midfielder sending a right hook across the forward's head. The dismissal came after an angry period of play and the blue touch paper was lit when Nigel Pearson aimed a studs-up lunge at Eric Cantona. The Frenchman walked away but Keane could not ignore the incident and ran almost 30 yards to remonstrate. A kick out by Robbie Mustoe as players were parted further raised the temperature. The heated contest continued for almost a quarter of an hour until Fjortoft pulled Keane's shirt. The Irishman didn't even wait for the notebook to come out. Ryan Giggs came in from the wing to cover in midfield.

Middlesbrough looked to play an open game which should have suited a team with a man advantage. Boro couldn't capitalise however, although they rallied after falling behind two minutes before the break. Gary Pallister punished a weak fist away by former United keeper Gary Walsh with a firm header. Cantona teed up a goal three minutes from the end to wrap up the points.

ARSENAL 1 MANCHESTER UNITED 0
Premiership - 4 November 1995

United tasted league defeat for the first time since their opening day reverse at Aston Villa allowing Newcastle to extend the gap at the top. Andy Cole in particular will not remember this game with any affection, the striker missed a host of chances as the Gunners backline was punctured countless times. Both managers had reason to be happy but on very different grounds - Bruce Rioch for the three points, Alex Ferguson at the level of performance which nine times out of ten would have won the game.

A lapse by Denis Irwin led to Peter Schmeichel being beaten after 16 minutes. The Irishman beat Dennis Bergkamp to David Platt's chipped pass, but under-hit an attempted backpass and when he tried to make good the error Bergkamp was far too quick, running in on Schmeichel before casually flicking the ball inside the right hand post. The home crowd sensed another could follow with Bergkamp and Wright forcing Schmeichel into saves.

All that kept United in the game was the threat of Ryan Giggs. Arsenal's pre-occupation with United's flanks allowed Cole more space but he failed to finish from 15 yards with only David Seaman to beat. Another pass slotted through the centre by Cantona gave Cole an opportunity to atone but a delay after the striker opted to take a touch allowed Adams to block. The roles were reversed when Cole gave Cantona a chance to level but an unusually heavy touch spoiled the angle he hoped to create and Seaman saved. Though vastly improved as a player Cole didn't look in the same class as Bergkamp, despite the pair commanding similar transfer fees. His uncertainty extended to an all-round game that looked shoddy in comparison.

Cantona's influence and contribution increased in the second half. It took two minutes before Seaman was given a second test of the afternoon - yet again the England stopper diverting a Cole effort. Another good chance came on the hour after Cantona and

Roy Keane weaved a route past Tony Adams and Steve Bould. Cole's best chance emerged after Cantona and Giggs carved an opening sending him clear on Seaman, the one time Highbury apprentice poked his shot inches wide.

Arsenal were pinned back for long periods, with Bergkamp and Paul Merson happy to help the defence. Yet the same duo were involved in a sweet move which almost yielded a second. Once Platt moved the ball forward they exchanged four crisp passes which ended in a Merson cross for Wright to send goalwards. Only an astounding save kept the gap at a single goal – enough as it turned out.

MANCHESTER UNITED 4 SOUTHAMPTON 1
PREMIERSHIP - 18 NOVEMBER 1995

WHEN UNITED WERE good they were almost unplayable here but their purple patch lasted barely 15 minutes. Ten of those minutes were at the opening of the game. Eric Cantona, in a mood to make the impossible look common place, found Ryan Giggs the perfect foil.

A Saints mistake at the kick-off allowed Cantona and Giggs to play a couple of quick passes which released Paul Scholes on the right. A centre to the far post was over-hit but Cantona pulled it back at the by-line for Giggs to fire past Dave Beasant. The Welshman had a brace within three minutes. Winning the ball off Richard Hall inside the Southampton half before unleashing an unerring shot. David Beckham struck the bar in the next foray downfield before, with just eight minutes gone, Scholes profited from an impudent dink from Cantona.

Bewildered Southampton never regained their composure as Cantona, acutely aware of Andy Cole's need to get back in the scoring habit, indulged the England international with a string of through balls. None paid off as his attempts to breach Beasant's defences failed before he finished a Beckham corner. Neil Shipperley replied, scrambling the ball in for a toe-poked consolation.

COVENTRY CITY 0 MANCHESTER UNITED 4
PREMIERSHIP - 22 NOVEMBER 1995

UNITED'S SCINTILLATING FORM helped halve Newcastle's lead over the field. Brian McClair grabbed a couple of deserved goals which, added to strikes from Denis Irwin and David Beckham, saw United ease past poor Coventry.

As had been the case against Southampton Ryan Giggs and Eric

Cantona were dominant figures and once more Andy Cole spurned a host of chances. While the goals were flowing it didn't cause much anxiety for Alex Ferguson but some feared that the striker's form would prove a major headache.

Coventry could point to a Dion Dublin goal that was incorrectly ruled out. Referee Keith Burge failed to see the striker's effort cross the line before Steve Bruce cleared, the linesman refused to signal a goal giving the senior official no option but to wave play on. Spurred by the injustice Coventry were the better side throughout the opening quarter. Peter Schmeichel denied Dublin and used his legs to keep a John Salako attempt out but once the Sky Blues fell behind they folded.

Giggs created the opener after 27 minutes, floating a corner on to Gary Pallister's head. Rather than divert the ball goalwards the centre back nodded it out to Denis Irwin who finished with a flourish. Two minutes into the second half Giggs made the most of loose control from Marcus Hall, picking out McClair with a reverse pass, the Scottish international netting from a dozen yards. An equally perceptive final ball from Cantona crafted the third though there was a rogue element. Nicky Butt failed to see David Rennie and when the two collided the attending defenders expected a whistle to sound. It never came and within the blink of an eye Cantona found David Beckham who scored with a low angled drive. A quarter of an hour from the end Giggs and Cantona combined with the latter standing the ball up for McClair to glance in.

NOTTINGHAM FOREST 1 MANCHESTER UNITED 1
PREMIERSHIP - 27 NOVEMBER 1995

DESPITE YET MORE incisive play from Giggs and Cantona, United struggled to convert chances at the City Ground. Nottingham born Andy Cole's worrying form continued and but for an Eric Cantona penalty in the second half, the Reds would have gone down to an undeserved defeat.

Forest had been hammered 7-0 at Blackburn in their last run out and most pundits believed that United could better that score - yet in goalkeeper Mark Crossley Forest had an insurmountable obstacle. Frank Clark took no chances with tactics, massing players behind the ball and relying on counter attacks. The ploy worked on 19 minutes, Colin Cooper's punt being helped on by Brian McClair. Bobby Howe attempted a snap shot which Gary Pallister could only divert towards Paul McGregor, the striker sweeping the ball in from 10 yards.

Crossley had already denied Cole by this point and Stuart Pearce got himself in the way of a David Beckham drive. Nicky Butt failed to bring a save from two efforts and Giggs fired a good drive against a post. Cantona and Giggs, always dangerous in the first half, resumed their devastating dual attack early in the second half, a spectacular back-heel from the Frenchman matched by a sumptuous Giggs run. The pair tracked each other over 30 yards and the return pass was a crisp one. Cantona may have preferred to shoot but once diverted wide by Crossley looked to find Cole in the centre. From nowhere the keeper saved the header then denied Paul Scholes who seemed certain to score with the follow up.

Scholes played Cantona in for a penalty conceded following Steve Chettle's crude tackle from behind. The Frenchman notching his 50th goal in 103 appearances. Cole was denied by another piece of excellence from Crossley with three minutes remaining.

MANCHESTER UNITED 1 CHELSEA 1
PREMIERSHIP - 2 DECEMBER 1995

ANDY COLE'S FAILURE to convert chances cost United another two points against Chelsea and with it there seemed a chance leaders Newcastle would disappear over the horizon. This time David Beckham spared United's blushes to equalise Dennis Wise's strike.

The visitors were without Ruud Gullit, Gavin Peacock and Terry Phelan. United had Kevin Pilkington starting his first league game with Peter Schmeichel out. Alongside him in a watching brief were Nicky Butt, Roy Keane, Ryan Giggs and Gary Pallister. A dull opening saw Chelsea happy to sit back and United strangely out of sorts. David Lee's shot across the face of goal was a rare moment of forward action, while Lee Sharpe fired wide and Paul Scholes' header forced Kharine into a fine stop.

After the interval, Steve Bruce headed a decent chance off-target before a defensive lapse gave Chelsea the lead. Sharpe's poor back-pass allowed John Spencer in on Pilkington, who parried the first effort but was helpless when Wise reached the rebound. Wise soon became a hero at both ends clearing a Bruce header off his own line when it seemed Andy Myers had handled but no penalty was awarded.

Home frustrations continued, Cantona earning a caution for a mistimed tackle on Eddie Newton. It was a rare lapse for the new look Cantona who preferred to set his sights on goal rather than retribution. Cole played an unwitting part in the equaliser when he fluffed a chance to test Kharine from Gary Neville's low centre, the ball ran for Beckham who calmly slotted into the top corner from the edge of the area. There should have been a winner when Cantona released Beckham but the youngster could only fire straight at the keeper.

United fans' appreciation towards their returning hero was reflected in a billboard advertisement opposite Old Trafford that thanked Cantona for "three amazing years". Eric's third anniversary was a reason for real celebration, his continued presence a calming influence on a talented if raw team.

MANCHESTER UNITED 2 SHEFFIELD WEDNESDAY 2
PREMIERSHIP - 9 DECEMBER 1995

FOUR YEARS BEFORE this game Sheffield Wednesday had resisted United's attempts to take David Hirst from Hillsborough, forcing the bid for Eric Cantona. The striker had suffered numerous and lengthy injury setbacks since that time. Interest had obviously subsided as a result. While Hirst visibly laboured on the afternoon, the man who eventually ended up at Old Trafford prospered.

During the early winter Cantona was saving games when colleagues failed to perform. Five missing faces - Ryan Giggs, Peter Schmeichel, Denis Irwin, Roy Keane and Nicky Butt – contributed to another disappointing result, but the Frenchman continued to perform like a virtuoso. The second of Cantona's two strikes against Sheffield Wednesday came just six minutes from time saving a season long unbeaten home run and reducing Newcastle's lead by a point after an unexpected loss at Chelsea.

Andy Cole, who had been described in his manager's programme notes as 'careless' against Southampton, was far from the worst performer in front of goal. His one and only chance came when Lee Briscoe dived at his feet as Cole readied himself to shoot. Lee Sharpe had the most gilt edged chance, hitting Kevin Pressman's legs from six yards under no pressure.

Cantona put United ahead with his first goal from open play since returning from suspension. A move in which Sharpe, Scholes and Cole played a crucial part, ended with a perfectly placed chip which caught Pressman unawares on 20 minutes. The lead would have doubled had Pressman not tipped a Cantona header turned against the post.

Chris Waddle, a former colleague of Cantona's at Marseilles, aped his former teammate in a play-making role and helped to level after an hour. Steve Bruce failed to deal with his cross allowing Mark Bright to apply a lobbed finish. Pilkington also had little chance with Guy Whittingham's header from a Marc Degryse centre. Yet Cantona saved the day once more with a spectacular volley from the edge of the area. His control of a ball which bounced high followed by a turn and shot which darted into the corner of goal marked out a great player.

Cantona earned praise from all corners but his manager was fulsome, "He was the best player on the field. Without him we would have lost the game, there's no question about that. He inspired all the good things that we did. His responsibility, his commitment to working off the ball was magnificent."

LIVERPOOL 2 MANCHESTER UNITED 0
PREMIERSHIP - 17 DECEMBER 1995

ROBBIE FOWLER CLAIMED the plaudits and ended a five game barren run with a brace as Liverpool got the better of United at Anfield for a second successive season. Had Peter Schmeichel not been in commanding form the damage would have been far greater. By contrast United rarely threatened David James as a four match run without a win left them seven points behind Newcastle.

Fowler served notice of his intent on 11 minutes, heading a Rob Jones cross narrowly wide, while Stan Collymore, who had something of a face-off with Schmeichel for most of the game, forced the Dane into two saves within a minute. David Beckham tested his own gloveman with a miscued clearance. The keeper was stranded and relieved to see the ball dip just over rather than under the bar.

United looked set to go into the break all square but with just seconds to go an alert Fowler spotted Schmeichel slightly off balance while looking to defend a free-kick from 25 yards out and curled the ball into the top right hand corner.

United produced little at the other end, David James was a spectator for the most part as the second half continued to be one-way traffic. Collymore was thwarted again by the angle of post and crossbar minutes after he had seen a penalty shout turned down.

In desperation, Andy Cole was withdrawn in favour of Paul

Scholes and Eric Cantona forced a save with a well placed header. James was then forced to pull of a sublime save from a Cantona volley following neat play between Giggs and McClair.

Liverpool wrapped up the points when McManaman teed up Fowler three minutes from the end. Fowler stepped inside before clipping in his 15th of the season.

LEEDS UNITED 3 MANCHESTER UNITED 1
Premiership - 24 December 1995

Successive defeats at two hated rivals piled more pressure on Alex Ferguson's young side. They seemed ill-prepared for an imminent meeting with runaway leaders Newcastle and lost Steve Bruce here to leave a struggling defence threadbare.

A controversial penalty both managers questioned after just five minutes set Leeds towards victory. Referee Dermot Gallagher punished Nicky Butt when he saw a hand make contact with the ball. Steve Bruce was irate and only stopped protesting when Peter Schmeichel intervened. McAllister's high spot-kick was emphatic as were Leeds who turned in a fine display through Tomas Brolin. The Swede provided the kind of creative edge missing since Eric Cantona's departure, setting up Brian Deane and Tony Yeboah with chances. Deane's best was a precise looking clip against the bar. Yeboah went one-on-one with Schmeichel twice but was denied on both occasions.

While Brolin was inspired, Cantona was subdued. Andy Cole equalised with his fourth of the campaign after Nicky Butt dispossessed Gary Speed and crossed for the striker to hit a low volley. Cole got more chances following promptings from Butt, Cantona, Keane and Beckham but their sporadic nature gave an air of inevitability about the final score.

Leeds could and should have scored their second well before the 35th minute when Paul Parker missed the ball allowing Yeboah to charge through, the Ghanaian chipping Schmeichel. The margin of victory threatened to be far more substantial and a third was overdue by the 73rd minute when Brolin took a pass from Carlton Palmer on the right. A dummy seemed to wrong foot the entire backline who were caught out by a lobbed pass towards the penalty spot where Deane headed powerfully home. Cantona needed stitches after a clash of heads although he wasn't likely to be ruled out of the mouth-watering clash with Newcastle just 72 hours later.

MANCHESTER UNITED 2 NEWCASTLE UNITED 0
PREMIERSHIP - 27 DECEMBER 1995

ANDY COLE RE-DISCOVERED THE goal scoring form that had persuaded Alex Ferguson to part with £7 million and Keith Gillespie for him just 12 months before with a stunning strike that kept United in the title race. This was the Red's first win in a month and victory was a huge fillip. The gap at the top would have extended to 13 points with a Newcastle victory.

The Old Trafford boss had noted a change in Cole during the defeat at Leeds. His accuracy had returned even if he failed to beat Mark Beeney more than once. Many had poured scorn on his post-match comments to that effect but there were few who felt inclined to do so now, even though there were poor misses to go along with a clinical strike.

Roy Keane and Nicky Butt laid the foundations of victory, taking control of midfield. As a result, United dominated from the start - Peter Beardsley lost out to Ryan Giggs who instigated the opening goal. The Newcastle defence, unnerved by Cantona's run, left a gap on the right in which Giggs found Cole, the striker's unerring effort beating Pavel Srnicek into the far corner.

Beardsley could have atoned for his error straight from the kick-off but with a chance to take aim at Peter Schmeichel missed the ball. A quarter of the match had passed before the travelling fans had something to cheer but Schmeichel denied Les Ferdinand. United sealed the points late on when a partially cleared corner found Keane who launched an unstoppable shot past Srnicek.

MANCHESTER UNITED 2 QUEENS PARK RANGERS 1
PREMIERSHIP - 30 DECEMBER 1995

WITH A PENCHANT for all things French at Old Trafford, United gave a debut to trialist William Prunier who had played with Eric Cantona at Auxerre. A holder of one full cap he had bought out his contract with Bordeaux and was seeking a new start across The Channel.

David May, Gary Pallister and Steve Bruce's absence meant he partnered Gary Neville at centre-half while Phil Neville took over at right-back, Denis Irwin retaining his brief on the left. He looked secure enough for the most part and supplemented a sound display with forward surges and a willingness to join attacks. His passing range was more than adequate though he had difficulty marrying up with Gary Neville.

Andy Cole got a welcome goal with Prunier playing a crucial part in the build up. The debutant also smashed an effort against the crossbar. Ryan Giggs provided a crucial second after QPR had gone close through Daniel Dichio. As well as he had performed, and somewhat against the general acclaim coming his way, there was a note of caution from Alex Ferguson who wanted to see a little bit more from the Bordeaux centre-half commenting: "We will play William and what we will see is how he defends away from home. There is always that thing about European defenders and how quickly they can pick up the pace. It's a far quicker tempo here. People get into the box more than they do abroad. Most of their attacking ends with just one or two in the area. In our game you will see four or five at times.

"I thought William improved as the game went on. He had the variety of facing Bradley Allen and then Daniele Dichio, who are both young. Teddy Sheringham is more experienced and we will have a better idea after seeing that."

TOTTENHAM HOTSPUR 4 MANCHESTER UNITED 1
PREMIERSHIP - 1 JANUARY 1996

WILLIAM PRUNIER GOT his chance to show some mettle away from Old Trafford but in a defence hit by injury - Denis Irwin was forced out - he struggled against a vibrant Tottenham front line. When Peter Schmeichel injured a calf during the warm-up and was forced off at half-time and Paul Scholes left unable to play due to illness United were in disarray and it showed.

The Reds held out for more than half an hour, though sometimes they had to rely on luck to protect a limping keeper. Just five minutes in Teddy Sheringham headed against the post after reaching a corner before his marker, then Chris Armstrong hit a rising effort from 20 yards against the junction of upright and crossbar. Still, United had their moments and with Cantona pulling the strings in a reserved role Ian Walker had to make a number of saves. Cantona, Beckham and Cole were all thwarted by good stops. However, the pattern of play changed when Tottenham went ahead ten minutes before the break.

Dean Austin evaded Phil Neville and crossed low for Sheringham who, after fluffing his initial attempt to score, was able to prod the ball past an ailing Schmeichel. An instant riposte came when Nicky Butt charged forward from the restart and the ball ran to Cole who finished from close range. Yet on the stroke of half-time Spurs regained the lead, Paul Parker, unwittingly squaring for Sol Campbell after Teddy Sheringham put him under pressure. Schmeichel had no chance.

A stooping Armstrong header after Ronnie Rosenthal had flicked Darren Caskey's centre on provided the home side with a third and the same striker grabbed a second after nodding an astute lobbed pass from Sheringham home. United laid siege to Spurs goal at times, Rosenthal was forced to clear off his own line, while Ian Walker was forced into last gasp heroics. Cole only just failed to find the target with a shot which passed the wrong side of the post.

United hadn't been beaten by a margin this big since losing at home to Queens Park Rangers almost four years ago to the day and the man at the helm for QPR that day, Gerry Francis, had also masterminded this win. Defeat handed Newcastle the initiative, their home win over Arsenal sending the Magpies seven points clear.

Alex Ferguson offered William Prunier the chance to extend his trial with Manchester United but with a permanent deal unlikely the player called time on his Old Trafford stay. Widely criticised after his White Hart Lane performance, it seemed offers back in France were far more attractive.

MANCHESTER UNITED 2 SUNDERLAND 2
FA CUP 3RD RD - 6 JANUARY 1996

FOR THE SECOND time in a month United were saved by a late Eric Cantona strike. With Sunderland threatening to knock the Reds out of the FA Cup at the first hurdle for the first time in 22 years, the Frenchman spared their blushes 11 minutes from time.

The match seemed likely to go to type after United took an early lead but the Rokerites, roared on by 8,000 supporters, dominated and scored twice within a few minutes. Even the loss of captain Kevin Ball failed to disrupt a side which seemed keen to prove itself against Premiership opposition. Prior to United's opener Sunderland had been the better side and Nicky Butt's deft chipped finish from the host's first potent move would have finished off most teams. But Peter Reid's side continued to dominate - Michael Gray striking an upright from 25 yards before Phil Gray feathered the ball after a quick turn in the area when a firmer touch would almost certainly have given Kevin Pilkington no chance.

Steve Agnew deservedly levelled when he hammered in a low

effort from just inside the area after Michael Gray had caused havoc with a mazy run. Pilkington was equally helpless with Russell's strike following Agnew's precise clip over a retreating defence.

The final quarter saw United finally dictate affairs but until Cantona got his head to a Lee Sharpe free-kick at the far post, an equaliser seemed unlikely.

MANCHESTER UNITED 0 ASTON VILLA 0
PREMIERSHIP - 13 JANUARY 1996

ANDY COLE HAD now bagged four in as many games but his profligacy returned against Aston Villa. With Newcastle taking to the field 24 hours later, United needed a win but the home side seemed intent on throwing away the initiative gained by their 2-0 win over the leaders a fortnight earlier.

Villa came looking for a stalemate and accomplished their mission despite being pegged back for lengthy periods. Ugo Ehiogu and Gareth Southgate were excellent, restricting Cole to a header from eight yards which he flicked wide and another from farther out that was blasted into the stands. Southgate shackled Eric Cantona throughout, forcing him so deep that the Frenchman became ineffective.

Ryan Giggs sparkled but even a player of his ability could do little on his own. Veteran Paul McGrath mopped up easily and Cantona only slipped the leash at a corner, Giggs' delivery producing a header that was comfortably saved. The Welsh winger also forced a save with a shot which kept low and Roy Keane's shot from range missed by a whisker as the anxiety levels rose at Old Trafford.

SUNDERLAND 1 MANCHESTER UNITED 2
FA CUP 3RD RD REPLAY - 16 JANUARY 1996

ANDY COLE WAS the centre of attention again, this time striking a last minute winner to send Sunderland out of the cup. Alex Ferguson, who had noted the lessons from the first game, selected a more defensive side playing five at the back with three centre halves. There was an opportunity for attacks to be supported but also a reliance on an isolated forward line to get the goals.

The Rokerites served further notice of their potential within 10 minutes - only a mix up between Martin Smith and Phil Gray saving United. Phil Gray was then denied by a well-timed Paul Parker interception before the deadlock was broken when a Steve Bruce clearance fell to Michael Gray who combined with Steve

THE COMPLETE ERIC CANTONA

Agnew before sliding the ball past Schmeichel. Sunderland should have doubled the lead soon after, Phil and Michael Gray outwitting the United defence, releasing Agnew who had the beating of Bruce. Schmeichel advanced to get a solid hand on the ball.

United produced little in the first period, but Lee Sharpe's introduction for Paul Parker saw the Reds dominate. Cantona missed a gilt-edged chance. Then United levelled on 70 minutes when Paul Scholes steered a left-sided Phil Neville cross home. Sunderland rallied and seemed set to force extra-time until Cole popped up to burst their bubble, converting a simple chance at the death.

WEST HAM UNITED 0 MANCHESTER UNITED 1
PREMIERSHIP - 22 JANUARY 1996

UNITED PAID THEIR annual visit to their bogey ground 12 points behind Newcastle who had already beaten Bolton Wanderers by the odd goal in three that weekend. Upton Park had seen previous United championship tilts fail, not least on their last visit when a win would have won the title. Yet United recorded only their second victory at the Boleyn in 21 years despite Nicky Butt's dismissal for a foul on Julian Dicks.

The vital goal came after just nine minutes, Eric Cantona finishing following Giggs' run and cross, the Frenchman steering his effort over Miklosko. Butt's dismissal came after Dicks had attempted a hack at Cole who was nimble enough to vault away from danger. Butt's tackle just seconds later was a form of retribution. Cole reacted so badly to the decision that he was shown a yellow card. Keen to ensure it didn't get worse his substitution followed immediately. West Ham threatened a barn-storming finish but foundered on United's much improved defence.

READING 0 MANCHESTER UNITED 3
FA CUP - 27 JANUARY 1996

READING HAD ONLY missed out on promotion to the top flight a season previously, losing the play-off final to Bolton Wanderers 4-3. Since then many of their best players had left and the Royals were never in this game, which only went ahead thanks to 20 tonnes of sand being spread on the pitch.

Joint player-managers, Mick Gooding and Jimmy Quinn, both 36, almost worked something between themselves before Quinn sent another effort goalwards which Trevor Morley deflected just wide. Gooding was making things tick on the pitch. He presented Lee

Nogan with a chance, his low cross was just missed by the striker.

When the change in emphasis came Cantona, who had seemed a little subdued, was at the heart of United's best play, providing a verve that was often absent. Sharpe set up the first goal, dispossessing Michael Gilkes close to the area and evading a challenge to shoot, Hammond parried and Giggs slotted home.

Paul Parker made sure of progress, registering his first goal in three years, although it appeared he was attempting to cross rather than shoot. The afternoon's final goal came with little more than a minute remaining, Nicky Butt's cross from the left and a Sharpe flick falling to Cantona who gave Hammond no chance.

When missiles came from the home sections of the crowd - one of which hit a linesman - they seemed aimed at Cantona who remained level headed and, although he returned a banana to the crowd, it was with no more than a gentle lob.

WIMBLEDON 2 MANCHESTER UNITED 4
PREMIERSHIP - 3 FEBRUARY 1996

IN RECENT WEEKS Eric Cantona had shown a restraint which would have done a pacifist proud but there were some who feared this lack of fire had nullified his game. A year and 10 days after the incident which led to his nine month ban, he returned to the scene of the crime, Selhurst Park. It may have daunted some but not Cantona whose two late goals proved vital. Then again Eric had to be on his best behaviour with his father Albert an interested onlooker in the Director's Box.

Although Wimbledon never led they still came close to upsetting the apple cart. But with Nicky Butt and Roy Keane in midfield United coped well despite the loss of captain Steve Bruce after just a quarter of an hour. Cantona took the armband while Keane deputised for Bruce at the back. The central defender came off to have 14 stitches inserted into his forehead after an accidental clash with Dean Holdsworth's elbow. The match was competitive but never dirty. Only one booking was made and that was for a succession of niggling fouls on Cantona by Steve Talboys.

Substitute David Beckham proved a perfect counter-balance to Cantona, his burgeoning partnership with Gary Neville down the right setting United on their way. Beckham was instrumental in the opener, lobbing the ball forward for Denis Irwin whose cross was met by Andy Cole with a perfectly timed run and jump at the far post. Seconds before half-time Lee Sharpe was felled just outside the box. Beckham curled a free-kick on goal which bounced off the underside of the bar, a disorientated Chris Perry flicking it into his own net to double the lead.

Marcus Gayle pulled one back from an Alan Kimble cross forcing United to up the pace. Cantona combined with Beckham whose centre the French international planted firmly past Sullivan. He headed for the crowd but there was no malice towards these supporters, as he joined the United fans in celebration before stewards stepped in. Jason Euell reduced the deficit to a single goal for the second time taking Keane's errant header past Schmeichel to shoot into an empty net. Cantona had the final word after Giggs had a shot handled by Kenny Cunningham. After scoring he looked to head towards the United supporters again but acknowledged the concerns of the stewards and waved instead.

MANCHESTER UNITED 1 BLACKBURN ROVERS 0
PREMIERSHIP - 10 FEBRUARY 1996

EVEN IF UNITED were not best placed to depose Blackburn Rovers as champions they were able to give the team which took their crown a bloody nose, although the narrow margin failed to do justice to their dominance. Ray Harford had taken the reins at Ewood Park with Kenny Dalglish becoming Director of Football. No longer the force they had been in the previous two seasons, Rovers away form and the absence of six players signalled a tough afternoon for the visitors.

With Mike Newell anonymous as a goal threat, Rovers only chances fell to Shearer just before the break. He headed a Kevin Gallacher cross over and sent a difficult volley wide when he may have expected to test Peter Schmeichel. The scraps he had to feed on were meagre, although a ring rusty backpass from the returning Gary Pallister was scrambled clear.

The winning goal came early with skipper for the day Eric Cantona, leading in the continued absence of Steve Bruce, setting up Lee Sharpe. The Frenchman playing a one-two with Andy Cole and hit a post, Sharpe scrambling the ball home. United didn't let up, a low Sharpe cross just evaded the number seven who had started the move back in midfield. Tim Flowers was also forced to claw a Denis Irwin effort which dipped and swerved as it flew towards the net away. It was United's first home win of 1996.

MANCHESTER UNITED 2 MANCHESTER CITY 1

FA Cup 5th Rd - 18 February 1996

A CONTENTIOUS PENALTY awarded by Alan Wilkie, the man who had indirectly triggered Eric Cantona's nine month ban, gave United a lifeline against City. The spot-kick was awarded for holding in the penalty area by Michael Frontzeck on Eric Cantona, an offence many believed was not worthy of such an award. Eric converted to give the hosts a parity they barely deserved.

Cantona, in contrast to his recent good behaviour, was unable to resist the provocation of the derby, going nose to nose with Michael Brown in the first minute. Roy Keane continued the theme with an uncompromising foul on Georgi Kinkladze. The Irish international was in danger of getting his marching orders and came close after he saw Brown lay his studs on a prostrate Nicky Butt. A group of players gathered to trade insults but not blows.

The reason for United's anxiety was a thorough examination by their neighbours who profited from some outstanding contributions by Kinkladze. The Georgian created the opening goal just 11 minutes in, splitting the defence with a pass which fed Uwe Rosler who lobbed an advancing Peter Schmeichel to send the blue hordes into ecstasy.

United finally found their feet in the dying moments of the opening period with the penalty that turned the game. A Giggs corner was floated over and Frontzeck and Cantona went for the ball, the German defender clearing. The referee pointed to the spot but it took a few moments before the crowd realised he had indicated a penalty.

United grasped the momentum, Giggs nodded slightly over with the goal gaping and Immel pulled off impressive saves from Keane and Sharpe to keep the prospect of a Maine Road replay alive until, with 78 minutes gone, Giggs found Phil Neville whose cross somehow fell for Sharpe who smacked his effort home.

MANCHESTER UNITED 2 EVERTON 0
Premiership - 21 February 1996

UNITED MADE THREE points up on Newcastle following the Toon's shock 2-0 reverse at Upton Park. Late goals in each half turned this hard fought contest. Andrei Kanchelskis, booed by sections of the crowd after his £5 million move up the East Lancs Road, was head and shoulders above everyone else in a blue shirt. The reception seemed not to concern the Ukrainian who caused no small measure of anxiety to his former employers.

Neville Southall was the busier keeper, forced to deny Phil Neville, following a wicked deflection off John Ebbrell. Andy Cole may have made the most of a David Unsworth error had Dave Watson not been so alert. Roy Keane had the honour of completing the finest move either side produced in the first half on 30 minutes, the Irishman bursting through the Everton rearguard to benefit from a one-two between Nicky Butt and Eric Cantona. The Frenchman, an otherwise peripheral figure, beat two men as he zipped through the gears on a sprint from halfway before locating Keane. Neville Southall attempted to narrow the angle but the ball was slid past him.

A light snowstorm fell on Old Trafford early in the second half but it was the Everton blizzard that threatened the United backline with the Merseyside club only deprived of an equaliser when a Schmeichel lunge denied Ebbrell's drive. The Dane also blocked Amokachi after a darting run. A betting man would have placed a fair wager on a draw at this stage. The Reds were looking far from a force in attack and doing no more than hanging on until, against the run of play, Giggs established a cushion. United broke following an Everton attack, Giggs taking a pass from Lee Sharpe, releasing Cantona who in turn sent Cole dashing towards goal with defenders trailing. The striker returned the compliment allowing Giggs to dab the cross over Southall. Although still half a dozen points behind, this was a win which lent greater significance to United's upcoming journey to St James Park.

BOLTON WANDERERS 0 MANCHESTER UNITED 6
PREMIERSHIP - 25 FEBRUARY 1996

WITH NEWCASTLE DROPPING more points following a 3-3 draw at Maine Road, United's crushing win at Burnden Park further closed the gap ahead of the top two's crunch meeting.

United wasted no time in crushing poor Wanderers - five minutes had elapsed when Roy Keane sent Ryan Giggs charging down an unguarded left, a chip over full back Keith Branagan and a shot which rebounded back off the bar allowed David Beckham to head in. Cole had a chance to double the lead soon after but his effort was kept out. However, it only delayed the inevitable. Steve Bruce nodding in from the resulting corner.

Bolton came back when Alan Thompson's free-kick caused some

anxiety but just under a quarter of the game remained when Cole lashed in the third. By the time a fourth arrived Cantona and Giggs had taken a seat on the bench. Cantona's replacement, Paul Scholes, scored within 100 seconds of being introduced and doubled his tally five minutes later, re-directing a Keane chance just to make sure. Nicky Butt completed the half dozen a minute from time. Between the final two strikes Nathan Blake thought he had pulled one back but his celebrations were cut short by an offside flag.

NEWCASTLE UNITED 0 MANCHESTER UNITED 1
PREMIERSHIP - 4 MARCH 1996

AT ONE STAGE Newcastle had held a 14 point advantage over the field and looked certain to clinch a first championship since 1927. However, there had been one or two stutters at St James Park while United went on a run of five straight victories. That lead was down to six points and this win halved that gap, yet it was far from straightforward.

Newcastle had the best home record in the top flight and had not suffered defeat at St James Park for almost a year. So it came as no surprise that the hosts burst out of the blocks. United were pinned in their own half for most of the opening 45 minutes with Peter Schmeichel producing one of the great performances to keep the Reds level. World class saves from Les Ferdinand and David Ginola kept the match goalless and the odd slice of luck helped as well: Peter Beardsley struck the crossbar with a free-kick and the normally assured Ferdinand somehow managed to spoon over from just six yards.

The second half didn't herald a complete change around but within six minutes of the resumption Andy Cole was able to get one over on his old club by supplying the cross from which Eric Cantona, pulling away at the far post, volleyed home. The move had seen United suddenly spark into life as an attacking threat for almost the first time and it was inevitable that Cantona would be the man to coolly accept the chance in an otherwise frenetic game.

The goal came completely against the run of play, in fact it was the visitors' first real attack and knocked the stuffing out of Newcastle and had ramifications for the wider title race. United were prepared for a Newcastle onslaught but the home side couldn't match their earlier zeal. As the game wore on Newcastle seemed to accept the inevitable, with some home supporters in tears at the final whistle.

MANCHESTER UNITED 2 SOUTHAMPTON 0
FA Cup 6th Rd - 11 March 1996

A below par United marched into the FA Cup semi-finals thanks to Eric Cantona who scored the opener before crafting a second in added time for Lee Sharpe. The win maintained Cantona's record of never having lost an FA Cup tie. He only signed for Leeds after United had knocked them out of the 1991-92 competition and missed the defeat by Sheffield United the following season when called up by France for a World Cup qualifier. The Reds won the trophy in 1993-94 and though the defence ended in the 1995 final, Eric was banned for the final. Southampton had a record of their own in the competition. They were the last team to beat Manchester United at Old Trafford in the FA Cup following their progress from the fourth round on penalties in 1992.

However when the whistle blew here they were irate about an incident midway through the second half when the Saints thought they had scored an equaliser. Neil Shipperley was ruled to have pushed Sharpe before heading past Peter Schmeichel.

In truth United should have been ahead long before that, the South Coast outfit riding their luck to survive a shaky start. Cantona was denied by Dave Beasant and a clearance off the line by Ken Monkou while Andy Cole should have done better having beaten his marker but his end product lacked pace as well as direction. The deadlock was broken four minutes before half-time - Giggs ran down the left, delaying his cross until Cantona ghosted towards the near post before hanging back buying himself the space to apply a simple finish.

Mark Walters forced Schmeichel to save with his legs when the Dane bought an initial dummy but with Southampton pushing for an equaliser and fuelled in that hunt by perceived injustice regarding the Shipperley 'goal', United countered on the right. Cantona eased past Simon Charlton, dragging the ball back for Butt and though his flick may well have been going in Sharpe made absolutely sure.

QUEENS PARK RANGERS 1 MANCHESTER UNITED 1
Premiership - 16 March 1996

Matters at Loftus Road were desperate and the Hoops must have feared the worst against a rampant, championship chasing Manchester United. Ten straight wins for Alex Ferguson's side contrasted with just one win in the same number of games for Rangers. They had to turn form on its head and had it not been for Eric Cantona's headed goal in the third minute of injury time they would have succeeded. For the Reds it may have looked like two points dropped but given the table it proved to be an important share of the spoils. It returned United to the summit with Newcastle kicking-off a day later, it also maintained an unbeaten run that stretched back to New Year's Day.

The hosts started brightly, Peter Schmeichel having to stretch to deny a Danny Dichio header. Simon Barker and Ian Holloway gave Roy Keane and Brian McClair a run for their money in the midfield and with it control for long periods. American keeper Jurgen Sommer began nervously but was soon in action denying Beckham, Giggs, McClair and Irwin as United threatened an opener.

Andy Impey's introduction at half-time gave QPR some much needed dynamism, the substitute hitting a forceful drive from the edge of the area which shaved Schmeichel's bar. Kevin Gallen should have done better with a whole net to aim at after Dichio had nodded Holloway's corner into his path before Rangers finally took a deserved lead when Holloway spotted a gap down the right, played in Dichio who finished unerringly from the edge of the area.

Sinclair wasted a chance to finish the visitors off in the dying minutes, sending his finish wide before a mad-cap finish. Cole skewered a chance wide and Keane clipped a post before Steve Bruce, pressed into service as a makeshift forward, out-muscled Impey and Alan McDonald to find Giggs. The Welshman's cross fell for Cantona heavily marked at the far post, the Frenchman's superb balance and control allowed him to convert his third vital goal of the month.

MANCHESTER UNITED 1 ARSENAL 0
PREMIERSHIP - 20 MARCH 1996

UNITED WERE QUICKLY becoming a two man team. The world class skills of Peter Schmeichel kept them in games, allowing Eric Cantona to win them. The same formula worked again here against a resurgent Arsenal. If Eric's 25 yard volley inspired the headlines, Schmeichel's late interventions to deny Glenn Helder and John Hartson drew praise from his team-mates, it was a formula that looked likely to deliver the championship.

Yet United should not have had to rely on their dynamic duo. Bruce Rioch later admitted that his team's goal had led a charmed life. It took only four minutes for United to rip through Arsenal's midfield and rearguard in a thrilling move which culminated with Ryan Giggs forcing David Seaman into a decent save. The Yorkshireman was grateful to his right-hand post on two occasions in quick succession. Roy Keane's drive was nearly turned in by Lee Sharpe before Andy Cole's effort from close range was somehow blocked. The same player was also denied following a poorly directed David Platt backpass.

Cantona, dodging tackles and would be interceptions from Arsenal players with the same élan as a matador, sold a host of dummies as he pressed to create for others. Sharpe laid on two chances for Cole who saw the first deflect off Andy Linighan and the second collected low by Seaman.

United remained dominant after the break but couldn't quite find the same momentum as the first 45 minutes. Nicky Butt had a penalty claim waved away after going down under pressure from David Hillier and David May skied an effort when there was time and space to do better before Arsenal, perhaps realising their luck was in, launched attacks of their own.

Peter Schmeichel somehow kept a Hartson drive out after Phil Neville had miscued a clearance and stuck out a right boot to clear from Helder. With United struggling to find their fluency, it was not a surprise to see Paul Scholes replace a frustrated Cole. Yet just when Arsenal were starting to look altogether more comfortable Cantona intervened. The striker glided onto Andy Linighan's hoofed clearance 25 yards from goal before unleashing a ferocious effort which dipped over Seaman and in off the underside of the bar. The win meant United now only trailed Newcastle on goal difference although they had two games fewer to play.

MANCHESTER UNITED 1 TOTTENHAM HOTSPUR 0
PREMIERSHIP - 24 MARCH 1996

THE COOLEST MAN in football had a further telling say in the destination of the title with a typical intervention in another tense game. Spurs, who had pulled off a 4-1 win at White Hart Lane, were in confident mood from the start and had the better of the opening exchanges forcing Schmeichel to pull off a great save from Teddy Sheringham before the Dane denied Chris Armstrong in a one-on-one duel.

Unfortunately the sometimes hapless Andy Cole let an easier chance go begging. An irony was that he very often created his own opportunities but failed to finish off that good work. Cole's sagging confidence in front of goal was underlined when, after an exchange of passes with Ryan Giggs he shanked the return ball tamely at Ian Walker.

Alex Ferguson, worried by Sheringham's movement, decided to deploy three centre backs. Late chances for the Londoners brought Schmeichel into action, the stopper finger-tipping a looping header to safety and making a point blank save to keep matters level.

But it was Cantona, as ever, who had the final word. The Frenchman broke following a Spurs corner and veered towards the right wing. The Tottenham players assumed he was about to cross but a subtle move inside allowed Eric to pull the trigger and fire left footed past Walker who had failed to make his ground. Giggs should have converted a fairly simple looking chance moments later but shot wide before pushing a teasing David Beckham cross against the bar.

Nevertheless, after Cantona's Miraculous March, United were somehow three points ahead of Newcastle albeit having played a couple of games more.

CHELSEA 1 MANCHESTER UNITED 2
FA Cp semi-final - 31 March 1996

Attention was diverted from the league for at least 90 minutes and with it the new, cosmopolitan air of English football was typified by an eagerly anticipated duel between Ruud Gullit and Eric Cantona. The pair were said to be running neck and neck for the Player of the Year awards and both made compelling cases for election here. Though the Dutchman fired Chelsea into a half-time lead he was ultimately surpassed by the mercurial French international who turned the match around in just five second half minutes.

Had the Villa Park pitch been in better shape this encounter could have been a classic but it was still an absorbing contest in which United had the early running. Already without Denis Irwin and Gary Pallister, Alex Ferguson lost Steve Bruce an hour or so prior to the start. It was a situation Gullit exploited before a quarter of an hour had been played. A one-two with Steve Clarke took him clear and although his lob beat Peter Schmeichel it drifted just over. 21 year old defender Michael Duberry almost showed his more illustrious colleague how a chipped finish should be done but struck the bar. Mark Hughes set up the opener ten minutes before the break, bursting through despite David Beckham's effort to clear a John Spencer pass. The Welshman fed an unmarked Gullit at the far post with a pin-point cross, the Dutchman couldn't miss.

In reply Cantona struck an upright from 25 yards in the last meaningful attack of the opening period after a poor attempt to clear. The equaliser came on 54 minutes when Phil Neville raided down the right after overlapping Beckham. Erland Johnsen attempted to clear but only guided the ball to Cantona who teed up Andy Cole. Before the hour mark had passed the deficit had been overturned with some assistance from the unfortunate Craig Burley whose backpass for Kevin Hitchcock was far too weak and rolled invitingly for Beckham who deceived the keeper, before stroking the ball home.

Within a minute Cantona preserved the advantage with a headed clearance off his own line, turning away a John Spencer volley with Schmeichel beaten. The Dane also played his part, denying Dennis Wise twice. Cantona could have provided a little more breathing space late on but his header was parried by Hitchcock's reflex save.

Soon after his side took the lead Roy Keane, who had been sent off for the Republic of Ireland in midweek, courted another dismissal after slapping Dennis Wise on the head. The Chelsea player reacted badly. Keane could have received a straight red but the official merely cautioned him.

MANCHESTER CITY 2 MANCHESTER UNITED 3
PREMIERSHIP - 6 APRIL 1996

NEWCASTLE UNITED HAD suffered perhaps their most damaging defeat in midweek, blowing a 3-2 lead at Anfield to a late Stan Collymore goal. While this was good news for United, the positive result meant that Liverpool still had a passing interest in the title run-in but would need United to fail. Although the time margins involved at Maine Road were not as tight, the drama was no less keen. United were twice pulled level but eventually made the advantage stick. Relegation battlers City had recently held a lead over Newcastle three times but were pegged back on each occasion with a draw the end result.

United opened the scoring on six minutes, Irwin's cross for Giggs saw the Welshman brought down by Nicky Summerbee, Eric Cantona sent Eike Immel the wrong way from the spot. A second spot-kick when Michael Brown appeared to handle David Beckham's cross was waved away soon after. City pushed for an equaliser with Niall Quinn coming close through a couple of headers before Michael Frontzeck, still smarting from the debatable penalty he conceded in the FA Cup clash, gained some recompense crossing for Mikhail Kavelashvili to convert from a few yards out.

The pendulum swung back towards United minutes later, Cantona slipping his man-marker Ian Brightwell before firing wide. The Frenchman then had a hand in giving United the lead just prior to half-time, flighting the ball for Andy Cole from the edge of the area, the striker guiding his shot home.

At the break City re-thought their plans and ended the practice of trying to hold Cantona at bay, Martin 'Buster' Phillips replacing Frontzeck. The substitute almost squared matters feeding Kavelashvili who was upstaging fellow countryman Georgi Kinkladze. A neat swivel and shot deserved more than to strike Schmeichel in the face. Taking Kavelashvili off may have appeared a strange tactic but with the Russian season in its opening stages and the English one in its final swings, he had received only four weeks training. And the decision seemed justified when his replacement, Uwe Rosler, took a Nigel Clough pass and charged into the area before firing past Schmeichel, the German striker angrily gesticulating at City manager Alan Ball during his celebrations.

Yet from the re-start Giggs put United back in control, the Welsh winger racing clear before firing a 20 yard rising shot past Immel. City tried to rally for a third time but only produced one telling shot despite plenty of possession, Schmeichel denying Rosler with his legs.

MANCHESTER UNITED 1 COVENTRY CITY 0
PREMIERSHIP - 8 APRIL 1996

AN HORRIFIC INJURY to Coventry's David Busst overshadowed this match. The defender challenged at the back post after just 90 seconds, he reached the ball but collided with Denis Irwin and Brian McClair. There was no suggestion of a foul by either player. Simultaeneous challenges from front and back shattered his lower right leg causing a compound fracture of the tibia and fibula. Such was the extent of the injury that the player ended up with one leg shorter than the other, his professional career over in an instant.

The nature of the injury had an effect on both teams, at one stage Peter Schmeichel appeared to be wretching at the sight of Busst's twisted leg. What followed was an understandably subdued affair that only sparked into life during the second half. United's winner eventually arrived following a Giggs run and cross that took a deflection off Liam Daish's heel and fell to Cole who squared for Cantona to slot home.

Coventry, perhaps inspired by the absence of their colleague, created a host of chances but failed to put one away. Noel Whelan was sent clear but Schmeichel denied him, Dion Dublin put a header wide and John Salako got a little too much on a shot. The Reds eventually established themselves with Andy Cole getting three very good chances. McClair just failed to hit the target as did David Beckham when he should have done far better.

By the time Cantona scored the winning goal Busst was undergoing emergency surgery at Salford's Hope Hospital. Players from both teams visited his bedside that evening and in the days which followed.

SOUTHAMPTON 3 MANCHESTER UNITED 1
PREMIERSHIP - 13 APRIL 1996

SOUTHAMPTON MADE A habit of indulging in late season runs which dispelled relegation fears and against well-fancied Manchester United they worked more South Coast magic here. Their first half performance bordered on the enchanting and ended United's long unbeaten run that followed their 1-4 reverse at White Hart Lane on New Year's Day - a run of 15 wins from 16 games. It gave Newcastle, in action a day later, a glimmer of a chance.

Matthew Le Tissier, a wizard at The Dell but only an occasional force elsewhere, usually saved his best for top ranking sides. When a free-kick was awarded following a Steve Bruce foul on Simon Charlton, Le Tissier's cross picked out Ken Monkou. Again Schmeichel saved but the header was only parried and the huge central defender lashed in the rebound. The Saints were all over United - Dodd fired wide and Le Tissier struck an upright from a tight angle before Giggs lost possession to Jim Magilton who released Alan Neilson on the wing. His low cross found Neil Shipperley who converted at the near post.

Southampton never allowed their guests to settle. Barry Venison and Jim Magilton snapped away in midfield providing protection for Le Tissier while Eric Cantona couldn't get into the game. Two minutes before the break Saints added a deserved third, Neilson centring, Schmeichel couldn't lay claim to the ball and Le Tissier drilled a shot into the far corner.

To some bemusement, United re-emerged for the second half in a different kit, the original grey jettisoned because, the manager claimed, they couldn't pick each other out against the background. Nevertheless, the new blue and white strip didn't change the flow of play which continued towards United's goal. Le Tissier juggled the ball on his feet and knees before crossing for Shipperley who glanced wide. The lone forward then sent a Charlton cross the wrong side of an upright before the Channel Islander struck a 25 yarder which moved in the air and caused Schmeichel problems.

Nicky Butt should have done better when sent clear by Andy Cole who forced Dave Beasant into one of just a handful of saves after Cantona had nodded Denis Irwin's free-kick his way. Then the keeper used his feet to great effect to deny Cole again. The Saints thoroughly deserved to end their dreadful record against United, although Ryan Giggs did convert a Gary Neville cross in the final minute.

MANCHESTER UNITED 1 LEEDS UNITED 0
Premiership - 17 April 1996

Lucas Radebe began his football career as a goalkeeper so when Mark Beeney was dismissed for handling outside his penalty area after just 17 minutes, the South African centre-half reprised his teenage years by donning the gloves. Radebe had been named as a substitute and with no replacement keeper to call on Howard Wilkinson had no option with Mark Ford making way.

Radebe excelled between the posts and was only beaten 18 minutes from time. With the exception of the opening seconds when Beeney saved from Cantona, Leeds had been the better side in almost every department until they went down to 10 men. The Leeds keeper, conscious of Andy Cole's presence, seemed to lose his bearings and rather than attempt a clearance he pawed at it. Under the laws there was no option for referee Keith Cooper.

The Reds enjoyed the lion's share of possession from that point on with the first test for Radebe coming just before the break from Brian McClair. The winner came when a Paul Scholes shot was parried as far as Keane. The midfielder shaped to pass for Lee Sharpe on the left, full-back Gary Kelly took the bait leaving Keane one-on-one with Radebe who stood no chance as the midfielder calmly picked his spot inside the left-hand post.

★

ON 20 APRIL 1996 it was announced that Eric Cantona had been named the Football Writers' Player of the Year and as was customary would be asked to accept the award at a special dinner held two days before the FA Cup Final.

Of the six man shortlist he had gathered 36 per cent of the vote with Ruud Gullit and Robbie Fowler trailing in well behind in second and third. The 49th winner of the accolade, it was the first time he had received the nod from the journalists rather than his peers. Manchester United winners had been rare. The last Old Trafford player to be honoured in such a way was George Best almost 30 years earlier in 1968. Just two other United players, Johnny Carey and Bobby Charlton, could share the distinction.

He also became the fourth non-British or Irish player to win the award following Germany's Bert Trautmann in 1956, Dutch midfielder Frans Thijssen in 1981, and holder Jurgen Klinsmann.

Learning of the news during a weekend in France he said. "I am very proud and privileged to have been voted Footballer of the Year. It is a tremendous honour for me and my country and it is a great tribute to my fellow players at Manchester United."

Alex Ferguson commented: "This award proves the value of British justice. It is well deserved because there is no doubt that Eric Cantona has been the best player in the country this season."

MANCHESTER UNITED 5 NOTTINGHAM FOREST 0
PREMIERSHIP - 28 APRIL 1996

HEADLINES PRIOR TO the game concerned the future of Andy Cole who was dropped in favour of Paul Scholes. Alex Ferguson had few qualms about leaving players out if it benefited his side, as Jim Leighton had discovered before the 1990 FA Cup final replay. The former Newcastle striker had endured a poor season in front of goal and seemed to be paying the price for a return of just 12 goals from 40 games.

Scholes on the other hand seemed to be a goal magnet and proved his worth here by snaffling a difficult chance to open the scoring after a frustrating opening period. Eric Cantona, playing further forward in Cole's place, meant a reliance on United's young midfield to create chances. Giggs and Beckham seemed to struggle with the responsibility yet they still crafted an opening for Lee Sharpe who sent a stooping header wide.

Sharpe caused problems for Mark Crossley with a volley from the edge of the area although when United did go ahead it was with the help of a Forest slip. Jason Lee lost possession to Roy Keane who found Giggs. The winger glided past Alf-Inge Haaland and though his cross seemed to be behind Scholes, the youngster somehow brought it under control before firing a controlled volley inside the far post. Crossley, who had done so much to keep the scores level, made a howler in choosing to punch a Beckham indirect free-kick, Cantona fluffed a volley but Beckham was alert enough to convert the loose ball.

Soon after the break Cantona sent Denis Irwin raiding down the left and a pass inside was dummied by Scholes for Beckham to convert. Cantona, drifting deeper, started another attack after Gary Pallister won a tackle deep inside his own half. A dash forward set up a simple finish for Giggs inside the area. Cantona rounded the game off with a sublime moment – finishing a volley after he had chipped his way past Colin Cooper. The vast array of French tricolours at Old Trafford in the last home game of the season were an indication of the home crowd's appreciation of their king. On the final whistle a lap of honour allowed all the players to be applauded.

Beating Forest so convincingly meant that Newcastle, who played Leeds 24 hours later, were six points adrift with two games in hand and seven goals behind in terms of goal difference. A defeat for Newcastle in either of the two fixtures Keegan's side had to play prior to the completion of the league programme in a week's time and the title - a third in four seasons - would be back at Old Trafford.

MIDDLESBROUGH 0 MANCHESTER UNITED 3
PREMIERSHIP - 5 MAY 1996

ALTHOUGH THE PREMIERSHIP trophy was lifted 123 miles away from home, the Reds were given a sporting ovation by Middlesbrough's fans at the Riverside Stadium. How much that had to do with denying Newcastle the prize was open to debate but no one could point a finger at the Boro players who gave their all.

Boro could have led after just 80 seconds when Juninho's cross found Neil Cox who shot over from inside the six yard box. The Brazilian was a livewire throughout and though rarely contained failed to set up either himself or a teammate. David May cleared when he got round Gary Pallister and took aim at goal. Nick Barmby headed wide before a Juninho run left Schmeichel exposed, Barmby again shooting wide.

David May was the unlikely first goalscorer, netting at the far post from a Giggs corner. Soon after Paul Scholes jinked his way into the area before setting up Nicky Butt, Cox blocking the goal bound effort. After an intense period of pressure Giggs shook his side out of a stupor by following Juninho's example and darting at defenders. It was one such run which set up the second. Giggs won a corner from which substitute Andy Cole scored with an instinctive hook-in from close range, his first touch since replacing Scholes just moments earlier. Giggs completed the scoring with ten minutes remaining, a slaloming run capped by a pin-point drive past Walsh.

MANCHESTER UNITED 1 LIVERPOOL 0
FA Cup Final - 11 May 1996

MOST UNITED FANS couldn't have thought of more fitting opposition against whom to complete an unprecedented "Double Double" than Liverpool. There was some antagonism caused by ex-Anfield stalwart Alan Hansen claiming that the Reds would "win nothing with kids" after a poor opening to the campaign. However those same youngsters were now Premiership champions and stood within an hour and a half of adding the FA Cup to their haul and becoming the first team to complete The Double twice. The Merseysiders would have loved nothing more than to thwart United's ambitions. Liverpool had gone so close to claiming the record themselves on several occasions in the 1970s and 80s, until their sole success in 1986, United having denied their rivals in 1977.

That year Liverpool wore white shirts but this afternoon it was the white cup final suits they would be most remembered for. The garments may have been created by Armani but there was nothing designer about the team's performance. For all the hype, this game settled into a defensive pattern that suited United more than their opponents. Alex Ferguson, working in the belief that Liverpool would struggle to break down his well-drilled midfield and defence, refused to open matters up and for long periods little of consequence happened.

As usual in these circumstances the sides cancelled each other out, although Andy Cole had an early opportunity but prodded his effort wide and mis-kicked when put in by Cantona. He wasted another great chance after David Beckham bought him space and time with a superb pass. David James denied the striker again with some smart thinking after a long clearance from his opposite number and his concentration was quickly tested by David Beckham who received a perfect ball from Giggs, before beating the ball to safety.

Steve McManaman had been a thorn in United's sides that term but without protection from Redknapp and robbed of the guile of John Barnes the wingman toiled and failed to make the most of the wide pitch that seemed tailor-made for him. Stan Collymore failed to settle and could only muster long range pot shots as United set about denying him service from midfield. Liverpool's failure to make any progress contributed to a snappy atmosphere and put paid to hopes of anything stylish being put together by either side.

James made a vital save from Cantona who showed he had the measure of Jason McAteer in the first attack of the second period but had little hope of placement with so little time to execute an effort on goal six yards out. Ian Rush came on for the last 15 minutes of the game and most likely his Liverpool career but the marksman couldn't find a way through.

Despite his earlier fine saves, David James showed just how easy it is for a keeper to turn from hero to zero when he applied a weak punch to a David Beckham corner in the closing stages. The ball fell awkwardly for Eric Cantona on the edge of the box. Between him and the goal stood a melee of players yet he somehow contorted his body into just the right shape to fire a shot through two or three players to score the winner and cap a remarkable season-long effort. Liverpool's players sank to their knees on realising that their chance had gone.

Eric Cantona invited injured club captain Steve Bruce to receive the trophy rather than lead the team up the steps himself but the central defender declined believing that the day's skipper and match winner should have that honour. The Frenchman, whose ban had ended in time for his return against the same opposition back in October, had scaled new heights on the English stage.

1995-96

THERE WAS NOW no doubting Eric Cantona's importance to United or his influence on the domestic game. His return following a nine month exile saw a new, better player who seemed inspired by adversity and capable of incredible of acts of goalscoring. In previous seasons he had been criticised for self-indulgence, this term he buckled down with a relentless determination to right the wrongs of his ban.

Perhaps, as the leader of a team shorn of some its more experienced players, Cantona felt he needed to cut out the showboating and teach his charges the professional elements required to succeed at the highest level. The emergence of Scholes, Beckham, the Neville brothers and Nicky Butt certainly seemed to change his style and add to the content. The new Cantona, keen to make a positive impression on the emerging members of United's side, steered clear of disciplinary problems. The only time his name was taken all season, at Stamford Bridge, was as a result of a mis-timed tackle.

Nevertheless some of his rescue acts still defied belief. Of the eight crucial 1-0 wins United recorded during the run-in, Cantona scored the vital goal on six occasions. During one remarkable period between late February and early April, he was almost single-handedly responsible for gathering 16 of the 18 points United registered (by scoring the winner or equaliser). The only other player with anything like the same degree of influence was Peter Schmeichel whose ability to single-handedly repel the opposition became another hallmark of United's success.

United had endured a poor Christmas period with defeats at Liverpool, Leeds and Tottenham lightened only by a 2-0 home win over Newcastle that kept the Reds in the title race. The Geordie frontrunners were 13 points clear in February and it took United's smash and grab duo of Schmeichel and Cantona to steal the 1-0 win at St James's Park that eventually decided the title.

United's run from New Year's Day until defeat at Southampton paved the way for the first part of the double. A cup run that saw them fortunate to beat Sunderland and Manchester City culminated in a come from behind win against star-studded Chelsea before Cantona's inspirational finish won the Cup against rivals Liverpool at Wembley.

Cantona ended his private feud with the press when he was named

Football Writers' Player of the Year. The media men in turn doffed their collective hats to a man who had shown his true footballing ability almost overnight. There was no condemnation forthcoming from the press, opponents, authorities and certainly not his club or the adoring supporters for whom he made the collection of more silverware a personal and imperative cause.

The changes Ferguson had made during the off-season had been controversial – the sale of Ince, Kanchelskis and Hughes looked ill-timed, especially with Cantona absent until October. Yet the manager was proved right about the quality of their replacements. United now carried a bigger threat, with pace from deep as well as out wide. As a result of his own experiences at the hands of Lucien Denis, Eric was also able to react better and ensure some unique talent was fostered rather than marginalised.

Despite a willingness to turn out for his country, France continued to omit him though he was not alone in being outside Aimé Jacquet's thoughts. Jean-Pierre Papin and David Ginola both went unselected from 1995 onwards as the manager concentrated on the 1998 World Cup.

In June there was a threat that Eric may quit the game following a quarrel over the use of his name on commercial products. A statement issued on Cantona's behalf read: "Eric Cantona will quit football if English companies do not stop associating his name with products that he has not given permission for his name to be used on." It went on to state, "[Some companies] have scandalously abused his name and have nothing to do with him or with Manchester United. The public must not be fooled by these advertising campaigns."

MANCHESTER UNITED - PREMIER LEAGUE 1995-96

DATE	OPPONENT	VENUE	SCORE	ATT'D	1	2	3	4	5	6	7	8	9	10	11	SUBSTITUTES
01-Oct-95	Liverpool	Old Trafford	2-2	34,934	Schmeichel	Neville G	Neville P	Bruce	Sharpe	Pallister	Cantona[1]	Butt[1]	Keane	Cole	Giggs	McClair (Scholes)
21-Oct-95	Chelsea	Stamford Bdg	4-1	31,019	Schmeichel	Neville G	Irwin	Bruce	Keane	Pallister	Cantona	Butt	Cole[1]	Scholes[2]	Giggs[1]	
28-Oct-95	Middlesbrough	Old Trafford	2-0	36,580	Schmeichel	Neville G	Irwin	Bruce	Keane	Pallister[1]	Cantona	Butt	Cole	Scholes	Giggs	Beckham (Butt) Sharpe (Scholes) McClair (Irwin)
04-Nov-95	Arsenal	Highbury	0-1	38,317	Schmeichel	Neville G	Irwin	Bruce	Keane	Pallister	Cantona	Butt	Cole	Scholes	Giggs	Neville P (Irwin) McClair (Scholes) Sharpe (Giggs)
18-Nov-95	Southampton	Old Trafford	4-1	39,301	Schmeichel	Neville G	Irwin	Bruce	Beckham	Pallister	Cantona	Butt	Cole[1]	Scholes[1]	Giggs[2]	
22-Nov-95	Coventry City	Highfield Road	4-0	23,400	Schmeichel	Neville G	Irwin[1]	Bruce	Beckham[1]	Pallister	Cantona	Butt	Cole	Scholes[1]	McClair[2]	Scholes (McClair) Sharpe (Beckham)
27-Nov-95	Nottingham F	The City Ground	1-1	29,263	Schmeichel	Neville G	Irwin	Bruce	Beckham	Pallister	Cantona[1]	Butt	Cole	McClair	Scholes	
02-Dec-95	Chelsea	Old Trafford	1-1	42,019	Pilkington	Neville G	Neville P	Bruce	Beckham[1]	May	Cantona	Sharpe	Cole	McClair	Scholes	Davies (Scholes) Cooke (Sharpe)
09-Dec-95	Sheffield Wed	Old Trafford	2-2	41,849	Schmeichel	Neville G	Irwin	Bruce	Beckham	May	Cantona[2]	Sharpe	Cole	McClair	Scholes	
17-Dec-95	Liverpool	Anfield	0-2	40,549	Schmeichel	Neville G	Irwin	Bruce	Beckham	May	Cantona	Sharpe	Cole	McClair	Giggs	
24-Dec-95	Leeds United	Elland Road	1-3	39,801	Schmeichel	Neville G	Irwin	May	Beckham	Parker	Cantona	Butt	Cole[1]	McClair	Keane	Scholes (Beckham) May (Parker/Neville P (Bruce)
27-Dec-95	Newcastle U	Old Trafford	2-0	42,024	Schmeichel	Neville G	Irwin	May	Neville P	Keane[1]	Cantona	Butt	Cole[1]	Beckham	Giggs	McClair (May)
30-Dec-95	QPR	Old Trafford	2-1	41,890	Schmeichel	Neville G	Irwin	Prunier	Neville P	Keane	Cantona	Butt	Cole[1]	Beckham	Giggs[1]	McClair (Cole) Parker (Neville P) Sharpe (Beckham)
01-Jan-96	Tottenham H	W Hart Lane	1-4	32,852	Schmeichel	Neville G	Parker	Prunier	Neville P	Keane	Cantona	Butt	Cole[1]	Beckham	Giggs	Pilkington (Schmeichel) McClair (Neville P) Sharpe (Keane)
13-Jan-96	Aston Villa	Old Trafford	0-0	42,667	Schmeichel	Neville G	Irwin	Bruce	Neville P	Keane	Cantona	Butt	Cole	Sharpe	Giggs	Scholes (Sharpe)
22-Jan-96	West Ham	Upton Park	1-0	24,197	Schmeichel	Neville G	Irwin	Bruce	Neville P	Keane	Cantona	Butt	Cole[1]	Sharpe	Giggs	Beckham (Cole)
03-Feb-96	Wimbledon	Selhurst Park	4-2	25,380	Schmeichel	Neville G	Irwin	Bruce	Neville P	Keane	Cantona[2]	Butt	Cole[1]	Sharpe[1]	Giggs	Beckham (Bruce) Perry o/g
10-Feb-96	Blackburn R	Old Trafford	1-0	42,681	Schmeichel	Neville G	Irwin	Bruce	Neville P	May	Cantona	Keane	Cole	Sharpe[1]	Giggs	
21-Feb-96	Everton	Old Trafford	2-0	42,459	Schmeichel	Neville G	Irwin	Bruce[1]	Keane	Pallister	Cantona	Butt	Cole	Sharpe	Giggs[1]	Beckham (Sharpe)
25-Feb-96	Bolton W	Burnden Pk	6-0	21,381	Schmeichel	Neville G	Irwin	Bruce	Keane	Pallister	Cantona[1]	Butt[1]	Cole[1]	Beckham[1]	Giggs	McClair (Giggs) Scholes (Cantona)
04-Mar-96	Newcastle Utd	St James Pk	1-0	36,584	Schmeichel	Neville G	irwin	Bruce	Keane	Neville P	Cantona[1]	Beckham	Cole	McClair	Giggs	Scholes (McClair) Sharpe (May/Butt (Beckham)
16-Mar-96	QPR	Loftus Road	1-1	18,817	Schmeichel	Neville P	Neville G	Bruce	Keane	May	Cantona[1]	Butt	Cole	Sharpe	Giggs	Scholes (Cole)
20-Mar-96	Arsenal	Old Trafford	1-0	50,028	Schmeichel	Neville G	Neville P	Bruce	Keane	May	Cantona[1]	Butt	Cole	Sharpe	Giggs	Beckham (Neville P) McClair (Cole)
24-Mar-96	Tottenham H	Old Trafford	1-0	50,157	Schmeichel	Neville G	Neville P	Bruce	Keane	May	Cantona[1]	Butt	Cole	Beckham	Giggs[1]	May (Bruce) Sharpe (Cole)
06-Apr-96	Manchester C	Maine Road	3-2	29,688	Schmeichel	Neville G	Irwin	Bruce	Keane	Neville P	Cantona[1]	Butt	Cole[1]	Beckham	Giggs[1]	Sharpe (Butt) May (Sharpe)
08-Apr-96	Coventry City	Old Trafford	1-0	50,331	Schmeichel	Neville G	Irwin	May	Beckham	Sharpe	Cantona	Butt	Cole	McClair	Giggs[1]	Scholes (Butt) Sharpe (Cole)
13-Apr-96	Southampton	The Dell	1-3	15,262	Schmeichel	Neville G	Irwin	Bruce	Beckham	Keane	Cantona	Butt	Cole	McClair	Giggs[1]	Scholes (Butt) May (Sharpe)
17-Apr-96	Leeds United	Old Trafford	1-0	48,362	Schmeichel	Neville P	Irwin	Bruce	Keane[1]	Pallister	Cantona[1]	Beckham[2]	Cole	Scholes[1]	Giggs[1]	May (Bruce) Scholes (McClair) Sharpe (Cole)
28-Apr-96	Nottingham F	Old Trafford	5-0	53,926	Schmeichel	Neville P	Irwin	May	Keane	Pallister	Cantona	Beckham[2]	Scholes[2]	Sharpe	Giggs[1]	Neville G (Neville P)
05-May-96	Middlesbrough	Riverside	3-0	29,921	Schmeichel	Neville P	Irwin	May[1]	Keane	Pallister	Cantona	Beckham	Butt	Scholes[2]	Giggs[1]	Cole (Scholes) Neville P (Sharpe)

FA Cup

DATE	OPPONENT	VENUE	SCORE	ATT'D	1	2	3	4	5	6	7	8	9	10	11	SUBSTITUTES
06-Jan-96	Sunderland	Old Trafford	2-2	41,563	Pilkington	Neville G	Irwin	Bruce	Keane	Pallister	Cantona[1]	Butt[1]	Cole	Beckham	Giggs	Sharpe (Beckham) Neville P (Neville G)
16-Jan-96	Sunderland	Roker Park	2-1	21,378	Schmeichel	Parker	Irwin	Bruce	Neville G	Neville P	Cantona	Butt	Cole[1]	Keane	Giggs	Sharpe (Parker) Scholes (Butt)
27-Jan-96	Reading	Elm Park	3-0	14,780	Schmeichel	Neville P	Irwin	Bruce	Neville G	Keane	Cantona	Cole	Butt	Sharpe[1]	Giggs[1]	Parker (Neville P)
18-Feb-96	Manchester C	Old Trafford	2-1	42,692	Schmeichel	Neville P	Irwin	Bruce	Pallister	Keane	Cantona[1]	Cole	Butt	Sharpe[1]	Giggs	
11-Mar-96	Southampton	Old Trafford	2-0	45,446	Schmeichel	Neville G	Irwin	Bruce	Neville G	Keane	Cantona[1]	Cole[1]	Butt	Beckham[1]	Giggs	Scholes (Cole) Neville G (Beckham)
31-Mar-96	Chelsea	Villa Park	2-1	38,421	Schmeichel	Neville G	Irwin	May	Sharpe	Keane	Cantona[1]	Cole[1]	Butt	Beckham[1]	Giggs	
11-May-96	Liverpool	Wembley	1-0	79,007	Schmeichel	Neville G	Irwin	May	Pallister	Keane	Cantona[1]	Beckham	Butt	Scholes[2]	Giggs	Keane (Cooke) Neville P (Sharpe)

League Cup

AU REVOIR

ALEX FERGUSON MADE five signings over the summer - Jordi Cruyff, son of Dutch legend Johann, Ronny Johnsen and Karel Poborsky arrived with prospects such as Ole Gunnar Solskjær and Raimond van der Gouw added as back up. Ferguson's aim being to bolster a squad that would now be stretched by European commitments.

There would have been more newcomers if the manager had his way but one possible departure would never have been sanctioned. During the summer Blackburn Rovers made an offer of £4 million for Eric Cantona. Though the Lancashire side would no doubt have followed their interest through, the bid was believed to be a reaction, if not a hands-off warning, after Manchester United attempted to take Alan Shearer from Ewood Park in a rumoured £12 million deal.

The Reds had competed for the striker's signature when he left Southampton and the failure to land him rankled with Alex Ferguson who remained an overt admirer. So much so that it tempted him to break his rule about never going back for a player he had once failed to sign. Blackburn chairman Robert Coar told reporters: "We have made a bid for Eric Cantona and are awaiting a response from United."

In an equally measured response United assistant secretary, Ken Ramsden said, "There is no way the matter will be considered. The offer has been rejected out of hand. Eric will not be going to Blackburn or anywhere else." Asked if he believed there was any tit for tat element to the bid Ramsden replied: "It is an unusual episode to say the least, but it is not for us to question other clubs' motives."

MANCHESTER UNITED 4 NEWCASTLE UNITED 0
CHARITY SHIELD - 12 AUGUST 1996

SHEARER REBUFFED FERGUSON'S approaches for a second time, although the player came close after talking with the United manager. Rovers owner Jack Walker was rumoured to be against any deal with the Reds but did not stand in the way of a world record £15 million deal with Shearer's boyhood club Newcastle United and a link up with his hero Kevin Keegan.

He lined up against United when the country's two best teams whetted the appetite nicely for the campaign to come. Shearer had little opportunity to show just why he had attracted a world record fee for his services. The Manchester United boss purred at the prospect of pairing the England forward with Eric Cantona, who he had made captain following the departure of Steve Bruce. Alongside Les Ferdinand, Shearer looked awkward, but just as satisfying as seeing his main transfer target blanked out was the performance of Cantona, who scored the first of four goals and had a hand in the two which followed.

That said a little of the old Eric returned. Cantona took exception to Philippe Albert tangling with Gary Neville early in the second half and sprinted across to grab the Belgian's shirt which he then used to haul him to ground. It being the Charity Shield referee Paul Durkin decided a charitable outlook was best and issued a yellow card. After the game Cantona smirked at the Newcastle player's reaction saying: "I must be very strong. I just pushed somebody and he fell down. It was nothing much." The referee was just as benevolent when deciding to book Roy Keane for seeming to want an altercation with the official himself.

Cantona scored the opener with 25 minutes gone having earlier spurned an opportunity when Paul Scholes and Ryan Giggs set him up - Pavel Srnicek sticking out a left leg to keep matters square before David Beckham skinned John Beresford and found Cantona who had no trouble beating the keeper at the second attempt. Another Cantona move secured the second on the half hour, Beckham taking a flick from his skipper before centring for Nicky Butt to head home. In the time remaining Butt suffered concussion after a clash of heads and was replaced by debutant Karel Poborsky.

Beckham made way on the flank though after he too settled. The man identified as one of the hottest young properties in football excelled in a central role, capped his performance four minutes from the close with a 30 yard chipped finish after a pass from Cantona. Keane, a little more subdued by the end, smashed the final goal of the afternoon profiting from a tapped Giggs' free-kick.

WIMBLEDON 0 MANCHESTER UNITED 3
PREMIERSHIP - 17 AUGUST 1996

THIS WASN'T ONE of United's better games but the three goals scored were all classic strikes. The tone was set by Eric Cantona's opener on 25 minutes, the Frenchman's sweet half volley from 15 yards struck following a typical Roy Keane surge. The Irishman beat Vinnie Jones and crossed to Nicky Butt who squared for Cantona to rifle home. It was a goal which deserved to win any match but the talking point was an equally stunning effort from David Beckham at the end.

Keane's contribution was immense against a team that relied on physical control. As a result the Dons struggled. Cantona was an immediate beneficiary as was Jordi Cruyff, wearing the number 14 shirt his father graced for Ajax, Barcelona and the Netherlands. He replaced the injured Ryan Giggs and linked well with Cantona.

The omnipresent Keane provided the pass for Denis Irwin to fire in from a tight angle just before the hour and at 2-0 up United seem prepared to play the game out. Cantona retreated to the bench 11 minutes from the end complaining of a pulled muscle in his buttock. Yet with 23 seconds of injury time played, David Beckham stole the headlines with a lob from just inside his own half that had Dons keeper Neil Sullivan beaten all ends up. Impeccably weighted, it dropped over the keeper and was quickly acclaimed goal of the season.

MANCHESTER UNITED 2 EVERTON 2
PREMIERSHIP - 21 AUGUST 1996

THE MUCH FÉTED David Beckham was moved into the centre of midfield to fill the gap left by the absence of Roy Keane. The Irishman was set to be out for three weeks with a knee injury. In his absence United struggled and trailed the Toffees 2-0 at half-time. By the end Alex Ferguson's cheer at escaping with a draw was tempered by outrage at Graham Poll's time-keeping and the denial of what he believed to be a blatant penalty for a foul on Ryan Giggs. Brian Kidd had to physically restrain his boss from approaching the official whose decisions took up a fair portion of the post-match press conference.

Everton, who had beaten Newcastle on opening day, stunned

the champions with a couple of Duncan Ferguson goals within the opening seven minutes. Former United winger Andrei Kanchelskis provided a killer ball for the first which Ferguson dispatched before Peter Schmeichel failed to claim Andy Hinchcliffe's cross from the left, Ferguson again converting from close range.

Poborsky was sacrificed at the break with Brian McClair introduced in his place. The change worked although Neville Southall, in his 701st league game, looked as spry as he had on his first 16 years earlier, denying Giggs with an astounding save. As the second half wore on the Reds enjoyed more possession and Southall had to rely on luck. The time he took re-starting the game was indicative of the pressure he was under. The United bench protested on every occasion, yet even when the keeper received a booking their ire failed to subside.

Instead United's determination got them through, an unmarked Jordi Cruyff heading in a Denis Irwin cross with twenty minutes remaining and, eight minutes from time, the left back centred again this time for Brian McClair on the far post. Defender David Unsworth attempted to avert the danger but could only steer the ball into his own net. Between those strikes the Toffees were fortunate not to concede a penalty. Craig Short seemed to have dragged Butt to ground but the referee decided the incident took place a few inches outside the area. An already fuming Alex Ferguson found little to lessen his blackened mood when no benefit was gained from the free-kick.

MANCHESTER UNITED 2 BLACKBURN ROVERS 2
Premiership - 25 August 1996

Blackburn Rovers came to Old Trafford in poor shape and poor form having lost their opening two games without scoring a goal and parted company with Kenny Dalglish. The man who led the Ewood Park club to the title just over 12 months earlier had left his Director of Football role days earlier. Ray Harford stayed in charge of first team matters and, but for the debateable rejection of a penalty, would have guided his side to an unlikely win.

The absence of Roy Keane and Nicky Butt from the middle played its part. It allowed Tim Sherwood and Lars Bohinen to dominate midfield and dictate a tempo which suited the visiting side and could have yielded more than the single goal scored during the opening 45 minutes. Rovers had knocked on the door several times before the impressive Kevin Gallacher saw another effort saved by Peter Schmeichel but this time the ball squirted to Paul Warhurst who tapped in.

United looked in awful spirits and even Eric Cantona failed to offer a route out of the doldrums. In fact he appeared a different player to the one who usually bestrode this arena. At times his frustrations looked set to spill over. A fortunate equaliser came five minutes after the break, although Colin Hendry would have been disappointed not to deal with Schmeichel's goal kick. Tim Flowers couldn't reach his header before Jordi Cruyff nipped in and flicked the ball over the stranded keeper. Rovers re-took the lead after Bohinen beat Denis Irwin on the right and cut inside before slamming the ball past Schmeichel at the near post.

New signing Ole Gunnar Solskjær, scorer of two goals for the reserves in midweek, was introduced for his debut just after the hour replacing David May and within ten minutes United were level. Cruyff, building on his impressive start as a United player, nodded the ball on for the substitute who sent a powerful volley that Flowers could only palm back to the 21 year old. Solskjær, the scorer of 31 goals in just 42 top flight games for Molde, notching his first in United red.

DERBY COUNTY 1 MANCHESTER UNITED 1
PREMIERSHIP - 4 SEPTEMBER 1996

UNITED WERE HELD for a third successive match and, like the previous two stalemates, got no more than they deserved against the Premiership newcomers. That teams such as Derby were not being dominated was a worry yet profligacy in front of goal was the true cause, Beckham snatching at a chance when played in by Cantona when he only had Russell Hoult to beat.

Before taking the lead midway through the first half the Rams had posted notice of their attacking intent and went ahead when Jacob Laursen fired a free-kick past Schmeichel. Hoult was the busier keeper as the interval neared and though he managed to tip a Ryan Giggs drive away he had no answer when the Welshman spotted Beckham's late run from midfield. The resulting shot from long range was exquisitely placed. While that may usually have heralded a siege on the hosts' goal Derby seemed to believe a major scalp was there for the taking. Even the introduction of Solskjær and Paul Scholes couldn't force a winner.

LEEDS UNITED 0 MANCHESTER UNITED 4
PREMIERSHIP - 7 SEPTEMBER 1996

THERE WERE FEW things an Elland Road crowd enjoyed more than a slice of misfortune for Eric Cantona and, though able to taunt their former favourite for failing to convert a penalty (the Frenchman's first in a competitive game) as *schadenfreude* goes it was pretty hollow. Eric's effort was poor, he shanked wide two minutes from half-time with United still only holding a slim 1-0 advantage. However, by the time Cantona had the final word, three minutes into injury time, none of the home fans were laughing.

Leeds did not force Peter Schmeichel to break sweat until the final few minutes when Ian Harte blazed over and Mark Hateley sent a header onto the bar. The home side looked to pump high balls forward although Gary Pallister's absence through injury wasn't felt. United took the lead after three minutes, a Karel Poborsky corner finding Ronny Johnsen's head. The effort went in, although it was untidy with Mark Ford and Harte getting touches before the ball deflected off Nigel Martyn's forehead.

In open play Poborsky showed his eye-catching performances for his country that summer had been no flash in the pan. Operating in tandem with Jordi Cruyff he pulled the Leeds' defence all over the park. The duo, who cost as much as the £4.5 million Leeds paid United for an ineffective looking Lee Sharpe, created huge amounts of room for Cantona, operating as a lone forward. Cruyff's excellence also won the spot-kick Cantona missed after David Wetherall felt he had no option but to grab the Dutchman in the area.

The second period mirrored the first. Cantona gave Poborsky reward for his persistence in the final quarter, releasing him into wide open spaces from halfway. Martyn, who made a couple of decent saves to keep his team in with a sniff, had no option but to come out but was exquisitely chipped. Cantona's *coup de grâce* came when he met an Ole Gunnar Solskjær centre at the far post and saluted the Don Revie stand. Rather than concentrate on the striker however, most of the home fans' ire was reserved for the man who sold Cantona to Manchester United - Howard Wilkinson.

JUVENTUS 1 MANCHESTER UNITED 0
CHAMPIONS LEAGUE GROUP C - 11 SEPTEMBER 1996

IN AN INTERVIEW held straight after the previous season's FA Cup final, Eric Cantona told Des Lynam that the Champions League was now the target for him and the club. He saw it as the crowning glory which made a good side a great one. Teams like the United vintage of 1968, Celtic's Lisbon Lions, the Liverpool sides who won four European Cups in eight seasons and the unfashionable Nottingham Forest side which won successive crowns were still talked about with reverence and Cantona wanted United to join that elite.

Leeds United were no real test of United's ability to compete with reigning European champions Juventus but the match served as a decent confidence boost. After this encounter in Turin and despite the close nature of the scoreline, most accepted that the Reds fared no better than the opposition they had pasted four days earlier as the Italians dominated possession to a ridiculous degree.

There was some irony that the scorer on 32 minutes was a man Alex Ferguson had tried to buy in the close season, Alen Boksic. The Croatian was a handful all night and had Christian Vieri been a little less profligate the game would have been over within 15 minutes. Boksic beat Johnsen and Neville in a mazy run with a dozen minutes played and centred for Antonio Conte but he volleyed into the turf and over. Vieri was next to spurn a Boksic centre - his header sailing wide. After Del Piero's shot was parried by Schmeichel, Gianluca Pessotto scored only for the effort to be ruled offside, even though the scorer was not the man transgressing.

A United corner - their first of the match - awarded after Eric Cantona's goal bound effort went out off Paolo Montero, gave Juventus the chance to break - Zinedine Zidane motoring upfield and finding Boksic whose pace and strength left Nicky Butt trailing before he lobbed Schmeichel.

McClair, Solskjær and Cole were all thrown into the fray during the closing stages but failed to make an impact. Although United had more of the game it made no difference. Cantona, who was asked to perform in a lone striker role, had nothing to work with and was an isolated figure. His task was made harder by the absence of Roy Keane in midfield. Without the Irishman's imposing presence, Juventus had control. Alex Ferguson was indebted to his keeper who made a world class save from Didier Deschamps to keep the score down. The group's other two sides, Rapid Vienna and Fenerbahce, shared a 1-1 draw in Austria.

MANCHESTER UNITED 4 NOTTINGHAM FOREST 1
PREMIERSHIP - 14 SEPTEMBER 1996

FOREST, WITHOUT STEVE Stone and leading scorers Kevin Campbell and Bryan Roy, shocked Old Trafford by taking the lead after just four minutes – Stuart Pearce's lofted ball allowing Alf Inge Haaland to slot past Peter Schmeichel. Forest continued to enjoy the bulk of possession, Saunders had a goal disallowed for offside and Denis Irwin was forced to block a Colin Cooper effort on the line.

Ole Gunnar Solskjær, made his first United start as Eric Cantona took a deeper role but the pair failed to gel for much of the opening period until combining on 22 minutes. Cantona took an incisive pass from Nicky Butt and found Solskjær, unmarked in the area, the Norwegian showing excellent technique in beating Mark Crossley. United's use of cross-field balls had proved profitable in the build up and Karel Poborsky's cross from the right soon found Giggs who nodded in.

Giggs was denied a second when Crossley tipped a shot away as the probing continued but it wasn't until the final eight minutes that the Reds made the points safe. A Giggs' free-kick was brought down with a sureness of touch by Cantona who clipped a measured shot in with assistance from an upright. It was no more than he deserved from the game but more was to come when Poborsky went down under a vigorous challenge from Chris Bart-Williams. Despite his recent miss at Leeds, Eric fired in from the spot.

ASTON VILLA 0 MANCHESTER UNITED 0
PREMIERSHIP - 21 SEPTEMBER 1996

A PROBLEM FREE return for Roy Keane was one of the positives to be drawn from a goalless draw at Aston Villa. With the Irishman came an added steel and, as far as Villa were concerned, an insurmountable obstacle. Villa were indebted to Ugo Ehiogu and keeper Michael Oakes for a point, the pair keeping out early efforts from widemen Jordi Cruyff and David Beckham.

In his primary role Beckham worried defenders through a series of pinpoint crosses. With Solskjær and Cantona beginning to flourish as a partnership, Ryan Giggs shared central midfield with Keane and the Welshman was able to push forward and interchange with Cruyff. Raimond van der Gouw was underused in his first outing of the season in place of Peter Schmeichel, who had fallen victim to a stomach bug, but there were worries at the other end where the solitary goal which seemed likely to be enough, remained elusive. Solskjær was sacrificed for Andy Cole who had shown great form with a midweek hat-trick for the reserves. The much maligned striker hit the bar after Giggs had seen an effort palmed on to a post. Dwight Yorke caught the eye, operating in a similar fashion to Cantona and created room for Savo Milosevic. The Trinidadian had a goal disallowed for a clear handball and his movement killed any thrust United had and with it their chances of victory.

MANCHESTER UNITED 2 RAPID VIENNA 0
CHAMPIONS LEAGUE GROUP C - 25 SEPTEMBER 1996

IF UNITED'S FIRST Champions League outing had seen them outclassed by champions Juventus, their second match proved that, on their night, they were more than capable at the very highest level. Rapid Vienna, undefeated in 13 matches from the start of the season, were blown away in just under half an hour.

It was the Viennese who were forced to waltz to Cantona's tune as the Frenchman finally found his feet in Europe. Having played only a peripheral role in Leeds victory over Stuttgart in 1992, been dismissed following ugly scenes in Istanbul in 1993 as a result of which he was banned for all but the final game of the 1994 campaign, Eric realised this was finally his chance to shine.

Rapid were on the back foot from the start - Solskjær wasting a chance in the opening minute before testing keeper Michael Konsel a couple of minutes later. The Norwegian then played Cantona in, Trifon Ivanov pulling off a timely tackle. Rapid were surviving on their wits at times with Ryan Giggs' corners causing problems. Ronny Johnsen should have planted a header into the net. Cantona would have but for Christian Prosenik on the line. Lone striker Rene Wagner enjoyed a couple of isolated chances, but they were the only touches he had for some time as once United opened the scoring, it was one way traffic.

Roy Keane's low cross from the right eluded all attempts to cut it out allowing Karel Poborsky to help it on for Solskjær who converted. The lead was doubled on 29 minutes, Peter Stoger under-hitting a back-pass, Beckham scoring at the second attempt. Solskjær had chances to add another when set up by Cantona but skewed the final effort wide. The Frenchman then hammered in a free-kick which was well saved by the Austrian keeper although the best stop of the night went to Schmeichel who launched himself across goal at full stretch to deny Zoran Barisic who caught hold of a shot from distance. It was part of a late rally from Rapid who captialised on a sloppy period from the home team.

MANCHESTER UNITED 2 TOTTENHAM HOTSPUR 0
PREMIERSHIP - 29 SEPTEMBER 1996

OLE GUNNAR SOLSKJÆR, scorer of a goal in each of his league appearances so far, proved as clinical against Tottenham Hotspur as he had been wasteful against Rapid Vienna. Yet it didn't start well for the Norwegian who was well patrolled by Sol Campbell until an early second half cross from Giggs put him under pressure. Campbell seemed sure that the diminutive Solskjær had no chance of reaching the centre but the Norwegian got their first, dragged the ball down and fired beyond Ian Walker.

Spurs, who had lost three of their last four games, had looked likely to end their slump until that point – their impressive play forcing United to defend for long periods in the first half. Andy Sinton nearly set up Rory Allen, who was inches away from connecting with his centre moments after Solskjær's goal. David Howells had a goal chalked off for handball following a telling Ruel Fox cross and Teddy Sheringham headed weakly just before the interval and was denied a similar chance after the restart by Schmeichel.

Jordi Cruyff and Eric Cantona combined to send Nicky Butt through the visitors backline to secure the points. Solskjær, in a menacing position to his left, had time to look up and curl home his shot. Spurs kept going, Sheringham feeding Allen whose cross for Fox was met with a spectacular mid-air volley that skimmed the bar. United almost had the last word, Butt's effort requiring Walker to make a fingertip save and concede a late corner.

MANCHESTER UNITED 1 LIVERPOOL 0
PREMIERSHIP - 12 OCTOBER 1996

LIVERPOOL WENT INTO the game as early Premiership leaders and with United just four days away from the Champions League clash at Fenerbahce which could define the course of the group, Alex Ferguson expressed concern about matches of this magnitude coming so close together. Fortunately for the Reds the continued absence of Robbie Fowler deprived the vistors of a cutting edge despite enjoying most of the possession. Much of the approach play Roy Evans' side put together was impressive but without any sharpness in the area, United always had a chance of nicking something.

With Pallister, Keane and Giggs missing, United played full backs Neville and Irwin in midfield for most of the game with Johnsen, May and Butt operating as a three-man backline. Though there was a numerical midfield advantage for United the six men often appeared confused and the dangerous Steve McManaman and Patrik Berger enjoyed more space than the United manager would have hoped. Had Stan Collymore not spurned his chances the result could well have gone the other way. As it was Schmeichel was never stretched despite the visitors enjoying more possession.

Midway through the first half Beckham, who had already shaved the woodwork with one curling effort, found what proved to be the winner. Some excellent close control and a perceptive pass found the midfielder just outside the area - lurking in the 'D' - from where he unleashed a shot which zipped low past David James and in off the right hand upright.

The Liverpool keeper looked likely to walk when he appeared to hack Solskjær to the floor but David Elleray gave him the benefit of the doubt. However, rather than dominate the game, United's doubts about their formation refused to go away. Liverpool remained on top for over an hour, freezing out Cantona, Beckham and others who barely managed to string more than a couple of passes together yet somehow the Merseysiders contrived to miss the target. McManaman could have had a hat-trick on another day but his shooting lacked accuracy and power. He spooned one over, headed straight at Schmeichel then sent a couple more wide of either upright. Collymore would have equalised, having worked himself some space with the goal gaping ahead of him, but managed to get the ball caught between his feet giving the defence vital seconds to clear. Michael Thomas spurned a close range chance and Berger found the keeper when he should have done better.

FENERBAHCE 0 MANCHESTER UNITED 2
CHAMPIONS LEAGUE GROUP C - 16 OCTOBER 1996

MANCHESTER UNITED'S TURKISH delight came after their most convincing European away performance for years. Eric Cantona made amends for his last visit to Istanbul by making the first and scoring the second in a superb individual and team display which combined attacking flair with defensive solidity. The unfancied home team counted on Nigerian international Jay-Jay Okocha, a prolific scorer in the Turkish Super League, to create and score goals but a well disciplined performance, which saw Ronny Johnsen deployed in midfield to take care of Okocha, allowed the Reds to exert almost total control.

The atmosphere was not as unwelcoming as that experienced at the Ali Sami Yen Stadium but still hostile enough. An hour before kick-off the floodlights failed. Flares and papers were lit and some of the flaming objects were thrown towards United fans. Okocha, encouraged by a raucous crowd, initially gave Johnsen and others a torrid time with only Peter Schmeichel's brilliance and a failure to make the most of those chances the keeper couldn't deal with, ensuring the game remained goalless. Emil Kostadinov and Elvir Bolic both wasted chances.

Once the home crowd were subdued the Reds took control and despite Fenerbahce's decision to kick their way out of a rut United kept their cool, Rustu making a superb save from a Cruyff volley before the break. Just before the hour Johnsen stole possession from Okocha and fed Cantona. Eric's slide rule pass released Solskjær down the wing. The Norwegian found Beckham who beat Uche Okechukwu before finishing from close range with a low finish Rustu got nowhere near.

Four minutes later Cantona added the second. Solskjær played his part in a one-two with Cruyff, the Norwegian's back-heel releasing the Dutch international to centre for his skipper standing in the six yard area. Cantona, who sprayed the ball around in the time remaining, appeared happy with his game for the first time in weeks. It emphasised not just the importance of his goal but the game and competition. A punch in the air at the end signified that this was the moment United and Cantona finally came of age in Europe.

NEWCASTLE UNITED 5 MANCHESTER UNITED 0
Premier League - 20 October 1996

NEWCASTLE'S MANAGEMENT, PLAYERS, officials and even their buoyant fans who sang about winning the league were only too aware of how early season promise could dissolve. Nine years and nine games had passed since their last win over Manchester United and this went some way to easing the pain of their championship meltdown of the previous season and maintained a run of seven successive wins.

This was the Reds' heaviest defeat since a loss by the same score at Everton in October 1984. For Alex Ferguson it was his worst reverse in 22 years of management on either side of Hadrian's Wall.

The result was all the more surprising when one considers that United hadn't conceded a goal in nine hours and nine minutes before the opener. Then again, matters might have been different. United managed as many attempts at goal the Magpies but couldn't finish while Pavel Srnicek coped with everything thrown at him.

Newcastle's victory owed much to Rob Lee and David Batty getting the better of midfield. The hosts forward line of Les Ferdinand, Alan Shearer, Peter Beardsley and David Ginola made hay as a result and by the end of the afternoon the French winger had run United ragged. The rout began on 13 minutes as Ginola's corner was flicked on by Shearer to Peacock who sent a downward header through a crowded six-yard box. It appeared the effort had been cleared off the line by Denis Irwin but referee Steve Dunn, who initially seemed to wave play on, spotted his assistant signalling the ball had crossed the line. TV pictures suggested it was the right decision but in the heat of the moment Peter Schmeichel was booked for his protests.

Soon after Karel Poborsky was denied a penalty when played in by Gary Neville and before the half hour the lead was doubled. Steve Watson's crossfield ball found John Beresford. Ginola surged on, beat Gary Neville with a deft touch before drilling a shot low into the far corner of goal. Soon after Shearer smashed an effort against the woodwork and United looked beaten but rallied in the second half, Poborsky's effort was well saved by Srnicek and Peacock blocked from Cantona. That was more or less United's last contribution.

After Les Ferdinand fluffed a straghtforward chance, Shearer offered his partner a chance of redemption a minute later, his run and cross from the right finding 'Sir Les', who nodded in off the bar. Shearer got reward for his industry soon after – setting up Beardsley for a shot that Schmeichel could only parry back to Ferdinand whose effort somehow landed at the £15 million man's feet inches from the line. As if to further gild the scoreline, Philippe Albert executed an exquisite lob over Schmeichel from 25 yards to round things off.

United were rarely chastened in this way and Cantona, riled by a personal feud with Albert, was booked and could consider himself fortunate not to be dismissed after rolling his studs down Beardsley's ankle.

SOUTHAMPTON 6 MANCHESTER UNITED 3
PREMIERSHIP - 26 OCTOBER 1996

FOLLOWING A 2-1 win over Swindon Town in the League Cup United experienced their second harrowing defeat in six days, taking the week's tally of goals conceded to a round dozen. The Dell had been the scene of a Matt Le Tissier masterclass during the run-in last term. This time United shot themselves in the foot – Roy Keane's early dismissal and the recurrence of Gary Pallister's back injury adding uncertainty to an already shaky performance.

Keane was cautioned for dissent when a penalty appeal was waved away after what he believed was a foul on Nicky Butt. A late challenge on Claus Lundekvam as the first quarter closed earned him a second yellow with the scoreline still 1-0. The Saints had taken an early lead when Eyal Berkovic flicked on for Egil Ostenstadt. The flick caught Pallister out allowing the Norwegian to power through – his shot was blocked but fell for Berkovic with just six minutes gone.

From the point Southampton gained a numerical advantage they looked favourites. Le Tissier hit one wide and had an effort smothered by Peter Schmeichel at close range. 'Saint Matt' made no mistake on 35 minutes, taking a pass from Berkovic, beating Brian McClair and David May before chipping Schmeichel. Beckham curled in a 25 yard free-kick before half-time that beat both Beasant and a man on the line but seconds before the break Berkovic sent Ostenstadt in again down the left. The Norwegian swept past David May's challenge to finish at the near post. Cantona, incensed by events, took out his frustrations on Ulrich Van Gobbel, the half-time whistle saving him from further sanction.

May reduced the arrears to a single goal by nodding in another excellent free-kick from Beckham early in the second period. Southampton looked to protect their lead and on most occasions this would have been suicidal but as United pushed up three goals in the final eight minutes ended all hopes of a revival. A partially cleared corner fell to Berkovic, and his volley into the top corner was the most eye-catching goal of the day. The Israeli turned provider again for Ostenstadt to claim a second and it became a hat-trick late on although Phil Neville got the final touch, before Paul Scholes scored from close range in time added on. This was the first time United had conceded half a dozen in any competition since a 6-0 defeat at Ipswich in March 1980.

A worry for United was the form of Cantona. Many believed the armband was weighing heavily on him, for the first time in months he looked frustrated and petulant. He was becoming a peripheral figure in contrast to the man who had only recently won championships single-handedly.

MANCHESTER UNITED 0 FENERBAHCE 1
CHAMPIONS LEAGUE GROUP C - 30 OCTOBER 1996

OVER THE 40 years and 56 games during which United had played host to the continent's elite, they had remained unbeaten at Old Trafford. Teams containing the attacking talents of Di Stefano, Maradona, Eusebio, Rivera and, just last season, Romario had managed no better than a draw. Yet Fenerbahce, one of the more unfancied clubs, left with a win netting the game's only goal 13 minutes from time following an insipid home performance that deserved little better.

Fenerbahce, beaten so easily in Istanbul, were far from comfortable with just one attempt at goal in the first half which Kemalettin Senturk volleyed over. United had only a handful of chances too but were equally profligate, Eric Cantona in particular would have been disappointed not to force Rustu into a save after being played in by Nicky Butt. He seemed to get no enjoyment from providing the focal point in an attack supported by Karel Poborsky and Jordi Cruyff who forced the keeper to save from an acute angle. Cantona started to drop deep but that just left United without an outlet. There was another chance for the Frenchman before the break after David Beckham rampaged through the centre, but Cantona shot wide.

On the restart Fenerbahce, bolstered by United's sloppiness, began to probe patiently - Emil Kostadinov connecting with Elvir Bolic's cross, guiding his effort over. Poborsky and Butt combined again but Rustu was quick to block before smothering Cruyff's attempted follow up. The Dutchman was replaced by Paul Scholes who struck the bar when he had looked to cross. Poborksy and Butt combined again but Rustu parried and Beckham was beaten to the loose ball. Jay-Jay Okocha and Bolic grew in confidence and the Croatian, chancing his arm after finding space on the left, launched the vital counter. He feinted inside David May's attempt to cover, the ball cannoning off May's shins, and ran on to beat Schmeichel with a deflected chip. It could have been worse as Kostadinov nodded against a post minutes later.

Wave after wave of United attack followed until the whistle.

The hosts seemed panicked by falling behind, and Beckham in particular, the best player on view by a comfortable distance, lost his composure. Peter Schmeichel pushed himself into attack for the last few minutes as the visitors were forced back but even this 'kitchen sink' approach came to nothing. Qualification for the quarter-finals would be difficult now - the Turks had been handed a lifeline.

MANCHESTER UNITED 1 CHELSEA 2
PREMIERSHIP - 2 NOVEMBER 1996

MATTERS WENT FROM bad to worse as United suffered a fourth defeat in five games and a first league reverse at Old Trafford for two years. Ruud Gullit's tactics handed Chelsea the win, countering United's re-shaped forward line by employing three centre backs and setting out to exploit the defensive frailties on view over recent weeks that included the sudden fallibility of Peter Schmeichel. The Dane, previously noted for miserliness, had let in 13 goals in four games and Chelsea, with Mark Hughes and Gianluca Vialli in their ranks, had just the strikers to take advantage.

Alex Ferguson omitted wide players Karel Poborsky and Jordi Cruyff in favour of strength through the middle – as Scholes and Solskjær came in. It almost worked with the Norwegian, prompted by Eric Cantona, looking the most likely. However, odd moments apart, Cantona's edge seemed to have deserted him and with their talisman subdued United's threat diminished.

Roy Keane had what proved to be United's best chance of the game, mistiming a leap at a David Beckham free-kick taken from near the corner flag to sky over. There was a visible change in the game within three minutes as a Dennis Wise corner was nodded in by an unmarked Michael Duberry. In Beckham and Giggs there were players on the pitch who could provide natural width but there was still a lack of penetration and the game was effectively put beyond the hosts on the hour when Frank Le Boeuf sprang the offside trap. Peter Schmeichel looked sure that a flag would be raised and was slow out of the blocks, giving Gianluca Vialli all the time he needed to steer a shot low through the keeper's legs.

Poborsky was introduced and pulled one back after his shot took a huge deflection off David May. Yet it always seemed likely to be nothing more than a consolation although there could have been an undeserved late equaliser had Cantona not got in the way of a goal bound Keane header three minutes from time. It was a moment typical of Eric's contribution and explained United's slump.

MANCHESTER UNITED 1 ARSENAL 0
Premiership - 16 November 1996

UNITED'S NIGHTMARE SEQUENCE of three games without a win ended against Arsenal courtesy of a Nigel Winterburn own goal. The Gunners, unbeaten in 10 games, had played the better football for over an hour but United finally got the break and ended their worst sequence of results since the Premiership began.

The Reds had equalled their guest's fervour but little else until a slice of fortune came their way. Roy Keane was a huge miss as the Gunners held control with a midfield of Patrick Vieira, David Platt and Paul Merson. David Beckham tried his best to counter that trio and although Nicky Butt was a presence the youngsters needed an older head among them. Again Eric Cantona was below his best and took time to impose any measure of authority. There was only one flicker of danger from the Frenchman who pulled a Gary Neville cross down and laid the ball off to Beckham. David Seaman made a lunge but never seemed likely to reach the shot and was relieved to see it bounce behind.

Denis Bergkamp had an effort from 20 yards spectacularly saved by Schmeichel before the Dutch international had a delightful lob chalked off for offside. Ian Wright seemed to have resurrected some of the bad blood which had dominated this fixture in recent years, sliding in on the keeper following a Bergkamp pass he only had a marginal chance of winning. The Dane's furious reaction had Wright responding in kind but the incident blew out quickly once others intervened.

The decisive moment came when Martin Keown attempted to clear but miscued. Seaman scrambled to prevent a corner but rather than push the ball to safety he only found Nicky Butt. His cross towards a gaping goal was intended for Cantona but Winterburn, desperate to deny the chance, tried to intervene only to divert the ball into his own goal. Arsenal did their best to gain parity. Schmeichel parried a Lee Dixon drive from distance and stopped Wright tipping the rebound past him. Platt ballooned a decent opening high before Wright latched onto a Lee Dixon high ball in the area. His turn and shot was denied by another first class block, Schmeichel rushing from his goal to gather the loose ball.

Still, United had the better of matters after the goal and kept their first clean sheet for exactly a month.

MANCHESTER UNITED 0 JUVENTUS 1
PREMIERSHIP - 20 NOVEMBER 1996

ONE EUROPEAN DEFEAT in 40 years at Old Trafford was turned into two within a fortnight as European Champions Juventus gave a lesson in ruthless efficiency. United performed admirably and would have beaten any of their domestic counterparts on this form but the Italians were a different proposition. Their silky passing made countless incisions keeping the Reds makeshift defence anxious and holding their midfield in check. With Denis Irwin and Gary Pallister out from the start there was a further blow when Phil Neville came off after 13 minutes. Brian McClair came on to cover in midfield while Roy Keane drifted back to fill the gap. The Irishman did an excellent job and McClair performed well but it took much away from an engine room that had started well.

The Reds raided successfully down the wings from the start, David May almost steering in a David Beckham corner, his header grazing the crossbar. Eric Cantona set up Beckham with a shot that fizzed wide and Giggs struck a post when McClair delivered from the wing. However, for all their efforts it was a piece of Italian trickery which led to the game's only goal. Alessandro Del Piero drawing a foul from Nicky Butt just inside the area, the Italian star took the spot kick himself and dispatched it high into the net.

The French tricolours had been waving from well before kick-off yet it wasn't Eric Cantona who held the attention but Zinedine Zidane, the man whom national coach Aime Jacquet had identified as the torch bearer for the hosts at the next World Cup. Along with countryman Didier Deschamps they made the most of Keane's withdrawal to dominate. Cantona could have equalised when sent through by Giggs but seemed flustered allowing Angelo Peruzzi to save. Later he hit the bar with a volley and much of the game resembled a basketball match as Juventus attacked before United countered. Giggs and Beckham had the best chances although Ole Gunnar Solskjær would have been disappointed to nod Beckham's free-kick wide. Keane was another just off target.

Cantona, back to something approaching his best as the game wore on, chested a Giggs corner down 20 yards out, his rising shot clipping the top of the bar. Another volley from outside the area was turned aside by Peruzzi yet Zidane and Alen Boksic could have stretched the lead. The latter had the best chance, rounding Schmeichel but ran too wide to make the chance count.

Another fortnight on and a draw could still see United reach the last eight should Juventus beat Fenerbahce at home - a distinct probability on this evidence as United had the edge in head-to-head meetings with the Turks. A Fenerbahce draw would mean United had to win to make the quarter-finals. A defeat or a Fenerbahce victory combined with any other result would see the Reds bow out.

MIDDLESBROUGH 2 MANCHESTER UNITED 2
PREMIERSHIP - 23 NOVEMBER 1996

ON THEIR FIRST visit to Middlesbrough's Riverside Stadium United had paraded the Premiership trophy. An early David May goal calmed nerves then. Now the defender's header 17 minutes from time looked likely to secure a first win on the road since early September before a controversial penalty allowed the hosts to level.

After a demanding midweek clash, Ferguson gave league debuts to John O'Kane, Ben Thornley and Michael Clegg. Paul Scholes was the other face brought in to the starting XI to partner Eric Cantona up front. Prior to Roy Keane finding the net after 17 minutes United looked comfortable in possession although Juninho had a couple of decent chances. He should have scored when found unmarked by a Craig Fleming pass but failed to control the ball a few yards out. He did far better with the next chance but fired just wide. Keane's goal came after David Beckham's volleyed pass across the area, Gary Walsh stood no chance.

Fabrizio Ravanelli tried to find an instant reply from 20 yards but his effort went inches wide yet just before the half hour the Italian levelled, beating Schmeichel with a low shot from the edge of the box following Juninho's pass. The Italian was denied again soon after, Schmeichel making an acrobatic stop from his header. Cantona had another disappointing afternoon but was in good company. Very few front players had a game to remember and David May looked to have bailed them out until referee Alan Wilkie decided Scholes had deliberately handled a Mikkel Beck free-kick. Craig Hignett fired home the spot-kick.

MANCHESTER UNITED 3 LEICESTER CITY 1
PREMIERSHIP - 30 NOVEMBER 1996

FOUR DAYS BEFORE journeying to Old Trafford, Leicester had knocked United out of the Coca-Cola Cup. The Foxes beat an under-strength United courtesy of goals from Steve Claridge and Emile

Heskey. Despite the Reds forthcoming season-defining European appointment in Vienna, United fielded a much stronger line-up here and welcomed back Gary Pallister with some relief. Recent defensive performances had left a lot to be desired and the home side looked far more comfortable going forward with a little solidity behind them.

Leicester made two enforced changes while only David May, Roy Keane and Jordi Cruyff survivors from midweek. Comfortably outplayed, Martin O'Neill's side somehow managed to stay on terms courtesy of some very poor finishing. It took the introduction of Ole Gunnar Solskjær to finally turn chances into goals. However, it was Keane who provided the first 15 minutes from time after he barged down the right and centred. The ball drifted towards the near post and despite the best efforts of Kasey Keller, Nicky Butt made the vital connection.

Close to the end Giggs also found his way round the back and from close to the byline dragged the ball back for Solskjær to net. A matter of seconds later Butt grabbed a second after swapping passes with Eric Cantona then getting clear. A minute from time Neil Lennon grabbed a consolation to give the scoreline a more accurate feel.

RAPID VIENNA 0 MANCHESTER UNITED 2
CHAMPIONS LEAGUE GROUP C - 4 DECEMBER 1996

ON A FREEZING winter night at the Ernst Happel Stadium, United became the first English side to reach the quarter-finals of Europe's premier club competition for 11 years. Fenerbahce, who could have qualified with a win in Turin, lost but despite a draw being sufficient there was no question of United settling for a point in Vienna. Although the margin of victory looked comfortable it was clear that United's form would have to improve before the Champions League reconvened in the spring.

Amongst some very ordinary play Eric Cantona stood out. Ryan Giggs, who netted after 23 minutes, was another leading light. His goal was created by Cantona who grabbed the second to dispel any prospect of an Austrian fightback. David Beckham was perhaps the stand out performer while Peter Schmeichel stood firm pulling off one of the best saves of his career at a crucial stage of the game.

United could have been ahead in the second minute when Andreas Heraf tried to clear a corner but almost put through his own net. During the next attack Beckham sped down the right. His cross eluded Ole Gunnar Solskjær but fell to Giggs who met it on the volley and lifted the effort narrowly over.

Having withstood that pressure Vienna countered, Peter Schottel's high ball for Rene Wagner cleared by Peter Schmeichel who had anticipated well. The keeper then denied Wagner again, flinging himself low to reach a stooping header which he pushed up and out of play. It was a save reminiscent of Gordon Banks' effort that denied Pele in the 1970 World Cup finals. From a little further out Wagner beat Pallister and crossed for Christian Stumpf. Schmeichel anticipated but could only paw at the ball and with the keeper prone Dietmar Kuhbauer blasted over.

A similar fate befell Solskjær who had collected a Cantona centre but somehow flicked his effort wide from four yards. Giggs quickly rectified matters after charging from the centre circle and linking with Cantona. A turn inside took the French international past Trifon Ivanov and give Giggs the return. Konsel came out but couldn't deny the Welshman. But the keeper made amends, denying Butt, Cantona and Solskjær before the interval.

Giggs wasted another opportunity on the resumption, Solskjær slipping two markers to lay on a chance, the winger blasting wide before Beckham dragged a shot wide and Cantona struck a post. United could celebrate when Beckham wriggled free down the right and crossed for his captain who slid the ball in at the far post.

Only injuries to Nicky Butt, Gary Neville and Roy Keane soured the evening. Keane's prognosis wasn't good after he was carried from the pitch and 30 stitches were inserted into a leg wound which punctured flesh right down to the bone.

WEST HAM UNITED 2 MANCHESTER UNITED 2
PREMIERSHIP - 8 DECEMBER 1996

UPTON PARK MAINTAINED its status as a bogey ground for United who squandered a two goal lead in the last 15 minutes. However, a point was far less than West Ham deserved as they dominated two thirds of the game while United, still in celebratory mode after their European exploits, looked lethargic and bereft of ideas and were thankful for two moments of football genius from Eric Cantona and David Beckham. The Frenchman's perfectly weighted pass allowed Solskjær to score before Beckham appeared to have rounded things off with a fantastic strike.

However, those two goals could have been mere consolations had the Hammers been able to take a similar percentage of the chances they created. United abandoned their open style in an attempt to save energy but Peter Schmeichel was called into action throughout the first half. When the Dane dropped a catch he had to react quickly to deny Ilie Dumitrescu, the Romanian's shot flashing across goal. Soon after a penalty claim for handball against Brian McClair was waved away by referee Peter Jones.

Not long after the restart United took the lead, Cantona rolled a pass to the Norwegian striker at a perfect speed for him to advance on the keeper and score. Within minutes United were two up, Beckham finding the top corner to put the visitors in total control.

Harry Redknapp's introduction of Florin Raducioiu changed the game, the substitute beating Ronny Johnsen before firing past Schmeichel just three minutes after Beckham's goal. Scenting blood the Hammers hemmed United in and within 90 seconds earned a penalty when Schmeichel knocked Hughes to the floor. Julian Dicks converted to leave United without an away league win since September.

SHEFFIELD WEDNESDAY 1 MANCHESTER UNITED 1
PREMIERSHIP - 18 DECEMBER 1996

CHRISTMAS WAS ALWAYS a key time in Alex Ferguson's planning. He believed that no matter the start to the season, if you could be within striking distance of the summit, a good festive period could turn things around. Yet it was the Owls who benefited from some early gifts as, despite being second best at Hillsborough, they led until a Paul Scholes equaliser restricted Liverpool's lead over them to just nine points.

Benito Carbone, who had arrived in South Yorkshire via Milan, was a constant danger, exposing a defence that continued to struggle. One of the Italian's shots veered so dramatically in the air that Peter Schmeichel was forced to alter his body posture and save with his chest. The Reds could have been ahead within a few minutes after Ryan Giggs, found by an incisive pass from Ronny Johnsen, beat Kevin Pressman but also the post. The Wednesday keeper then tipped a Scholes header over when the midfielder met a Giggs cross from the left.

Schmeichel seemed certain to be beaten but Guy Whittingham fluffed his chance, the Dane also denied Mark Pembridge, his parry reaching Whittingham who whipped the follow up across goal. It was inevitable that the pressure would tell and Carbone was the deserved beneficiary on 57 minutes, Orlando Trustfull jinking his way through the United defence before finding the Italian who curled home from the edge of the box.

United took just four minutes to respond. Schmeichel punted the ball high and as it dropped Steve Nicol lost out in a tussle with Ole Gunnar Solskjær. Scholes ran on to score. Eric Cantona was rarely involved in the game and placed his only chance to score into the jubilant home fans on the Kop.

MANCHESTER UNITED 5 SUNDERLAND 0
Premiership - 21 December 1996

This thumping win drew the Reds within six points of Liverpool, as the Merseysiders would play Newcastle United 48 hours later. With European matters to one side United could now concentrate on the league and showed renewed vigour for the title race with an emphatic performance that featured the return to form of Eric Cantona who grabbed his first brace since September.

At the back the Reds were resolute with five men protecting Peter Schmeichel who for the first time in weeks had a leisurely 90 minutes. Solskjær made the breakthrough on 36 minutes mopping up after a Ryan Giggs cross from the left was fired in by Paul Scholes, a stunned Lionel Perez, a former teammate of Cantona's at Nimes, made a save but had no control over the rebound as the Norwegian forward slid in. The incident clearly rattled the keeper who was beaten by his international compatriot from the spot after he brought Nicky Butt crashing to the ground. It seemed a critical moment for Cantona who had allowed the ball to slip from his usually eloquent feet within the first ten minutes. His authority seemingly gone, Eric appeared slow in thought and movement but it returned after the penalty.

With Eric back to his best United moved smoothly through the gears, a long throw out by Schmeichel was gathered by Solskjær who forced himself ahead of Dariusz Kubicki before slotting home. On the hour a fourth was added, Butt glancing home a Giggs corner. The fifth was a thing of beauty – a piece of art fit to grace The Louvre. United broke down the right, Cantona played a one-two with McClair and without glancing at the target executed the most exquisite lob over Perez, the ball glancing off the angle of post and bar before falling into the Sunderland goal. Cantona's statuesque celebration, as if to say 'What did you expect?' rounded off a perfect moment, a summation of his Old Trafford career.

NOTTINGHAM FOREST 0 MANCHESTER UNITED 4
PREMIERSHIP - 26 DECEMBER 1996

ALEX FERGUSON PROVIDED Nottingham Forest caretaker manager Stuart Pearce with a lesson he'd never forget. The left back had led his charges to a win over Arsenal in his first game but was unable to do the same to United.

David Beckham, recalled to the side after spending a few games on the bench, got matters underway with a crafty chip over Mark Crossley after Eric Cantona and Ole Gunnar Solskjær had created space. When Paul Scholes had a shot saved it was only delaying the inevitable for a few seconds, Nicky Butt dispatching the loose ball.

Pearce knew he had to do something at the break and withdrew Dean Saunders who had been operating as a right winger. However, Forest just didn't have the resources to stem the flow which continued when Cantona struck the bar with a subtle effort off the outside of his foot, Solskjær nodding in the rebound. Andy Cole, given 20 minutes from the bench to boost his confidence, grabbed the final goal.

This crushing win moved United into third place with a game in hand over table toppers Liverpool and served notice that the Reds were bang in form.

MANCHESTER UNITED 1 LEEDS UNITED 0
PREMIERSHIP - 28 DECEMBER 1996

LUCAS RADEBE WAS the given the brief to mark Eric Cantona and the South African stuck to him like glue for almost the entire match, save for the decisive penalty Eric took in the 10th minute.

The spot-kick came about when Cantona managed to outwit the South African with an adroit lay-off to set Ryan Giggs charging down the left. Radebe was dragged towards the ball as Cantona looked to guide the winger into the area. They traded touches before the Welshman moved through the gears. Gary Kelly, who was beaten for pace, brought him down. Having missed from the spot when the teams met earlier in the season, the pressure may have affected some but not Eric as he sent Nigel Martyn the wrong way.

The goal proved that having a tight rein over your man was only half the battle with some players able to outwit any defensive cover on their day. There was a hint of controversy when it appeared Cantona kicked out at Radebe who needed attention before carrying on. That incident apart Leeds were comfortable at the back but that single goal was always going to be enough as at the other end they had all the impact of a powder puff. Their labouring strikers included the now impotent Tony Yeboah who had returned from injury in poor shape. For their part United looked secure at the back and took their foot off the gas in the closing stages.

MANCHESTER UNITED 0 ASTON VILLA 0
PREMIERSHIP - 1 JANUARY 1997

UNITED'S INABILITY TO find the target was a source of frustration as Villa's gameplan succeeded on New Year's Day. The return of Roy Keane was important for United's title quest and his midfield presence lent the hosts a stability they had missed for some months.

Keane's impact was instant, the Irish international setting Eric Cantona in motion downfield, to cross for Giggs who blasted wide. Giggs tried to make amends, winning the ball on the edge of his own area and speeding away before releasing Cantona. With only Mark Bosnich to beat most anticipated a goal but Eric's feeble shot allowed the Aussie to grab the ball.

There was so little shown after Cantona's failure to finish that Villa started looking for their own chances and possibly should have had a penalty after Keane's heavy challenge on Savo Milosevic. Andy Townsend and Mark Draper had goal attempts blocked, the Yugoslav international also tested Peter Schmeichel though to everyone's relief Dwight Yorke was not the man on the end of the chance.

Ole Gunnar Solskjær was replaced by Andy Cole who had just seconds to shape himself and send an effort goalwards when the ball fell kindly for him, Bosnich smothered. Villa's Tommy Johnson forced Schmeichel to make a reflex save to preserve the stalemate with a whipped volley in the last meaningful act of the game.

MANCHESTER UNITED 2 TOTTENHAM HOTSPUR 0
FA CUP 3RD RD - 5 JANUARY 1997

As TIES OF the round went this clash between the two most decorated sides in the FA Cup took some beating. Yet Tottenham, who had conceded seven goals the last time they ventured from White Hart Lane, were missing half a dozen important names. Each department of the team was affected and the visitors employed a cautious approach as a result.

Nevertheless they began well, seeing plenty of the ball but doing little with it. Their teenage forward line, consisting of Rory Allen and Neale Fenn, enjoyed little service. United manufactured far fewer opportunities but made Ian Walker work. An unfortunate feature of those chances which went begging was the errant shooting of Andy Cole. The striker failed to gel with Cantona who seemed to give up trying to find his colleague. Ryan Giggs passed up other opportunities, with the most clear cut - a simple header from David Beckham's cross - placed too close to the keeper.

For all his troubles in front of goal during the build-up Cole was like a flashing blade and contributed to the opener, finding Beckham before playing Paul Scholes in who finished from 12 yards out. Allen soon had a chance to draw level after linking up with his partner but sent his effort wide.

United dominated the closing stages with every forward thinking player chancing their arm. Cantona and Giggs put chances marginally wide and Cole seemed to have fashioned himself an easy opportunity after gliding round Walker but was forced wide and scuffed his effort. A free-kick awarded when Giggs was upended by Colin Calderwood 25 yards out allowed Beckham to bend his effort over the wall and past the keeper's outstretched right hand.

TOTTENHAM HOTSPUR 1 MANCHESTER UNITED 2
PREMIERSHIP - 12 JANUARY 1997

DAVID BECKHAM PROVED Spurs' nemesis for the second time in a week, grabbing a late goal against the club he had trained with as a youth. The returning Gary Pallister provided a welcome boost to a backline shorn of Denis Irwin and Phil Neville. David May was due to undergo surgery on a hernia just days after the game which seemed to have accounted for Ronny Johnsen's participation in the short term. The Norwegian left the field carrying a limp at the end.

Spurs were able to welcome Steffen Iversen back and the forward provided a prolonged test for Pallister and worried Schmeichel who fielded many more attempts on his goal than had been the case at Old Trafford. Iversen thought he had beaten Schmeichel with a volley before the first quarter ended, but the Dane recovered well, then Iversen danced past Johnsen and struck a rocket from 25 yards but the ball came back off the bar, Andy Sinton wasting the follow-up.

It proved an expensive miss as within a few minutes United led, Solskjær taking a long ball from Keane, before playing a one-two with Eric Cantona, the Norwegian sliding the ball in from the left. It could quickly have been 2-0 as Ole released Ryan Giggs but Walker calmly watched the ball fizz across his six yard area. Tottenham's last chance of the first half was converted to give them a deserved equaliser. A corner won by David Howells' persistence was floated in by Sinton for £3.7 million signing Ramon Vega. The Swiss defender's goal bound effort billowed the net courtesy of Rory Allen's head.

Alex Ferguson made tactical switches at the break switching Johnsen to left back and adding an extra man to midfield. Yet neither side threatened until Karel Poborksy's introduction on the right hand side changed the game. Cantona headed wide, Giggs passed up another decent opening and lofted over the bar, but it was Beckham, whose day was crowned by receiving his Young Player of the Year award, who gave United the lead 15 minutes from time with a 30 yard curler. Just seconds prior to the shot being unleashed it seemed nothing was on. Spurs closed down space but there was just enough room for the shot. The win put United in second, a season long high, and most importantly two points behind Liverpool.

COVENTRY CITY 0 MANCHESTER UNITED 2
PREMIERSHIP - 18 JANUARY 1997

UNITED'S PLAYERS RAN out at Highfield Road following Alex Ferguson's announcement that he would be retiring when his current contract ended. The absence of David Beckham, who had been a creative force over recent weeks, saw fewer chances fashioned and a win was only claimed by a large dose of cheek from Ryan Giggs.

One fierce long shot from Paul Scholes hit the crossbar, Ronny Johnsen was inches away from picking up the pieces. Veteran stopper Steve Ogrizovic made a reaction save from Ole Gunnar Solskjær who had been teed up by Eric Cantona. He also denied Gary Pallister from short range later in the game. Solskjær had a second chance laid on by Cantona but volleyed wide. The manic nature of play only stopped when Cantona put his foot on the ball and began to dictate the game.

Despite their rank as strugglers, Coventry could not be taken for granted. They had done United a favour by beating Liverpool recently and Gordon Strachan, opposing his old boss for the first time as manager, had the dangerous Darren Huckerby, a young, quick striker, who had a burgeoning reputation. Huckerby thought he had won a penalty soon after the interval when chasing a pass over the top from Noel Whelan. He seemed to have been caught by Gary Neville but the referee waved appeals away.

Soon afterwards Giggs unleashed a rising drive which Ogrizovic failed to get close to. Remarkably the Welshman passed up a simple chance when fed by Solskjær just in front of goal before, from a similar position, he ended a goalmouth scramble after Giggs aided by Cantona repaid the favour. It ensured United continued their 11 match unbeaten run which had so far yielded 25 points.

MANCHESTER UNITED 1 WIMBLEDON 1
FA Cup 4th Rd - 25 January 1997

A number of late home goals had saved the Reds recently and most thought they had won this game following a Paul Scholes strike with minutes remaining. But Wimbledon, who were never fazed, came back to claim a draw and a replay at Selhurst Park.

Wimbledon clearly fancied their chances from the start but a pattern soon established itself of visiting attacks being broken down and counter-attacks being launched. Keane wasted a glorious opportunity from one of these moves, knocking the ball over from a few yards out after Eric Cantona and Ryan Giggs tore down the left flank. Giggs then set Cantona up but the Frenchman's header was mistimed and those gilt-edged chances aside the Dons had the better of it, Schmeichel repelling a couple of efforts from Efan Ekoku, one stop in particular was superb after the giant striker met a corner. Marcus Gayle should have converted a Robbie Earle cross, while Dean Blackwell failed to force home a Vinnie Jones centre.

The break marked a transformation in the game as United started to pour forward with Cantona the focal point. There was a fear that the inexperienced defence could be caught out in the latter stages. Cantona set up Keane who sent a shot wide then, after being fed by Giggs, he thought he may have won a penalty when falling under Alan Kimble's challenge. When Scholes stooped to head in a Cantona cross in the closing minutes, it seemed the next round beckoned until Robbie Earle nodded in a Kimble free-kick with seconds of injury time remaining.

MANCHESTER UNITED 2 WIMBLEDON 1
Premiership - 29 January 1997

Wimbledon agreed to reschedule the league fixture, which would now be sandwiched between the two FA Cup encounters, to assist United's European ambitions. Yet the Dons looked set to take all three points and score an important psychological boost ahead of the Selhurst Park FA Cup replay before a couple of goals in the final quarter of an hour turned the match on its head.

Alex Ferguson welcomed back Beckham, Pallister and Solskjær.

Vinnie Jones was absent through injury. Rather than get themselves on the front foot Wimbledon sat back. Solskjær showed his sharpness had not been dulled by his time on the bench but though he beat Neil Sullivan with a pair of well executed shots both rebounded back to safety off the crossbar.

Wimbledon had the first chance of the second half and it took a superb save from Peter Schmeichel to deny Marcus Gayle. A huge hand tipped the forward's effort on to the woodwork. However, there was no answer when Chris Perry finished from close range after Robbie Earle flicked on an Alan Kimble corner soon after.

Cantona, who had a quiet game by his own standards, was another to see a fine effort - a rasping and well controlled volley – hit the bar but an equaliser arrived courtesy of a Giggs header from what initially appeared an under-hit Beckham corner. Andy Cole, who had missed with a header when unmarked, then finished off a goalmouth scramble following a parried Solskjær shot to claim all three points. It was a win which allowed United to top the table for the first time all season.

MANCHESTER UNITED 2 SOUTHAMPTON 1
PREMIERSHIP - 1 FEBRUARY 1997

THERE WAS AN admirable boldness about Southampton's confident play, no doubt bolstered by the memory of those six goals they had put past United at The Dell earlier in the season. Matt Le Tissier and Eyal Berkovic, playing as converted wingers, drew first blood after just 11 minutes. Egil Ostenstad, who had already seen an angled drive from the right saved, converted after Jim Magilton outmuscled United's rearguard. An equaliser came quickly from an unlikely source. Gary Pallister chested down an Eric Cantona corner before rocketing the ball into the top corner.

The Saints, victims of Stockport County in the last eight of the League Cup, withstood an all out assault after the break. Ryan Giggs, enjoyed a better second half, teeing up Solskjær, Keane, Neville, Poborsky, Beckham and Cantona for chances before the Frenchman finally made the most of a teasing centre, converting at the far post. Then another Giggs dribble took him past five players, the lay off for Poborsky was just as breathtaking but the Czech couldn't apply the finish. Nor could he beat the keeper with three further chances.

Again Cantona appeared somewhat awkward, sending two chances wide and allowing Alan Neilsen to intercept when he hesitated. There was however one moment of sheer brilliance - an overhead kick which seemed sure to beat Maik Taylor but was blocked by Charlton. Keane should have converted what seemed a 'gimmie' with Taylor struggling to make his ground. Magilton struck a post in the closing minutes but there were no further scares and some measure of revenge was gained for that early season humiliation.

WIMBLEDON 1 MANCHESTER UNITED 0
FA Cup 4th rd replay - 4 February 1997

THREE MATCHES WITH Wimbledon in just over a fortnight ended with victory for the Dons. It meant United, who never looked likely winners here, lost a cup tie at a ground other than Wembley for the first time in four years and it also meant Eric Cantona's first ever defeat in the FA Cup before his two match ban kicked-in.

Joe Kinnear picked three centre forwards in Marcus Gayle, Efan Ekoku and Dean Holdsworth and the squally conditions clearly favoured the home side. Ekoku got a header wrong from just six yards out with Peter Schmeichel exposed before the same player turned provider, setting up Holdsworth and Oyvind Leonhardsen in quick succession. A point blank save from an Andy Cole effort aside, United barely had a sniff until the early stages of the second period when David Beckham's 30 yard strike whistled just over. Yet once Gayle scored from a Kenny Cunningham cross near the corner flag, with just over an hour gone, belief seemed to disappear from the away side.

United changed their system, pushing three into attack by introducing Ole Gunnar Solskjær and Brian McClair but couldn't level. Beckham missed from 15 yards with a snap shot when the ball broke to him and Gary Pallister's late header was turned round a post. A late charge upfield by Peter Schmeichel seemed to have paid off when the Dane hooked the ball in until he noticed a flag had been raised and the effort disallowed.

February proved a mixed month for United with only two league matches scheduled after the FA Cup exit. Eric missed both the 2-1 win at Highbury and a 1-1 draw at Chelsea.

MANCHESTER UNITED 3 COVENTRY CITY 1
Premiership - 1 March 1997

TWO OWN-GOALS within a 50 second spell gave the Reds a chance to focus on the forthcoming visit of Porto. Before play began David Busst, whose career had been ended following the horrific broken leg suffered in the last year's fixture, was a guest of honour. Coventry's players lined up to applaud their former colleague and were followed by the entire ground, which would stage a testimonial later in the year.

It took Eric Cantona just four minutes to forge a breakthrough. His hope to play Andy Cole in on the edge of the area was anticipated by Gary Breen but an attempt to divert the ball away from danger ended up sliding past Steve Ogrizovic. Then Beckham, given a central role in the absence of Roy Keane, released Giggs. Ogrizovic saved but the ball rolled kindly for Jordi Cruyff whose low cross intended for Cole found its way into the net off Eoin Jess. There should have been more within the quarter of an hour which followed. Cruyff set up Cole who side-footed wide. Cantona looked rusty in front of goal missing a series of chances he would normally have expected to convert.

Dion Dublin, who had started the game as a striker, was pushed back into central defence by Gordon Strachan after just half an hour. Debutant Alexandr Evtushok was soon replaced by Peter Ndlovu and Coventry, without a goal in seven previous visits, finally started to offer a threat.

A third home goal was something of an inevitability – Cruyff and Cole combining to set up Karel Poborsky's low finish from the edge of the box. With the game safe preparations for Porto began as Beckham, Irwin and Giggs were benched. Coventry converted one of their late chances – Huckerby's mazy run capped by an accurate shot across Schmeichel. Nevertheless the win opened up a four point gap over Liverpool who lost 24 hours later to a late goal at Aston Villa.

MANCHESTER UNITED 4 PORTO 0
CHAMPIONS LEAGUE QUARTER-FINAL 1ST LEG - 5 MARCH 1997

PORTO WERE WELL regarded in Champions League terms and most anticipated a stiff test of United's credentials. They had been beaten for the first time all season just a week previously but the Portuguese champions were unbeaten away from their own imposing Das Antas Stadium. They gave notice of their attacking intent, almost going ahead within 80 seconds, Artur's shot flew wide after he was played in by Edmilson, but that proved to be almost the last chance the visitors crafted. United quickly found their feet, Andy Cole just failing to connect with a Cantona cross from the right that fell for Gary Neville who ballooned over. Nevertheless it set a tempo on and off the pitch that added impetus to United's quest to reach the last four.

Giggs, deployed in a free role, was a constant worry for Porto and outstanding throughout meaning that the injured Roy Keane wasn't as great a loss as first feared, with Ronny Johnsen deputising in the middle. David May should have converted a Cantona cross just minutes in but could only direct his header at goalkeeper Hilario. The 21 year-old was forced into a sensational back-pedalling save from a Cole header soon after and with every United player bar Peter Schmeichel camped in the opposition half, Gary Pallister met a David Beckham cross that Hilario couldn't collect and David May sent the loose ball crashing into the net.

Just past the half hour Cantona, who was proving an excellent foil to Cole and Solskjær, doubled the lead. Schmeichel's huge goal-kick was fielded by Solskjær who found Cantona in acres of space. Aloisio got a foot to the ball but stumbled and the striker ran on before drilling his effort home. Brazilian striker Jardel came on soon after but the scorer of almost 30 goals that campaign failed to make much of a difference despite Porto seeing more of the ball. Cantona retreated to cover as a full back at one stage but one Jardel centre aside, which May cut out, there was no serious threat to the United goal.

The interval was the only respite Porto were able to enjoy all evening. Beckham thrust an effort inches wide after the resumption and Cole should have done better with a chance when clear. There was no let up at any stage of play and Giggs gained just reward with little more than an hour played. United's counter was breathtaking, Cantona playing a exquisite ball down the line for Cole that allowed the striker to run at a worried central defence. Jorge Costa dropped off and Cole found Giggs with a delicious reverse pass - the winger flicking the ball past Santos before arrowing an effort inside the near post. With 10 minutes left United added a fourth, Johnsen winning the ball from Barroso then finding Cantona. Like a matador confronting a tired bull, Eric looked to apply the killer blow. Cole, whose confidence had grown since teeing up Giggs, made a run behind Costa, the Frenchman laying the perfect ball into his path, and the striker chipped Hilario.

This was one of the most convincing European nights in United's history and it seemed a turning point in Alex Ferguson's European ambitions. Previously the Scot had talked about succeeding at the highest level but, for one reason or another – inexperience, tactical shortcomings or the foreigner rule – his team seemed some way short. Defeat at the hands of second rate teams such as Galatasaray and Gothenburg were proof that United lacked something at this grade. Now, with Europe sitting up and taking notice, they had crushed the Portuguese champions with fine, attacking football. From this point on United would feature in the latter stages of the competition for the next 10 years, a record only rivalled by Real Madrid.

SUNDERLAND 2 MANCHESTER UNITED 1
PREMIERSHIP - 8 MARCH 1997

SUNDERLAND, WHO HADN'T tasted victory for two months and had just been spanked 0-4 at home by Tottenham, took advantage of United's European hangover to cause a shock. In five previous domestic fixtures following Champions League commitments United had lost three and drawn two.

Alex Ferguson rested Cole and Solskjær but perhaps most crucially Ryan Giggs who, though named as a substitute, stayed on the bench after tweaking a hamstring during the warm-up. McClair, Cruyff and Poborsky came in and while they should have been fresher the latter two were clearly struggling with the relentless pace of English football and looked spent by the break. Gary Pallister was forced out and Ronny Johnsen partnered Denis Irwin and David May in the centre with Phil Neville coming in as a wing-back complementing his brother Gary on the opposite flank.

A couple of second-half goals, when United looked weary, won the game but Sunderland were the better team throughout. Cole, sent on for a final push after one was pulled back, had a great chance to snatch an equaliser in injury time but had he been successful it would have been rough justice on the home side.

Michael Bridges and John Mullin were tireless up front, even if they produced few clear cut chances. United's attack was a stark contrast. Hallmarked throughout by sloppiness, Eric Cantona appeared in woeful touch. Few of the passes he tried came off and, with the exception of a shot from just outside the area minutes before the break, for once his contribution was negligible.

The Rokerites took the lead following a Gareth Hall cross. Mullin made a challenge that prevented Schmeichel from fielding the ball which allowed Michael Gray to tap into an empty net. Mullin gave the scoreline a more accurate feel 14 minutes from the close, Hall's ball over the top catching out a United defence pushing up to find an equaliser. Schmeichel got a touch but couldn't save. Andy Melville gifted an own goal soon after but that late Cole chance aside there was nothing which worried the home defence unduly.

A first Premiership defeat since November along with Arsenal beating Nottingham Forest meant the title race was still open. Liverpool retained their hopes with a 4-3 Anfield win over Newcastle.

MANCHESTER UNITED 2 SHEFFIELD WEDNESDAY 0
PREMIERSHIP - 15 MARCH 1997

UNITED, KEEN TO put the Sunderland game behind them, rediscovered a little of their swagger with a goal either side of the break. Ryan Giggs, who shook off a slight hamstring problem to start, was the spark which ignited many moves alongside Cantona, who reverted to a withdrawn role and looked far more comfortable than of late. The pair combined to set up the opener. A Giggs ball slipped through the middle set his captain free and Eric's clever lay-off found Cole who drilled a low shot across Pressman. It was only the striker's fifth of the season, a poor return despite limited appearances.

Wednesday came out for the restart with a determination to try and grab a share of the spoils but once Poborsky scored following a well crafted move by Cantona and Solskjær on the right the result was never in doubt. The Frenchman's final contribution to the move - a flick as he pirouetted in mid-air - was typical of his contribution which was marked by flair and attacking intent. Solskjær was the recipient of possibly the most audacious manipulation of the ball, as Cantona dummied the entire Wednesday defence with a deft reverse pass.

PORTO 0 MANCHESTER UNITED 0
CHAMPIONS LEAGUE QUARTER-FINAL 2ND LEG - 19 MARCH 1997

PORTO HAD NO choice but to launch an all out assault on Peter Schmeichel's goal in a vain attempt to turn around the four goal deficit. The Reds, without Ryan Giggs and Andy Cole, picked a solid midfield of Roy Keane, Nicky Butt and Ronny Johnsen to counter any threat. Content to remain unadventurous for lengthy periods, United were well prepared to ride out the storm then strike when they could.

It took some time for that pattern to establish itself as Jardel set about restoring some pride. The Brazilian had two early chances - the first a diving header which he did well to force towards goal, following a one-two with Rui Jorge before Edmilson got behind the United backline leaving Schmeichel no choice but to advance. His ball for Jardel seemed to offer the Brazilian a gift-wrapped chance but he took far too much time to line up his effort, allowing David May to intervene. Porto were soon forced to try long shots which were meat and drink for Schmeichel.

United rarely threatened but a David Beckham free-kick from 35 yards shook the crossbar before Phil Neville and Cantona linked up, Hilario saving again. Porto pushed more men forward as the end neared, if only to restore pride. Substitutes Arnold Wetl and Grzegorz Mielcarski added weight to the attack but United were never truly threatened. Their best chances came when Fernando Mendes found Edmilson deep inside the area but headed over. Gary Neville was forced to make a superb tackle on Ljubinko Drulovic who had powered through the middle. The same player rounded the Dane a few minutes later but was forced too wide.

In control of the game for the last quarter it became United's turn to pass up opportunities, the most gilt-edged of which fell for Cantona after a delightful ball from Solskjær. Though the Porto defence was beaten the end product was easily fielded by Andrzej Wozniak.

At the whistle United had reached the European Cup semi-finals for the first time since 1969 and would meet Borussia Dortmund following the Germans' slim win over Auxerre. However European Footballer of the Year Matthias Sammer would miss the first leg after picking up a yellow card. United would have no such handicaps with all players coming through without a hitch.

EVERTON 0 MANCHESTER UNITED 2
Premiership - 22 March 1997

Everton, who had frittered away a two goal advantage at Old Trafford earlier in the season, had a decent record against the champions which gave Liverpool and Arsenal, who would meet each other on Monday evening, some hope that points might be dropped. However, the Goodison Park club had struggled of late and came into the game on the back of nine defeats from a dozen games.

Again the Reds were far from rampant but much stronger than their hosts and won with goals from Cantona and Solskjær. The six point lead looked comfortable although Pallister and Beckham suffered injuries which threatened their participation in an upcoming

England game if not Manchester United's next fixture two weeks on.

Midfield control was wrested from Everton at the start. Joe Parkinson, Claus Thomsen and Gary Speed may have been considered a formidable trio but were no match for Roy Keane and Nicky Butt. Yet there were few chances until Beckham cut inside from the right to fire narrowly over from 25 yards.

Everton focussed on high balls to Duncan Ferguson, the Scottish striker got his head to a Nicky Barmby free-kick but ballooned over. Another Ferguson chance went closer but for the most part he was well marshalled by David May and Pallister. The Scot's frustrations boiled over when he put an arm across May's face as they tussled in a chase for a long ball.

Schmeichel began the move which gave United the lead, his long clearance finding Cantona who released Solskjær with a trademark flick. Dave Watson was held off before the Norwegian smashed in a shot with his left foot. Paul Gerrard, in for the dropped Neville Southall, seemed to have it covered but the ball slipped through his hands.

When Pallister went off with a back injury Duncan Ferguson may have hoped to profit and there were claims for a penalty when Ronny Johnsen grabbed hold of Graham Stuart. The incident appeared to be inside the area but the offence was ruled to have taken place just outside. Speed wasted the free-kick, smashing his effort into the wall. From another counter Cantona ran clear to score with 11 minutes left. Again Gerrard would have been disappointed with his attempt to stop the ball crossing the line.

MANCHESTER UNITED 2 DERBY COUNTY 3
PREMIERSHIP - 5 APRIL 1997

UNITED'S TITLE HOPES were dealt a blow with an unlikely win for relegation strugglers Derby County courtesy of a late Dean Sturridge goal. Matters could have been so different if Cantona and Giggs had taken their chances. Derby made the most of their reprieves on 29 minutes. Paul Trollope, who took a moment off from his superb man-marking of Cantona, crossed for debutant Paulo Wanchope to head on for Ashley Ward who hit his shot into the ground but just under the bar. Six minutes later the unorthodox Costa Rican striker scored a sublime second, his mazy run taking him past four defenders before beating Schmeichel.

Nicky Butt made way for Solskjær after the break and it was the Norwegian's diagonal pass out of midfield that dragged the Reds back into things. Cantona took a touch to kill the ball then dabbed it past the advancing Mat Poom. Derby, who had been composed until that point, began to fear they would be hauled back after Wanchope was forced out with cramp. Solskjær was now a focal point of every attack though somehow the danger was ridden out.

Schmeichel and Pallister made a rare error on the edge of the penalty area which Sturridge punished by heading a bouncing ball beyond them. The ball striking a post before the striker followed up. Solskjær hit in a dipping shot within 60 seconds but otherwise there was little on offer from the home side with ex-Old Trafford centre half Paul McGrath in control for the Rams.

BORUSSIA DORTMUND 1 MANCHESTER UNITED 0
CHAMPIONS LEAGUE SEMI-FINAL - 9 APRIL 1997

DEFINITIONS OF A good result in Europe had changed since the days when Matt Busby guided the club against the continent's elite. A 1-0 away defeat with a home leg to come was on paper something which should not stand in United's way but Dortmund's deflected winner on 76 minutes in a game the Reds dominated was a huge blow, especially as the Germans were under strength. Along with the suspended Matthias Sammer there were five other regulars missing including creative force Stephane Chapuisat, first choice defender Jurgen Kohler and forward Karlheinz Riedle. Paulo Sousa took over the playmaker role and Heiko Herrlich looked the player most likely to make the most of his colleague's promptings.

United would have claimed a win had the woodwork been a little kinder to Nicky Butt and had David Beckham not had a shot cleared off the line. The Reds were forced to play without Peter Schmeichel, who withdrew an hour before kick-off with a back injury. Raimond Van Der Gouw, who had played just a handful of times since coming to Old Trafford, looked tentative early on and took a knock from Gary Pallister when he came for a ball intended for Herrlich. However the Dutchman's composure grew as play wore on, he fielded a fierce Rene Tretschok volley well and was able to deny Herrlich twice.

On 28 minutes United fashioned their first chance - David Beckham linking with Nicky Butt to set up Eric Cantona on the edge of the box who shot over. Dortmund were dogged in defence and always had an answer to United's direct play. It wasn't until after the break that United picked up the pace, Cantona releasing Nicky Butt. Stefan Klos had no choice but to come out but a shot was hammered past him only to rebound off a post. Solskjær was first to the loose ball but his left-foot volley went wide.

Dortmund then dominated and United's only opportunity came on the break, Cantona teeing up Beckham who charged 50 yards to hit a low effort that beat Klos only for Martin Kree to stretch out a leg and clear. Borussia forced United back as the half wore on - Butt nearly put through his own goal after getting the top of his head to a corner, Cantona clearing via the woodwork. But there was no reprieve the next time the ball took a deflection. Paulo Sousa went past Cantona, found Rene Tretschok whose 20 yard shot skimmed off Gary Pallister and into the top corner.

Roy Keane, who had mopped up countless German threats, received a booking for a challenge on Sousa and would miss the second leg.

BLACKBURN ROVERS 2 MANCHESTER UNITED 3
PREMIERSHIP - 12 APRIL 1997

THERE MAY ONLY have been a goal separating the Reds from a side which took their Premiership title from them just two years before but the gulf between the teams was far larger. The damage had already been done in the first half when Andy Cole finally looked worth his £7 million transfer fee. He scored an opener at a crucial time and played a substantial part in the two goals which followed. Cole prospered as part of a three man attack alongside Cantona and Solskjær with Paul Scholes providing a link from midfield. It was a formation the manager favoured as it allowed players to support attacks.

As if to verify the theory Keane and Pallister both found the woodwork in the opening minutes before Nicky Butt was fouled by Jeff Kenna on 22 minutes. Uncharacteristically the spot kick was a poor effort which Tim Flowers had no problems stopping. It was Eric's first penalty miss since Elland Road in September. It took 10 minutes for Cole to rectify the situation. The striker got up off the floor to beat three men before placing a low effort beyond the keeper.

Blackburn looked to strike back quickly and gained parity when Billy McKinlay saw a bobbling shot from 30 yards escape Raimond

Van der Gouw's clutches but United regained the lead three minutes before the break, Cole finding an unmarked Scholes who scored from the right hand edge of the area.

The lead was only extended in the 80th minute, Cole making another thrust through the Rovers defence before cutting the ball back for Cantona. Paul Warhurst scored with two minutes remaining and Van der Gouw had to be alert to deny Per Pedersen who had a free header during injury time.

LIVERPOOL 1 MANCHESTER UNITED 3
PREMIERSHIP - 19 APRIL 1997

A STRAIGHTFORWARD WIN at Anfield effectively removed the hosts from title contention leaving only Arsenal, five points behind, capable of preventing United from retaining their crown. Gary Pallister scored a brace of headers from badly defended corners, before David James gifted Andy Cole a third to round things off. However, it would be wrong to lay the difference between the sides at these lapses by the keeper. The superb running and intuitive forward play of Cole deserved reward as did the constructive play of Cantona and Beckham.

For long periods an entertaining and enterprising Liverpool were only kept out by some dogged defending. There was the odd slice of luck too yet the chances carved out by the visitors were more clear cut. Cantona almost lashed a volley in but the effort dipped just over before Pallister grabbed the first on 12 minutes out-jumping Mark Wright at the near post to nod Beckham's corner past James. Cole should have done better after rounding the keeper following a woeful back header from Stig Inge Bjornbye but screwed the ball wide. Liverpool levelled soon after, McAteer's centre finding John Barnes who flicked the ball past Peter Schmeichel.

Robbie Fowler, about to start a three match ban after being sent off against Everton, seemed too eager at times and snatched at a number of chances. While Ronny Johnsen came close to converting another corner before the break before, at the next one, Pallister diverted the ball in at the near post after getting the better of Wright once more. Liverpool made changes in an attempt to regain parity but United were too cute and the Merseysiders threats were isolated. Fowler was denied at point blank range before Cole was gifted a third.

MANCHESTER UNITED 0 BORUSSIA DORTMUND 1
CHAMPIONS LEAGUE SEMI-FINAL 2ND LEG - 23 APRIL 1997

IF THERE WAS one course of events United could have done without it was the concession of an early away goal and when Lars Ricken, a 20 year-old born in the city of Dortmund, struck after seven minutes the Reds needed to find three goals in the remaining 83 minutes. Ricken profited from an Andreas Moller through-ball that caught United's back-line napping before hitting a powerful cross shot past Schmeichel.

From that point on United had an almost impossible task against a team that welcomed back the impressive Jurgen Kohler and Matthias Sammer. United still carved out chances through David Beckham and Nicky Butt. Andy Cole tried as hard as anyone but the inspiration of his strike partner Eric Cantona was sadly missing. A wily guiding hand could possibly have tipped the scales but the Frenchman squandered his best chance of the game with little more than a quarter of an hour gone, a Solskjær burst down the right finding Andy Cole whose quick cross was only half-cleared by Stefan Klos. Normally Cantona would have instinctively flicked the ball in but he took too long over shooting and allowed Kohler to knock the ball to safety.

Nevertheless United continued to press, Solskjær heading over before Ronny Johnsen's shot was deflected to safety. Another cross from the right by Beckham found Cole but the angle made the resulting header difficult and Kohler was on hand to nod the ball out. Ryan Giggs came on to offer a spark and had a couple of efforts saved. He provided plenty of centres but no one could apply the finishing touch. Cantona seemed to have finally found a way through after heading over Klos but yet again a spare man was able to clear on the line.

It was a disappointing exit for United but at least Alex Ferguson could point to the progress of his team at the highest level in Europe. Two long range strikes had handed Dortmund a berth in the final in which they shocked holders Juventus (and the rest of Europe) with a 3-1 triumph.

LEICESTER CITY 2 MANCHESTER UNITED 2
PREMIERSHIP - 3 MAY 1997

WINNING THE TITLE was a slim possibility at sun-kissed Filbert Street before kick-off but in the event the point earned allowed United to clinch the Premiership at Old Trafford 48 hours later. The early kick-off seemed to catch many United players out as relegation battlers Leicester exploited some sloppy defending to take a two goal lead within 20 minutes and offer other title challengers a lifeline in the process.

Leicester opened the scoring on seven minutes, Steve Walsh charging from deep to convert a far post corner. A few minutes later the hosts extended it, a goal-kick from Keller ended with David May and Marshall tussling for a flick. In the end neither got a touch but the Leicester man was able to react first and nutmeg Gary Pallister before sweeping the ball beyond Schmeichel. Leicester pressed for a third, Marshall curling wide, Claridge pilfering the ball from Schmeichel but finishing poorly before Muzzy Izzet's claims for a penalty were denied.

United found a route back towards the close of the first half. A Pallister clearance sending Scholes clear. The midfielder's incisive ball found Cole who squared for Solskjær to lash home. A lack of width was a handicap to United as attempts to break through the middle were predictably met by massed ranks of defenders. Even Eric Cantona failed to operate effectively when space was this limited. David Beckham came on at the break. Just five minutes after the restart Cole shot for goal from 18 yards, Keller saved but had no luck as the ball fell for Solskjær who stabbed in. A potential winner was threatened soon after, Keane capping a dynamic run with an angled drive which Keller managed to control as Solskjær and Cole closed in. And the latter should have profited from a Beckham centre but chested the ball softly into Keller's gloves.

As disappointing as this draw may have been United still had three home games left within six days. A win on Monday against Middlesbrough would wrap the title up although another point would be needed to make the victory mathematically sure.

MANCHESTER UNITED 3 MIDDLESBROUGH 3
PREMIERSHIP - 5 MAY 1997

RELEGATION BATTLERS 'BORO pooped United's title party, denying them the win that would have gift-wrapped the championship. The conditions may have been a crucial factor as the visitors acclimatised themselves better to the heavy pitch despite being second best during the opening minutes.

Once called into action for the first time Peter Schmeichel was by far the busier keeper. Fabrizio Ravanelli's early effort grazing an upright before Juninho instigated and finished off the move which opened the scoring. The Brazilian was involved in the move four times before rounding matters off, converting Craig Hignett's intelligent flick. United set about getting on terms quickly, Andy Cole centring for Cantona who was only denied by a clearance on the line. Further chances fell to Solskjær, who had a header saved and then a shot collected by Roberts. Soon after a Cole run was halted by Gianluca Festa before he was able to take aim but the ball ran for Keane who fired low past Roberts to equalise. Many would have expected United to dominate after that but Boro had other ideas.

An injured Ravanelli was replaced by Ben Freestone. The young substitute, who might suddenly be playing for a cup final place given the top scorer's withdrawal, made the most of a lapse in concentration from Gary Pallister when Juninho centred, getting goalside to play in Emerson who fired low and hard to regain the lead. It got worse for Alex Ferguson's men moments later - Hignett converting a Robbie Mustoe cross. However, as accomplished as the visitors' attack could look, they remained vulnerable at the back. Just before half-time Cantona found Gary Neville who cut inside to score his first senior goal for United, striking the ball accurately and securely past Roberts.

The equaliser was provided by the unlikely source that scored the second. Gary Neville crossed for Solskjær who stole between two defenders and glanced a header into the far corner. The crowd sensed a winner could be found in the final quarter and with Middlesbrough ceasing to be an attacking force it almost did. Nigel Pearson was called on to deny Cole twice with well-timed challenges. The centre back was also on hand to repel a succession of Beckham centres. There was a late penalty shout when Cantona, who had been otherwise out of sorts, released Denis Irwin in the area, Phil Stamp sending the Irishman tumbling. It was a challenge referee Dermot Gallagher ruled to be fair.

Another draw should have left United fretting about their next fixture against Newcastle but the challengers fell by the wayside. Liverpool losing by the odd goal in three at Wimbledon while the Magpies shared a goalless draw with West Ham. That result assured the Hammers of their top-flight status and made United uncatchable.

MANCHESTER UNITED 0 NEWCASTLE UNITED 0
Premiership - 8 May 1997

Reds partied and sang throughout the dampest of squibs safe in the knowledge that the title had been retained. United had all but completed their season and with both hands now on the Premiership trophy after a gruelling programme of three games in six days had an excuse for taking their collective feet off the pedal but Newcastle's reticence considering that the second Champions League spot was up for grabs was inexplicable. It meant they coasted to a second successive 0-0 draw.

Providing a guard of honour could have put many in the wrong frame of mind as the generosity of that welcome onto the pitch stretched beyond the first whistle. With United in party mood and Newcastle happy to sit back yet toothless in attack, the game petered out.

MANCHESTER UNITED 2 WEST HAM UNITED 0
Premiership - 11 May 1997

Prior to the game Alex Ferguson urged his men to go out and put on the finest show possible for the fans who would see the Premiership trophy officially handed over. Or at least handed back. His bidding was also prompted by the failure to win in four home games spread over two months.

It took a few minutes for the carnival atmosphere that gripped Old Trafford to subside, Karel Poborsky latching on to a long ball down the right before crossing for Beckham whose cut back to Eric Cantona was deflected over. Ronny Johnsen was first to the resulting corner finding Paul Scholes whose 20 yard effort crashed against the underside of the bar. The ball thudded down, apparently bouncing on the line and back into play. West Ham were slow to react allowing the always alert Ole Gunnar Solskjær to profit and make sure but TV replays suggested Scholes' shot had crossed the line in any case.

With notable absentees across the field West Ham tried to keep things tight and only became an attacking threat in the second half. Stan Lazaridis' effort was comfortably saved by Peter Schmeichel before the Australian winger fired in from distance but straight at the Dane.

Cantona almost set up a second with an inspirational piece of skill after being fed by Solskjær. Substitute Jordi Cruyff anticipated the back-heeled flick but was hustled out of possession. The Reds reasserted themselves at the finish, Johnsen was inches from registering his first goal in Manchester United colours from one corner before Cruyff tested Miklosko from distance. A diagonal pass of 40 yards from Cantona found the Dutchman clear on goal, his finish was composed.

Schmeichel was keen to get a goal, he had gone an entire season without doing so, but did no more than lurk around halfway just in case the chance presented itself. One of his predecessors in the United goal, the increasingly well travelled Les Sealey, came on for West Ham during injury time when Miklosko was unable to see the game out and received a standing ovation.

The entire playing and coaching staff from seniors to juniors took the applause of Old Trafford when the game ended and with good reason. Each of those squads had been crowned champions of their respective leagues. The Reserves topped the Pontin's League, the 'A' team Division One of the Lancashire League and the 'B' team Division Two. Ken Doherty the recently crowned World Snooker Champion displayed his trophy at half-time to add to the glint of silverware.

1996-7

ERIC CANTONA, AN English champion in five of the last six seasons, lifted the trophy after a trademark United charge from the turn of the year that saw off all-comers. Liverpool, who had led for the early part of the season, were so shaken by their 3-1 Anfield defeat that they failed to profit from a late United slump and fell away. It seemed the future was bright and all was set well.

Manchester United were a fine footballing side but as the season entered a crucial stage any pretensions about style and entertainment were quickly dispelled. With a four-way challenge looking likely and a major distraction in Europe, United's ability to churn out the wins proved crucial. As for Eric Cantona, his contribution wasn't as great as it had been in previous seasons but then again Clark Kent would have struggled to reprise his 1996 performances that seemingly won the title single-handedly.

A two game suspension, during which United garnered four points out of six at Highbury and Stamford Bridge, underlined the development of the team and the growing presence of David Beckham. As someone who had a similar work ethic to Cantona and followed his example of repetition exercises after training, the young England international was pivotal during the run-in, as was the emerging Scholes, a player nicknamed 'Little Eric' by the Old Trafford faithful for his uncanny finishing ability and his perceptive approach play.

Yet the greatest progress was made in Europe. Cantona seemed to save his best for the Champions League, his performances at Fenerbahce and Rapid Vienna were vital in finally getting United through the group stages. However he was disappointing in the two leg tie with Dortmund, even if United were unlucky to bow out to two long range efforts.

Cantona seemed adversely effected by these matches. When the whistle blew at the end of the campaign he trooped from the pitch with a forlorn look and many pondered whether this was the moment when he decided to call an end to his playing career. Alex Ferguson said Cantona informed him of a wish to retire just 24 hours after United's European exit to Borussia Dortmund.

Theories abounded as to why Eric Cantona and Manchester United struggled to match their domestic triumphs in Europe.

Clearly United had struggled to adapt their pacy, counter-attacking style to the continent's more considered approach. Ferguson's tactics had been described as 'naïve' by some but when one bears in mind the long absence of English clubs from the top European competition and the fate of Arsenal and Leeds in the same tournament, reaching the last four was no mean feat.

Dortmund's victory proved that to lift the European Cup you needed the run of the ball. The Germans had a decent team and were well organised but most considered the team they beat in the final, Juventus, their superiors tactically and technically. On the night Borussia were inspired and got the breaks, as they had in the semi-final.

CANTONA MADE HIS future known to Alex Ferguson on 8th May 1997 just a few days before the final league game at a private meeting. It was agreed that no official announcement would be made for almost a fortnight so as not to overshadow the club's achievements and David Busst's testimonial. After a little more contemplation Cantona confirmed his decision to Martin Edwards, stressing that he had talked to the manager and neither he nor anyone else could dissuade him. Speculation grew later that a host of European clubs were interested in signing him but it soon became clear that Cantona had retired.

In more general terms Eric had, for the first time since arriving at Old Trafford, stumbled through a season. When he was on song he remained without equal but all too often his performances had been indifferent. As he had always promised, he went out at the top. He had seen other players descend to lower levels after going beyond 30 but accepting a place outside the first team was never Eric's style. In any case United were well equipped to deal with his loss, Andy Cole was finally beginning to hit form after a poor start while Ole Gunnar Solskjær had been a revelation.

The news became public knowledge on 18 May 1997 at a press conference held almost a week to the minute after Cantona had lifted the Premiership trophy. The news stunned the public. A few days earlier he had been filming an advert on London's Hackney Marshes alongside Ian Wright and Robbie Fowler. He was playing with a host of Sunday leaguers for somewhere in the region of six hours filming a new Nike advert. There had been no hint of retirement.

On the previous Friday he had scored a brace in a testimonial for David Busst whose career had ended at Old Trafford just over a year ago. Before making the decision public he wanted to turn out for the ex-Coventry man. He signed the shirt he wore and handed it to Busst at the end.

Eric himself summarised the news by saying: "I've played professional football for 13 years, which is a long time. I now wish to do other things. At Manchester United I have reached the pinnacle of my career and I always wanted to retire at the top. I've had a marvellous relationship with the manager, coach, players and not least the fans. I wish United even more success in the future."

Ferguson commented, "Eric has done so much for this club he is very much in credit. He's been a fantastic player for us. Eric has had a huge impact on the development of our younger players. He has been a model professional. He is one of the most gifted and dedicated players that I have ever had the pleasure of working with. Whenever fans discuss United's greatest side, you can be sure that for many Eric's name will be very high up."

He later added: "He has a million faults but the best thing he did at our club was to drive home the importance of practice to attain perfection."

MANCHESTER UNITED - PREMIER LEAGUE 1996-97

DATE	OPPONENT	VENUE	SCORE	ATT'D	1	2	3	4	5	6	7	8	9	10	11	SUBSTITUTES
17-Aug-96	Wimbledon	Selhurst Park	3-0	25,786	Schmeichel	Neville P	Irwin¹	May	Keane	Pallister	Cantona¹	**Beckham¹**	Butt	Scholes	Cruyff	Johnsen (Butt) McClair (Cantona)
21-Aug-96	Everton	Old Trafford	2-2	54,943	Schmeichel	Neville P	Irwin	May	Poborsky	Pallister	Cantona	Beckham	Butt	Giggs	**Cruyff¹**	McClair (Poborsky), **Unsworth o/g¹**
25-Aug-96	Blackburn R	Old Trafford	2-2	54,178	Schmeichel	Neville P	Irwin	May	Johnsen	Pallister	Cantona	Beckham	McClair	Giggs	**Cruyff¹**	Neville G (Neville P) Solskjaer (May)
04-Sep-96	Derby County	Baseball Gd	1-1	18,026	Schmeichel	Neville G	Irwin	May	Johnsen	Pallister	Cantona	**Beckham¹**	Butt	Giggs	Cruyff	Scholes (Cruyff) Solskjaer (May)
07-Sep-96	Leeds United	Elland Road	4-0	39,694	Schmeichel	Neville G	Irwin	May	Johnsen	Butt	Cantona¹	Beckham	**Poborsky¹**	Giggs	Cruyff	Cole (Cruyff) McClair (Beckham), Solskjaer (Poborsky), **Martyn o/g¹**
14-Sep-96	Nottingham F	Old Trafford	4-1	54,984	Schmeichel	Neville G	Irwin	Butt	Johnsen	Pallister	**Cantona²**	Beckham	Poborsky	**Solskjaer¹**	**Giggs¹**	McClair (Butt) Cole (Solskjaer)
21-Sep-96	Aston Villa	Villa Park	0-0	39,339	V d Gouw	Neville G	Irwin	Keane	Johnsen	Pallister	Cantona	Beckham	Cruyff	Solskjaer	Giggs	Cole (Solskjaer) Poborsky (Cruyff)
29-Sep-96	Tottenham H	Old Trafford	2-0	54,943	Schmeichel	Neville G	Irwin	May	Butt	Pallister	Cantona	Beckham	Poborsky	**Solskjaer²**	Giggs	Cruyff (Giggs) Scholes (Poborsky)
12-Oct-96	Liverpool	Old Trafford	1-0	55,128	Schmeichel	Neville G	Irwin	May	Butt	Johnsen	Cantona	**Beckham¹**	Poborsky	Solskjaer	Cruyff	Scholes (Poborsky) Giggs (Solskjaer)
20-Oct-96	Newcastle Utd	St James Park	0-5	36,579	Schmeichel	Neville G	Irwin	May	Johnsen	Pallister	Cantona	Beckham	Butt	Solskjaer	Butt	Cruyff (Solskjaer) Scholes (Poborsky) McClair (Johnson)
26-Oct-96	Southampton	The Dell	3-6	15,253	Schmeichel	Neville G	Neville P	**May¹**	Keane	Pallister	Cantona	**Beckham¹**	Butt	**Scholes¹**	Cryuff	McClair (Butt) Irwin (Pallister/Solskjaer (Cruyff)
02-Nov-96	Chelsea	Old Trafford	1-2	55,198	Schmeichel	Neville P	Irwin	**May¹**	Poborsky	Johnsen	Cantona	Beckham	Butt	Solskjaer	Scholes	Poborsky (Scholes)
16-Nov-96	Arsenal	Old Trafford	1-0	55,210	Schmeichel	Neville P	Irwin	**May¹**	Keane	Johnsen	Cantona	Beckham	Butt	Solskjaer	Giggs	**Winterburn o/g¹**
23-Nov-96	Middlesbrough	Riverside Stad.	2-2	30,063	Schmeichel	Clegg	O'Kane	**May¹**	**Keane¹**	Johnsen	**Cantona²**	Beckham	Butt	Scholes	Thornley	Cruyff (Thornley) McClair (O'Kane)
30-Nov-96	Leicester City	Old Trafford	3-1	55,196	Schmeichel	Neville G	Irwin	May	Keane	Pallister	Cantona	Beckham	**Butt²**	Cruyff	Giggs	Solskjaer (Cruyff) Poborsky (Giggs)
08-Dec-96	West Ham	Upton Park	2-2	25,045	Schmeichel	Johnsen	Irwin	May	Poborsky	Pallister	Cantona	**Beckham¹**	McClair	**Solskjaer¹**	Giggs	Neville P (Poborsky)
18-Dec-96	Sheffield Wed	Hillsborough	1-1	37,671	Schmeichel	Neville G	Irwin	May	Neville P	Pallister	Cantona	**Scholes¹**	Butt	Solskjaer	Giggs	Beckham (Neville G) Neville P (Johnsen)
21-Dec-96	Sunderland	Old Trafford	5-0	55,081	Schmeichel	Neville G	Irwin	May	Neville P	Pallister	**Cantona²**	Scholes	**Solskjaer²**	**Butt¹**	Giggs	McClair (Pallister) Poborsky (Solskjaer) Thornley (Giggs)
26-Dec-96	Nottingham F	The City Gd	4-0	29,032	Schmeichel	Neville G	Irwin	May	**Butt¹**	Johnsen	Cantona	Scholes	**Solskjaer¹**	**Beckham¹**	Giggs	Cole (Solskjaer) McClair (Butt) Poborsky (Giggs)
28-Dec-96	Leeds United	Old Trafford	1-0	55,256	Schmeichel	Neville G	Irwin	May	Keane	Johnsen	**Cantona¹**	Scholes	Beckham	Solskjaer	Giggs	Butt (Scholes) Solskjaer (Cantona)
01-Jan-97	Aston Villa	Old Trafford	0-0	55,133	Schmeichel	Neville G	Irwin	May	Keane	Johnsen	Cantona	Butt	Beckham	**Solskjaer¹**	Giggs	Cole (Solskjaer) Scholes (Butt)
12-Jan-97	Tottenham H	W Hart Lane	2-1	33,026	Schmeichel	Neville G	Irwin	May	Keane	Pallister	Cantona	Scholes	Beckham1	**Solskjaer¹**	Giggs	Poborsky (Scholes) Casper (Johnsen) Cole (Solskjaer)
18-Jan-97	Coventry City	Highfield Rd	2-0	23,085	Schmeichel	Neville G	Irwin	Pallister	Keane	Johnsen	Cantona	Scholes	Poborsky	**Solskjaer¹**	**Giggs¹**	Casper (Johnson)
29-Jan-97	Wimbledon	Old Trafford	2-1	55,314	Schmeichel	Neville G	Irwin	Pallister	Keane	Clegg	Cantona	Scholes	Beckham	Solskjaer	**Giggs¹**	**Cole¹** (Scholes)
01-Feb-97	Southampton	Old Trafford	2-1	55,269	Schmeichel	Neville G	Irwin	**Pallister¹**	Keane	Clegg	**Cantona¹**	Poborsky	Beckham	Solskjaer	Giggs	Cole (Poborsky) Johnson (Clegg)
01-Mar-97	Coventry City	Old Trafford	3-1	55,230	Schmeichel	Neville G	Irwin	Pallister	May	Cruyff	Cantona	**Poborsky¹**	Beckham	Cole	Giggs	Neville P (Irwin) McClair (Beckham) Johnsen (Giggs) **Breen o/g¹, Jess o/g¹**
08-Mar-97	Sunderland	Roker Park	1-2	22,225	Schmeichel	Neville G	Irwin	May	Neville P	Johnsen	Cantona	Beckham	McClair	Poborsky	Cruyff	Cole (Cruyff) Solskjaer (Poborsky) Melville o/g
15-Mar-97	Sheffield Wed	Old Trafford	2-0	55,267	Schmeichel	Neville G	Irwin	May	Butt	Pallister	Cantona	Beckham	Beckham	Solskjaer	Giggs	Poborsky (Cole) Scholes (Solskjaer)

Date	Opponent	Venue	Score	Att												Subs / Scorers
22-Mar-97	Everton	Goodison Pk	2-0	40,078	Schmeichel	Neville P	Irwin	May	Keane	Pallister	**Cantona**[1]	Butt	**Solskjaer**[1]	Beckham	Giggs	Johnsen (Pallister); McClair (Beckham)
05-Apr-97	Derby County	Old Trafford	2-3	55,243	Schmeichel	Neville G	Neville P	Johnsen	Keane	Pallister	**Cantona**[1]	Butt	Cole	Beckham	Giggs	**Solskjaer**[1] (Butt) Irwin (Neville G) Scholes (Pallister)
12-Apr-97	Blackburn R	Ewood Park	3-2	30,476	V d Gouw	Neville G	Neville P	Johnsen	Keane	Pallister	**Cantona**[1]	Butt	**Cole**[1]	**Scholes**[1]	Solskjaer	Beckham (Scholes)
19-Apr-97	Liverpool	Anfield	3-1	40,892	Schmeichel	Neville P	Neville P	Johnsen	Keane	**Pallister**[2]	Cantona	Butt	**Cole**[1]	Beckham	Scholes	McClair (Scholes)
03-May-97	Leicester City	Filbert St	2-2	21,068	Schmeichel	Neville G	Neville P	May	Keane	Pallister	Cantona	Butt	Cole	Scholes	**Solskjaer**[2]	Beckham (Butt); Johnson (Solskjaer)
05-May-97	Middlesbrough	Old Trafford	3-3	54,498	Schmeichel	**Neville G**[1]	Irwin	May	**Keane**[1]	Pallister	Cantona	Johnsen	Cole	Beckham	**Solskjaer**[1]	Scholes (Johnsen)
08-May-97	Newcastle Utd	Old Trafford	0-0	55,239	Schmeichel	Neville G	Neville P	May	Keane	Johnsen	Cantona	Scholes	Cole	Beckham	Poborsky	McClair (Keane) Solskjaer (Cole)
11-May-97	West Ham	Old Trafford	2-0	55,249	Schmeichel	Irwin	Neville P	May	Butt	Johnsen	Cantona	**Scholes**[1]	Solskjaer	Beckham	Poborsky	Clegg (Irwin) **Cruyff**[1] (Scholes) McClair (Poborsky)

FA CUP

Date	Opponent	Venue	Score	Att												Subs / Scorers
05-Jan-97	Tottenham H	Old Trafford	2-0	52,495	Schmeichel	Neville G	Irwin	May	Keane	Johnsen	Cantona	**Scholes**[1]	**Beckham**[1]	Cole	Giggs	McClair (Irwin) Solskjaer (Cole)
25-Jan-97	Wimbledon	Old Trafford	1-1	53,342	Schmeichel	Neville G	Irwin	Casper	Keane	Clegg	Cantona	**Scholes**[1]	Poborsky	McClair	Giggs	Solskjaer (Poborsky), Cole (McClair)
04-Feb-97	Wimbledon	Selhurst Pk	0-1	25,601	Schmeichel	Neville G	Irwin	Pallister	Keane	Johnsen	Cantona	Poborsky	Beckham	Cole	Giggs	Solskjaer (Poborsky) McClair (Irwin)

CHAMPIONS LEAGUE

Date	Opponent	Venue	Score	Att												Subs / Scorers
11-Sep-96	Juventus	St. Delle Alpi	0-1	50,000	Schmeichel	Neville G	Irwin	Johnsen	Cruyff	Pallister	Cantona	Butt	Beckham	Poborsky	Giggs	McClair (Giggs) Cole (Cruyff) Solskjaer (Poborsky)
25-Sep-96	Rapid Vienna	Old Trafford	2-0	51,831	Schmeichel	Neville G	Irwin	Johnsen	Keane	Pallister	Cantona	Poborsky	**Beckham**[1]	**Solskjaer**[1]	Giggs	May (Johnsen) Cole (Solskjaer) Butt (Poborsky)
16-Oct-96	Fenerbahce	Turkii Stad	2-0	26,200	Schmeichel	Neville G	Irwin	Johnsen	May	Pallister	**Cantona**[1]	Butt	**Beckham**[1]	Solskjaer	Cruyff	Poborsky (Cruyff)
30-Oct-96	Fenerbahce	Old Trafford	0-1	53,297	Schmeichel	Neville G	Irwin	Johnsen	Keane	May	Cantona	Butt	Beckham	Poborsky	Cruyff	Scholes (Cruyff) Solskjaer (Poborsky) Neville P (Neville G)
20-Nov-96	Juventus	Old Trafford	0-1	53,529	Schmeichel	Neville G	Neville P	Johnsen	Keane	May	Cantona	Butt	Beckham	Solskjaer	Giggs	McClair (Neville P) Cruyff (Solskjaer)
04-Dec-96	Rapid Vienna	Prater Stad	2-0	40,000	Schmeichel	Neville G	Irwin	May	Keane	Pallister	**Cantona**[1]	Butt	Beckham	Solskjaer	**Giggs**[1]	McClair (Keane) Poborsky (Butt) Casper (Neville G)
05-Mar-97	FC Porto	Old Trafford	4-0	53,415	Schmeichel	Neville G	Irwin	**May**[1]	Keane	Pallister	**Cantona**[1]	Beckham	**Cole**[1]	Solskjaer	**Giggs**[1]	
19-Mar-97	FC Porto	Stad Das Antas	0-0	40,000	Schmeichel	Neville G	Irwin	May	Johnsen	Pallister	Cantona	Beckham	Solskjaer	Keane	Butt	Scholes (Solskjaer) Neville P (Irwin) Poborsky (Beckham)
09-Apr-97	B. Dortmund	Westfalen Stad.	0-1	48,500	V. d. Gouw	Neville G	Johnsen	Keane	Pallister	May	Cantona	Butt	Solskjaer	Beckham	Giggs	Cole (Solskjaer) Scholes (Giggs)
23-Apr-97	B. Dortmund	Old Trafford	0-1	53,606	Schmeichel	Neville G	Neville P	Johnsen	May	Pallister	Cantona	Butt	Cole	Beckham	Solskjaer	Giggs (Solskjaer) Scholes (May)

CHARITY SHIELD

Date	Opponent	Venue	Score	Att												Subs / Scorers
11-Aug-96	Newcastle Utd	Wembley	4-0	73,214	Schmeichel	Neville P	Irwin	May	Pallister	**Keane**[1]	**Cantona**[1]	Scholes	**Butt**[1]	Beckham1	Giggs	Poborsky (Butt) Neville G (Irwin) Cruyff (Scholes)

THE HISTORY MAN

ERIC CANTONA BROKE the mould at Old Trafford. Over the three decades since the sixties golden age, so many players had been purchased with huge expectations but failed to deliver. The list of failures included high-profile internationals and players with sackfuls of medals. When Eric arrived in the autumn of 1992, the shadow of Matt Busby hung over everybody at the club and threatened to consume Alex Ferguson's reign as it had those of McGuinness, O'Farrell, Docherty, Sexton and Atkinson.

1992 proved to be a turning point. Following another agonising league title defeat Ferguson knew he needed a player with the X-Factor, a man who could give a talented squad the confidence to take that extra step and shed the heavy hand of history. A chance phone-call that October, just five months after the despair of Anfield defeat, proved the catalyst for 16 years of domestic domination.

Asked to sum the player up Ferguson later said, "Eric was born to play for United. Some players, with respected and established reputations, are cowed and broken by the size and expectations. Not Eric. He swaggered in, stuck his chest out, raised his head and surveyed everything as if to ask: `I'm Cantona, how big are you? Are you big enough for me?'"

All of a sudden, almost overnight, the mood at the club changed. 26 years of frustration discarded by the strut of a player who expected to win. On signing a three year extension to his contract in 1995 Eric described his time with United as a 'love story.' His affection for the fans and the confidence he gave them, was reflected back, as United supporters abandoned their self-mocking pre-Eric chants such as 'Always Look On The Bright Side of Life' and quickly adopted a more arrogant self-satisfied tone.

Eric was venerated at Old Trafford like no one before or since. Denis Law, the 1960s King of the Stretford End, was perhaps the last player to have received such a level of hero-worship, but he played alongside the likes of Best and Charlton, world class players who perhaps took the focus away from him at times. More recently

Cristiano Ronaldo, who joined the 60s trio to become the fourth United winner of the 'Ballon d'Or' or European Footballer of the Year, was admired for his record-breaking goalscoring feats, awesome skill and his ability to wind up opponents but, as his move to Madrid became inevitable, the relationship soured.

Cantona came at a unique time in the club's history, a moment when the club needed a catalyst. As a result he quickly became referred to as a deity. "Dieu" was certainly an apt moniker given a creative instinct as keen as the killer impulse he possessed in front of goal. He did things no one had seen at Old Trafford since George Best.

However, just like Best his certain belief in his ability sometimes got him in trouble with authority. Although, unlike the Irishman this wasn't as a result of his frustrations with his own team but a clear-eyed vision of instant justice. If Eric made a robust challenge it would be as brazen as his outrageous skills. There was never any question of a sly flick or dig off the ball. He would dispense justice in the cut and thrust of open play. If that meant a caution or red card he would take the consequences on the chin.

Sometimes the two extremes would be evident in the same game. His recklessness was evident throughout a career in France and it emerged at points with Leeds. It was also something Alex Ferguson knew he was buying and perhaps it was an attribute the Scot felt United needed. The Reds had been criticised for being too nice in the pre-Eric years, the purchases of Cantona and Keane added the steel that all champions need.

Trouble brewed for Cantona in 1994. Dismissals at Swindon and Arsenal ruled him out for six games. Then, when his temper truly got the better of him at Selhurst Park in January 1995, he was suspended for nine months. Yet his return only reinforced his iconic status. Without him they had looked short of inspiration and stalled on the title run-in. Now he was back United ruthlessly hunted down leaders Newcastle and completed The Double thanks to Cantona's match-winning performances.

His retirement was met with disbelief. Just seven days after hanging up his boots he was back. But it was purely as a one-off with Manchester United's full permission. The Reds would retain his registration for the year remaining on his contract. It was even rumoured they would continue to pay his £15,000 per week wages in the hope he would change his mind.

A couple of old friends were behind the return to the Stade Grimonperz-Jooris, home of Lille. Brothers Pascal and Stephane Plancque, who had started their careers with Les Dogues - Cantona played alongside the former at Auxerre during 1987 - were having a joint testimonial.

Just over a hundred Manchester United fans swelled the crowd with flags worshipping Eric draped over hoardings. Jean Pierre Papin, Bernard Lama and former Aston Villa midfielder Didier Six were among the other stars present. Eric represented a North of France side in the number seven shirt against a Lille XI and scored a second-half goal in his side's 4-2 defeat. He prompted a few attacks including one perfectly weighted and measured lobbed pass which those United fans cheered.

The reality of Eric's exit dawned as United embarked on preparations for the 1997-98 season by winning at Wembley courtesy of £3.5 million recruit Teddy Sheringham. The King would be missed but a bright future without him appeared sure even if their victory over Chelsea was earned via a penalty shoot-out.

Sheringham was almost a like-for-like replacement for Cantona - a quick thinking, intelligent player able to see passes his peers couldn't. Almost but not quite. The Londoner, for all his vision and undoubted ability, could never quite match the technical wizardry of the Frenchman, nor gain the unfettered adoration of the fans.

POST UNITED CAREER

Cantona has returned to Old Trafford to play in a few games since his retirement. In August 1998, 457 days after deciding to call it a day, he played in a special match to raise money for the Munich Memorial Fund captaining a European Invitation XI against a Manchester United representative side. As the teams came out of the tunnel there was a huge wave of expectation. Necks craned for a first glimpse but those present received a helping hand from the stadium announcer who boomed out of his speakers: "He's been away far too long."

Eric emerged holding the hand of his eight-year-old son Raphael. The stadium erupted with colour - the red, white and blue of French tricolours mixing with United's red, white and black. The noise was ear splitting and naturally included hearty renditions of "Ooh Aah Cantona" to the tune of the Marseillaise.

As first touches went the ball he played to Pascal Vahirua was a good one and brought the crowd to its feet. But what they wanted to see had to wait until a dozen minutes from time. Cantona sauntered through the cover, which may not have been as serious at closing him down as it might have been, and chipped in a goal that was a sight to behold.

Ryan Giggs had scored early on. Jean-Pierre Papin and Laurent Blanc established a lead but just before half-time Paul Scholes equalised. Martin Dahlin and Old Trafford youngster Mark Wilson put the guests 4-2 up before United grabbed six without reply. Added to Cantona's strike were goals from Jordi Cruyff, Phil Neville, Nicky Butt and two from Alex Notman.

Eric played for the Reds in the second half and David Beckham donned a number 16 shirt so Cantona could turn out with that iconic seven on his back. He also took the armband and at the end took to the microphone to address the crowd.

"It's a special night for me," he said. "I lost my passion for the game and I'm sorry about that. I gave everything for 10 years and had five wonderful seasons here, the best of my career. I love you all."

He then performed a lap of honour. United won 8-4 with Cantona netting the seventh goal. 55,121 people raised over £1 million for those who survived the air crash in 1958 and the dependents of those who perished.

October 1999 marked another return, This time to pay tribute to Sir Alex Ferguson. His testimonial raising a seven figure sum, most of which would go to good causes. Manchester United fielded a team of past legends and present stars against a Rest of the World XI winning 4-2. Eric Cantona was among those to start but matters were closed by those past greats who along with David Beckham saw out the last quarter.

There was a more competitive edge than the game 14 months earlier and Gianluca Vialli, who had just guided his side to a 5-0 win over the Reds in the last league game, opened the scoring for the world XI, George Weah and Cafu fashioning a tap-in. Teddy Sheringham levelled after being teed up by Phil Neville. The striker celebrated by jumping on Peter Schmeichel's back. The Dane, who had left United following the 1999 season, skippered the opposition and left the field with Cantona soon after the restart to rapturous applause. The Frenchman watched as Careca made it 2-1.

That Rest of the Word side became an ex-Manchester United XI on 68 minutes when the entire team went off. Only Beckham, who was using the occasion to gain fitness after a hamstring injury, was currently on the club's books. Cantona and Schmeichel slipped back into the action along with Gary Pallister and Steve Bruce, Bryan Robson and Mark Hughes. The latter put in a trademark volley to make it 3-1. He got another and set up a Cantona goal six minutes from the end. Instead of playing in a pass he curled the ball into the top right hand corner of goal. Paul Scholes pulled one back late on though the referee blew up with a full minute remaining.

As preparation for the 2001-02 season Ryan Giggs had a testimonial against Celtic. Juan Sebastian Veron and Ruud van Nistelrooy made their Old Trafford bows before a 67,000 strong crowd almost none of whom knew there would be a surprise guest for the last 15 minutes – Eric Cantona.

There was never any question about the seriousness of this game as Celtic were to face Ajax in a Champions League qualifier and this was perfect preparation. The Hoops took an early lead when Chris Sutton netted from a Didier Agathe cross. Neil Lennon increased the advantage. Most of the United team had only returned from a pre-season tour to Thailand 24 hours earlier and the 13 hour flight told.

Van Nistelrooy was able to make the most of a Paul Scholes' flick but Celtic put their foot down again. Henrik Larsson linked with Sutton on the edge of the area, Paul Lambert scoring. During the second half Veron sent in a dipping volley from outside the area to reduce the arrears. Substitute Lubomir Moravcik netted with a 30 yard free-kick Fabien Barthez should have done better with.

Cantona's presence at the expense of Scholes was a delight but he had too little time to exert much influence though he did have a hand in events when van Nistelrooy struck again once again from close range.

AROUND CHRISTMAS 2001 it seemed Eric Cantona may be set for a return to the game with Australian National Soccer league side Melbourne Knights. He had been asked to guest in the club's derby against South Melbourne in February of the following year. Former England striker Peter Beardsley had ventured Down Under for a couple of appearances with the same side who were not averse to letting the media know about their ambitious plans for short term captures. General manager Robert Hrzic told the *Sydney Morning Herald* that his side was "looking at everyone and Eric Cantona is a name that has been bandied about. We have found out who is available and it is now a matter of whether we can agree on terms." A figure of up to £17,630 for a game was mooted but the deal never happened.

There was one last return to play at Old Trafford in Sir Alex Ferguson's testimonial in which he featured for Manchester United against an All-Star XI. Around the same time he was voted the club's greatest player of all-time by fans. Soon after suggesting that his acting career would be coming to an end in 2001 Cantona was named as one of Manchester United's youth coaches on an informal basis for the 2001-02 campaign to enhance his bid to obtain the necessary badges to go into the profession. Sir Alex Ferguson, who was due to leave the club at the end of the season, would act as mentor and said, "Eric wants to get back into the game so we've given him the opportunity to help coach the young players at the start of next season. It's not an appointment but a casual arrangement to allow Eric to gain some experience of coaching."

The appointment never happened as Cantona's acting career took off but there were doubts cropping up within six weeks of the possible appointment. An evasive Cantona told reporters who asked him: "I'm not sure I will like it. I will try it for one or two weeks and maybe if I like it, I will come back. It is like a woman being seduced. She thinks yes. She thinks no. She thinks, do I need someone to seduce me? But I don't know. I am not a woman."

Eric's main involvement in the game has been in beach football and not long after leaving Old Trafford, Cantona was named captain of France's national team. Though he no longer wears the armband Eric continues to represent his country and other teams in tournaments.

In 2001 and 2002 he played in England at events sponsored by Kronenbourg held in London and Brighton. For the English capital's first experience of the game 480 tons of sand were poured into an area close to Knightsbridge Barracks in Hyde Park. Cantona was voted the Most Valuable player. He received a copious amount of the sponsor's product in return which he handed out to the Manchester United fans present. It said much about the relationship between the two parties.

As a manager he guided France to victory at the inaugural FIFA Beach Soccer World Cup at Rio de Janeiro's renowned Copacabana Beach in 2005. A year later his side finished third. They ended up a rung lower 12 months on but when France were hosts for 2008 they met with defeat in in the quarter-finals to eventual runners-up Italy.

FILM CAREER

CANTONA'S ACTING CAREER has built slowly but his role in Ken Loach's 2009 Palme D'or nominated film 'Looking for Eric' seemed to be a turning point. The film, set in Manchester, saw Eric play himself, a figure who inspires a down-trodden United fan to transform his life uttering the immortal line 'I am not a man, I am Cantona'.

Previously Eric had directed a short film 'Apporte-moi ton amour' in 2002 and played a role as the French ambassador in the movie 'Elizabeth', starring Cate Blanchett in 1998. He also guest starred as a mysterious bar-room philosopher in independent British film 'Jack Says' and co-starred as Thierry Grimandi in 'French Film'.

THE LEGACY

IN 1999 MANCHESTER UNITED completed a unique treble of Premiership, FA Cup and European Cup – in the hyperbolic phrase of Clive Tyldesley 'everything their hearts desired'. It was some achievement but few doubt that it could have happened without the influence of Eric Cantona.

In the years since his retirement United have won the league seven times in 12 seasons and the European Cup twice. It is by some distance the most successful period in the club's history. Eric's commitment to training, his ability to tutor players, his influence on diet and his attitude to alcohol transformed United. If one considers the 'drinking club' image Manchester United had in the 1980s and the detrimental effect it had on the careers of Whiteside, McGrath and even Bryan Robson, the transformation seems even more acute.

That his name is still sung by United supporters (particularly at Christmas) is another clue of a continuing influence. Given a freehand a majority would pick him as a successor to Sir Alex Ferguson with perhaps Ole Gunnar Solskjær or Ryan Giggs as assistant.

After all Eric didn't just help United end 26 years without a league title. He didn't just help knock Liverpool 'off their f**king perch', he allowed United to dominate English football for the first time and his methods eventually brought consistent European success.

For that, United fans will be forever grateful.

IC CANTONA SEASON-BY-SEASON CAREER BREAKDOWN

SEASON	CLUB	LEAGUE	LEAGUE APPS	LEAGUE GLS	CUP APPS	CUP GLS	LGE CUP APPS	LGE CUP GLS	EUROPE APPS	EUROPE GLS	TOTAL APPS	TOTAL GLS
FRANCE			LEAGUE		COUPE DE FRANCE		COUPE DE LA LIGUE		EUROPE		TOTAL	
83/84	Auxerre	DIVISION 1	2	0	-		-		-		2	0
84/85	Auxerre	DIVISION 1	5	2	-		-		-		5	2
85/86	Auxerre	DIVISION 1	7	0	-		-		1	0	8	0
85/86	Martigues	DIVISION 2	15	4	-		-		-		15	4
86/87	Auxerre	DIVISION 1	36	13	-		-		-		36	13
87/88	Auxerre	DIVISION 1	32	8	5	1	-		2	1	39	10
88/89	Marseille	DIVISION 1	22	5	-		-		-		22	5
88/89	Bordeaux	DIVISION 1	11	6	-		-		-		11	6
89/90	Montpellier	DIVISION 1	33	10	8	8	-		-		41	18
90/91	Marseille	DIVISION 1	18	8	5	1	-		3	1	26	10
91/92	Nîmes	DIVISION 1	17	2	2	2	-		-		19	4
ENGLAND			LEAGUE		FA CUP		LGE CUP		EUROPE		TOTAL	
91/92	Leeds Utd	DIVISION 1	15	3	0	0	0	0	-		15	3
92/93	Leeds Utd	PL	13	6	0	0	1	0	5	1	19	7
92/93	Man Utd	PL	22	9	1	0	0	0	0	0	23	9
93/94	Man Utd	PL	34	18	5	4	5	1	4	2	48	25
94/95	Man Utd	PL	21	12	1	1	0	0	2	0	24	13
95/96	Man Utd	PL	30	14	7	5	1	0	0	0	38	19
96/97	Man Utd	PL	36	11	3	0	0	0	10	3	49	14
COUNTRY	FRANCE		198	58	20	12	-		6	2	224	72
	ENGLAND		171	73	16	10	7	1	21	6	215	90
TOTAL			369	131	36	22	7	1	27	8	439	162

NOURS:

UE 1 (2): 1989, 1991 (MARSEILLES)
UPE DE FRANCE (2): 1989 (MARSEILLES), 1990 (MONTPELLIER)
JTBALL LEAGUE FIRST DIVISION (1): 1991-92 (LEEDS UNITED)
ARITY SHIELD (4): 1992 (LEEDS UTD), 1993, 1994, 1996 (MANCHESTER UNITED)
EMIER LEAGUE (4): 1992-93, 1993-94, 1995-96, 1996-97 (MANCHESTER UNITED)
CUP (2): 1993-94, 1995-96 (MANCHESTER UNITED)

IVIDUAL:

PLAYERS' PLAYER OF THE YEAR 1994, FWA FOOTBALLER OF THE YEAR 1996

FRANCE 1987-1995

DATE	OPPONENT	COMP	VENUE	SCORE	ATTD	1	2	3	4	5	6	7	8	9	10	11	SUBSTITUTES
12-Aug-87	West Germany	F	Berlin	1-2	31,000	Bats	Ayache	Le Roux	Battiston	Amoros	Toure	Fernandez	Poullain	Passi	Papin	**Cantona**	Buscher (Papin) Martini (Bats)
14-Oct-87	Norway	ECQ	Paris	1-1	11,308	Martini	Sonor	Senac	Boli	Amoros	Toure	Fernandez	Anzani	Bijotat	**Fargeon**[1]	Cantona	Ferreri (Anzani)
18-Nov-87	East Germany	ECQ	Paris	0-1	16,851	Bats	Amoros	Boli	K'deuch	Le Roux	Germain	Bijotat	Poullain	Zenier	Cantona	Bellone	Fargeon (Bijotat)
27-Jan-88	Israel	F	Tel Aviv	1-1	5,000	Martini	Ayache	Le Roux	K'deuch	Amoros	Toure	Fernandez	Poullain	Passi	Papin	Bellone	**Stopyra**[1] (Bellone) Dessevroux (Fernandez) Ferreri (Toure)
23-Mar-88	Spain	F	Bordeaux	2-1	14,441	Bats	Sonor	Sauzee	Boli	Di Meco	Ferreri	**Fernandez**[1]	Deschamps	Durand	**Papin**[2]	Cantona	Boli (Amoros) Dib (Bijotat)
16-Aug-89	Sweden	F	Malmo	4-2	16,619	Bats	Amoros	Sauzee	Le Roux	Di Meco	Ferreri	Pardo	Deschamps	Perez	**Papin**[2]	**Cantona**[1]	Blanc (Ferreri)
05-Sep-89	Norway	WCQ	Oslo	1-1	8,564	Bats	Amoros	Sauzee	Le Roux	Di Meco	Ferreri	Pardo	Deschamps	Perez	**Papin**[1]	Cantona	Silvestre (Le Roux) Blanc (Ferreri)
11-Oct-89	Scotland	WCQ	P. Princes	3-0	22,651	Bats	Silvestre	Di Meco	Le Roux	Sauzee	Pardo	**Deschamps**[1]	Perez	Durand	Ferreri	**Cantona**[1]	Casoni (Le Roux) Bravo (Perez) Nicol og
18-Nov-89	Cyprus	WCQ	Toulouse	2-0	34,687	Bats	Silvestre	Sauzee	Casoni	Amoros	Pardo	**Deschamps**[1]	Perez	Ferreri	Papin	Cantona	**Blanc**[1] (Perez)
21-Jan-90	Kuwait	F	Kuwait	1-0	5,000	Roussett	Silvestre	Boli	Sauzee	Amoros	**Blanc**[1]	Dib	Pardo	Garde	Cantona	Vahirua	Deschamps (Pardo) Ferreri (Vahirua) Boli (Amoros) Dib (Cantona)
24-Jan-90	East Germany	F	Kuwait	3-0	1,500	Martini	Amoros	Sauzee	Casoni	Di Meco	Blanc	Ferreri	Pardo	**Deschamps**[1]	Ferreri	**Cantona**[2]	Garde (Ferreri) Silvestre (Sauzee) Boli (Amoros) Dib (Blanc)
28-Feb-90	West Germany	F	Montpellier	2-1	22,000	Martini	Amoros	Boli	Casoni	Di Meco	Blanc	Garde	Deschamps	**Papin**[1]	**Cantona**[1]	Ferreri	Blanc (Boli) Vahirua (Ferreri)
28-Mar-90	Hungary	F	Budapest	3-1	12,000	Martini	Silvestre	Boli	Casoni	Amoros	Pardo	Fernandez	Perez	**Cantona**[2]	Tibeuf	Ferreri	Durand (Amoros) Divert (Tibeuf) Boli (Fernandez) Blanc (Sauzee)
15-Aug-90	Poland	F	Paris	0-0	15,919	Martini	Amoros	Sauzee	Petot	Casoni	Pardo	Perez	Fernandez	Papin	**Cantona**[1]	Ferreri	Boli (Fernandez) Vahirua (Ferreri) Durand (Amoros)
05-Sep-90	Iceland	ECQ	Reykjavik	2-1	8,000	Martini	Amoros	Blanc	Boli	Casoni	Blanc	Pardo	Deschamps	Perez	**Papin**[1]	**Cantona**[1]	Durand (Blanc) Fernandez (Cantona)
13-Oct-90	Czechoslovakia	ECQ	Paris	2-1	38,249	Martini	Amoros	Blanc	Casoni	Durand	Angloma	Deschamps	Sauzee	**Papin**[2]	Cantona	Vahirua	Fernandez (Angloma) Silvestre (Vahirua)
20-Feb-91	Spain	ECQ	Paris	3-1	41,174	Martini	Boli	**Blanc**[1]	Blanc	Casoni	**Sauzee**[1]	Pardo	Durand	**Papin**[1]	Cantona	Vahirua	Fernandez (Pardo) Deschamps (Vahirua)
20-Mar-91	Albania	ECQ	Paris	5-0	24,181	Martini	Amoros	Boli	Blanc	Durand	**Sauzee**[2]	Pardo	Cocard	**Papin**[2]	Cantona	Vahirua	Balili (Vahirua) Deschamps (Sauzee)
12-Oct-91	Spain	ECQ	Sevilla	2-1	20,000	Martini	Amoros	Boli	Blanc	Casoni	Amoros	Deschamps	**Fernandez**[1]	Perez	**Papin**[1]	Cantona	Garde (Perez) Durand (Fernandez)
20-Nov-91	Iceland	ECQ	Paris	3-1	27,381	Martini	Angloma	Boli	Casoni	Amoros	Deschamps	Fernandez	Perez	**Simba**[1]	**Cantona**[2]	Vahirua	Boli (Casoni) Durand (Fernandez)
19-Feb-92	England	F	Wembley	0-2	58,723	Roussett	Amoros	Angloma	Fernandez	Boli	Casoni	Blanc	Deschamps	Perez	Cantona	Perez	Durand (Petit) Fernandez (Vahirua) Simba (Perez)
25-Mar-92	Belgium	F	Paris	3-3	22,894	Martini	Sauzee	Boli	Casoni	Petit	Angloma	Angloma	Deschamps	Perez	Cantona	Cantona	Durand (Petit) Fernandez (Vahirua) Amoros (Sauzee)
27-May-92	Switzerland	F	Lausanne	1-2	21,000	Martini	Angloma	Casoni	Blanc	Boli	Durand	Deschamps	Sauzee	Perez	**Divert**[1]	Cantona	Silvestre (Boli) Petit (Casoni) Fernandez (Deschamps) Gardie (Sauzee) Cocard (Cantona)
05-Jun-92	Holland	F	Lens	1-1	40,000	Martini	Angloma	Casoni	Blanc	Boli	Petit	Sauzee	Deschamps	**Papin**[1]	Cantona	Vahirua	Amoros (Petit) Durand (Angloma) Fernandez (Sauzee) Divert (Papin) Perez (Vahirua)
10-Jun-92	Sweden	ECF	Stockholm	1-1	30,000	Martini	Amoros	Blanc	Casoni	Deschamps	Sauzee	Blanc	Boli	Vahirua	Cantona	Angloma	Perez (Vahirua) Fernandez (Angloma)
14-Jun-92	England	ECF	Malmo	0-0	26,535	Martini	Amoros	Fernandez	Boli	Casoni	Blanc	Sauzee	Deschamps	Papin	Cantona	Durand	Angloma (Sauzee) Perez (Fernandez)
17-Jun-92	Denmark	ECF	Malmo	1-2	25,763	Martini	Amoros	Blanc	Casoni	Deschamps	**Papin**[1]	Perez	Boli	Divert	Vahirua	Cantona	Fernandez (Vahirua) Cocard (Perez)

Date	Opponent		Venue			Martini	Sassus	Boli	Sauzee	Casoni	Durand	Fournier	Deschamps	Papin	Cantona	Gravelaine	
14-Oct-92	Austria	WCQ	Paris	2-0	39,186	Martini	Durand	Boli	Roche	Casoni	Lizarazu	Sauzee	Deschamps	Papin¹	Cantona¹	Gravelaine	Gnako (Fournier) Vahirua (Gravelaine)
14-Nov-92	Finland	WCQ	Paris	2-1	28,630	Martini	Durand	Boli	Roche	Casoni	Lizarazu	Sauzee	Deschamps	Papin¹	Cantona¹	Gravelaine	Karembeu (Durand) Vahirua (Gravelaine)
17-Feb-93	Israel	WCQ	Tel Aviv	4-0	30,000	Lama	Boli	Roche¹	Blanc²	Lizarazu	Sauzee	Le Guen	Deschamps	Ginola	Papin	Cantona¹	Petit (Ginola) Loko (Lizarazu)
28-Apr-93	Sweden	WCQ	Paris	2-1	43,134	Lama	Angloma	Boli	Blanc	Petit	Sauzee	Le Guen	Martins	Deschamps	Cantona¹	Ginola	Vahirua (Ginola) Lizarazu (Martins)
28-Jul-93	Russia	F	Caen	3-1	19,000	Martini	Boli	Roche	Blanc	Petit	Deschamps	Le Guen	Sauzee¹	Martins	Papin¹	Cantona¹	Lama (Martini) Dugan (Boli) Lizarazu (Martins) Gravelaine (Petit) Pedros (Sauzee)
22-Aug-93	Sweden	WCQ	Stockholm	1-1	30,530	Lama	Desailly	Roche	Blanc	Lizarazu	Deschamps	Le Guen	Sauzee¹	Pedros	Papin	Cantona	Vahirua (Pedros)
08-Sep-93	Finland	WCQ	Tampere	2-0	8,000	Lama	Desailly	Roche	Blanc¹	Petit	Deschamps	Le Guen	Sauzee	Martins	Papin¹	Cantona	Pedros (Martins) Guerin (Deschamps)
13-Oct-93	Israel	WCQ	Paris	2-3	30,000	Lama	Desailly	Roche	Blanc	Petit	Deschamps	Sauzee¹	Le Guen	Papin	Cantona	Ginola	Lizarazu (Roche) Djorkaeff (Ginola)
17-Nov-93	Bulgaria	WCQ	Paris	1-2	48,402	Lama	Desailly	Roche	Blanc	Petit	Deschamps	Le Guen	Sauzee	Pedros	Papin	Cantona¹	Ginola (Papin) Guerin (Sauzee)
16-Feb-94	Italy	F	Napoli	1-0	20,000	Lama	Karembeu	Roche	Desailly	Di Meco	Gnako	Deschamps	Djorkaeff	Le Guen	Cantona	Ginola	Guerin (Gnako) Cyprien (Karembeu) Martins (Desailly)
26-May-94	Australia	Kirin	Kobe	1-0	16,743	Barthez	Angloma	Blanc	Petit	Di Meco	Karembeu	Ferri	Dugarry	Papin	Ginola¹	Cantona	Martins (Dugarry) Pedros (Ginola)
29-May-94	Japan	Kirin	Tokyo	4-1	60,000	Lama	Angloma	Blanc	Desailly	Di Meco	Deschamp	Le Guen	Djorkaeff¹	Papin¹	Ginola²	Cantona	Lizarazu (Di Meco) Ouedec (Djorkaeff)
17-Aug-94	Czech Republic	F	Bordeaux	2-2	15,000	Lama	Angloma	Thuram	Blanc	Ngotty	Di Meco	Desailly	Cantona	Martins	Dugarry	Ginola	Lizarazu (Ginola) Zidane² (Martins)
07-Sep-94	Slovakia	ECQ	Bratislava	0-0	14,238	Lama	Angloma	Blanc	Roche	Di Meco	Djorkaeff	Deschamps	Le Guen	Pedros	Cantona	Ginola	Dugarry (Pedros) Lizarazu (Djorkaeff)
08-Oct-94	Romania	ECQ	St Etienne	0-0	31,144	Lama	Angloma	Blanc	Roche	Lizarazu	Karembeu	Le Guen	Pedros	Loko	Cantona	Ouedec	Zidane (Ouedec) Dugarry (Loko)
16-Nov-94	Poland	ECQ	Zabrze	0-0	20,000	Lama	Angloma	Blanc	Roche	Di Meco	Karembeu	Desailly	Le Guen	Pedros	Cantona	Ouedec	Djorkaeff (Pedros) Dugarry (Ouedec)
13-Dec-94	Azerbaijian	ECQ	Trabzon	2-0	4,000	Lama	Angloma	Blanc	Roche	Di Meco	Desailly	Le Guen	Pedros	Loko	Cantona¹	Papin¹	Ferri (Desailly) Martins (Pedros)
18-Jan-95	Holland	ECQ	Utrecht	1-0	15,000	Lama	Karembeu	Blanc	Desailly	Di Meco	Ferri	Cantona	Le Guen	Pedros	Loko¹	Papin	Angloma (Le Guen) Ouedec (Papin) Thuram (Karembeu)

BACK FROM THE BRINK
by Justin Blundell
The Untold story of Manchester United in
the Depression Years 1919-32

IN THE RICH HISTORY OF MANCHESTER UNITED THERE
HAVE BEEN SEVERAL GREAT CRISES - BACK FROM THE
BRINK TELLS THE STORY OF THE MOST SIGNIFICANT OF
THEM ALL...

SPECIAL OFFER: £8
PAPERBACK

If Manchester United revelled in innocent childhood during the Edwardian era, winning two leag
titles and an FA Cup within 9 years of the club's establishment, it endured a painful adolescence
the inter-war years saw it absent from the honours lists. In this amusing, irreverent and fascinati
account, Justin Blundell traces the events of the club's lost youth between the end of the Great W
and the worldwide economic crisis that almost scuppered the club yet ushered in a new era und
James Gibson.
Blundell's punchy account deserves to stand alongside the many volumes written about the pos
war glory years - it tells the story of how United survived the Depression Years and came ba
from the brink.

Morrissey's Manchester
by Phill Gatenby
Second Edition

Lyrically unique, Morrissey saw 1980s Manchester differently. Where most
recognised the derelict remains of a Victorian warehouse, he saw humour,
where others saw post-industrial squalor, he felt the frisson of romance.
As a result the city became as much a part of The Smiths output as the
guitars, drums and vocals. Unusually, these places still exist and provide the
devotee with a place of pilgramage. Now updated, Morrissey's Manchester
has added new places to visit, more lyrical references and more background
information on one of the world's most influential bands.

SPECIAL OFFER: £6
PAPERBACK

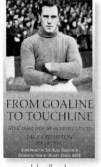

Hardback
Special offer £12

From Goal line to Touch-line
My Career with Manchester United
by Jack Crompton

Jack Crompton is one of the surviving members of Manchester Unite
swashbuckling 1948 FA Cup winning side and the first to pen l
autobiography. Jack served the club as goalkeeper, trainer and caretak
manager for over 40 years playing a major part in the triumphs of t
immediate post-war years and witnessed the rise of the Busby Babes fi
hand before leaving for a coaching role with Luton Town in 1956.
Now a sprightly octagenarian, Jack is in a unique position to discuss t
considerable changes in the game during his lifetime and look back or
seven decade long association with Manchester United.

18 TIMES AND THAT'S A FACT!
BY JUSTIN BLUNDELL
400PP · PAPERBACK · £10.95

This was the season when Sir Alex Ferguson's long-held wish to 'knock Liverpool off their f**king perch' was made flesh. A season so successful that even European Cup Final defeat to Barcelona couldn't fully diminish the club's achievements. Justin Blundell tells the story of United's triumphs in a punchy, rabidly red-eyed review of every single match and goal.

Written with an eye for the humour and pomoposity surrounding the modern game, Justin Blundell brings the matches, goals and managerial spats back to life in an entertaining, minute-by-minute guide to the matches that really mattered. "18 times" is a book for everyone who lives and breathes United, not just on match day but every single day.

SPECIAL OFFER: £8
PAPERBACK

Memories... Of a Failed Footballer
AND A CRAP JOURNALIST
BY PAUL HINCE

PAUL HINCE BEGAN his football career with boyhood heroes Manchester City under the legendary Mercer-Allison partnership of the late 1960s before continuing his first class football career at Charlton, Bury and Crewe Alexandra. After retiring from the game he worked his way up to the heights of Manchester Evening News Manchester City correspondent and, later, that paper's first, and only, 'Chief Sports Writer'. Famed in later years for getting up the noses of both United and City fans in equal measure courtesy of his weekly columns, Paul retired from the Manchester Evening News in 2006.

SPECIAL OFFER £7

BEFORE THEY WERE FAMOUS
the story of NEWTON HEATH 1878-1902
Charbel Boujaoude
Published: 12th January 2010

THIS IS THE rivetting story of Newton Heath's formation. Told as a prequel to Justin Blundell's acclaimed Back from the Brink published in 2007, it seeks to answer the age old question: what was exceptional about the bunch of Victorian railway workers that formed the football club that would go on to be Manchester United? Relying on extensive research and written in a snappy style, Charbel Boujaoude brings to life a late Victorian era where football mushroomed to become the national pastime.

SPECIAL OFFER £9

Reminiscences of Manchester
And its surrounding areas from 1840
by Louis M Hayes · Originally published 1905

WRITTEN OVER THE course of his lifetime, Louis Hayes' memoirs of Manchester life 'Reminiscenes of Manchester' is an evocative look back at the city's formative years. As well as outlining the social changes in the city, Hayes profiles the key characters, many he knew personally, to make a mark in Manchester life.

An invaluable guide to those keen to know more about the formative years of the city and those who wonder what life was like for Mancunians over a century ago, Reminiscences of Manchester is a remarkable work reprinted here in full with additional footnotes and the illustrations published in the original edition.

special offer £9

PUBLISHED FEBRUARY 2010
OLD TRAFFORD
100 YEARS OF THE THEATRE OF DREAMS
by Iain McCartney
Order via: www.empire-uk.com

Old Trafford endures as a monument to the vision of Manchester United's founder and f patron John Henry Davies. Built during football's first boom, it was originally planned a 100,000 capacity stadium, and was described as "the most spacious and the most remarka arena I have ever seen" when it opened in February 1910.

Laterly it has become a world class venue capable of hosting anything from wo title boxing fights to rock concerts. To celebrate its centenary, Iain McCartney profiles construction and re-developments of this legendary venue over the past century comp with previously unpublished photographs and memorabilia.

EMPIRE PUBLICATIONS

Dear Reader,

If you have read this far it's probably safe to say you've enjoyed the book. As the list opposite indicates we are an independent Mancunian publisher specialising in books on the sport, music and history of our great city.

If you would like to receive regular updates on our titles you can join our mailing list by email: **enquiries@empire-uk.com**, by sending your details to: **Empire Publications, 1 Newton St., Manchester M1 1HW** or by calling **0161 872 4721**.

We also update our website regularly: **www.empire-uk.com** with our latest title information.

Cheers

Ashley Shaw
Editor

COMPLETIST'S DELIGHT - THE FULL EMPIRE BACK LIST

ISBN	TITLE	AUTHOR	PRICE	STATUS†
1901746003	SF Barnes: His Life and Times	A Searle	£14.95	IP
1901746011	Chasing Glory	R Grillo	£7.95	IP
190174602X	Three Curries and a Shish Kebab	R Bott	£7.99	IP
1901746038	Seasons to Remember	D Kirkley`	£6.95	IP
1901746046	Cups For Cock-Ups+	A Shaw	£8.99	OOP
1901746054	Glory Denied	R Grillo	£8.95	IP
1901746062	Standing the Test of Time	B Alley	£16.95	IP
1901746070	The Encyclopaedia of Scottish Cricket	D Potter	£9.99	IP
1901746089	The Silent Cry	J MacPhee	£7.99	OOP
1901746097	The Amazing Sports Quiz Book	F Brockett	£6.99	IP
1901746100	I'm Not God, I'm Just a Referee	R Entwistle	£7.99	OOP
1901746119	The League Cricket Annual Review 2000	ed. S. Fish	£6.99	IP
1901746143	Roger Byrne - Captain of the Busby Babes	I McCartney	£16.95	OOP
1901746151	The IT Manager's Handbook	D Miller	£24.99	IP
190174616X	Blue Tomorrow	M Meehan	£9.99	IP
1901746178	Atkinson for England	G James	£5.99	IP
1901746186	Think Cricket	C Bazalgette	£6.00	IP
1901746194	The League Cricket Annual Review 2001	ed. S. Fish	£7.99	IP
1901746208	Jock McAvoy - Fighting Legend *	B Hughes	£9.95	IP
1901746216	The Tommy Taylor Story*	B Hughes	£8.99	OOP
1901746224	Willie Pep*+	B Hughes	£9.95	OOP
1901746232	For King & Country*+	B Hughes	£8.95	OOP
1901746240	Three In A Row	P Windridge	£7.99	IP
1901746259	Violet - Life of a legendary goalscorer+PB	R Cavanagh	£16.95	OOP
1901746267	Starmaker	B Hughes	£16.95	IP
1901746283	Morrissey's Manchester	P Gatenby	£5.99	IP
1901746313	Sir Alex, United & Me	A Pacino	£8.99	IP
1901746321	Bobby Murdoch, Different Class	D Potter	£10.99	OOP
190174633X	Goodison Maestros	D Hayes	£5.99	OOP
1901746348	Anfield Maestros	D Hayes	£5.99	OOP
1901746364	Out of the Void	B Yates	£9.99	IP
1901746356	The King - Denis Law, hero of the...	B Hughes	£17.95	OOP
1901746372	The Two Faces of Lee Harvey Oswald	G B Fleming	£8.99	IP
1901746380	My Blue Heaven	D Friend	£10.99	IP
1901746399	Violet - life of a legendary goalscorer	B Hughes	£11.99	IP
1901746402	Quiz Setting Made Easy	J Dawson	£7.99	IP
1901746410	The Insider's Guide to Manchester United	J Doherty	£20	IP
1901746437	Catch a Falling Star	N Young	£17.95	IP
1901746453	Birth of the Babes	T Whelan	£12.95	OOP
190174647X	Back from the Brink	J Blundell	£10.95	IP
1901746488	The Real Jason Robinson	D Swanton	£17.95	IP
1901746496	This Simple Game	K Barnes	£14.95	IP
1901746518	The Complete George Best	D Phillips	£10.95	IP
1901746526	From Goalline to Touch line	J Crompton	£16.95	IP
1901746534	Sully	A Sullivan	£8.95	IP
1901746542	Memories...	P Hince	£10.95	IP
1901746550	Reminiscences of Manchester	L Hayes	£12.95	IP
1901746569	Morrissey's Manchester - 2nd Ed.	P Gatenby	£8.95	IP
1901746577	Before They Were Famous	C Boujaoude	£10.95	TBP (12/1/10)
1901746585	The Complete Eric Cantona	D Phillips	£10.95	IP
1901746593	18 Times	J Blundell	£9.95	IP

* Originally published by Collyhurst & Moston Lads Club + Out of print PB Superceded by Paperback edition
† In Print/Out Of Print/To Be Published (date)